THE WORKING CLASS IN THE LABOUR MARKET

CAMBRIDGE STUDIES IN SOCIOLOGY
Editors: R. M. Blackburn and K. Prandy

This series presents research findings of theoretical significance on subjects of social importance. It allows a wide variety of topics and approaches, though central themes are provided by economic life and social stratification. The format ranges from monographs reporting specific research to sets of original research papers on a common theme. The series is edited in Cambridge and contains books arising from work carried out there. However, suitable books, wherever they originate, are included.

Forthcoming titles

A. Stewart, K. Prandy and R. M. Blackburn:
SOCIAL STRATIFICATION AND OCCUPATIONS
K. Prandy, A. Stewart and R. M. Blackburn:
MOBILITY AND MILITANCY: THE WORK EXPERIENCE AND
  UNIONISM OF WHITE-COLLAR EMPLOYEES

The Working Class in the Labour Market

R. M. Blackburn
and
Michael Mann

© R. M. Blackburn and Michael Mann 1979

First published 1979 by
THE MACMILLAN PRESS LTD
London and Basingstoke
Associated companies in Delhi
Dublin Hong Kong Johannesburg Lagos
Melbourne New York Singapore Tokyo

Printed in Great Britain by
Unwin Brothers Limited
Gresham Press, Old Woking, Surrey

British Library Cataloguing in Publication Data

Blackburn, Robert Martin
    The working class in the labour
    market. – (Cambridge studies in sociology)
    1. Labor supply – England – Peterborough region
    2. Labor and labouring classes – England –
    Peterborough region
    I. Title   II. Series
    331.1   HD5766.P/

    ISBN 0–333–24325–0
    ISBN 0–333–24326–9 Pbk

Contents

List of Tables and Figures

TABLES

vii

FIGURES

Preface

The project on which this book is based is part of the sociological research programme of the Department of Applied Economics in the University of Cambridge. It was carried out with the help of a grant from the Social Science Research Council, and a small grant from the Engineering Employers Federation.

Large-scale fieldwork is only made possible by the friendly co-operation of many people. Our thanks go out to all of them. First and foremost we owe a debt to the management and workers of the nine participating organisations, those of Baker-Perkins Ltd., Bettles the Builders, British Rail (Peterborough District), Combex (and parent company Dunbee-Combex-Marx Ltd), Farrows (and parent company Reckitt and Coleman Ltd), Horrells Dairies, London Brick Company, Perkins Engines (and parent company Massey-Ferguson), and Peterborough Corporation. Well over 1000 people in these organisations gave generously of their time, knowledge and other resources. Many others in the town of Peterborough — including union officials, other managements, the staffs of the Employment Exchange and of the New Town Development Corporation — also gave us much help.

Our research team has also been numerous. The Department of Applied Economics has been our project's home, and most of its staff have contributed in one way or another to this book. Carol Stocking of the N.O.R.C. unit in Chicago helped in the early stages when we were studying the firms and setting up the interviewing programme. This programme was carried out with the help of Sheila Abrams, Paola Begey, Valerie Blackburn, Meg Brian, Kay Coe, Wendy Nicol, Rosemary Parker, Penny Pollitt and Mary Riddell, all of whom also helped in a number of other ways. Our data analysis was assisted by Margaret Clarke, not forgetting the staff of the creed room, while programming owed much to Mike Hughes, Roger Smith, Dr Joyce Wheeler and Dr Lucy Slater. For the typing and production of questionnaires, research instruments, and various drafts of this book we wish to thank the secretarial staff of the D.A.E. and also Linda Peachey of Essex University and Elizabeth O'Leary of the London School of Economics.

To our colleagues in the D.A.E., Ken Prandy and Sandy Stewart, we owe a large intellectual debt. The sharing of ideas, fieldwork experience and techniques of analysis between our various research projects has been so extensive that often we cannot remember where a particular idea originated. Other colleagues, especially in the Essex University Sociology Department and in the Stratification Seminar of the Social Science Research Council, have given helpful advice and criticism. We would like to single out especially Frank Bechhofer, John Goldthorpe, David Lee, David Lockwood, Howard Newby, Frank Wilkinson and Stephen Wood.

Despite all this, however, we take and claim responsibility for the contents of this book.

1 The Working Class and the Labour Market

The labour market is a central area of capitalist society. It has also been of crucial importance in the development of theory in both sociology and economics. Yet, apart from economists' studies of wage-rates, there has been a remarkable dearth of empirical research on the labour market. In this book we hope to go some way towards remedying this by presenting the findings of the most comprehensive empirical study of a labour market yet undertaken. In the period 1970–2 we conducted a cross-sectional study of a large and varied urban labour market – the town of Peterborough in the East Midlands of England. Concentrating on non-apprenticed male manual workers, we interviewed almost 1,000 workers, collected extensive background data on wages, conditions of employment, etc., and observed at length all of the individual jobs they were doing. It is our ability to relate together the "subjective" and the "objective" aspects of the labour market – the workers' experience and the actual structure of the market – that has enabled us to make a substantial contribution to knowledge in this area. Our major findings are summarised at the beginning of Chapter 10. We recommend the reader who is anxious to know our result to turn there now.

The defining characteristic of the worker within capitalism is that he sells his labour power to the employer within a free market. By selling himself, he places himself under the control of the employer and his management agents. Yet he has freely sold himself and is free at any time to choose to sell elsewhere. Whether this is a "real" choice is an old and important question among defenders and critics of capitalism alike. At issue is freedom itself, for, as MacPherson (1966) has observed, political freedoms in liberal democracy are founded upon a model of economic freedom, with the individual "proprietor of his own person" able to exercise choice within a market. Whether the worker experiences his job choice as "freedom" is thus of the utmost importance in contemporary Western society. Important practical as well as theoretical issues flow from this. For those concerned with practical improvements in industry

1

from whatever social, political or economic standpoint, the rationality and perhaps the efficiency of the system is related to the amount of choice it generates – the more workers and employers are able to choose, the more rational the system will become, and the more meaningful the workers' experience. Work experience, in turn, influences involvement in the wider society.

Our knowledge of these problems depends critically upon the answer to a simple two-part question:

Does the labour market objectively allow to the worker a significant measure of choice over his economic life?
Does he subjectively perceive this as choice?

This may be seen as the central question to which our study addresses itself, although its simplicity is rather deceptive as the problem is much wider than the question appears. It concerns the actual market processes which constrain and define areas of choice, and how they are experienced by workers. This has significance for the workers' lives in general and for social stratification, as we will demonstrate in the later chapters of this book.

In sociological theory, the labour market has played an important role. Marx recognised its centrality to capitalism, though some contemporary Marxists like to deny this, asserting the primacy of production over market relations. In a sense, this primacy is true of Marx's general theory of materialism, but it is a different matter when we come to the capitalist mode of production. Marx's definition of the capitalist mode actually includes the existence of a market: the market for commodities exchanged between what he called Departments I and II of the economy (i.e. sectors manufacturing production and consumption goods). Without this exchange there can be no extraction of surplus value, and with it there must, of necessity, be a labour market. Thus labour in capitalism is a commodity, bought and sold on the market. An adequate account of capitalism and of classes within it must, in Marx's scheme, merge production and market factors (as Emmanuel also argues, 1972: 326–30). In particular, the actual selling of labour power and the terms under which the worker has to sell it are fundamental to the class structure. Thus the clear-cut contrast usually drawn with the other major theorist of stratification, Max Weber, is rather crude. True, Weber sometimes defined classes only in terms of market capacities. But empirically within capitalist societies, we cannot sharply distinguish the productive from the market sphere. In this study, describing the condition of employment of workers invariably involves both. Moreover, workers with a common position in production relate similarly to the market, and vice versa. The abstract theoretical dispute need have no bearing on our analysis.

Weber also distinguished stratification related to consumption, in terms of status, and a similar approach may be seen in the use of "class" in an American tradition following Lloyd Warner. However, we would again question how far differentiation in consumption patterns can be significantly independent of production and market factors in capitalism. In any case, in all uses of the consumption approach we find the market situation involved through occupation and income. Even if we turn to the functionalist theory of stratification, we find it is based on an assumption of market forces of supply and demand for different types of workers, although we doubt if anyone really takes the theory seriously any more.

There seems little need to discuss further the theoretical importance of the labour market; its centrality is unmistakable, and its neglect in empirical research is correspondingly remarkable. Of course our contribution applies directly to only one specific capitalist society, Britain in the 1970s. However, we would argue that, because of the issues involved, the analysis is highly relevant to any form of capitalism, and has some bearing on any society where there is a market for labour.

We are not directly concerned here with the market situation of the working class, or a segment of it, in relation to the *total* market structure, nor with the economic and social forces determining it. These are unquestionably relevant but for present purposes they belong to the context rather than the subject of analysis. The aim is to look at a significant section of the market, to examine processes within it and the way in which the processes are structured. In particular, we are concerned with the way in which the market is experienced by those who come to form an unqualified proletariat. This approach means that we can largely ignore theoretical disputes concerning the nature of capitalism or even of class structure. Instead, we concentrate on understanding processes within this particular yet central area of capitalist society. Indeed, it is only in the final pages that we relate our analysis of the market to theories of class. However, although wider theoretical issues are not dealt with directly, this is not to say they have not influenced our approach. Similarly, although the conclusions are not drawn out until the end, the relevance of the analysis to more general theoretical concerns will be apparent.

At the outset we are confronted by one peculiar difficulty. The labour market falls between the provinces of two established and mutually suspicious academic disciplines, economics and sociology. When the academic practitioners of each discipline found that their inquiries were leading them into the others' territory, they grew timid and drew back, often rationalising their timidity with a loudly voiced contempt for the other – for the "softness" of sociology or the "blinkered narrowness" of economics. Economists long ago realised that the market was not God-given but socially determined; they also knew that the worker could and did calculate the non-economic rewards of employment; sociologists realised that the worker's relationship to his work is critically affected by economic variables; yet neither has responded with research that is very helpful to the problems faced by the other discipline.

In recent years the upsurge of the "radical political economists" both here and, especially, in the United States has begun to focus attention on interdisciplinary issues again. But to find thorough, large-scale research uniting the disciplines we have to go back over 20 years, to Lloyd Reynolds's *The Structure of Labor Markets* (1951), a study of a U.S. labour market in the late 1940s (disguised, but recognisable as New Haven, Connecticut). Reynold's book is a model attempt by an economist to incorporate a sociological approach into his research. We hope that as sociologists we can reciprocate.

Because previous research belongs to two separate theoretical and empirical traditions it is quite difficult to summarise it in a unified way. As a preliminary to the task of integrating the two approaches we will first present the various alternative models of the labour market into which actual research can be fitted.

CONDITIONS NECESSARY FOR JOB CHOICE

Let us first analyse the various possible forms of workers' subjective experience of the labour market. Then we will turn to the objective structure of the market.

In considering job choice it must be seen against a background of economic constraint. Normally a man (and many women) must find paid employment in order to live adequately as a member of society. Although he is free in principle to withhold his labour from the entire labour market, this "choice" is not often made in practice and is apt to make him a social outsider. We will largely ignore it.

Choices are based on comparisons. The worker may be comparing the attractions of the jobs open to him or he may be comparing his job opportunities to some other standard. If the jobs open to him fall a long way short of what he would really like, then the differences among them may not appear as significant or salient to him. As we are studying jobs near the bottom of the stratification system, we should prepare ourselves for this possibility. In studying variations in actual job structures, we must not overlook the possibility that wider structural factors might make these variations seem trivial to the participants. We shall term this the *alienation hypothesis*. As they must work *somewhere*, we might expect "alienated" workers to exhibit conservative, security-conscious behaviour in the labour market and to be relatively uninterested in job differences.

Even if we rejected the alienation hypothesis, we would not yet be in a position to demonstrate that, where different jobs were available to workers, they were able to experience choice. For this depends also on the structure of their preferences.[1] If all workers possess the same preference, their common interests are best served by jobs being identical (and congruent with their preferences), i.e. by no job choice; otherwise jobs have different but equally desirable or undesirable combinations of attributes[2] or there is competition for the better jobs, and there is still no scope for choice. Choice depends on the *differential* distribution of preferences. If this does not exist from the point of view of the workers, jobs are hierarchically ordered. Then *either* the better jobs go to workers who are more valued by employers, *or* if there were no basis for stratification to occur among the workers, we might expect that the operation of equal net advantages would ensure that the more desired jobs eventually declined to the level of the others. Hence meaningful job choice depends on differential preferences.

So in dealing with any social stratum there are at least three ideal types of job choice experience:

1. the workers share a common *class* experience of constraint and alienation;
2. the workers share common goals but are internally *stratified* in terms of opportunities to pursue their goals;
3. the workers possess *differential* goals which gives them a theoretical equality in the exercise of choice.

This is the "subjective" side of the problem.

Quite regardless of the worker's consciousness, objective features of the labour market must also be present if he is to be in a position to exercise "choice". Clearly there must be objective differences in the jobs corresponding to the different preferences of the workers. However, the point is rather more complicated. Insofar as there is not perfect congruence between the distribution of preferences in the labour force and the supply of available jobs optimising the corresponding rewards, then there will be competition for the more popular jobs and the market is hierarchical. For instance, if jobs which meet a demand for intrinsically interesting work are scarce, there will not only be competition for these jobs but the unsuccessful will also be competing against other workers for their alternative choices, and so on, resulting in competition for most of the jobs in the market. Now, it is highly improbable that such perfect congruence will ever exist, especially as only a limited number of jobs are available to be filled at any one time. Hence we may conclude that there must always be a hierarchical element in the market, causing competition between workers and constraint on their possibilities for choice.

Further, to exercise choice the worker must potentially be in control of the job allocation system. Yet there are at least two other types of possible system. Firstly, it might be controlled not by the workers but by management. Alternative jobs might be available, but workers applying for them might be at the mercy of managerial selection procedures. Insofar as there are relevant differences between firms, the workers have an element of control in who applies to each, but selection among applicants rests with the management. To the extent that this is based on recognisable criteria such as education, skill level of previous jobs, or health and strength it is at least predictable for the worker. But this may imply not greater choice on his part but rather an extension of constraint through the introduction of fine degrees of stratification. If workers can be placed in a hierarchy and allocated jobs according to their characteristics, then their possibilities of control become limited to the initial attempt to obtain qualifications. The more stratified the labour market, the less choice and control for the worker. However, management selection may be based upon more qualitative assessments of the worker's character and co-operativeness. Managements may operate with certain rule-of-thumb guidelines or "screening devices" to this end, (e.g. having had periods of unemployment or gaps in employment for other reasons, and having worked for many employers are usually considered bad signs). The sense of being judged according to standards of "responsibility" and "co-operativeness" may raise the dialectic between the worker's sense of constraint and his need for co-operation to a higher level of tension. He is at the mercy of management's judgments, but he has no clear knowledge of what they are. Whereas formal qualifications may divide the workers from each other by introducing further stratification, qualitative judgments may place them in a common class position of uncertainty, and either unite them in a class consciousness of constraint or render them dependent and compliant.

The second type of allocation system is that *neither* workers nor management is in control; instead, the labour market is chaotic from both viewpoints. Obviously, this serves nobody's interests particularly well. What is normally at the root of this situation is that the labour market (or rather the "external" labour market) is cross-cut by the *internal* labour market, the distribution of jobs within each organisation. If jobs vary as much within organisations as they do between them, the worker in "choosing" an organisation is only in control of his allocation if he has knowledge of the organisation's internal structure and if he can determine in which department and job he will be placed. This knowledge must be quite extensive, going beyond the characteristics of the jobs actually available to him now, to those to which he may be later promoted. For the "port of entry" jobs may be only a small section of the organisation's job structure and the "better" jobs from all points of view may be normally attained by internal promotion.

For management to attain control of this process, it must not only possess a unified system of job and departmental transfers but must also overcome trade union insistence that promotions be determined by seniority. Unpredictability may often result in practice from the partial autonomy of departments and the acceptance of seniority as a principal but not the sole criterion of promotion. A "balance of power" between central management, departmental management and trade unions over these issues may mean that none of them has any effective control.

In one respect the interests of management and workers coincide. Management would like workers to possess knowledge about *differential* employment opportunities, so that they can find their way to the jobs which best suit their abilities. However, where the opportunities are *stratified* it is only in the interests of the "better" employers and workers for knowledge to be freely available. When it comes to the actual exercise of control, the conflict of interests between workers and management is universal.

Hence there are two stages at which workers may be thwarted by either management or the complexities of the labour market; they may simply not possess the *knowledge* on which choice must be based, or, despite having knowledge, they may be unable to *control* the actual process of job allocation. To this we must add the *subjective* problem already discussed of whether workers see these objective variations as significant in relation to their goals. The obstacles to the exercise of informed job choice are thus considerable. If worker preferences are to be the decisive element in job allocation, no less than six conditions must be met:

1. the labour market contains a variety of employment types;
2. these are available to all workers (i.e. they are not stratified);
3. information about these alternatives is available to all workers;
4. the workers possess that information;
5. the workers possess differing preferences;
6. there is a matching between the number of each type of preference and the number of corresponding jobs, both overall and for those jobs and workers actually in the market at any given time. Each job need not correspond exactly to a preference, in the sense of providing the optimum situation for the worker concerned, but it must be the best choice for just one preference.

It is highly unlikely that each of these conditions will be perfectly met within any labour market, and we must be prepared for more imperfect situations. The trouble with previous research, to which we now turn, is that these conditions have usually been investigated separately in ones and twos without consideration of the implications for the whole model.

The bulk of relevant research data on labour markets has been provided by economists, but they have been unable to unify their findings because of two unsolved dilemmas. Firstly, they have long realised that non-economic considerations may enter into workers' choices, but have doubted their own ability to investigate these or to avoid the danger of tautology brought to the concept of rationality if *any* factor can be held to influence job choice. Secondly, they have been somewhat doubtful about the possibility of using their model of "rational man" in the face of apparent evidence that workers do not make "rational" choices between employment opportunities, but are usually ignorant of them. Disagreement exists on these problems. (See the debate between Rottenberg and Lampman, in Galenson and Lipset, 1960.) Nevertheless, we must note that virtually all economists have equated rationality with "informed job choice". However, there are two other situations in which workers may be said to be acting rationally without choosing between jobs. The first is that the external labour market may not offer the worker as much "choice" as the internal market. If job differences *within* firms are far greater than the differences between firms, the worker may not regard the selection of a firm as a significant decision and may make his decisions carelessly and "ignorantly". In that case it would be his subsequent behaviour within the firm that revealed his rationality. The second alternative returns us to the alienation hypothesis, for workers may be acting quite "rationally" in carelessly selecting their employment if they regard *all* available employment as being equally constraining, in the sense that any differences between jobs are not meaningful to them. The fact that this possibility has not been traditionally considered by economists shows the ideological uses to which they have put the concept of rationality. If workers are ignorant about the precise nature of employment differences, it may not be the workers who are irrational but the labour market itself.

A brief word of qualification is called for, as it may be objected that the rational course if all work is undesirable is to stay away from it altogether. The alienation hypothesis assumes the economic need to work, but that rational choice is possible in terms of minimising personal inconvenience or interference in non-work life. It may be expressed in various ways, such as staying put in a job, or taking one near home, as well as staying away from work as much as possible. However, these rational responses to meaningless "job choice" have not, as such, been adequately considered.

THE NEO-CLASSICAL MODEL

The Demand Side and "Worker Quality"

Most of the research conducted by economists on the labour market has been from within the framework of neo-classical orthodoxy. This states that the labour market is the locus of the intersection of supply and demand, and applies an appropriate model to each. The employer's demand for labour is governed by its marginal productivity over other factors of production, so the employer views labour according to its productive quality. This is an essentially *stratified* structuring of the market, for workers are assumed to have a definite place in the labour "queue" assigned to them on the basis of their potential productivity. Employers assess this on such worker qualities as ability, education, experience and on-the-job training, which may be regarded as "human capital" and rewarded accordingly. To some extent the stratification varies by type of employer since some desired qualities are specific to certain sorts of work, though such occupational qualifications may also be taken as another indicator of general ability. The supply side is dominated by the "rational economic man" model of the worker – he weighs up each employment offer in terms of his preferences and trades off potential costs and benefits to himself before accepting any offer. This is a *differential* model, and the overall market is therefore a combination of the employer's attempt to stratify and the worker's attempt to retain the larger area of choice offered by differential opportunity. Obviously both imply choice, in the first place by the employer, and in the second place by the worker.

Labour economists generally test their models by deriving from them predictions about wage-rates. On the demand side, the strength of this orthodox model has always lain it its ability to predict stable differences in wages according to productive quality (i.e. skill differentials) and differences over time according to fluctuations in supply and demand. Yet one of its weaknesses has been its failure to predict stable differences in wage-rates between groups who do not necessarily differ in their productive qualities – men and women, and different ethnic groups, being the main ones. These "institutional" differences originate outside the market itself. This criticism has been voiced increasingly in the last few years, especially in the United States by labour economists advocating the related *dual labour market* and *radical* models. We will consider these rival approaches later on. For the moment we will incorporate some of the points they make into a general critique of the neo-classical orthodoxy.

The "demand" side of the neo-classical view of the labour market has concentrated on the hierarchical ordering of workers by employers. However, in some circumstances employers might generate differential demand patterns. Employers offering a very distinctive kind of work are naturally interested in finding workers with congruent aptitudes and preferences. For example, an important differentiating characteristic revealed by our own study is whether employment is offered indoors or outdoors, and we found a fairly distinct sub-group of workers (indeed, *the* most distinctive sub-group) who preferred to work outdoors (see Chapters 6 and 7). The "demand" concerns not the quality of workers but their preferences. Yet the only previous research on differential situations and preferences has been conducted by sociologists. We will discuss this "orientations" approach later in the chapter. For their part, economists have concentrated on their favourite variable of wages, which is, of course, hierarchical (everyone wants higher wages). They have shown that across the whole manual labour market there are positive correlations between wages, other desirable job features, and indices of worker "quality". The fact that wages are positively correlated with both fringe benefits and pleasant working conditions (Lester, 1952: 487; Reynolds, 1951: 220–2; Mackay *et al*. 1971: 92) is an important check to any differential model – in these three respects the labour market is divided into *better* and *worse* jobs, whatever other compensatory differences it may also contain. In Chapter 3 we extend this kind of analysis to *all* work rewards to see the extent to which they vary directly or inversely.

Economists' research has also revealed a tendency for "better" jobs to be filled by "better" workers. Our own analysis of this problem is contained in Chapter 9. In previous literature, skill differences between workers are associated with wage differentials, in the sense that the broad census groups of skilled, semi-skilled and unskilled workers are on a descending hierarchy of wages. This is obvious enough, but it is reinforced by data on wage differences between workers in the same overall skill category. The major evidence is from the study of the Chicago labour market conducted by Rees and Schultz. They found that within individual job categories, wages were positively related to two conventional measures of worker "quality" – years of schooling and seniority (as a measure of experience on the job). They also found "clear evidence of wage differentials in favour of males over females, whites over non-whites and other whites over those with Spanish surnames . . . Employers may view these preferences as indexes of quality, but there is no reason for the objective observer to do so" (1970: 220). The authors' scepticism about these measures of quality actually opens up wider problems than they realise, for there are good reasons for doubting not only race and sex but also education and seniority as indicators of worker ability. Seniority raises the specific problem of the internal labour market, which we will delay discussing for the moment. However, the general issue of "worker quality" must be faced up to here. The major difficulty with demand side of the neo-classical approach is that "worker quality" in the conventional sense is not simply badly measured in the selection methods used by the employer: it is not even relevant to his needs. We will consider these points in turn.

Most writers characterise employer selection procedures for manual workers as haphazard. Only a minority conduct tests of aptitude, intelligence or literacy, and the normal reliance is on informal, highly subjective interviews conducted by personnel managers or production foremen (Mackay *et al*, 1971: 360; Gordon and Thal-Larsen, 1969: 280). But what kind of systematic information should the employer gather? Objectively there is little difference between workers. In all Western countries an apprentice-training or its equivalent gives to a minority of the working class a clear, generally recognised guarantee of skill. Apart from this, no readily discernible criteria exist. In a country which offers relatively equal educational opportunities, like the United States, years of schooling might be thought to give some criterion of "ability" to employers. Yet radical economists have charged that this criterion does not measure "ability" but rather such character qualities as perseverance, co-operativeness and acceptance of authority (Gintis, 1971; cf. also Collins, 1971). Edwards (in Edwards, Reich and Gordon, 1975: 12) has summarised these as "habits of predictability and dependability", (More of this in a moment.) And in a country like Britain with a less egalitarian education system this criterion does not even exist. In our sample, for example, 95 per cent had no formal educational qualifications. Other indicators of quality are also lacking – on-the-job training qualifications are rare (apart from apprenticeship), experience cannot be greatly found or sought, for over a man's work history, inter-industry moves have been found to approximate to randomness (Reynolds, 1951: 32–6; cf also Miernyk, 1955: 144–5).

Why have measures of skill not been generally devised? The answer is that the employer has no great incentive to measure worker quality (in the economist's sense), for the jobs he offers at the manual level do not vary greatly by skill. This may seem a surprising statement, but it is one of our main findings. In Chapter 4 we present some results of our analysis of the Peterborough job structure. Using technical notions of "skill" we find that almost all workers use less skill at work than they do, for example, in driving a car. In other words, nearly all the manual skills required of workers are readily found among the labour pool. Indeed, if we investigate which workers could not undertake which jobs, we find only five pockets of non-transferability: workers with mental or physical deficiencies, workers who are non-literate (usually immigrants), workers nearing retirement and losing both strength and adaptability, jobs requiring unusual physical strength, and high-skill jobs requiring complex decision-making. We have estimated that in Peterborough about 85 per cent of the workers possess the necessary ability to undertake 95 per cent of the jobs, and though these figures might vary in other "unqualified" labour markets we do not consider them atypical.

How is this to be reconciled with the fact that employers do search for worker quality? Though employers do not operate very rigorous selection procedures, they do make an attempt to be selective. We discuss their attempt in Chapter 4. Instead of using direct measures of ability, they use what the economic literature terms "screening devices", that is, they assume that some readily observable characteristic (like race) can serve as an indicator of a certain degree of ability, and select according to that. The most common screening devices are race, sex, previous job history, age, marital status and (in countries where it is appropriate) years of schooling. In the first stage of the selection procedure for "good jobs" are weeded out the blacks, the women, those with several jobs over a recent short period, the very young and the very old, the single and the school drop-outs (Lester, 1954; Mackay *et al.* 1971: 359–3; Rees, 1966: 562). In the United States extensive and open reliance is also placed upon police records to weed out "trouble-makers" (Gordon and Thal-Larsen, 1969: 291–8). This practice remains covert in Britain and its incidence is unclear: the study by Hill *et al.* (1973: 65–8, 94–5) found no clear relationship between criminal record and length of unemployment. However, there are no good data on the experience of political militants. What all these criteria have in common is that they seem aimed less at "ability" than *stability*. The sought-after worker is less the skilful initiative-taking worker than the worker who will arrive on time, do what he is told, and not quit. Gayer and Goldfarb (1972: 715) have noted that management in the United States even treat the worker's high-school diploma in this way: "He was motivated enough and reliable enough to stick it out through high school, so that he is likely to be motivated enough and reliable enough to show up every day at the job." And the conclusion of Mackay and his colleagues about selection procedures in the British engineering industry is that the screening procedures are:

> to eliminate manifestly unsuitable candidates, which in effect meant those individuals whose attitudes and values were not felt suitable, given the requirements of the plant. Particular stress was placed on the need to identify and reject the groups who were likely to display a high wastage rate (1971: 361).

Note the key terms "attitudes and values", not IQ or aptitude! The ideal worker is male, around 30, married with small children, related to other employees and with a stable educational and work history. He is not necessarily cleverer than other workers, but his commitments are less likely to make him jeopardise his job. It seems then that *co-operation* and not ability is in short supply. Our own evidence in Chapter 4 confirms this.

If most workers are ranked by employers according to their degree of co-operativeness, does this offer a stable basis or *stratification* to occur within the working class? Here we must consider the nature of the "screening devices" used by employers. On inspection, the list we have already given appears extremely varied. Some of the most important refer to the worker's life-cycle—the youth, the single person, the older worker are less attractive than the married man with young children. Obviously this is only a "temporary" discrimination and, though it may divide the working class, it is not a stable basis for stratification in the sense that most workers will not occupy the same position on the queue for their entire work-lives. By contrast the *ascriptive* criteria of race and sex offer the clearest basis for permanent stratification. We will consider this later when dealing with both the dual labour market and the radical theories.

The discussion of worker quality has pointed to the reverse of the neo-classical "human capital" view of worker productivity. Workers may be ranked not according to their possession of attributes of quality, but according to their closeness to the minimum required level of compliance with managerial directives. This would not invalidate the neo-classical approach (for the marginal productivity of workers can still be estimated in these terms) but it would give to the model a somewhat less optimistic tinge than is normally found in labour economics. More importantly, it gives us a way of understanding the inadequacies of the model on the *supply* side, and it is to this that we now turn.

The Supply Side and Worker Choice
The neo-classical model operates with a "rational man" model of job choice. Workers estimate the costs and benefits of the employment available to them, and choose according to their preferences (though the objective state of the market or employers' preferences may frustrate them). Is this what actually happens?

The research on the subjective experience of workers in labour markets is somewhat fragmentary. The most comprehensive studies are the oldest, conducted in the 1940s and early 1950s in the United States (Miernyk, 1955; Myers and Schultz, 1951; Palmer *et al.*, 1962; Parnes, 1954; Reynolds, 1951; Reynolds and Shister, 1949). Since then the research has concentrated either on unemployed workers (Aiken *et al.*, 1968; Kahn 1964; Wedderburn, 1965; Wilcock and Franke, 1963; Sheppard and Belitsky, 1966; Hill *et al.*, 1973; Herron, 1975; Martin and Fryer, 1972; Parker *et al.*, 1971) or on whole labour markets but using only the economists' characteristic variables—wages, race, seniority, etc. (Mackay *et al.*, 1971; Rees and Schultz, 1970). Yet this research does throw out several challenges to the neo-classical model.

Firstly, the earlier studies demonstrated that only a small minority of workers — between 10 per cent and 20 per cent — were "really" in the labour market, in the sense that they might be available to employers. Those looking for employment were overwhelmingly either involuntarily unemployed or they had only just started a job and were restless and dissatisfied in it. Those who had been stably employed even for as little as a few months did not characteristically survey the market at all. Only the minority were likely to be attracted by short-run changes in wage-rates and other rewards, and thus the classical relationships between supply and demand could only work for them. This is not a death-blow to the theory, however. Reynolds observed that the neo-classical labour market can operate with this 10 per cent of workers, as long as there are sufficient workers responding to marginal adjustments in demand (cf. also Palmer *et al.*, 1962: 60–1).

Secondly, the research showed that even those actually in the labour market usually possessed very incomplete knowledge of it. Reynolds claimed that few workers could make exact comparisons between wages available at different firms — still less between other work rewards. Only a small minority possessed any precise knowledge about several companies. Typically workers did not "shop around" between many companies, making comparisons between them. Rather they accepted the first job offered them provided it was minimally acceptable (cf. also Parker *et al.*, 1971: 92; Martin and Fryer, 1973: 138–41). Exploring this minimum, Reynolds found it to be composed simply of a certain level of take-home pay combined with some crude notion of the intrinsic job activities. The idea of a minimum was maintained by the worker while in employment — only 15 per cent of Reynold's sample of recent voluntary movers had left a "satisfactory" job in order to take a better one (the rest had been actively dissatisfied) (1951: 85–6, 101, 108–9).

Two points can be made about the low level of knowledge. As we shall show with respect to our own data in Chapter 5, employers publicise little about the jobs they are offering. They are not concerned to let workers look them over; *they* wish to exercise choice. This ensures that any worker who does wish to compare companies is often forced to try working at them. Yet any worker who moves frequently will be discriminated against by employers, for they consider him "unreliable". Thus the employer discourages "rational man". But the second point is that the neo-classical model does not require workers to have *perfect* knowledge of market opportunities. Even a quite crude ranking of firms would be sufficient: the worker need not know a firm's exact wage-rate, only that it is offering "good wages". In presenting our own research data in Chapter 5 we will be careful to distinguish precise job or company information from vaguer stereotypes, and to note that it is usually the latter that enables workers to make rational job choices. In previous literature failure to make this distinction has been a stumbling block. Parnes (1954) noted that no agreement existed as to what constituted "ignorance" – worker responses classified as containing accurate information in one study would be regarded as "vague" in another. Yet there has been progress made in the field of industrial sociology on this point in recent years, progress which offers help to the neo-classical approach. We refer to the theory of "worker orientations".

A SOCIOLOGICAL NEO-CLASSICAL VIEW–ORIENTATIONS TO WORK

In previous research one of us defined an orientation as "a central organising principle which underlies people's attempts to make sense of their lives" (Beynon and Blackburn, 1972: 6). Orientations can only be of interest to the social scientist given two assumptions: that people's cognitive beliefs have an underlying structure and unity, and that such beliefs have some causal efficacy in the world. Such assumptions are voluntaristic, embodying what has come to be known in sociology as "action theory", and emphasising the ability of the individual to make sense of, and to change, the world, though the extent to which he can do either is still problematic. Voluntarism is deeply embedded in contemporary social thought and, from Max Weber onwards, has repeatedly surfaced in sociological studies of economic life. For example, it has characterised the industrial sociology studies of Gouldner (1954), Dalton (1959) and Touraine (1964, 1966). In general the approach is complementary to neo-classical economics, fleshing out what is merely an assumption in the latter, that the economic actor has the ability to choose rationally between alternatives according to his scale of priorities. In particular, the approach has an obvious application to the supply side of the labour market, that is to job choice, and recently this connection has been explicitly made in the British "affluent worker" studies (Goldthorpe, 1966; Goldthorpe *et al*, 1968). However, orientations do not necessarily imply a neo-classical model of the labour market based on rational choice, though what we may call an "orientations model" is certainly of this type. Given that workers do have orientations, it remains an empirical question how far the resultant preferences actually contribute to the operation of the labour market.

In the "affluent worker" studies, the term "orientation to work" is used in a rather narrower sense than in the previous paragraph. It assumes that the "central organising principle" in a person's attitudes toward work is a type of, or a collection of, work rewards. Thus, for example, "instrumentalism" is considered an important orientation to work. It denotes a worker unusually motivated and dominated by financial concerns, so that his entire attitude to work, and perhaps to non-work aspects of life too, is significantly coloured by this. It can be appreciated that, if the labour force is composed of persons with contrasting orientations of such type, then one of the preconditions for real job choice is met. Furthermore, with such relatively simple and structural preferences, workers would not need extensive labour market knowledge. An economistic worker should merely know the level of wages offered and whether the level of other rewards fell within the range he was prepared to "trade off" for wages. Thus the orientations approach comes to the aid of the neo-classical model in a much-needed way: it requires far less than perfect knowledge (which – as we have just seen – does not exist). Yet the approach embodies several problems which we now discuss. [3]

The most basic problem is whether orientations can be said to exist at all, in the sense in which the term has been used. Certainly workers have attitudes to their work, but it may be argued that these are purely a response to their work experience. Orientations must have a degree of independence of the immediate situation and of stability across different frames of reference if they are to be truly "central organising principles".

A particular problem here is the degree of generality of the orientations. The issue is whether orientations are merely work-specific or whether they "spill over" into non-work life. This may be illustrated by comparing "instrumentalism" as presented by Goldthorpe *et al* with "economism" (Ingham, 1970). Economism refers to an unusual concern with the level of wages, while instrumentalism also includes the wider set of attitudes that is supposed to accompany this – low moral involvement in work, a calculative attitude to work, and social privatisation. While both need to be understood in a wider context than the present job, the reference of economism is work-specific while instrumentalism is also an orientation to non-work life. In Chapters 6, 7 and 8 we first test for orientations in the work-specific sense and then explore their integration in the worker's life as a whole.

The third problem is really another aspect of the question of generality. Whether we use instrumentalism or economism, it is a *single* orientation, and workers are characterised by having this orientation. Yet it is far from clear that most workers can be characterised in this sort of way. The instrumental workers of the "affluent worker" study made it clear they would like better intrinsic and social rewards. Thus it seems reasonable to argue that instrumentalism or economism only refer to the dominant character of an orientation, not its totality. This being so, we may ask if the totality can be characterised by a single dominant feature or whether it should be seen as a whole set of wants and expectations on different aspects with different priorities. To deal with this we introduce in Chapter 6 a distinction between a strong and a weak sense in describing orientations. At this stage it is important to note that the strong sense, where the worker is characterised by an orientation with a single dominant aspect,[4] allows a much simpler model of job choice. This is the sense which has been used in most of the literature, and is entailed in a straightforward "neo-classical orientations" model of the labour market.

The question of job choice brings us to the fourth type of problem: the orientations model implies a degree of job choice by the worker, but this is always within certain limits. The manual worker cannot actually work in one of the professions even if his "orientation" is to do so. Orientations can only operate within each hierarchical stratum and functional specialism. Furthermore, strong orientations relating to a specific reward, such as economism, may be characteristic of only one social stratum, the manual working class. It is perhaps only here that men *have* more or less completely to sacrifice other work rewards in order to receive the one which is most salient, such as relatively high wages — "managers, for instance, usually have more rewarding work on all aspects, including pay" (Beynon and Blackburn, 1972: 5). Therefore such orientations, embodying a certain degree of choice, may only occur amid an environment of constraint. This point is accepted in principle by Goldthorpe *et al* (1968: 38), although they continue to emphasise the degree of choice available to their sample.

Fifthly, different orientations may not so much be held by different workers in the same section of the labour market as characterise non-competing sections of the labour force. Let us consider, for example, the orientations referred to by the "affluent worker" research team. While their analysis is focused on instrumentalism they do mention two contrasting orientations, though they have no empirical data on them. The first is a "bureaucratic orientation", a strong and moral commitment to a steady long-term career. The second is a "solidaristic orientation", a strong and loyal commitment to a work-group and the work it shares (Goldthorpe *et al.*, 1968: 39–41). But previous research shows that these orientations are found among different *hierarchical* social strata: the bureaucratic orientation among certain middle-class groups, and solidarism among highly skilled manual workers and some professions, together with some rather isolated occupational communities among manual workers. This raises a problem for the orientations approach: to the extent that orientations are *stratified*, they are non-competing and cannot be alternatives within the same labour market. In previous research one of us has shown how very different orientations to work are found among male and female workers. But as these groups are not competing for the same jobs, the differences do not help either to find congruent work (Beynon and Blackburn, 1972). We do not doubt that different social and occupational groups have different attitudes to work. But unless these groups compete in the *same* labour market, their orientations may have no effect at all on job *choice*.

A final problem arising from orientations research is the actual measurement of orientations. For both Goldthorpe *et al.* and Ingham, economism is best measured by directly questioning workers about the attractions of their present job, why they stay at it, and how it compares with other jobs. If they reply in terms of wages, they are classified as economistic. The difficulty with this is that we could hardly expect workers in high-paying but unpleasant jobs to give any other reply unless they admit to being irrational. Workers who found their way into such jobs quite by chance might be expected to rationalise their own situation in terms of "choosing" this work. The difficulty is that *ex post facto* economism is consonant with *three* courses of action:

1. the workers did previously possess this orientation and selected employment according to it;
2. the workers did previously possess this orientation, were unable to choose employment according to it, and so were initially distributed randomly, but then selective turnover left only workers with congruent orientations there;
3. the workers did not previously possess this orientation, and have been "socialized" into it by their experience in this employment.

The second of these is only a modification of the orientations approach; it accepts the difficulties for choice presented by labour market structure. The third is quite contrary to the orientations approach. All three entail a congruence between orientations and present employment, which is assumed in such questions as why they stay in the job. However, there is a fourth possibility which is also contrary to the orientations approach. Present attitudes may be a reaction against the present job, producing a situation of incongruence. Reasons given for staying would then be rationalisations or would reflect inertia and the need to be in *a* job. It thus seems essential not to base a measure of orientations merely on attitudes to the present job. We have accordingly measured orientations differently, as can be seen in Chapter 6.

Having clarified conceptual problems surrounding orientations, it remains to ask about the empirical basis for this model of the labour market. If all workers have the same preferences then the differential, orientations model falls to the ground, and we must replace it with either the class or the stratified model. Reynolds made this step in his study of the New Haven labour market. Using a series of open-ended questions concerning both job movement and job satisfaction, he concluded:

> Preference systems of workers in this area seem to be broadly similar. The workers interviewed tended to mention the same job elements and to give them about the same relative weight. A "fair wage", moderate physical effort, some degree of interest in the work, and "a good boss" stood out consistently as the prime requisites of a satisfactory job . . . The meaning of a good job is thus reasonably uniform throughout the area. Given complete information about any two jobs, most workers could express the same preference between them (1951: 220–1).

Reynolds, in fact, abandons the differential model in favour of a stratified one, although he does not explicitly discuss the latter.

This is quite a severe check to the differential model – one that is matched by the correlation between objective job attractions to which we referred earlier. However, our own data, based on a more thorough and rigorous methodology, do not permit such a sweeping dismissal. Furthermore, the objective labour market is more complex than the simple correlation reveals. There certainly do exist some jobs which offer unbalanced work rewards – the automobile worker, highly paid but highly alienated, is the traditional example. There are opportunities for workers with distinctive preferences to exercise them, and the studies we have mentioned have produced some, though inconclusive, evidence that distinctive preferences also exist. We are already finding that elements of *all three* models, class, stratified and differential are found in the labour market, and that our main problem is delineating their precise interaction. Previous research fails to do this.

The neo-classical model has so far survived, though in somewhat modified form. We have changed the meaning of "worker quality", noted that the responsiveness of labour supply is confined to 10 per cent of the labour force, noted that workers' knowledge is at best crude, and have reported inconclusively on workers' preferences. But if the model is capable of explaining some labour market behaviour, it is appropriate to ask whether another model explains more. David Gordon (1972) has argued that both the "dual labour market" and the "radical" models are competing "paradigms" to the neo-classical model. Can they do better?

THE DUAL LABOUR MARKET MODEL

This model arose from the union of two hitherto separated problems, the persistence of discrimination within the labour market, and the internal labour market. Neo-classical theory had always experienced difficulty with the former. Like any theory which contents itself with analysing existing market forces, it can only take as "given" the parameters of that market. If discrimination between races and sexes is built into the structure of the market, the theory must content itself with an explanation of rational choice made within that structure. To explain discrimination itself, a wider historical and sociological approach would be necessary. The dual labour market model does not actually provide such an approach, but it does attempt to provide a fuller description of discrimination, and to note its peculiar contemporary links with internal labour markets.

As its title suggests, this model asserts that the labour market is increasingly divided into *primary* and *secondary* sectors. Into the primary sector go the monopolies, capital-intensive, highly profitable and technologically advanced firms and industries. Into the secondary sector go small, backward firms located in competitive markets – in retail trade, services and non-durable manufacturing industries such as clothing or food processing.[5] The primary sector is high-wage, highly unionised and contains internal labour markets. In this sector, to quote the major "dualists":

. . . differences between the skills and abilities of the labour force and the requirements of jobs are reconciled through a series of instruments which are controlled within the internal labor market. These instruments – recruitment procedures, training, compensation, and the like – exist because a number of functions conventionally iden- tified with the competitive labor market have been internalised by the enterprise (Doeringer and Piore, 1971: 189–90; see also Kerr, 1954; Mann, 1973b).

In the extreme form of the internal labour market, only the lowest manual jobs are filled from outside. The remainder are filled by promotion from within, either by seniority, ability or a mixture of the two. More normally, however, at least two levels of "port of entry" job will exist, at the unskilled and at the skilled levels.

According to the dual theorists two interconnected processes have brought about the development of the internal labour market. Firstly, the growth of economic concentration has given the large corporation an unprecedented degree of control over its product market. As production needs are stable and secure, the employer's need for stability from his workforce becomes even greater. He is less interested in hiring and firing according to fluctuations in the product market, and he wants, above all, to reduce labour turnover and to count upon steady production from his workers. Secondly, technological developments have led to an increase in capital-intensity in this primary sector, and so unsteadiness from any worker will result in greater damage than ever before. Furthermore, the specialised nature of the costly equipment needs, not conventional skills, but *experience*, and so the employer retains his labour force by promoting them through more-and-more specialised jobs. Alongside this, he will increase the "golden chains" of fringe benefits, and will link sickness pay, holiday pay and pensions to length of service. One of us has described this in previous research as an increase in *mutual dependence* – neither employer nor worker wishes to expose himself to labour market uncertainty (Mann, 1973b).

Yet these processes only affect part of the economy. The data on economic concentration show not only an increase in the market shares of the largest companies, but also an increase in the number of very *small* companies (for U.S. data, see various articles in Andreano, 1973). Furthermore, Suzanne Berger (1972) has shown that in the case of Italy, the monopoly sector and the small, competitive sector are now in a symbiotic relationship with each other. The low-wage competitive sector can make technologically-simple products very cheaply, and so the monopolies have hived off simpler aspects of their production to them. Thus, by preserving the competitive sector, they can keep down both wage levels and the level of unionisation in the economy as a whole. Thus – at least in Italy – the primary and secondary sectors are now in a stable, functional relationship.

Such a bifurcation has important consequences for the workers.

While the primary sector is looking more than ever for the stable worker, the secondary sector needs to use turnover and redundancy to adjust employment volume to unpredictable product markets. Thus secondary employers abandon the "queue" and look for *unstable* employees – women, ethnic minorities and other marginal and relatively docile groups. The result is a stratified labour market.

These are the arguments of Doeringer and Piore and their dualist colleagues (Bosanquet and Doeringer, 1973; Doeringer, 1973; Doeringer and Piore, 1971; Piore, 1973a and 1973b). We should note at once that they have produced very little hard data to support their arguments, which are really interesting hypotheses rather than established fact.

Yet they make life difficult for themselves by one methodological error, pointed out by Barron and Norris (1976). The dualist argument depends on demonstrating that there is actual *segregation* in the labour market. Yet the only supporting evidence produced concerns *average differences* between, say, the wages paid to men and women, whites and blacks, and workers in manufacturing and service industry. The evidence needed, however, concerns the degree of overlap between the groups. Social stratification involves two elements, inequality and segregation. It is highly unlikely that stratification within the working class can occur, or that the stratified groups can attain separate consciousnesses, without some degree of segregation. There are two main criteria of labour market stratification readily available to us: segregation in terms of wage levels and segregation of actual jobs.

Though wages data are plentiful, a simple and comprehensive distributional analysis for men and women, blacks and whites, etc. has not yet been undertaken. The clearest analysis is by Barron and Norris (1976), of sex differences in wages in Britain in 1962. They found that the area of overlap between the hourly earnings of men and women is less than a third of the area of the combined distribution. This is an astonishing degree of segregation, apparently unrivalled among the ethnic groups. Most data on the latter came from the United States, and though they reveal the expected differences between whites and blacks, these are only about half of the sex differential (Morgan *et al.*, 1974) and the distributions are much closer together (Wohlstetter and Coleman, 1972). They have also been decreasing in the period 1950–70 (Freeman, 1973; Szymanski, 1975). There is no good distributional analysis for Britain, though sample surveys have revealed that the average earnings of Commonwealth immigrant groups are only between 10 per cent and 30 per cent lower than indigenous averages – probably insufficient for clear segregation (Jones and Smith, 1970: 91–2; Political and Economic

Planning, 1976: 84–8). Much of this difference is actually accounted for by the fact that immigrant job levels are considerably lower than those of native British workers. Comparing immigrants and natives doing similar jobs produces a much lower wage difference (as we will see in Chapter 9), although it ignores that part of discrimination attributable to job rather than wage processes. So let us turn to job segregation.

In investigating the occupational segregation of men and women, Barron and Norris (1976) note that the job categories used in national censuses are too broad to permit reliable conclusions but that they nevertheless indicate considerable segregation. A study like ours is able to use much more precise job categories over a smaller area. In Chapter 2 we note that in the town of Peterborough occupational segregation is virtually complete – men and women are almost never interchangeable as individuals in the manual labour market. Of course sexual discrimination is too obvious really to need specialised sociological investigation. It is so uniform that *everyone knows* that women are rarely allowed to do men's jobs, that where they are they are paid less, that their shifts are restricted, that they are rarely allowed to supervise men. In both Britain and the United States recent legislation has attempted to remedy the worst abuses, yet discrimination is thoroughly built into the institutional framework of industrial relations, so that, for example, redundancy practices often entail the laying-off of women before men. This points us to the conclusion that effective stratification in the labour market may need a legal or institutional framework, outside of the immediate market, to be effective.

This is a conclusion that is highly relevant to the recent growth of "bonded labourers" in Western capitalist countries. By this we refer to the use by almost all Western countries of immigrant labour which does not enjoy traditional labour market freedoms. In all European countries, for example, an immigrant worker cannot initially change his employer without permission from the immigration authorities. Restrictions are sometimes removed after a certain period of stay – in Britain, four years (Castles and Kosack, 1973: 98–107). In the United States, Mexican immigrants cannot change employment within the first two years (although thereafter they are free). In Britain, those Commonwealth and Irish citizens who arrived after 1971 do not possess full labour market rights. In all these cases the immigrants are naturally at the mercy of their employer. Furthermore, all these legalised schemes have created an illegal underworld of smuggled immigrants, certainly a majority in the case of Mexicans in United States, although probably minorities elsewhere. These workers are even more helpless.

This is a dual labour market with a vengeance, separating the working class into free and semi-free legal statuses reminiscent of feudalism rather than capitalism. Yet it is not the kind of dualism posited by Doeringer and Piore, and it does not apply at all to the group that the dual model was really devised for. Blacks in the United States – and Puerto Ricans, too – have full citizen rights and full freedom on the labour market. So, too, do most immigrants to Britain. It is the countries of continental Europe (and the State of California) which most practise this form of dualism. In this system, the discrimination is not merely, or even primarily, in terms of wages, but in terms of the discipline the employer is able to enforce on the worker and of the inability of the worker to negotiate his conditions of employment.

How segregated are both free and semi-free immigrant groups in terms of the occupations they hold? This is where the various Western countries diverge, mainly according to the proportion of immigrant or ethnic group workers in the total employed population. In Switzerland, this proportion is highest, with nearly 40 per cent of all factory workers being foreign-born. This gives rise to high concentration figures among manual workers in a few industries: 63 per cent in clothing, shoes and linen and over 50 per cent in textiles, hotels and catering, and construction. The lowest stratum of occupations in these industries is probably entirely filled by immigrants. Thus Switzerland is the exemplar of the dual labour market. Elsewhere, concentration on this scale is unusual. In France it appears confined to the building industry, where the smaller (low-paying) firms are almost exclusively filled by foreigners (a study quoted by Castles and Kosack, 1973: 107). But immigrant workers have also penetrated the high-paying but extremely unattractive industry of automobile assembly. This happened early in France and Germany, though it is more recent in Britain (Political and Econimic Planning, 1976: 69).

In Britain, concentration is lower. Immigrant males did not constitute more than $5\frac{1}{2}$ per cent of the workers in any industry according to the 1966 Sample Census. The proportions among females are even lower. Even using finer occupational classifications we find that immigrant males constitute at most 26 per cent of males in any occupation – the highest being for "winders and reelers" in textiles. Again, the proportions among females are lower: the highest, among hospital orderlies, is only 7 per cent. (Jones and Smith, 1970). Again we would undoubtedly find higher concentrations if we were able to use finer occupational categories at the lowest manual levels. Furthermore, national figures conceal regional variations, which are very great in all

Western societies because of the residential patterns of immigrants. So, bearing in mind that high concentration at the "macro-level" of industries is comparatively rare, we will turn to micro-studies for a more realistic view of segregation in employment.

First we will consider micro-studies of internal labour markets. This is the most critical aspect of dual theory. Here we encounter international differences. In the United States internal labour markets are more highly developed than in Europe, probably not because of either immediate economic or technological differences but because of the U.S. tradition of plant-bargaining. Plant unionism tends to privilege present employees *vis-à-vis* other workers in the labour market, and, in particular, to develop formal seniority rules for promotion. In Britain, seniority governs redundancy practices more than it does promotion. A study of three labour markets in the engineering industry found that " ports of entry" existed at every skill level. Very few semi-skilled workers were upgraded, and although rather more unskilled were promoted, nevertheless internal mobility contributed less than mobility between firms to promotion (Mackay *et al.*, 1971: Chapter 11).

Even the United States is not dominated by internal labour markets. Reynolds noted that steady upward movement, where it occurred, tended to be internal, yet only a minority of workers had moved steadily up. Only 28 per cent said that they had moved to a better job since starting with their present employer, and even among the longest-service group only one-half had moved up. Yet overall, 38 per cent of these who had started in semi-skilled positions had risen to skilled, while 67 per cent of those who had started in unskilled jobs were now in semi-skilled or skilled ones. In fact much upward mobility is irregular, not to say haphazard (1951: 134–151). These data are over 25 years old, of course. The Bay Area Study gives us more recent information on employer policy in the United States and shows that it is quite diverse. About two-thirds of employers in manufacturing industry said that promotion from unskilled to semi-skilled jobs occurred frequently, but all the employers in other industries said it occurred only infrequently (Gordon and Thal-Larsen, 1969: 347–8).[6] In all countries, therefore, the internal labour market normally co-exists with the external market.

This is important, for in the overall market the internal and external elements may cross-cut each other. All firms contain some "bad" jobs, even if the firm is itself in the primary sector. Thus a high-paying job may be a high job in a low-paying firm, or a medium or high job in a high-paying firm. There is additionally a third determinant of wage-levels, the type of payment system involved. British research shows that unskilled piecework jobs often receive higher wages than skilled timework (Mackay *et al.*, 1971: Chapter 5). One study of part of the Coventry and Glasgow labour markets concluded that internal and external labour markets and payment systems interact in such a confused way that the overall wage structure is chaotic (Robinson *et al.*, 1970). Some other work rewards are similarly distributed. Fringe benefits are generally granted to all the employees of a company, but the tendency to relate benefit level to length of service may confuse the simple inter-firm hierarchy. Security also incorporates both an inter-firm (expanding or contracting) and an intra-firm ("first in, last out") hierarchy. There is obviously considerable complexity in the distribution of these and other work rewards. No study has yet delineated the precise relationship of internal to external markets for all major rewards. In Chapter 4 we attempt this.

Finally, we must consider the supply side of the dual argument, the characteristics of the workers in the supposed primary and secondary sectors. The micro-studies reveal that there are relatively few firms that are composed overwhelmingly of immigrants or ethnic minorities. Indeed, employers often deliberately resist such concentration, fearing trouble from their existing workers if they allow numbers to creap past 10–15 per cent (Wright, 1968: 63–6; cf. also Gordon and Thal-Larsen, 1969). Thus discrimination may reduce segregation. Yet one uniformity remains – that immigrants have little opportunity for promotion. Employers in Europe say that they will not generally consider this for fear, again, of alienating native-born workers (Wright, 1968: 81; Castles and Kosack, 1973). And in the United States, Piore found that Puerto Rican workers in Boston had few advancement possibilities (1973: 11 – 12). It seems probable, however, that current "Affirmative Action" programme in the United States are reducing this handicap, at least for blacks. Apart from this possible improvement, however, we confront an odd paradox: promotion may be largely confined to highly segregated industries and firms. It is only there that minorities can supervise minorities. The P.E.P. national study of England and Wales, conducted in 1974, found that only 18 per cent of Asian and West Indian men were supervising other people, compared to 40 per cent of white men. Even so, however, Asians and West Indians were more likely to be supervised by their compatriots than by white men (P.E.P., 1976: 98–9). The probable result is that the average level of wages and other work rewards of immigrant groups is less than that of the natives, but the overlap between the two groups is considerable.[7]

The explanation would seem to be that the labour market contains not one but several hierarchies that can often cross-cut each other. These are, firstly the rival internal and external labour markets, where jobs can be desirable in certain respects either because the firm is "good" (even if the job level is low), or because the job is a high-level one (even if the firm is "bad"). Secondly, there are jobs which offer unusually unbalanced work rewards, such as assembly-line work, foundry work, many kinds of heavy labouring, where secondary workers can earn high wages doing unpleasant work. We have already noted that immigrants have penetrated to the automobile industry. Physical strength and youth can generally earn high wages if the worker is prepared to incur other severe costs. Thirdly, piecework systems often escape market forces.

Thus there may be effective segregation only at the extreme of the market: secondary workers will only rarely have jobs which offer high rewards on all dimensions, and primary workers will rarely have generally "bad jobs", but in the middle there is considerable overlap. This receives some support from Lester's (1954) somewhat impressionistic and now rather old study of hiring practices in manufacturing industry in one U.S. labour market. He observed that differences in wage-rates between firms were only related to differences in "worker quality" (as seen by management) in the few firms right at the top and at the bottom of the hierarchy.

Thus segregation between ethnic groups within the labour market is far from complete. It is also far less complete than segregation in other spheres of life. The degree of residential and educational concentration of ethnic minorities and immigrants is certainly higher than in employment in most countries. The dual argument in the United States has thus involved considerable discussion of the "ghetto" (Harrison, 1972 and 1974). And, although Western societies have a rather weak tradition of organising around urban and educational issues, interracial strife is generally fiercer there than in the sphere of labour relations.

Only segregation between the sexes reaches the proportions envisaged by dual labour market theorists – and this is, of course, traditional. Powerful discriminatory forces have also traditionally existed in the position of ethnic groups. Yet the competitive, and often chaotic, forces of the market and of the firm prevent these from ossifying into dualism. Only two changes in that direction can be observed. The first is the growth of the internal labour market. Yet, as we have seen, this development is uneven, greater in the United States than elsewhere. More importantly, unless industrial structure became simplified to the point where the entire labour force of all primary firms were located within an internal labour market, the internal market must often cross-cut the hierarchy of the external market and reduce dualism. The second change is the highly sinister recent development of unfree immigrant labour, most notably in the European countries, but also involving Central Americans in the American South-west and East Coast. With this main exception, we are sceptical of the extent to which real labour markets, certainly in Britain, approximate to the dual model.

Furthermore, we should remember that some other characteristics of secondary workers are not stable sources of stratification. Both adolescents and older workers disproportionately occupy secondary-type jobs. The former have reasonable chances of primary employment on reaching the age of 18 or 21, the latter may have already held such employment. The problem of old age is that the extent of demotion, with failing powers, is often unpredictable. Some firms have benign reputations, "carrying" their workers nearing retirement, others are more ruthless. All older workers are aware that they stand little chance on the external labour market. Thus the older workers hang on to present employment with a grimness and a wariness that often depresses the outside observer (e.g. Palmer *et al.*, 1962). This is the more negative side of the internal labour market, indicating that it may not offer a better job to the worker, but rather the *only* job. The powerlessness of old age in the labour market is often added to by ill-health or disability, sometimes predictable from childhood but sometimes incurred in the course of work itself. These are fears which are almost uniform throughout the manual working class – they do not lead to stable social stratification within it.

THE RADICAL MODEL

To the sociologist, the interest of the model offered by radical political economists lies in its attempt to give an explanation, couched in historical and social-structural terms, for the evolution of the capitalist labour market. It also attempts to link together two features of economic life which are all too often separated in academic social science: the labour market and the productive process. In this there is an obvious debt to Marx.

The model started empirically from the observation of dual labour market processes, including the tendencies toward stratification between primary and secondary sectors, between men and women, between races. Yet it does not depend on the existence of a simple duality in the market, for it accepts that these stratification lines within working-class employment do not necessarily coincide. Rather they are alternative ways for the capitalist to divide the working class, thereby reducing the level of wages and of working-class resistance. As Gordon says:

> It seems likely that members of the capitalist class have sought increasingly to encourage and permit the development of several *objectively defined classes* in the American labour market, each in objective competition with the others, in order to heighten the stratification of the labour force (1972: 79; cf. also various contributors to Edwards, Reich and Gordon, 1975).

This familiar Marxist argument underlies the whole model. From it are developed specific explanations of the use of race, sex and primary/secondary differentiation of the labour force. Even the internal labour market is included within its rubric: whatever the "technological necessity" of its emergence, it also represents a "divide-and-rule" strategy by the employer, enabling him to exercise a "top down" authority through the creation of hierarchical divisions within the working class. Also, seniority rules, firm-specific fringe benefits and "welfare capitalism" in general are all ways of dividing employees of a company from the rest of the working class. All these forms of segmentation are functional for the survival of capitalism (Gordon, 1972: 70–9; Reich, Gordon and Edwards, 1973) and one study has attempted to demonstrate that in the case of the U.S. steel industry this is precisely why segmentation developed (Stone, 1975).

There is an obvious functionalism in the argument (as there is in so many varieties of contemporary Marxism). Capitalism is said to "require" the development of segmentation if it is to function. Furthermore, this necessity is sometimes said to be consciously recognised by capitalists. One can certainly criticise the model at this point for an exaggerated conspiratorial view of history, but this is not the vital point. Even, indeed, without any consideration of employer policies the functional version of the radical model would be upheld provided segmentation, however caused, actually did keep down levels of wages and working-class consciousness. It is not at all implausible, in fact, to assert that employers are normally conscious of the utility of segmentation in keeping down wage levels, and that segmentation does keep down wages, even if employers are not normally conscious of any need to preserve the structure of capitalism.

As we have already noted, the division between the sexes is the most clear-cut form of labour market segmentation. It is certainly in the interests of capitalists to have such an elastic and undemanding source of cheap labour as women. Yet the economic subordination of women pre-dates capitalism, and permeates the values of almost all men and women, be they capitalists or workers. In any case, it is not clear that it is in the interests of capitalists to preserve women, or indeed any other group, as a separate segment of the labour force. If women, blacks, adolescents or other secondary groups were suddenly interchangeable with white adult males, might not the latter's average wages fall, just as the former's might rise? That is certainly the prediction made by the trade unions who represent the latter. And, as women are underemployed in the economy at large, to increase their wages might further encourage their entry into the labour force, increasing the volume of labour supply and thereby reducing wages in general. Thus, it is not at all clear that to retain segmentation keeps down the general level of wages, and there is no evidence to show that employers believe this. (For a discussion of the theory, see Arrow, 1972, and Prager, 1972–3).

A second problem with this radical argument is that the level of segregation and discrimination is not constant; indeed, it tends to decline throughout periods of economic expansion. As capitalism has expanded considerably throughout its history, there has been a secular decline in the level of discrimination against its most exploited groups of labour. Wallerstein (1974) has noted that on a global level when capitalism has first penetrated a new area it tends to use, not free wage-labour, but slave and semi-free labour. With time, however, these systems tend to be ameliorated. Similarly, ethnic immigrant minorities tend to improve their position *vis-à-vis* the native-born. Szymanski's thorough documentation of this improvement for U.S. blacks had led him to reformulate the radical position. Noting that blacks are now being replaced at the bottom of the U.S. hierarchy by Latin American immigrants, he concludes: "Racism is indeed an inherent aspect of capitalism. But no one group is its special victim forever . . . Racism persists: only the victims change." (1975: 6, 18). Provided we note that "racism" need not actually be confined to ethnic groups, but could apply to women, child labour or indeed *any* highly exploited group, this seems broadly acceptable.

Let us examine the employers' motivation in the matter. Throughout the history of capitalism, employers have sought to expand their markets and therefore, as a general rule, the labour force. They have persistently encouraged the entry of these "secondary" groups into the labour market. There are two reasons for this. Firstly, they seek to increase the volume of labour supply, especially in periods of under-supply of "primary" workers. Secondly, they are pleased to be able to use cheap docile labour with low employment aspirations. Moreover, it can be to the advantage of the employers to keep this labour *totally* segregated from the rest of the market, so that wages are set in comparison to non-market factors (unfree labour's subsistence levels; married women's need for an extra wage; immigrants' comparison with wages back home). But such protection from the market needs legal or institutional backing, and either extensive repression or general cultural acceptance of different relationships to production. Employer encouragement of segregation must take the form of backing for semi-free (or slave) statuses for "secondary" workers. Capitalists have two broad alternative strategies in terms of "divide-and-rule". They can use legal and coercive means to keep secondary workers out of the primary market altogether, but if they are unable to achieve this, then the pressure of market efficiency will push them towards the opposite extreme, the interchangeability of all labour.

Moreover, the radical account tends to leave out the worker's interest in segmentation. Collaboration between employers and established workers against newcomers is a normal feature of industrial relations throughout the development of capitalism. In the case of the treatment of foreign labour in Europe, native workers and their trade unions have generally supported the discriminatory legislation. Convinced that "over-full" employment retards the growth of the economy, they consent to the importing of labour provided that it does not possess full labour rights, that it can be sent back home again if unemployment rises, that it cannot compete on the open labour market. This is merely a modern instance of an historic trend. Collaboration with craft workers was a necessity for employers from the beginning of the Industrial Revolution, because crafts were already exercising a monopoly within the market. The employer was not dividing a hitherto united proletariat – there never was a united proletariat. The second stage in the history of collaboration came later, with the realisation by the employer that it was not practicable for him to replace the whole of the workforce if he was in dispute with them. Thus the collaboration now moved to a plant-wide basis, and the employer was prepared to grant special privileges to his workers (which in turn became "golden chains" for them). The third stage brings us to the technological and market forces, noted by dual and radical theorists alike, which developed the internal labour market. Throughout the history of industrial relations, on the first and third of these issues the employer normally resisted pressures for segmentation emanating from established workers, by challenging craft restrictive practices and refusing to regulate the internal labour market exclusively by seniority. We do not therefore agree that capitalists have consistently encouraged segmentation – though they may have done so in particular circumstances.

Insofar as the radical theorists identify the principal obstacle to the development of a united working class as the cunning of the capitalist, they are wrong. It would be more correct (as well as more truly Marxian) to identify that obstacle as the development of the forces of production themselves. As capitalism has expanded throughout the world, new groups have been brought into the labour market, possessing differing values and skills from those already there. The assimilation of rural immigrants, women, slaves and international migrants into the existing working class has been slow. Each group has at first constituted a kind of *lumpenproletariat*, or secondary labour force. It has been in the immediate economic interests of the primary workforce to keep them in that position, but as the primary group's skills are objectively low (as we saw earlier) it has had to fight hard through trade unions to preserve its existing job property rights. If the legal and institutional means are available to keep the new secondary group in a totally segregated position (as in the former slave-owning Southern states of the United States or with women until now), the employer will acquiesce in this stratification. Otherwise he will encourage market forces to break it down. Few manual workers bring more than an undifferentiated labour power into the market, and so any stratification among them is precarious. We discuss these issues further in Chapter 10.

CONCLUSION–CLASS EXPERIENCE OF UNCERTAINTY

In our review of the literature, we found that elements of all three models of the labour market specified earlier – class, stratified and differentiated – coexist for the manual worker, sometimes in a confused and contradictory way. Yet there is a possibility that such complexity might actually lead us to support a class model of the labour market, albeit of an amended kind. If the sociologist or economist is uncertain about how to make overall sense of the market, why should not the worker be in the same position? If internal and external markets, piecework, stratification processes in both supply and demand, common alienating tendencies all exercise their force, might not all workers feel uncertain about their economic destiny?

Let us add two labour market features that might add to uncertainty.

The most important is the dynamism of the economy itself. Even if concentration is reducing competition within the economy of the nation-state, international competition is still largely unregulated. Both individual firms and whole national economies can suffer profit and loss which is unpredictable, at least to their manual workers. Prosperity and redundancy, overtime and short-time working are perennial possibilities for the worker. Studies in both the United States and Britain show that the worker has a better-than-even chance of being unemployed at some point in his work-life, and that although there are tendencies for unemployment to be concentrated both among certain socio-economic groups (races, regional groups, unskilled workers) and at predictable points in the life cycle (the first and last five years of work), the threat is sufficiently real yet unpredictable to worry most workers.

Then we must consider the non-permanent elements of stratification and differentiation. At various points we have noted that the life cycle plays an important role in affecting both worker and employer preference. Workers go through the same basic life process, though the effects of this upon their labour market chances are neither uniform nor entirely predictable.

Thus we conclude tentatively that the labour market does not seem to allow a significant measure of choice to most workers because it tends to be either constraining or unpredictable. Yet there is enough uncertainty in the literature (as well as perhaps in the minds of workers) to justify more intensive research into the labour market. Our own effort now follows.

2 The Choice of a Labour Market

We wished to undertake an intensive study of one labour market, and this obviously involved setting boundaries to our study. Our first empirical problem was to delineate our labour market both geographically and occupationally. Geographically we were looking for a town within reach of our base of operations, Cambridge, which would offer three things:

1. a high degree of self-containment as a labour market, so that we could study the entire range of choice available to the worker in it;
2. a low level of unemployment, so that "choice" was not merely a question of working in any job or remaining unemployed;
3. a high degree of employment variety so that meaningful choices would appear to be possible.

Six towns appeared to meet these criteria to some degree, and we spent some months visiting, and collecting data on, Bedford, Cambridge, Colchester, Ipswich, Norwich and Peterborough. Then we chose the last-named as our labour market; in a moment we will describe Peterborough more fully. But even this choice did not end our search, for we had obviously to concentrate our study on a particular occupational stratum, or (at most) on a collection of strata. Even manual work is too varied in certain respects for one intensive study. Thus we will also explain our occupational coverage. Finally, having settled our boundaries, we had to devise sampling and other methodological procedures adequate to our purpose. This chapter will set the scene in three ways, describing in turn Peterborough, the problem of sub-markets within the manual working class, and our sampling and other methodological procedures.

THE TOWN OF PETERBOROUGH

Peterborough is an unremarkable medium-sized English town. Its fine Norman cathedral stands isolated among undistinguished urban architecture and attracts fewer tourists than it deserves. Its strategic position beside the main rail and road communications between Northeast and South-east, and between the Midlands and East Anglia, ensures that it has no very pronounced local or regional character. Its soccer team hovers around what we suspect to be its rightful place in the Football League – exactly half-way up the four divisions. Politically it is also mid-way, having continuously given highly precarious majorities (of between 4,584 and 3) to its Conservative M.P. between 1950 and 1974, when it fell to Labour. The outside world takes note of Peterborough only for two reasons, for its industry and for the persistence with which local Icaruses with artificial wings attempt to fly over the River Nene from the roof of Brierley's Supermarket. If any of them actually succeeded in flying, the town would be deprived of one of its most dependable sources of entertainment and publicity.

Peterborough's industrial structure is noteworthy, however. It is one of the oldest industrial towns in England, for its sprawling brickworks date from the period of the Roman occupation. They still dominate the local landscape, and their smell – strangely like burning rubber – makes Peterborough memorable to motorists passing along the Al as the place where they stopped to check their tyres (although the town remains invisible to them). In the second phase of the Industrial Revolution its strategic position made it an important railway town, and from the railway workshops came other engineering concerns. These concerns have kept pace with 20th-century technological developments and now stand as a highly representative sample of modern engineering firms – manufacturing a range of products from printing presses to washing machines, from machine tools to diesel engines. Finally, its communications and its position close to the most mechanised and profitable agricultural area in Europe, East Anglia, have made it an attractive location for food-processing firms. That three major industries – bricks, engineering and food-processing – are found in such a small town gives Peterborough an unusual variety and volume of employment.

In the early 1960s, when prosperity and population growth seemed to threaten the engulfing of Britain's major cities, Peterborough's buoyant industrial base (together with a large supply of vacant and reclaimable land, from its brickmaking industry) seemed to make it an ideal candidate for planned expansion away from existing areas of congestion. Designated a New Town in 1967, its Development Corporation was empowered to raise the population from around 81,000 to almost 200,000 by the early 1980s. This plan is still formally in operation, although at the time of writing (early1977) the population is still under 100,000, and national economic stagnation is tending to retard the development. As our fieldwork was largely completed in 1972, the expansion had had little effect on the town that we studied.

The detailing of local population and employment statistics is complicated by the boundary changes brought about by the New Town. The area covered by the New Town is a more meaningful unit than the old town's boundaries, and the 1971 census revealed its population to be 87,568. This reflected about a 15 per cent increase over the previous decade, indicating the steady industrial expansion of the town (Census, 1971a : Part I, Table 3). The unemployment rate has been below the national average since the Second World War. (Hancock, Hawkes and Associates, 1967). During the course of our field research it moved up from the exceptionally low point of 1 per cent in June 1969 to 3 per cent in April 1972, but this reflected the drift upward from 2.2 per cent to 3.9 per cent in Great Britain as a whole in this period. In fact, the employment provided there is greater than the town's population would suggest, for many commuters are attracted from the hinterland. Of the 48,620 persons employed there, 14,080 commuted into the borough from outside (Census, 1971c : Table 6). These commuters are of especial interest for us, for rural-urban differences have been stressed in the sociological literature dealing with worker orientations. Peterborough enabled us to collect a sample of workers of diverse urban/rural residence, for most of its commuters are from rural areas. As these predominantly rural commuters far outweighed the borough residents who worked outside, the Peterborough labour market meets our specification of a large degree of self-containment.

Peterborough offers an unusual volume of employment to manual workers. It is predominantly an industrial town and has more employment in manufacturing industries, and less in service industries, than the national average. As a consequence manual workers predominate, as Table 2.1 reveals.

We can see that all manual workers, and especially semi-skilled workers, are over-represented in the town. It is at the overlap of the skilled and semi-skilled categories that Peterborough seems most over-represented, offering a good sample frame for highly specialised occupations such as engine testers, furnacemen, drivers, and railway employment. So to

Table 2.1   Percentages of economically active males in certain occupations, 1971

	S.E.G. 9	S.E.G. 10	S.E.G. 11
	Skilled manual	Semi-skilled manual	Unskilled manual
	%	%	%
Peterborough New Town	31	17	9
East Anglia	27	12	7
Great Britain	30	13	8

Source: Census 1971b: Table 37; Census 1971c: Table 4.

Note: These three socio-economic groups exclude supervisory, self-employed, personal service, and agricultural workers.

volume we must add variety, for it is the diversity of specialised manual jobs available in Peterborough that most attracted us to the town. To the main manufacturing industries of engineering, food-processing and bricks, we must add the range of non-manufacturing employment (public services, construction, transport), and this amounts to a great diversity of employment types. If all these types of employment were available to the same workers at the same time, the Peterborough working class would have considerable job choice. Here is a labour market where job choice and work orientations should be observable if they are at all important in working-class behaviour. Furthermore, it is broadly identifiable as one labour market, relatively isolated from other industrial centres. Only small market towns of under 20,000 population are within practicable commuting distance of the town; beyond that lie Cambridge and Bedford at a distance of 35 miles. These are the reasons why we picked Peterborough.

By the same token, of course, we cannot claim that Peterborough is a "typical" town (whatever that would mean). Its industrial structure is admittedly unusual, its geographical position unique in more than just a map reference sense. Even its lack of local character might seem peculiar. We will not therefore conclude that our findings are simply representative of Britain (still less of Western capitalism) as a whole. We discuss the problems raised by generalising from our findings at the end of this monograph.

SUB-MARKETS WITHIN THE MANUAL WORKING CLASS

So far we have discussed job choice in very general terms, as if there were only one labour market for the manual part of the working class as a whole. Yet even the most cursory glance at real productive processes and labour markets reveals divisions which are sufficiently important to create a tendency toward non-competing sub-groups. The two main divisions are those provided by sex and by the training requirements of "skilled" manual jobs. We are writing at an interesting period in the history of the division of labour between the sexes, when (in this, one of the most socially advanced capitalist countries) equal pay and anti-discrimination legislation are intended to erode the clear boundary hitherto existing between working-class men and women in the labour market. There are many reasons for doubting its effectiveness, however. Peterborough in the early 1970s had not yet seen any of this process: we found no cases where male and female adult labour, identical except as regards their sex, was interchangeable. Excluded from all skilled trades, from supervising men, from nightwork, from driving, building, brick-making, heavy engineering, and railways, women were interchangeable only with special categories of males – juveniles, physically handicapped, seasonal students, and (some) blacks.[1] Thus men and women from the manual working class do not generally compete as individuals in the same labour market – a statement that is also true for both Britain as a whole and for most Western capitalist countries (Barron and Norris, 1976). We did not have the resources to study both these groups, and so we drew our sample only from the larger group, the men.

Even among male manual workers, sub-groups appear to exist. One of these seems to stand out in importance, that of "skilled workers". The existence of a distinct category of skilled workers appears to be vouched for by every Western census, by virtually every system of industrial relations, and by popular speech, which understands by such terms as "craftsman" and "tradesman" not merely a job title but a separate work ethos and attitude to life. Indeed, within the labour market the fully qualified craftsman and the labourer are only very rarely in individual competition for jobs. The former has undergone a long period of formal learning, and has an exclusive right to his job, guaranteed by paper qualifications and trade-union power. The labourer, it is generally agreed, is not qualified for such jobs. This differentiation might seem to cut like a knife right through the heart of the working class. In Britain, about 30 per cent of the whole employed population (and about 60 per cent of manual workers) are classified as skilled workers by the Office of

Population Censuses and Surveys (formerly the Registrar-General's Office), and this is a fairly typical figure for Western capitalist countries. Yet how many of these approximate to the fully qualified, ideal-typical craftsman? The O.P.C.S. category covers a very much wider range, including the foremen of all manual workers, all sorts of drivers outside agriculture, and most jobs which would be popularly regarded as semi-skilled. Thus, for example, apart from those specifically defined as labourers, all the manual jobs of workers in wood, paper, leather or rubber, and nearly all in glass and ceramics, metal and engineering are classed as skilled. For only a minority of "skilled" jobs is recruitment through an apprenticeship training, though some of the others require just as much skill. A random sample survey of household heads conducted in the United Kingdom in 1968–9 found that only 35 per cent of those in the O.P.C.S. Social Class 3, Manual (skilled workers) had even begun an apprenticeship period.[2] And a study conducted in 1971 by O.P.C.S. discovered that 64 per cent in the men in this group (and 85 per cent of the women) had no qualifications of any kind, including apprenticeship (O.P.C.S., 1973: 243).

The formality of apprenticeships themselves is often overestimated. Only a tiny minority of those apprentices in Britain registered for the City and Guilds training programmes successfully complete their courses, yet all are recognised as craftsmen if they have served their necessary time. Actual learning practices for skilled trades vary enormously according to industry, region, firm and trade-union strength. It is also possible for unskilled and semi-skilled workers to be promoted into craftsman positions, but this also varies by industry, etc. In factories where formal apprenticeships are closely adhered to, such upgrading is regulated and formalised. Those promoted are referred to as "dilutees" and their numbers agreed with the trade unions representing skilled workers. Yet in most factories upgrading is more informal and gradual. Occupational mobility surveys show that only 42 per cent of British skilled workers in 1949 had started in skilled positions while under 20 per cent of U.S. craftsmen in 1962 had done so, although the categories are rather wide and it should also be borne in mind that some first jobs are fill-ins before commencing apprenticeships. (Thomas, n.d.; Blau and Duncan, 1967: 498; cf. also Palmer, 1954).

Even in the engineering industry, where it is generally believed that the apprenticeship system is at its strongest, one study of 14 firms found that only a bare majority of skilled tradesmen in engineering crafts had served apprenticeships (Robinson, 1970: 58–60). Whether a clearly differentiated "aristocracy of labour" of skilled craftsmen actually existed in the 19th century is now becoming a matter of dispute among historians. Insofar as the term is used to describe skilled artisans rather than the labour leadership of the period, it is clear that their relative advantage was principally in terms of job security (Gray, 1974) coupled with higher pay, when compared to unskilled, frequently casual labour. Security prospects and incomes of manual workers have subsequently become much more equally distributed.[3] Thus if one uses the term today one should not mean by it the majority of skilled workers. Indeed, whether any manual group in manufacturing industries today can be regarded as an "aristocracy" is extremely doubtful. They rarely now possess, for example, their own trade unions ensuring restriction of access to their trade. The fact that British industry is now largely organised by general and industrial unions is a preliminary indication of some degree of class homogeneity among manual workers.

All this shows that the skilled group which does not compete in the labour market with less-skilled workers is far smaller than might be expected. Those craftsmen who have served a fairly formalised learning period when young, and who possess generally accepted credentials, may have been in a substantially different labour market from, say, labourers all their working lives, but they constitute only a minority of skilled workers, perhaps a small minority. Most skilled workers have at some point — and probably for several years at least — competed for jobs with non-skilled workers. As with women, we felt that the fully qualified craftsmen would necessitate a separate study (involving more investigation of technical education and youth employment than with other male workers). Therefore we have omitted them from our sample.

This study is concerned with the labour market for unqualified male manual workers. By "unqualified" we refer to a man in any manual job for which a formal apprentice-training, recognised by employers in general, is not required. Thus we include a few men who have served apprenticeships but are not following their trade, since they do not have qualifications relevant to their present jobs.

We should point out that this is a far broader stratum than the term might suggest. We include not only the O.P.C.S. entire unskilled and semi-skilled "social classes" but also a substantial majority of the skilled class. This accounts for three-quarters or even four-fifths of the male manual working class. In our sample we have highly specialised workers like engine testers and train drivers as well as some who are labelled by both their own management and unions as "skilled tradesmen" but who are in practice "dilutees" not easily able to transfer their skills to any employer in their industry. Some of these "dilutee" arrangements are formalised between unions and management, but many are not, especially in non-union firms and in small firms employing only a few craftsmen, whose wages and conditions of employment are probably substantially below those of most craftsmen. We have one such firm in our sample (Combex), where the engineering craftsmen are non-apprenticed, serving under only moderate employment terms, and without the possibility of moving into the engineering industry proper as craftsmen. They may be said to inhabit the same labour market at the rest of our sample.

If we have excluded women and fully skilled tradesmen from our sample, we must not also exclude their effects upon our sample. Precisely because they do not compete as individuals, they compete as groups within the labour market. Employers try continually to reduce their labour costs through technical innovation, and one of the avenues open to them is to substitute unskilled for skilled, and female for male, labour. Trade unions representing the group already established have, of course, resisted this. Thus the conditions of employment of each of the three groups are partially determined by the strength, both in numbers and in bargaining power, of the others. In Peterborough the conditions of our sample, the "middle group", have been very obviously affected by both the other groups. The importance of skilled engineering trades within local industry has tended to increase the wages of less-skilled workers at the same time as rendering promotion to the skilled stratum more difficult. Yet in the food-processing industry the predominance of female labour has depressed the wages of more-skilled workers there. These are merely examples – which would have to be investigated more fully – to show that the labour sub-market with which we are dealing is affected by other sub-markets.

THE SAMPLE : FIRMS, JOBS AND WORKERS

Within the Peterborough labour market we wished to study the work situation and attitudes of male non-skilled workers. This involved us in drawing a sample. As we noted in Chapter 1, a significant unit in any labour market analysis must be the individual employing organisation. Thus the obvious first step was to sample firms. With the aid of the Peterborough Employment Exchange we were able to draw up a list of all firms employing more than 50 persons. Their industrial distribution is detailed in Table 2.2, as is the sample we drew from this list.

This table reveals the two principles by which we sampled firms –

Table 2.2 Major employers in the Peterborough Employment Exchange Area by industry, 1968

Size Range	Food A	Food B	Engineering A	Engineering B	Bricks A	Bricks B	Other Mnfg. A	Other Mnfg. B	Construction A	Construction B	Other A	Other B	Total A	Total B
50–200	4	1	6	0	0	0	6	0	6	1	4	0	26	2
201–500	2	0	2	0	3	0	2	1	1	0	3	0	13	1
501–2000	2	1	2	0	0	0	0	0	1	0	3	2	8	3
2000	0	0	3	2	1	1	0	0	0	0	0	0	4	3
Total	8	2	13	2	4	1	8	1	8	1	10	2	51	9

A = No. of employees
B = No. included in study
Source: Peterborough Employment Exchange, unpublished

coverage of the major industries of the town, and over-representation of the larger firms. Our aim was to collect data on the productive process and the labour market as they might appear to the workers themselves. This entailed a dual coverage of the main types of work and the main employing organisations, for it seemed clear that workers could select their employment on the basis of either job or firm characteristics. Thus we expected (and found) that workers would refer to our building firm, Bettles, almost solely as a provider of outside construction jobs, whereas their references to the old-established engineering firm of Baker-Perkins would be dominated by its local image as a benevolent firm. As we wanted to give the latter type of "firm-stereotype" a chance to emerge, we overweighted our sample with large firms, where local stereotypes would presumably be clearer. Indeed, we tried to include all the largest firms in the sample and were prevented only by one refusal of co-operation. A further, rather obvious reason for including the large firms is that they provide a very substantial part of the employment in the area. As it is, our sample includes firms which together employ over three-quarters of the male unqualified manual workforce of the town.

We are aware that our sample of firms cannot be regarded as "typical" of Peterborough industry. It contains no agricultural employment and no firms with less than 50 employees; nor indeed could any nine firms represent the immense diversity and complexity of a large labour market. It is indeed difficult to see how typicality could be achieved, except by a lavish and wasteful research budget. Our intentions are somewhat more modest – to provide *examples* of the major non-agricultural types of employment situation available in one labour market, and to collect systematic objective data on them which can be related to the subjective opinions of the workers themselves.

The general characteristics of the nine sampled firms and of the workers interviewed in each are given in Table 2.3. Within the larger firms we sampled by two stages, first selecting groups of workers in the same vicinity, to enable us to study the social and physical context in which each man worked. This meant, for example, that the London Brick sample was drawn from just two brickyards and one pit. Also, our concentration on exemplary job types affected our sampling procedures within firms. Firstly, we wished to include the types of job for which the firm might be well known in the locality. For example, the reputation of the Perkins Manufacturing Company is for highly repetitive assembly-line work. Yet only about 1,000 of Perkins's 6,700 manual workers actually work on the assembly tracks, and a random sample of the firm's labour force might contain too few track workers for

Table 2.3: Companies participating in the study and the distribution of the sample

Organisation and product	Main types of labour surveyed	Approx. size of male manual labour force	Sample size	No. of respondents
Baker-Perkins (manfg. of industrial machinery)	Machinists, (inc. dilutee craftsmen), foundry workers, factory labourers	2000 +	223	159
Bettles (builders)	Building workers	80	43	16
British Rail (Peterborough Area)	Engine crews, signalmen, porters and labourers	1500	218	161
Combex (plastics)	Machine operators, fitters, warehousemen	75	60	36
Farrow's (food-processing)	Machine operators, warehousemen	120	62	53
Horrell's (dairy)	Milkmen	50	54	32
London Brick (brick manufacturing)	Open-cast pit workers, burners, labourers, machine operators, drivers	3000	215	180
Perkins (diesel engine manufacturing)	Assemblers, machinists, engine testers	6000	234	190
Peterborough Corporation	Gardeners, road gangs, dustmen, dilutee craftsmen	250	171	124
Totals			1280	951

Note: Response rate is 74.3 per cent. The non-respondents included 58 workers who had apparently left the company some time previously. If we exclude them from the calculations, the response rate rises to 77.8 per cent and rises disproportionately at Combex and Bettles.

statistical analysis. Thus we built up our samples within firms by deliberately including sub-groups, like the Perkins track workers, which were of especial theoretical interest.

So, even within the firms this was not a random sample. As with the firms, we over-represented work with a distinctive character and sought to obtain examples of the main types of work available. As a consequence we paid little attention to the size of the firms in sampling within them. We simply divided them into two groups according to size, in the larger ones aiming for a sample of around 200, and in the smaller ones of around 50. In both cases the aim was to adequately represent the types of work which especially interested us, though in the smallest firms it meant taking all relevant workers.

We carried out an extensive systematic observation of the work processes, and we also talked to workers and supervisors to gain a better understanding of what was involved. Further information about the firms and conditions of employment was gained from company records and from discussions with management and unions. As well as data on things of direct concern to workers, like wages, hours and fringe benefits, this provided more general background material on such items as the size and composition of the labour force, accidents and labour turnover, together with details of the employers' recruitment policies. Some of the information we collected was more or less equally relevant to all jobs in a firm, but a great deal applied to specific jobs.

Our attempt to compile precise and systematic data on all aspects of the jobs, and not just on the pay and hours, has been a distinctive feature of this research. In effect, we have undertaken our own work-study analysis – differing from industry's own such schemes, of course, by the fact that we were not using it to rank jobs or to legitimise a particular payment system! We scored all jobs on 31 different criteria of job content, ranging from environmental conditions, through skill components, to promotion chances, autonomy, interaction with other people, shift systems, and so on. We refer to these, perhaps rather arrogantly, as the *Objective Job Scores*. The full scheme is contained in Appendix II.

The scheme derives from the work of Turner and Lawrence (1965) – the only other systematic attempt to measure jobs in the sociological literature[4] – although we found immediately that their categories were of little use for non-factory employment. The subsequent modifications we made are another indication of the amount of employment variety contained within our sample. Most items are scored from 1 to 5 and are quite explicitly scales. However, in two cases, the Payment System (28) and the Incentive Philosophy underlying this system (29), the categories are not ordered, so these items are used differently, and separately, from the remainder. One or two presented some difficulty in measurement, either because it was not realistic to differentiate as many as five categories, as happened with Danger, or because they are, like Responsibility, rather more complex than our unidimensional scales imply. However, we have found it fruitful to use these measures as they stand.

As our term "Objective Job Scores" indicates, our aim was to measure objectively the characteristics of the jobs. However, we were well aware of an inevitable subjective element in almost all measures; we scored items according to our perceptions. Let us illustrate this with the scoring of noise. In principle this could have been done with measurements on a meter, with the scale based on established physiological relations, but even this would not have been so simple as it sounds. Quite apart from practical measurement problems we would still need to interpret variations within one job. What we actually did was to relate Noise to difficulty in communication, on a range from normal conditions to where it was virtually impossible for us to talk or understand. Such noise *we* found almost unbearable, yet the workers would stick it day after day and were even able to "talk" if necessary.[5] On this and all other items we were careful to observe its relevance for the men concerned – not least to protect us from being overimpressed by unfamiliar features. However, men will put up with all sorts of things if they have to, so it was important to base the measures largely on our own "unadjusted" perceptions. Our method was a combination of observing and talking (to the workers), together, where necessary, with doing the job ourselves. Ideally it might have been better to couple this method with the use of measuring instruments, but there were few cases where this would have been possible; noise is one thing, but what instrument measures dirt or danger? The only technical aids we used were our wrist watches and here we had to be careful not to be mistaken for time-study men. With a whole battery of technical apparatus we might well have found the job impossible. We would certainly have produced different results. For example, one of the most difficult scoring problems we encountered was how to deal with workers who invested a great deal of skill and ingenuity in doing virtually no work at all and, indeed, in rendering themselves invisible for long periods. We gave to them not high scores but our respect! Had we appeared with a battery of equipment they would undoubtedly have performed – as they usually do for job-evaluation experts – the elaborate but largely unnecessary set of work routines they are formally required to do.

The scores, from 1 to 5, given to each item may be taken as points on a continuum. For much of the analysis we have treated them in this way, particularly in correlations. However, five values is a very short range, and this fact must be added to the usual considerations of measurement error (it is hardly conceivable that we were perfectly consistent in our scoring). The possibility of non-linear relationships also makes for caution in interpreting correlation coefficients. On the other hand, the main distortion is likely to be general under-estimation of the level of relations, which is relatively easy to allow for. Furthermore, factor analysis copes well with crude indicators and is appropriate for use with the objective job scores. It is employed extensively in the next chapter, both in exploring the structure of inter-relationships between variables and in simplifying data. The structure is, of course, a direct concern of the research, while 29 variables is a lot to work with concurrently, so that simplification into a smaller number of factors was useful as well as instructive. But such simplification inevitably entails some loss of information. Thus we have also worked with the basic variables at many points.

We have two alternative ways of using these data on jobs (either in raw or factored form) in building up a picture of the diversity of the labour market. First, we can consider the different *jobs*. We have data on 368 jobs, but our interview samples included men in only 275 of them. For the latter we were able to calculate the average wages and hours of the men doing them. Thus at any point where we want to incorporate wages and hours in the analysis, the smaller set of jobs is used. Elsewhere we found that it makes very little difference which sample of jobs we use, which is reassuring on grounds of reliability, but we preferred the larger sample where it was suitable. However, this sample limits us to an approach which does not give us any real idea of the typicality of jobs, for it weights equally a job existing for only one worker and a job for 41 (our highest figure). For some purposes, therefore, we have used a second approach in which we have weighted each of the 275 jobs by the number of respondents occupying it. Each of these methods is more suitable for certain purposes.

The Objective Job Scores are the most original part of our methodology. We feel that the year spent collecting the data for this pioneering venture has been justified by the results we have obtained. For the first time in industrial sociology we are able to give a detailed description of the job alternatives available to workers. We also wished to relate these alternatives to workers' attitudes and behaviour, and this led to the second main area of our research methodology, our interview survey.

We obtained interviews with 951 of the workers occupying the 275 jobs already mentioned. We interviewed them in works time, and generally received very great co-operation from managements and trade unions in organising this. Difficulties were greatest where the firm was highly decentralised (as in building) or where the workers could not be interrupted in their work and were in effect doing the interview in their own time (as among railway footplate staff and dustbinmen). Only in the building firm is the response rate inadequate. The interviews took about an hour each and were conducted by one of the authors (Mann) and a team of six women interviewers, selected and trained by us. The interview schedule and its accompanying check-list can be found in Appendix I.

A special problem in interviewing workers arises in virtually all contemporary European countries, that presented by immigrant workers speaking a different language from the natives. In Britain, Pakistanis and Indians are now found in large numbers in many labour markets and Spaniards, Italians and other Mediterranean peoples in certain regions and industries. In Peterborough foreign immigrants form about 11 per cent of the male population; they are of diverse origins, but Italians and those from the Indian sub-continent form the largest groups among them, followed by refugees from eastern and central Europe (2.4 per cent, 2.2 per cent and 1.4 per cent respectively of the male population; Census, 1971a: Table 14). As noted in Chapter 1, the position of immigrant groups in the labour market is a vital part of advanced capitalist economies, and we do not wish to neglect them. However, they present logistical and budgetary problems. This was especially so for the Indians and Pakistanis (we interviewed before the secession of Bangladesh), for whom the nearest to a common language was actually English. We did not have the resources to employ interviewers speaking Urdu, Bengali, Hindi and the lesser languages. Italian was another matter, however, and we were able to secure both the necessary professional advice and an expert interviewer to proceed with an Italian version of the questionnaire.[6] Apart from the Italians, we were forced to reject from our sample all those workers whose English was inadequate. This must tend to bias our sample towards the more educated among Indians and Pakistanis. We discuss this in Chapter 9.

We interviewed from August 1970 to May 1971. This was near the end of the low unemployment years, and subsequent to our fieldwork the national slump hit Peterborough. One of our companies (Farrows) closed down completely, and all the other private firms in the sample announced redundancies. We will comment on this in our concluding chapter.

THE NINE FIRMS

We provide systematic data on the conditions of employment and the job structure of the nine firms in Chapter 4. But we will first give a sketch of their more general characteristics.

Baker-Perkins is a medium-sized company with three main factories, of which the largest (the headquarters) is in Peterborough. Its turnover of around £40m. per annum in 1971 is based on the manufacture of machinery for the food industry and of printing presses. The former tends to be small batch production of ovens, moulds, etc., while the latter is dominated by "one-off" manufacture and assembly of very large presses. During the period of our fieldwork, the centre of the factory began to be dominated by the bulk of a huge offset-litho colour press. Such a product demands high-precision engineering and a high proportion of fully skilled labour. Thus our sample in Baker-Perkins is drawn from under one-half of the labour force. It includes foundrymen and fettlers, mates, labourers, semi-skilled machinists, and some dilutee craftsmen. All work on the one site, though spread between several buildings.

The company is not a member of an employers federation and so deals exclusively with local unions. Labour relations are good in both a formal and informal sense. Formally, these is a very stable system of consultation with the shop stewards of the major unions. The A.E.U.W. predominates amongst skilled workers and therefore in the factory as a whole, but shares representation among the semi-skilled and unskilled with the T. & G.W.U. and the G. & M.W.U. All workers must join one of these unions. Informally, the co-operative atmosphere is clear to the outside observer. Around the construction of the printing presses can be seen groups of craftsmen, foremen and managers discussing work problems on a more egalitarian basis than in most factories. However, it must be pointed out that our sample, as relatively unskilled workers, are somewhat marginal to this process, as they are indeed to the company's main interests in labour relations.

The company is well liked by its employees and has a reputation locally as a "good firm to work for", as we will see in Chapter 5. It does not pay especially good wages, but has good fringe benefits. Its reputation for providing secure employment took a dent after the completion of our interviews, when almost 200 men (out of 2,700 male manual workers) were made redundant in 1971. This year was a bad one for the company, though it has subsequently revived.

Bettles is a small but expanding building firm, owner-managed by a father (a self-made man) and his son. We appear to have received their co-operation partly because the then Director of our Cambridge department went to the same public school as the son! The firm had doubled its turnover in the period 1967–9 to nearly £1m., and had moved into the highly competitive field of tendering for single contracts. It engages in much sub-contracting, thereby reducing the fluctuations of the labour force which are so characteristic of the industry. As well, it has regular maintenance contracts with two air force bases near by which involve keeping permanent labour forces at the bases. Security reasons denied us access to one of these, a U.S.A.F. base. A large joinery shop was also excluded from the sample, as the workers there were apprenticed craftsmen. Except for the base workers, our sample worked in small groups, moving frequently between sites around Peterborough.

The conditions of employment resemble those of the building industry generally, except that security is higher. Wages are highly negotiable, according to the day-to-day jobbing needs, and fringe benefits are negligible. Relations with management are highly individualised and no formal negotiations with trade unions take place (though many workers are union members). Most workers feel that their employer is the building industry rather than the firm of Bettles, though there is a core of long-service workers who are intimate with the firm and know the family. Subsequent to our fieldwork Bettles has continued to expand profitably.

British Rail (Peterborough Area) We presume that British Rail's activities are public knowledge. We sampled from the normal range of railway jobs – porters, parcels-handlers, cleaners, shunters, signalmen, guards, footplate staff (drivers and firemen), etc. We conducted part of our pilot survey in the railway workshop and the Peterborough subsidiary station and so these were excluded from the main survey. A peculiarity of Peterborough is the large parcels-sorting depot for the region (which moved during our fieldwork from a former passenger station to a site adjacent to a mail-order warehouse), and so our sample included a large number of unskilled parcels-handlers. But the largest group were the footplatemen, based in Peterborough, but working routes, covering the east of the country, between Doncaster and London. Their hours are highly irregular and unpredictable because of continual re-scheduling to ensure that there is always a driver available with the necessary route knowledge. Most other railwaymen work shifts, but these are less erratic. British Rail fringe benefits are generous.

Industrial relations are like those in any other railway region. Two strong unions represent our workers, A.S.L.E.F. representing almost all footplatemen (drivers and firemen) and N.U.R. representing the remainder. All our sample belonged to one or the other. A.S.L.E.F. consciously adheres to the historical tradition of "the aristocracy of labour", and industrial relations at the national level see almost as much conflict between the two unions as between them and management. Relations between management and men are good at a local level, partly because many of the conflict issues are negotiated nationally, and partly because railwaymen have traditionally shared a strong interest and pride in their industry. This pride is felt to be on the decline, however, and clearly did not exist among a non-traditional occupation like parcels-handling.

Combex is the Peterborough factory of the Dunbee-Combex-Marx group, manufacturers of plastic toys and toiletries. At Peterborough are made low-cost plastic toys and ladies' cosmetics. The firm made high profits by keeping re-investment low, and this makes for rather poor working conditions, fringe benefits and wages. Demand for the products is somewhat seasonal, rising to a peak before Christmas, and some temporary labour is recruited. The company is generally short of labour when unemployment is low, and it employs all the groups which might be thought to inhabit the "bottom" of the labour market – women, blacks, juveniles and registered disabled persons. Combex certainly does not practise discrimination against any of these groups! The technology is very simple and the factory is divided into several largely autonomous departments, one for each main type of product. The jobs are mostly of low skill – machine operating, assembling, and stores and warehouse work. The skilled maintenance workers are not usually apprenticed, and we included them in our sample.

About half the workers were in the T. & G.W.U., which was recognised by management but was not very well-organised or militant in the period of our fieldwork. As we found most of the workers had rather low aspirations, industrial relations were more harmonious than the conditions of employment might lead one to expect. Subsequently, the expansion of the firm and its widely advertised high profits of 1971 and 1972 have led to rather more union activity and successful short strikes over wages and conditions. Combex was at the end of a particular period in its history when we studied it, and has clearly undergone important changes since then.

Farrow's is a brand label of the canned fruits and vegetables sold by the Norwich-based Reckitt & Colman food-processing group. Most of the Peterborough factory was devoted to the fairly simple technology involved in canning fresh food (and making peanut butter) although one floor was occupied by a more complex continuous-process plant manufacturing preserves, while a small, bee-infested area mixed and bottled Gale's Honey. We use the past tense because the entire factory was abandoned in 1971–2 and production transferred to Norwich. The whole labour force was declared redundant except for a few key workers who were transferred. There had been very little warning of the shut-down, and the company had been very stable for the previous 20 years, but the dilapidation and inefficiency of the factory were fairly evident to us beforehand.

Farrow's was in many ways a typical small cheap-food factory. Working conditions were somewhat messy, and half the labour force were women. As many of the men were Pakistani, it can be guessed that the company was near the bottom of the labour market. To cope with the seasonality of canning, the company also recruited a large number of student workers in the summer. Though wage-rates were low, very long hours of overtime brought actual earnings above the local average. Fringe benefits were quite good. However, these benefits were not readily visible to outsiders, and the company's local reputation was unduly poor (as we shall see in Chapter 5). Day work was the norm.

No formal negotiations were entered into with trade unions, though most employees did belong to one. The difficulties of organising such a diverse collection of workers were great. Industrial relations did not seem either particularly good or bad. The atmosphere varied considerably between sections. The cooking areas were environmentally unpleasant, in the bottling/canning areas the pace of work was somewhat pressurised by the speed of the machines, but in the large warehouses there was an easy, friendly working atmosphere which permitted quite extensive card-playing.

Horrell's Dairies is a local, family-managed, dairy and milk delivery firm, supplied by its own farm (which we did not study). Apart from half-a-dozen machine operators and crate-humpers in the dairy, the labour force consisted of milkmen. After loading their vans, around 3.30–4.30 a.m., the milkmen went on their rounds until about 9.30–11.30 a.m., when they unloaded their empties before knocking off. (There was a fair amount of flexibility in starting times, and some men would choose to start late, but to begin delivery after 6 a.m. was rare.) Obviously the most distinctive feature of this work is the hours, which though short, are early and demanding – the milkmen work right through for five weeks and then have a week off. However, the level of working autonomy is high, as are the chances for social contact while at work. Ability to deal with money calculations is, of course, required.

Interestingly, the company calculate that horse-drawn floats are more economical to run than either electric or petrol power, but claim that they cannot attract men who can or will look after horses.

Wages were only average, though this works out at a very high rate per hour. Normal fringe benefits were poor, and, we are sorry to report, we could find no evidence of the additional fringe benefit popularly accredited to the milkman.

Trade unions were not recognised and there was no demand voiced for them by the workers. We showed in an earlier article (Blackburn and Mann, 1975: 150) that the Horrell's workforce was the most conservative in our sample. Both management and men believe the milkman to be an individualist, out to "get on" by his own unaided efforts. Relations with management thus tended to be good or bad according to individual personalities. Horrell's seemed to possess few characteristics as a firm that would distinguish it from other dairies.

The London Brick Co. Ltd is the largest brick manufacturer in the world and occupies a near-monopoly position within the British market. The supply of bricks is so strategic to the British building industry that it is inconceivable that the company could make a long-term financial loss, but its profits have in the past been generally rather low. In 1969 it made only a 9.6 per cent return on capital employed, a low return for the dominant producer in a static industry. However, it is somewhat vulnerable to short-term national recessions.

The company has two main centres of activity, – at Bedford (its headquarters) and Peterborough, which are the two main locales of the special Oxford clay on which its prosperity is based. Oxford clay has the unusual property of containing its own igneous material.[7] Thus it needs little independent fuel and no elaborate system of firing. A continuous fire is maintained, which is allowed to pass from chamber to chamber round the kiln, as required, with just a small addition of coal dust – "smudge" – from time to time to keep it going. The "Fletton brick" (named after a village near Peterborough) derived from this clay is thus cheaper than other bricks of a comparable quality.

Traditionally brickmaking has not been highly mechanised and so the optimum unit of organisation has been the largely autonomous individual brickyard, employing anything between 50 and 250 men. In the late 1950s there were about 20 of these in the vicinity of Peterborough. However, technical innovations then reduced both the number of yards and men required. For 20 years until 1970, yard closures and redundancies dominated industrial relations within the company.[8] It was thought that this period had ended in 1970, and profits did increase, but further cut-backs have followed.

Brick manufacturing involves a number of contrasting operations. The first stage is the quarrying of the clay in the open-cast pits. In the most modern pits this can be an awe-inspiring sight. Sheer cliffs of dark green clay, 100 feet high, are swept by the blades of an enormous shale planer. At most pits, however, the clay is dug from above by a dragline excavator. One excavator takes off the top 12 feet or so of ordinary soil and a second digs the clay (or "knot") which may go down for another 100 feet. The clay is broken up in a "Kibbler" and transferred to the shed, which may be a considerable distance away, usually on a conveyor but sometimes in lorries. The work involved (to keep the clay moving, maintain equipment, move the conveyor with the digging, etc.) varies widely in content and effort, but entails some heavy labouring, and it can be very dirty. Above all, the men have a high degree of freedom and share a sense of working on their own as a team.

When the clay arrives at the sheds it is pulverised, sifted and machine-pressed into "green bricks". At this stage the jobs are largely routine machine-minding, although the processing of clay calls for activities rather different from most jobs of this sort, such as moving around between hoppers and poking the clay with a long pole to stop it sticking. The green bricks are then stacked rather elaborately by "setters" working by hand. Fork-lift trucks transfer the stacks to the kiln chambers, which are arranged in long double rows making up a kiln. The outer side of each chamber is left open to form an entrance, and when the chamber is ready this is sealed with a "wicket" of rough brickwork. The bricks then dry out until the burner, working on the flat roof of the kiln, begins the firing by allowing the fire to enter from the next chamber. The burner controls the process of heating, baking and cooling, which is at a different stage in each chamber, moving steadily round the kiln in a 14-day cycle. His is a complex and responsible job. When the bricks are cooled, the wicket is knocked down and the bricks, now red, are removed ("drawn") by fork-lift truck into the yard. They are then stacked by hand, by "blockers", or bound by "banders" ready for delivery. This, like setting, is hard, demanding labouring. The brickyard itself is either dusty or muddy and this adds to the unpleasantness.[9]

Several kinds of distinction can be made between the jobs: between the contrasting environments of pit, shed and yard, between those on piecework who earn high wages (setters, blockers, banders, fork-lift drivers) and those on day rate who usually earn rather little, between the different types of mental and manual skill involved, between day shift and night shift. The burner stands somewhat alone, physically isolated on his roof, working a rotating three-shift system, and with a job of unique mental demands. There is also ethnic diversity in the yards. In the wartime and post-war labour shortages, the company recruited large numbers of displaced European refugees and Italians. They stayed, the recruitment of Italians has continued, and now some Indians and Pakistanis have been added. Almost half the labour force is of non-British origin.[10] Yet this diversity is welded together by the common culture of the brickyard. This has not changed greatly since its portrayal in Victorian novels. Management and men liked to exaggerate the toughness of the yards, warning us of the dangers lurking there for our female interviewers (nothing untoward actually happened). Fringe benefits are poor and are expected to be. Eccentricity is also cultivated. Traditionally, the three burners entrusted with each kiln (one to each shift) kept a dog up on the kiln roof. The dog provided company and was unable ever to leave the roof. We were told a typical story by a local union official. One day, he said, the burners from a yard threatened with closure stormed into his office, shouting and swearing against management and loudly demanding immediate militant action against redundancy. "But", said the official, "I thought we'd sorted out the redundancy issue. Management are transferring you to another yard." "It's not us," said the men, "it's the dog. What's going to happen to him? There's already a dog at the other yard."[11]

Industrial relations are tough, and disputes are easily inflamed. Almost all workers belong to a trade union, about two-thirds to the G. & M.W.U. and most of the remainder to the T. & G.W.U. During our period of fieldwork, the latter union began to increase its membership at the expense of the former. The widely reported militancy of the new T. & G.W.U. local officer (who subsequently went over to the other side by taking up a management position elsewhere) greatly attracted the brickworkers. Despite all this, we would hesitate to describe industrial relations as "bad", for disputes are relatively quickly settled through negotiation. Rather, both sides cultivate a tough style.

Perkins Manufacturing Co. Ltd. is easily the largest organisation in the Peterborough district. It employs around 8,000 people, while the value of its products is over £40m. a year. Perkins makes a single product, diesel engines, and has a dominant position in the world market for lower-priced engines. Originally a small Peterborough family firm, it was taken over in 1958 by Massey-Ferguson, the Canadian machinery group. Until the national recession of 1970–1, it had steadily expanded and prospered under Massey-Ferguson. The parent company has other British plants, and its European headquarters are on the same site in Peterborough.

Perkins is a very tightly-organised firm. The effort to cut down overhead costs is apparent at once to the outsider, and there are only 1,300 office staff out of the 8,000 employees. Production is highly mechanised and lower management is allowed little discretion. Labour relations are partly determined at national Massey-Ferguson level, and partly through three-year (later reduced to two-years) contracts signed between Peterborough management and union officials. Hence working arrangements are highly rule-governed, and personal relations between the men and their immediate supervisors are more than usually irrelevant to production. Supervisors are frequently ignored as the workers' hierarchical system of shop stewards, senior stewards and convenors quickly take grievances to higher management. There is 100 per cent union membership, largely of the A.E.U.W., although other unions are represented.

Labour relations could only be regarded as "tough" in our period of study. The terms of the contract were so important for both sides that strikes were regarded by both as being a normal part of the bargaining process. Towards the end of the contract period there was a noticeable build-up of tension. The typical pattern was then that the convenor and deputy convenor who negotiated the last agreement were voted out of office by the men, then a large wage demand was made, countered by a minimal management offer, then the strike was threatened. In 1968–9 a three-week strike occurred; in 1971 it was averted only because the threat of redundancies obviously weakened the men's bargaining position. In 1973 and 1974 long strikes and lock-outs occurred over a claim for parity of wages with Massey-Ferguson in Coventry.

The dominating factor in industrial relations was top management's willingness to grant high wage concessions in return for absolute control over working practices between contracts. Toughness was recognised by both sides as "the normal means of doing business". In other ways Perkins was quite a benevolent employer. Its fringe benefits were quite good. And its highly organised consultative system with unions prevented arbitrary use of prerogatives such as dismissal. General job security was only fair, for demand for the company's product is highly susceptible to the buoyancy of the national economy. In the difficult year of 1971 approximately 10 per cent of the labour force was made redundant on a "voluntary" basis, while most of the factory was on short-time working for a period of several weeks.

However, Perkins's most salient feature is its wages. It is the highest payer of the sampled firms, and probably in the Peterborough district, whether we consider weekly or hourly earnings. The hours worked are short but somewhat inconvenient, and almost all the workers we interviewed were required to work alternate fortnights on days and nights.

The principal sacrifice the men must make for their high wages is work autonomy. The closely controlled system of mass-production has led to extreme sub-division of tasks. Here we find the ideal-typical modern assembly worker who, throughout his whole workng day, fits three screws on to a machine part, with a job cycle of 12 seconds. The majority of the manual workers at Perkins, whether machining or assembling, are required to do the kind of short, repetitive, mindless tasks which Chris Argyris (1957) has observed are more effectively performed by mental defectives than by normal healthy adults. Not surprisingly, therefore, the commitment of Perkins workers to their employment is minimal. This worries the more liberal and sensitive Perkins managers during periods of labour shortages, though less during periods of high unemployment (when the theory is that fear of the dole keeps up the level of commitment.) In short, Perkins is the type of mass-production plant so often studied by the industrial sociologist – the home of the mythical assembly-line worker, privatised, instrumental and affluent. Even the more skilled jobs tend to carry their unpleasantnesses. After the bought-in rough parts are machined and then assembled, the completed engines (or a sample of them) are tested by an individual worker for periods ranging from 20 minutes to 24 hours. This provides a longer work cycle, and a more skilled job, but unfortunately the noise level surrounding the testers is appalling. However, among our sample of machinists, assemblers and testers, the work of one group had improved considerably in recent years. The machinists of the 4.236 diesel engine (Perkins's smallest-capacity engine) now supervise "transfer machinery", giving them a less pressurised, more responsible job with a longer work cycle.[12]

Peterborough Corporation was responsible for the normal range of local authority services. At the period we did our fieldwork, the New Town Development Corporation was a separate organisation, largely concerned with forward planning. The old town corporation was carrying on normally and the designation of Peterborough as a New Town did not affect this part of our research.

We interviewed workers in the Parks, Cleansing, Sewerage, Maintenance, and Building Departments. Therefore our sample includes gardeners, groundsmen, dustbinmen, road and building labourers and craftsmen (dilutees), sewage workers, and drivers of various kinds. This is a very varied collection of jobs, though a certain uniformity is engendered by the low pay, lack of shiftwork (except for the sewage workers and a few others), very high job security, excellent fringe benefits (especially pension and sick pay), and the generally weak nature of managerial control. Despite labour shortages, very few women or immigrants are employed, and this indicates either the presence of discriminatory practices or the local belief that they exist there.

Most workers belong to N.U.P.E., and, as in most public services, relations between unions and management are highly institutionalised. Many of the conditions of employment are negotiated at national level, but the tendency towards local productivity schemes has increased local negotiations. In Peterborough the building workers and the dustbinmen were particularly involved in this, the latter with some degree of militancy.

These nine firms, then, represent a considerable diversity of employment conditions. They include limited companies and public services; the profitable, the stagnating and the collapsing; the non-union, multi-union and closed shop. The range of jobs is enormous, from milkmen to millers (both food- and machinist), from dustbinmen to drillers. In order to surmount this heterogeneity—which exists in most towns, of course— we clearly had to undertake a highly quantitative form of analysis.

We make no apology for the extensive statistical analysis of this report. Although our observational studies, together with some of the interview data, would allow us to write descriptively about subjective meanings and so on, we do not think this would be appropriate or fruitful at this stage. We have taken account of what we learned through all the methods that we used. But what is needed in this area is a study with sufficiently wide coverage to enable a rigorous analysis to clarify some basic problems. Such an approach calls for statistical analysis, whether the data be qualitative or quantitative. The only difference is that the more qualitative the data, the more difficult the statistical analysis. However, we have endeavoured to keep the analysis as simple and comprehensible (to non-statisticians) as possible.

We make quite extensive use of "tests of significance", which have come in for severe criticism from time to time. (For a valuable set of criticisms presented in a rather aggressive editorial context see Morrison and Henkel, 1970.) This is not the place for us to attempt an adequate statement of our position, but a brief comment may be helpful since our usage conforms to the expectations of neither conventional users nor — obviously — those who regard their use as a sin. Part of the problem is the misleading terminology, which is often taken (by supporters and critics) to imply that if the measures are of any use they must *test* something, generally accepted as hypotheses, on the basis of statistical (not substantive) significance. Of course, this reflects their original purpose and conventional use. Yet what the "tests" actually do is provide estimates of probabilities concerning relationships in data. We see no virtue in deliberately ignoring this information, although any decisions should take account of all the circumstances and information.

It might be argued that probability measures add nothing to measures of association, which we also use extensively. However, a correlation coefficient is not a substitute for a "significance" level (nor vice-versa), any more than a regression coefficient is for a correlation measure. In any case, there are difficulties associated with the measurement of association, as we shall see, so we cannot afford to neglect the additional information on probabilities.

Since we are engaging in sociological analysis, not attempting to carry out a social survey, we are not using "significance tests" as criteria for generalising to a population. Throughout this report they are used as estimates of the probability of a degree of association as great as, or greater than, that observed arising by chance. The interpretation of this probability is not entirely unproblematic, although it is no more difficult than that of most correlation statistics of association. Roughly we may say that the less the probability, the more seriously we take the observed association.[13] We refer to "significance" in conventional terms and use conventional cut-off points to divide data, but these should be seen as arbitrary divisions chosen for their usefulness. Where appropriate we make equally arbitrary but useful divisions on other variables. In fact, our general approach to the area of statistics is pragmatic; we do whatever we think best helps to further understanding. Statistics should serve, not dominate, research.

3 Jobs in the Labour Market

We come now to a consideration of the jobs available to the manual workers without relevant occupational qualifications. Our aim in this chapter is to examine the ways in which the different job characteristics vary together, to establish the extent to which the labour market is *hierarchical* or *compensatory* in form: that is to say, do desirable job features vary directly or inversely? If they vary directly the labour market is hierarchical, for then there exist only generally "better" and "worse" jobs, not jobs that offer equally desirable but different features. The opportunity for workers to exercise choice depends on a compensatory structure, where rewards on less salient aspects can be sacrificed for those which are most desired. Hierarchy, on the other hand, entails constraint, since it means competition for the better jobs, while decisions about who gets them are in the hands of the employers and workers' preferences are irrelevant.

Despite the dominance of a neo-classical and compensatory theory in labour economics its detailed research findings would tend to lead us to a hierarchical view. It is now well established that fringe benefits vary directly with wages: those with higher wages receive more generous benefits (Lester, 1952: 487; Mackay *et al.*, 1971: 92; Rees and Shultz, 1970: 77–9; Reynolds, 1951: 202). Researchers note that working conditions also seem better in high-wage plants, though no one has devised adequate quantitative techniques for measuring this (Mackay *et al.*, 1971: 92; Myers and MacLaurin, 1943: 59–61; Reynolds, 1951: 221). Distance travelled to work is the only aspect of work which has been found to compensate for wages: that is, the higher-paid travel farther (Mackay *et al.*, 1971: 92, 251–2; Rees and Shultz, 1970: 169–75). In order to pursue this type of enquiry more rigorously, and to extend it to other conditions of employment, we have used our Objective Job Scores, described in the last chapter. Our analysis will proceed in two stages. To begin with, in this chapter, we look at the jobs as a whole, and the patterns of relationship of different aspects. Thus we are ignoring an important aspect of the real labour market, the fact that jobs are grouped in *firms*, which are normally the actual recruiting mechanisms within the market. We will consider this in the next chapter.

We examine the structure of hierarchical and compensatory relationships in three stages. Firstly, we consider the relations between a wide range of individual job attributes. Then we explore the structure with the aid of factor analysis. This provides a basis for us to construct a number or theoretical factors to represent general job aspects related to the main clusters of individual attributes. With these we can then proceed to a more adequate evaluation of hierarchy and compensatory structure. This is done first for the set of individual jobs, and then we consider the effect of weighting them by numbers of occupants, to come closer to the actual distribution of jobs in the market. We must warn the reader that the analysis which follows in this chapter is necessarily somewhat complicated and statistical, though the actual techniques used are not particularly difficult.

RELATIONSHIPS BETWEEN INDIVIDUAL JOB ATTRIBUTES

Our first step is to see whether desirable job characteristics tend to be found together in the same jobs (i.e. *hierarchy*), or whether different jobs have their own attractions (i.e. *compensatory*). From our job scores, and adding wages and hours, we have selected those characteristics which appear most likely to be viewed by the sample as desirable or undesirable. We assume for this purpose that workers prefer higher wages, shorter hours, a quieter, cleaner working environment, greater freedom of movement, higher degrees of skill but lower physical effort, and the most obvious interpretations of the other job features which appear in Table 3.1. These desirable and undesirable characteristics have been inter-correlated for the 275 jobs in our sample.[1] Correlations which indicate a hierarchical view of the labour market (i.e. where desirability varies together on the two aspects across jobs) are in heavy type, those indicating a compensatory view are in italics.[2]

Hierarchical relations predominate (115 to 40), but until we consider the meaning of the items, we cannot decide whether this is an artefact or an indication of the dominance of hierarchy. For example, one partial artefact is constituted by the number of highly inter-correlated measures of "mental abilities", which tend to over-weight the matrix. We will consider this further when we look at the factor patterns.

If we start at the other end, with the few compensatory correlations,

Table 3.1 Job characteristics, correlations (275 jobs)

	(1)	(2)	(3)	(4)	(5)	(6)	(7)	(8)	(9)	(10)	(11)
1. Exposure	1.00										
2. Fumes, dirt, etc.	0.03	1.00									
3. Noise	-0.40	0.35	1.00								
4. Danger	-0.05	0.43	0.20	1.00							
5. Quantity of physical effort	0.28	0.30	0.10	0.16	1.00						
6. Pace of physical effort	0.11	0.18	0.09	0.09	0.52	1.00					
7. Manual dexterity	-0.01	0.15	0.28	0.13	0.04	0.18	1.00				
8. Work cycle length	0.41	0.00	-0.13	0.01	-0.01	-0.26	0.10	1.00			
9. Object variety	-0.25	-0.10	0.12	0.01	-0.21	0.17	0.31	0.21	1.00		
10. Mathematical calculation	-0.12	-0.12	0.03	0.03	-0.10	-0.22	-0.00	0.26	0.49	1.00	
11. Reading, writing	-0.09	-0.32	-0.09	-0.02	-0.20	-0.17	0.09	0.32	0.59	0.68	1.00
12. Memory	-0.02	-0.33	-0.07	-0.08	-0.17	-0.14	0.46	0.39	0.63	0.52	0.72
13. Visualisation	0.01	-0.11	0.08	0.11	-0.17	-0.18	0.63	0.40	0.52	0.31	0.45
14. Complexity of decisions	-0.18	-0.10	0.14	0.09	-0.15	-0.14	0.55	0.34	0.60	0.42	0.55
15. Autonomy of decisions	0.25	-0.10	-0.13	0.01	-0.13	-0.30	0.31	0.65	0.35	0.23	0.42
16. Pace choice	0.41	-0.11	-0.36	-0.04	-0.13	-0.35	-0.13	0.54	0.08	0.18	0.19
17. Responsibility	0.04	-0.24	-0.05	0.09	-0.19	-0.11	0.33	0.32	0.23	0.22	0.40
18. Supervision: absence of	0.59	-0.05	-0.35	-0.08	0.05	-0.15	0.01	0.48	-0.07	0.08	0.17
19. Optional interaction	0.22	-0.16	-0.31	-0.19	0.07	0.02	-0.18	0.36	-0.04	0.01	0.11
20. Promotion chances	-0.01	-0.01	-0.06	-0.03	0.01	-0.02	-0.33	-0.00	-0.04	0.02	0.03
21. Hours: irregularity	-0.00	-0.13	0.08	-0.08	-0.05	-0.22	-0.01	0.19	-0.09	0.08	0.16
22. Hours: length	-0.01	-0.04	-0.17	0.07	0.05	0.09	-0.04	0.17	-0.02	-0.09	-0.03
23. Wages per week	-0.23	0.06	0.19	0.12	-0.03	0.14	0.17	0.07	0.13	0.16	0.17

	(12)	(13)	(14)	(15)	(16)	(17)	(18)	(19)	(20)	(21)	(22)	(23)
11. Reading, writing												
12. Memory	1.00											
13. Visualisation	**0.75**	1.00										
14. Complexity of decisions	**0.75**	**0.78**	1.00									
15. Autonomy of decisions	**0.56**	**0.55**	**0.51**	1.00								
16. Pace choice	**0.20**	0.12	0.06	**0.58**	1.00							
17. Responsibility	**0.57**	**0.66**	**0.58**	**0.46**	**0.11**	1.00						
18. Supervision: absence of	**0.24**	**0.20**	0.07	**0.48**	**0.52**	**0.26**	1.00					
19. Optional interaction	0.04	-0.05	-0.07	**0.24**	**0.35**	-0.03	0.09	1.00				
20. Promotion chances	*-0.12*	*-0.23*	*-0.18*	*-0.12*	0.04	-0.08	-0.02	**0.13**	1.00			
21. Hours: irregularity	0.11	*0.13*	0.08	0.09	-0.12	*0.24*	0.02	0.01	*0.10*	1.00		
22. Hours: length	0.02	0.08	0.08	0.06	0.05	*0.11*	0.01	0.10	*0.12*	*-0.11*	1.00	
23. Wages per week	**0.18**	**0.19**	**0.30**	-0.04	-0.20	0.08	-0.30	-0.13	-0.03	*0.21*	*0.36*	1.00

Italics   denotes compensatory relationships, i.e. an association between a desirable and undesirable characteristic.
Bold Type   denotes hierarchical relationships, i.e. an association between two desirable characteristics.

we find some quite important ones. The *hours of work* stand out here. Apart from its relation with control over the pace of work, regularity of hours*(i.e. absence of shiftwork or less variable and more predictable shifts) is associated with unattractive features: dirty work, a fast pace, a short repetitive cycle, low mental components, little responsibility, poor promotion prospects, long hours and low pay. Although the correlations are small, this indicates some possibility of choice between pleasanter work or more convenient, regular hours. Similarly the significant correlations of Length of hours are all in the compensatory direction, although again they are fairly low. Short hours are also associated with low pay, a short job cycle, low responsibility, poor promotion chances and noisy work.

This appears to give scope for a kind of "alienated instrumentalism", where the possibility of finding intrinsically meaningful work is rejected in favour of minimising the time that has to be spent at work. As we noted in Chapter 1, this is one of the variant forms of economism, which entails selling one's labour for purely economic returns. Of course, willingness to spend time in increasing the returns will vary with the relationship between expectations and actual levels of extrinsic rewards. Similarly, instrumentalism must imply minimising the inconvenience for non-work life of the hours that have to be devoted to work. In fact, length and regularity of hours do tend to compensate each other slightly, and so act as alternatives. Short hours have the advantage for instrumental choice of going with higher wage-rates *per hour* ($r = 0.33$, not included in Table 3.1), though not, of course, with high weekly wages.

However, when we turn to "economism" where the predominant concern is to maximise wages regardless of hours and shifts, we find a rather more complicated pattern. Long hours and inconvenient shifts do tend to bring in higher weekly wages. Also, high weekly wages go with a high noise level, danger, a hard pace of physical effort, low pace choice, close control by supervision and few possibilities for interaction with others. Hence they might be said to compensate for these six unpleasantnesses. However, high weekly wages are also associated with being protected from the elements, with manual dexterity, with variety in job content, and with all the mental skill components. Of course, nobody would seriously deny that both hierarchical and compensatory

* Where we name a variable which is one of the Objective Job Scores we start the name with a capital letter. Similarly, when we come to name constructed factors we shall do so in quotation marks. However, to aid readability we shall drop these conventions where there seems to be no risk of misunderstanding.

factors operate within the labour market, or that it is likely that some job characteristics will be associated with one and some with the other. In this case, most of the skill components correlate positively with wages, as we would surely expect them to do, while compensation operates through different mechanisms, notably autonomy and the "toughness" of a job. This complexity might make it more difficult for workers to select employment on the basis of "economism" than on the basis of the more negative kind of instrumentalism which seeks to avoid work as much as possible. Choosing work which minimises interference with home life is likely to entail a clash between short or convenient hours.

Turning to other aspects of the job, we see the most important compensatory characteristic is *Exposure to the weather*, i.e. working out of doors or being poorly protected from the elements. This is quite highly correlated with low noise, long, varied work cycles, autonomy of decisions, pace choice, little supervision and the opportunity for sociable interaction. Of course, exposure to the weather also carries its own intrinsic compensation when the weather is nice, but Peterborough hardly enjoys the climate to make this a general attraction! Thus working indoors or outdoors, or more precisely the degree of exposure, is a fundamental characteristic differentiating the jobs in the town. It is closely related to another aspect of where people work, not yet considered, which we will see is extremely important. This is the extent to which they work outside, in the sense of being away from the central site. Thus it ranges from typical factory work to jobs which involve being on a distant site or moving around and often being exposed to the elements. Thus working outside is an obvious source of autonomy. It is also readily apparent which jobs are outside.

Not only are there different degrees of exposure, but the extreme jobs are themselves quite varied. At lower levels of Exposure are most sorts of drivers, many of whom have unheated cabs and most of whom have to work outside their vehicle on occasion. Milkmen come at the extreme, having to spend considerable time in the open in all weathers, though with few other hardships except the early start. Most jobs in the brickyards involve moderate exposure. The sheds where, for example, setters and belt attendants work, offer fair protection but are partially open-sided. Out in the yard itself conditions are tougher – dusty or muddy according to the weather – and the worker may have no sort of shelter. Signalmen and pointsmen on the railways, secure in their "boxes", probably have the most comfortable conditions which are not actually "indoors". In contrast shunters are moving around out on the track all the time. Building and the local authority provide employment with the most exposure (though many council jobs are not at the highest level). The jobs include tough dirty work like digging trenches. However, the corpoation also provides what must be one of the most attractive lines of work for lovers of the open air: gardeners have relatively interesting, pleasant jobs in a setting of fresh air and freedom, and they have fairly comfortable huts where they can usually shelter from the worst of the weather. There is, then, a considerable variety of jobs outside the factory. Yet all share a variability dependent on the weather. A flooded clay pit in the depths of winter is very different from the same place on a sunny summer's day. The contrast is not always so dramatic, but all degrees of exposure carry with them some element of hardship.

A third group of compensatory relationships centres on the other aspects of *working conditions* – noise, danger, dirt and fumes. Noisy work, especially, is compensated for with high weekly wages, short hours and the opportunity to use manual dexterity. In fact, the chance to use manual skills varies directly with all these aspects of environmental unpleasantness, as well as with a fast pace of work which is not under the worker's control, with lack of opportunities for social interaction on the job and with poor promotion prospects. Nonetheless, the various conditions are also hierarchically related to rather more job characteristics, and these conflicting results reveal that the job structure is not uniform. A narrow segment of jobs offer skill of a particular kind with bad working conditions – such is the distinctive combination of engine testers, fettlers and the like, stressful machining work contained in the most unpleasant factory areas. But there is no uniform relationship between skills in general and unpleasantness.

Promotion chances appears to be a compensatory variable, as it tends to compensate six variables of Table 3.1, and also wages per hour. However, to a large extent this may be seen as itself a reflection of the hierarchical nature of the job market. Some lower-status jobs have scope for moving up, while the better jobs have less room for improvement without moving out of the "unqualified" market, which is sometimes possible, but is not a predictable feature of any "unqualified" job. It is noteworthy that a measure of within-firm status, in spite of ignoring variations between firms, is correlated -0.25 with promotion chances – the lower status the job, the better the prospects. While the compensatory element is important, it is of an essentially different kind.

These, then, are the main types of compensation possible within the Peterborough labour market: short or regular hours are found in jobs which are otherwise unattractive; high weekly wages can be obtained by making sacrifices of working conditions, autonomy and time (although there are also other pleasanter ways of making high wages); working outside in the cold and wet brings freedom but low pay and high effort; and unpleasant or dangerous working conditions within a factory can bring high wages and certain skill opportunities. None of these is particularly surprising, especially when we name a few examples of jobs that contribute highly to these four types of relationship. The first two tend to include assemblers and simple machine operators at low and high levels of technology respectively – thus the latter are relatively highly pressurised and highly paid. The third involved building operatives and clay-pit labourers; the fourth, as already mentioned, engine testers and fettlers. But at least we have established that these, and not *other* possibilities, are the main compensations available. These are the main objective possibilities for choice.

We turn now to the hierarchical relationships, or more precisely the relationships, where the more desirable (or less undesirable) job features occur together, which make the labour market hierarchical. These are predominantly concerned with autonomy, variety, mental qualities, skill and physical effort—all factors concerned with the *actual performance of the job*. The first point to note is that where there are several measures of different aspects of a broader characteristic, as there are for mental skill and autonomy, they all tend to go together, and generally the correlations are quite high. Thus there tends to be no opportunity for choosing one aspect of, say, mental skill, in exchange for another. Furthermore, all these factors go together, apart from the few exceptions, already mentioned, involving manual dexterity. Working conditions in terms of fumes and dirt, noise and danger, but not exposure, go together and this aspect tends to be positively related to the other hierarchical features (particularly the quantity of physical effort and optional interaction), with manual dexterity again the main exception.

THE STRUCTURING OF JOB ATTRIBUTES

To explore the structure further we use factor analysis. The basic assumption of factor analysis is that an observed set of correlations between variables is due to an underlying regularity in the data. The observed variables are taken as indicators of one or more common factors, such that the values of each variable are due partly to the common factors and partly to extraneous influences. The factors can therefore be regarded as a limited set of underlying variables determin-

Table 3.2   Factor matrix (orthogonal) of Objective Job Scores, wages and hours

Variable				*Factor*					
	1	2	3	4	5	6	7	8	9
1. Outside	—	0.80	—	—	—	—	0.21	—	—
2. Exposure	—	0.83	—	—	—	—	—	—	—
3. Fumes, dirt, heat	—	—	—	0.29	—	—	-0.23	—	—
4. Noise	—	-0.45	0.37	—	0.69	—	—	—	—
5. Danger	—	—	—	—	0.40	—	—	—	—
6. Effort: quantity	—	—	—	0.64	0.62	—	—	—	—
7. Effort: pace	—	—	—	0.77	0.22	—	—	—	—
8. Manual dexterity	0.22	—	—	—	—	—	—	—	—
9. Work cycle length	0.31	0.59	0.78	—	—	—	0.23	—	0.44
10. Object variety	0.74	—	—	—	—	0.26	—	—	—
11. Mathematical calculations	0.72	—	—	—	—	—	—	—	—
12. Reading, writing	0.83	—	—	—	—	—	—	—	—
13. Memory	0.78	—	0.28	—	-0.20	—	0.33	—	—
14. Visualisation	0.55	—	0.48	—	—	—	0.47	—	—
15. Concentration	0.21	-0.27	0.72	—	0.21	—	0.22	—	—
16. Complexity of decisions	0.68	—	0.44	—	—	—	0.31	—	—
17. Autonomy of decisions	0.38	0.52	0.21	-0.30	—	—	0.22	—	—
18. Pace choice	—	0.64	—	-0.33	—	—	—	—	0.38
19. Responsibility	0.38	0.20	—	—	—	—	—	—	0.31
20. Supervision: absence of	—	0.77	—	—	—	—	0.65	—	—
21. Required interaction	—	—	-0.27	0.39	0.23	—	—	—	—
22. Optional interaction	—	0.21	0.22	—	-0.21	—	—	—	—
23. Promotion time	0.68	—	—	—	—	0.26	—	—	0.55
24. Promotion chances	—	—	-0.42	—	—	—	-0.24	0.23	—
25. Promotion from outside	—	—	0.22	—	—	-0.55	—	—	—

26. Learning	0.78	—	—	—	—	—	—	-0.23	—	—
27. Qualification ties	0.25	-0.23	—	—	—	—	—	—	-0.65	—
28. Hours: irregularity	—	—	0.48	—	—	—	0.68	0.20	—	—
29. Status in firm	0.71	—	—	—	—	—	—	—	0.25	—
30. Wages per week	0.27	-0.25	—	—	—	—	0.30	—	0.65	—
31. Hours: length	—	—	—	—	—	—	—	—	0.65	—

Number of Jobs = 275
Rotation   = varimax
Variance explained = 75%
Loadings < 0.2 are omitted

ing the data. How well each factor represents a variable is given, for orthogonal factors, by the "loadings" of the "factor matrix", which are the correlations between the factors and observed variables and also the regression weights for each variable expressed in terms of the factors. Thus the higher a particular loading, the more closely is the variable related to (and the more determined by) the factor.[3] There are thus two main ways in which we can make use of factor analysis: firstly, we will use it to explore the underlying structural regularities of the labour market, then later on we shall replace the detail of many job aspects by a few factors to make the general analysis both simpler and more effective.

The initial step is to establish whether a suitably limited number of factors can be extracted, which is in fact the case. This means that we can meaningfully consider an underlying structure rather than confine ourselves to the set of separate job aspects. Given this, the aim here is to see if underlying factors are hierarchical or not, in the sense of whether a factor is positively related to a set of desirable attributes. Table 3.2 presents the results of an orthogonal factor analysis for all 29 scaleable Objective Job Scores, together with wages and hours (for clarity of presentation all factor loadings of less than 0.2 are ignored). Because we have included wages and hours only 275 jobs are used. However, if the analysis is limited to the Objective Job Scores very similar results are obtained using 368 or 275 jobs, and in the latter case the result is essentially the same as in Table 3.2, except that factor 8, which is primarily wages and hours, disappears. Indeed, we experimented with various procedures and types of rotation with overwhelmingly consistent results.[4] We have chosen to present orthogonal factors here to make it easier to grasp the structure of interrelationships. Since orthogonal factors are definitionally uncorrelated, we need only consider the pattern of correlations (i.e. the loadings) of the variables with each factor separately. In fact, the oblique factors are also very largely independent of each other; two-thirds of the interfactor correlations are less than 0.1 and only one (between factors 2 and 9) is greater than 0.3. We note any important difference between oblique and orthogonal factors in the following discussion.

The first point to note is that factor 8 is mainly one explaining the common variance of *wages per week and hours worked*. Length of hours[5] is not related to any other factor, and wages are only weakly related to three others. There are two more variables weakly related to factor 8, Status and Promotion time, to which we shall return presently. However, what this points to above all, is that the way to high weekly wages is through long hours. In general, a worker seeking high wages can expect to do so at the cost of his leisure time, regardless of other job characteristics. This suggests that truly "instrumental" workers, as defined in Chapter I, might be forced to adopt a privatised life-style to accommodate their financial needs, but we shall see that this is not what happens (see Chapter 8).

Turning to the other factors we see that factor 1 is overwhelmingly *the mental abilities required for the job* (variables 10–14, 16 and 26). Concentration, which in this context may be seen more as a demanding feature of the job rather than as a wholly desirable opportunity to use the mind, is not really included here. Visualisation of shapes and relationships is less highly correlated than the other "mental" variables, being more strongly related to factor 3, and with oblique rotation the association is further reduced. However, it is unquestionably associated with this factor and, as we shall see, it is well related to a specific "mental abilities" factor. Variety in the equipment and materials used in the job (Object variety) entails mental ability in the number of different things to be mastered, but may also be seen as a separate, hierarchically-related item measuring variety, which is how we shall treat it. The other variables strongly related to factor 1 are Status level within the firm and Promotion time – the time which normally has to be spent in a firm to attain a job. These are both general indicators of hierarchical position within a firm. Then come indicators of autonomy and responsibility, followed by wages, Qualification ties – the extent to which the worker's capacity to move to a comparable job is limited because such jobs normally require qualifications he does not possess[6] – and Manual dexterity.

The first factor, then, gives a powerful indication of hierarchy in two ways. In the first place, it gives a fair indication of a single factor of "mental abilities", which we shall measure presently. This means, in effect, that opportunities to use different mental abilities tend to vary together leaving little scope for enjoying one aspect at the expense of another. Secondly, the other variables associated with the factor add up to a more general hierarchical structure; those using their mental abilities have *better*, not merely distinctive jobs.

We also have here some indication of the importance of the internal labour market. The two main "non-mental" variables associated with this factor are Status level and Promotion time, which clearly give an indication of standing in the firm. This may also be seen as attachment to the firm in an objective sense, particularly the latter variable which directly measures the extent to which the job is removed from availability in the open market. A further variable, Qualification ties, also is an indicator of attachment to the firm. Jobs which allow the worker to use his mind, are generally acquired by staying with one firm. It will be recalled that Status and Promotion time were also related to the "Wages and Hours" factor. When hours are dropped from the analysis, a new factor emerges with substantial loading on these two variables (0.62 and 0.65), together with moderate loadings on Qualification ties (0.40) and Wages (0.47). Thus high weekly wages are also quite dependent on success in the internal labour market. We can therefore conclude that the internal labour market plays the main part in distinguishing between jobs that are simply and generally "better" and "worse".

Factor 2 explains the variance of *Outside and exposed work*, together with indicators of *autonomy*. Outside refers to working away from the factory and not surprisingly is related to Exposure, since these aspects coincide at the lowest levels – in the factory – while working away entails some element of exposure to the elements. It is, however, also a source of autonomy since it tends to remove the workers from management and allow greater freedom in the way the job is carried out. Thus factor 2 may be seen as essentially in autonomy factor, the main loadings apart from Exposure being Outside, Length of work cycle, Autonomy of decision-making, choice in the pace of work and absence of close supervision. Length of work cycle, although a reasonable indicator of autonomy, may be regarded more as a separate characteristic giving variety to the work, and in that sense is hierarchically related. The other variables related to this factor suggest both hierarchical and compensatory aspects. Most striking is the compensatory relation of exposure. As we have already noted, autonomy may be gained by sometimes suffering the cold and wet. Low weekly wages also tend to belong in this pattern. On the other hand, low noise, for which we have already observed the compensatory relation with exposure, is seen to be hierarchically associated with autonomy.

When we consider autonomy itself it is not so internally hierarchical as the "mental abilities" factor, i.e. it is not so homogeneous. Indeed, we see factor 9 is *another "autonomy" factor*. The job characteristic most closely related to this latter factor is Optional interaction with other people (usually workmates, but not always). This is only weakly related to factor 2. The other characteristics featuring here – Object variety, Autonomy of decisions and Pace choice – are three of the ones well related to factor 2 (with oblique rotation the direct explanation of these variables is greater from this factor and less from factor 2).[7] However, Supervisor interaction and Outside work do not feature at all.

This can be taken further with a factor analysis limited to these various indicators of autonomy. For this exploratory analysis we have included Work cycle length, though for subsequent measurement of an autonomy factor it was excluded. It is worth noting that its exclusion would make little difference to the structure described here. We find that one factor accounts for only 53 per cent of the variance, while the addition of a second explains a further 18 per cent and would be used following normal conventions (eigenvalue >1). Even two factors do not give a clear picture, and the optimal rotation is more or less inde-terminate. The reason is that there are three different aspects of autonomy involved. One is "technical" autonomy in the job itself, with work cycle length, autonomy of decision-making and choice of work pace all well related together; the others are the two social aspects of freedom from close supervision and the opportunity to talk with workmates, etc. Working outside relates to all three, but above all to the absence of close supervision and least to optional interaction with people. The technical aspect is fairly well related to the other two. Rather surprisingly, however, closeness of supervision is almost unre-lated to the chance to stop and have a chat. This is in itself quite an interesting finding, for it seems that social relationships at work are dependent on the technical rather than the supervisory control in the job.

Thus one factor gives a fairly good representation of autonomy. Two factors do not clarify the situation, as one at least will be more or less uninterpretable (perhaps this is best seen graphically as three positions competing for two axes). So three are needed to effect any improvement on one, and these will be interrelated. However, using three does little to simplify the data from their original form. So we have chosen to measure the different aspects of autonomy by their appropriate variables, e.g. supervisor interaction, alone. For autonomy in general we will use the single factor. It must be borne in mind, however, that this factor does some violence to the complexity of autonomy in work, and in particular that there is some scope for trade-off between the different aspects.

Returning to the main analysis, factor 3 concerns the *skill of a job*. Its main indicators are Manual dexterity, Concentration, Visualisation of shapes and relationships, and Complexity of decision-making. The first two of these are the items most closely related to the factor and the others are in a group of fairly well-related variables, together with status in the firm – a predictable hierarchical feature – and lack of promotion chances, reflecting to some extent the absence of better jobs to which the more skilled workers might be promoted. Other variables with some relation to this factor entail both compensatory and hierarchical aspects, including high noise, low optional interaction, but (in line with the foregoing observations on autonomy) freedom of choice in decision-making. The mental skills involved do, of course, overlap with those of factor 1 ("mental abilities") and we see the variables are related to each factor, though in quite different patterns, giving meaningful independent factors. This is confirmed by a separate analysis on variables of skill and mental ability. Two orthogonal factors strongly differentiate mathematical and verbal abilities from manual dexterity and concentration, with the remaining four variables related fairly strongly to both.[8]

Physical effort, in terms of quantity and pace, is the basis of the factor 4, which is hierarchical in the sense that all other items associated with the factor are undesirable features, such as lack of control over one's pace and low autonomy of decision-making. We are aware that the quantity of physical effort is not necessarily disliked in itself. In fact, it may be considered a desirable feature within the particular type of working-class sub-culture which assigns dignity and prestige to hard "man's work" — for example, in mining communities. The assumption underlying Table 3.1, that there is consensus regarding desired features of work, is therefore a little dubious with respect to physical effort, though no worker in our sample mentioned it as an attraction (see Chapter 5). Here we see that — whatever its intrinsic attractiveness — it is associated with less problematic, undesired features to form a distinctive bundle of job attributes. In particular, it is highly correlated with high effort to cope with the pace of work, which is always considered unattractive.

The interpretation we have offered of factors 3 and 4 is supported by a separate factor analysis covering the eight variables of skill and effort. This gives two clearly independent factors; even with oblique rotation the angle between them is about 91°. There is no relationship at all between the skill factor and the two measures of effort, though the skill variables do relate slightly to the effort factor (concentration and dexterity being related positively and the other four negatively). If we take the effort and skill sets of variables separately, each gives a clear single factor.

The physical conditions of work are represented in factor 5, particularly fumes, dirt and heat, and danger, with noise also quite well related. With oblique rotation these variables are more clearly related to the factor and the relation of all other variables becomes negligible, emphasising the coherence of this factor. As it stands, this is a hierarchical factor, but there is one significant omission. Another basic aspect of working conditions – the degree of exposure to the weather – is not at all related to the factor. Separate analysis of the four relevant variables gives two factors: exposure is unrelated to the first, while the second entails the compensatory relation between exposure and noise which we noted earlier, with the other two variables unrelated. In other words, there is a general "conditions" factor comprising the three variables, while exposure is a quite separate factor, largely independent but carrying the compensation of freedom from excessive noise.

The remaining two factors are rather different, in that they are not readily interpretable as aspects of the job. Factor 6 is, indeed, the only one which is essentially compensatory. Primarily, inconvenient hours are set against promotion to the grade above being from within the firm. This latter is clearly an indicator of promotion prospects, and we may note that although Promotion chances does not feature here it is related to the comparable factor in versions (368 or 275) which do not include both length of hours and wages. (These two "promotion" variables combine quite well and have been used in a single factor.) Higher wages and long work cycles also tend to make up for irregular hours, as we noted in Table 3.1.

Finally, there is a generally hierarchical factor relating to responsibility, the requirement of formal qualifications for the job, and to a lesser extent various aspects of skill. This seems merely to reflect the distinctive character of the driving jobs in the sample.

The overall picture of the labour market is now quite clear. It is essentially hierarchical, particularly in relation to the content of the jobs. The different elements of general categories, such as skill or physical effort, vary together to a considerable degree, and relations with other variables are also often hierarchical. While the argument points clearly to a hierarchical market structure, we must not overstate the position. Firstly, we have been dealing with trends, not absolute relationships, which allow an amount of variation. That is to say that although some desired characteristics usually occur together there may nonetheless be situations where a choice of one at the expense of the other is possible. Also, there are two basic compensatory mechanisms. One operates through exposure to the weather, primarily as a way of gaining autonomy, although the chance to avoid excessive noise might also be felt worthwhile. The significance of exposure emerged clearly in both the correlation and the factor analyses. The other concerns the possibility of instrumentalism, at least in the negative sense of working hours which entail least cost to the enjoyment of non-work life. This did not show up in the factor structure, apart from the overwhelming extent to which wages depend on the number of hours worked. But in considering the individual variables, we saw that length and irregularity of hours are related in a compensatory way to many other variables. Short, convenient hours bring many disadvantages.

Furthermore, while the existence of coherent factors indicates a limitation on the possibility of choice in one way, it may actually facilitate choice in another. By simplifying the structure of alternatives it may make it easier for workers with similarly general orientations to identify jobs where the rewards are congruent with their orientations. For example, workers giving primacy to opportunities to use their minds are faced with a clear hierarchy on this characteristic and so are likely to be able to identify the "best" jobs, while those with an "autonomy" orientation will find the situation a bit more complicated.

HIERARCHICAL AND COMPENSATORY RELATIONSHIPS

The crucial question now becomes whether choice in these simplified terms is possible. Are these general characteristics related in a compensatory or a hierarchical way? To answer this we need to establish meaningful measures of the characteristics, which will also serve at other points in the analysis.

The orthogonal factors we have been considering are not suitable, since they are necessarily unrelated (by definition), and so can give no indication of hierarchy or compensatory relations. Furthermore, each factor includes all job attributes to some extent, regardless of their different types. On the other hand, these factors do provide an indication of which aspects actually combine together. Accordingly, we carried out a series of factor analyses, including only meaningfully relevant variables in each factor. For example, the "autonomy" factor is derived from those attributes which may be regarded as aspects of autonomy. In this way we created measures of seven basic, general characteristics of the jobs.* For certain other aspects the individual Job Scores remain appropriate.

These new factors are not, of course, logically independent, and how they interrelate is our prime concern at this point. In Table 3.3 we

---

* The derivation of the factors used to measure general job characteristics is presented in Appendix III. Two very general factors concerning skill and interest, which are not included in Table 3.3, are also presented there.

3

Table 3.3 Job characteristic correlations: constructed measures and other variables, 275 cases, weighted and unweighted[9]

weighted (949 jobs) — upper triangle; *unweighted (275 jobs)* — lower triangle

	1.	2.	3.	4.	5.	6.	7.	8.	9.	10.	11.	12.	13.	14.
1. Exposure		−0.07	0.19	−0.03	0.41	−0.28	−0.06	0.65	0.13†	−0.07	−0.16	−0.17†	0.13†	−0.32
2. Conditions (F)	−0.06		0.29	0.04	−0.09	−0.05	−0.33	−0.24	−0.27	−0.04	−0.09	−0.20	−0.02	0.06†
3. Effort (F)	0.22	0.27		−0.16†	−0.34	−0.37	−0.36	−0.29	−0.28	0.03	−0.24†	−0.15	−0.04	0.11†
4. Skill (F)	−0.10	0.09	−0.01		0.43	0.55	0.67	0.25	0.63	−0.25	0.58	0.13†	0.04	0.19
5. Work cycle length	0.41	−0.02	−0.16	0.24		0.26	0.52	0.73	0.45	−0.04	0.32	0.17	0.24	−0.05
6. Object variety	−0.25	−0.06	−0.22	0.52	0.21		0.66	0.06	0.27	−0.20	0.52	−0.07	−0.03	0.04†
7. Mental abilities (F)	−0.11	−0.24	−0.22	0.62	0.38	0.70		0.41	0.62	−0.15	0.62	0.24†	−0.05	0.13
8. Autonomy (F)	0.61	−0.15	−0.16	0.16	0.69	0.09	0.32		0.45	−0.14†	0.08	−0.04	0.20†	−0.38
9. Responsibility	0.04	−0.18	−0.17	0.52	0.32	0.23	0.52	0.33		−0.13†	0.42	0.30	0.05†	0.06
10. Promotion opportunity (F)	0.06	−0.06	0.02	−0.35	0.06	−0.14	−0.19	−0.05	−0.13		−0.11	0.35	−0.01	0.14†
11. Position in hierarchy	−0.13	−0.04	−0.10	0.55	0.27	0.55	0.65	0.08	0.31	−0.15		0.23†	−0.16†	0.49
12. Hours: irregularity	−0.00	−0.10	−0.15	0.05	0.19	−0.09	0.12	0.01	0.24	0.27	0.08		−0.19	0.38
13. Hours: length	−0.01	−0.05	0.08	0.02	0.17	−0.02	−0.00	0.04	0.11	0.05	−0.03	−0.11		0.08†
14. Wages per week	−0.23	0.11	0.07	0.26	0.07	0.13	0.23	−0.25	0.08	0.02	0.52	0.21	0.36	

(F) = Constructed factor

Italics denotes compensatory relationships

Bold type denotes hierarchical relationships

† denotes relationship only observed in either weighted or unweighted data (only weighted are so marked).

present the correlations between these factors and several other important variables.† The lower, left-hand part of the table (i.e. below the diagonal) is comparable to Table 3.1, giving correlations between the new factors and those variables of the earlier table which are not included in the factors. The half above the diagonal gives the same for weighted data, to which we shall return presently.

Looking at the unweighted 275 cases we see the pattern is much as we would expect from the previous discussion. However, the general structure of the market is more clearly discernible. Most importantly, we see that the hierarchical nature of the market is not confined to the existence of factors in which similar types of rewards coincide. Relations between factors and with other variables also tend to be hierarchical in the ratio 2:1. Even this tends to underestimate the difference, because several of the compensatory relations involve "promotion opportunities" which are mainly confined to moving within this section of the labour force and so are necessarily greater in the poorer jobs. Excluding promotion opportunities, there are 36 hierarchical relationships and only 13 compensatory ones, a ratio of almost 3:1. Of course, some of these correlations were included in Table 3.1. If we look only at the new correlations their importance for the hierarchical structure may be seen from the fact that the ratio jumps to 6:1 (excluding promotion opportunities). Indeed, among the factors there are no compensatory relations apart from those involving promotion.

The major source of compensatory rewards shows up even more clearly as hours of work, both in terms of length and irregularity. These two variables are involved only in compensatory relationships with other variables and account for half of the total number of such relations. Other compensatory relations involve exposure to the elements being suffered to gain autonomy and a long work cycle (as already observed), and wages making up for low autonomy and bad conditions (as well as bad hours of work).

The factor measure of "position in hierarchy" is included here. As it is specific to each firm it was not considered appropriate to include its components in the detailed analysis, but it is interesting to include it at this more general level. Relationships are predictably hierarchical, especially with the intrinsic job rewards. It correlates 0.70 with our general factor measuring interest, skill and variety (see Appendix III), while we see a correlation of 0.64 with the "mental abilities" aspect alone

† Where we want to make clear that we are naming a factor, the name is given in quotation marks. It will be recalled that the comparable practice for Job Scores is to start the name with a capital letter.

and high correlations with the other aspects. Also, it is strongly related to wage levels.

THE ANALYSIS WITH "WEIGHTED" JOBS

So far our analysis has been strictly in terms of jobs, with all jobs counting as equal. We have been concerned to see how job aspects vary together from job to job, without taking account of availability. While this may be seen as a more fundamental approach, it is also possible to look at characteristics in the particular labour market by counting a job each time it occurs in the sample. Because non-sampled jobs are omitted this tends to give excessive weight in the correlations to the more common jobs. Nevertheless, it is interesting to compare the results from this approach with those of the preceding analysis.

The main point to note is a substantial similarity. Correlations are different, of course, but for the most part the differences are not great and the associated factor patterns are largely the same.

The upper half of Table 3.3 gives the relevant data for this set of variables, which give a good overall indication of the similarity and the main differences. While not presenting all the individual correlations between the job scores, we will note any changes that are of interest at this more detailed level.

The most striking change is a decline in the relationship between wages and hours, from $r = 0.36$ to $r = 0.08$. However, this has to be interpreted with care because the values used are averages for each job and generally there will be variance "within" the job. It is to be expected, therefore, that the relationship of longer hours bringing in more pay will be greater if taken over individual workers in the labour market. But at the level of typical wages and hours for jobs the relationship disappears, reflecting the hierarchical distribution between firms of wages per hour, with longer hours serving to raise wages to comparable levels in the poorer firms.[10] We shall discuss this in the next chapter.

Length of hours also changes in its relationship to other variables. A compensatory relationship with autonomy emerges clearly, both with the general factor and with the separate variables, apart from Outdoors, (co-efficients from 0.15 to 0.21). On the other hand, there are now hierarchical relations with Exposure and "position in hierarchy" and also with three component variables of other factors, namely Danger (0.22), Maths (0.14) and Reading and writing (0.11), though apart from Danger they are only weak. Also, the previous weak relation with

Responsibility is gone. The distinctive nature of the length of working hours as a source of compensatory rewards is significantly reduced.

On the other hand, the compensatory character of Regularity of hours shows yet more strongly, encompassing 11 of its 13 relationships in Table 3.3. In the case of "working conditions" it conceals a mixed situation, with regular hours accompanying both low noise and danger. However, the general pattern of inconvenient hours having to be suffered to gain other advantages is extremely clear.

The pattern of relationships of wages with other variables also changes, although it remains mixed. In addition to changes shown in the table, autonomy in decisions (− 0.21) joins other measures of autonomy in a compensatory relation to wage levels, strengthening the general pattern. The work available in Peterborough seems to pose a definite alternative where autonomy can only be enjoyed by accepting relatively low wages and long hours.

In general, correlations tend to be greater than in the previous analysis, particularly those which were significant before. To be sure, some coefficients fall below our previous minimum level, but usually the change is slight. On the other hand, several new relationships emerge, although again they are usually at a low level, as shown in Table 3.3. At the level of detailed job characteristics, the most significant not yet mentioned mainly concern autonomy, with complexity of decision-making going with control of work pace (0.23) and freedom from supervision (0.24), while the use of mathematical ability also goes with the latter (0.19). Finally, the use of mathematical calculations tends to accompany high noise levels (0.21). Overall, the general hierarchical pattern is, if anything, even more evident, though as we have said, changes are small in most cases.

The peculiarities of the wages and hours variables inevitably have some effect on the structure revealed by factor analysis. In particular, and predictably, there is no longer a clear "wages and hours" factor. There is instead a factor in which hours are the only dominant variable. Wages are also positively related to this factor but less so than danger. Wages are now much more strongly related to factor 6, the one compensatory factor. This means high wages go with inconvenient rather than long hours.

Apart from this effect, the factor pattern is substantially the same. This we were able to confirm by comparing the analyses of weighted and unweighted job scores without wages and hours,[11] which give very similar factors. Table 3.4 gives nine factors for data including wages and hours, as in Table 3.2, but this time there are only eight significant factors. We show the structure with nine factors because this is most similar to the eight-factor version without wages and hours,[12] which is directly comparable to the equivalent structure using unweighted job scores, and because it makes comparisons with Table 3.2 easier. The "hours" factor in the table is roughly the same as with only the eight significant factors, except that danger is no longer related to it, and so is also rather different from its counterpart in the earlier analysis. Otherwise the factors are directly comparable, although the order is a little different as indicated in the note to Table 3.4 where, for comparison, they are in the same order as in Table 3.2.

The first factor is essentially unchanged, except that the weighted data provide more of a common factor in that loadings are generally higher. This makes its hierarchical character clearer than ever; for instance, high quantity and pace of physical effort and high fumes or dirt can be seen to go with low mental components, whereas previously the loadings were below the level we are considering (in fact, they were -0.15, -0.16 and -0.19 respectively).

Factor 2, which primarily concerns autonomy and exposure to the weather, also looks more hierarchical. We now have easy work pace and two more mental skill variables – memory and visualisation – tending to accompany high autonomy. The loadings on autonomy variables are rather higher, while the second autonomy factor (factor 9 in Table 3.2) disappears as a significant factor. However, when the number of factors is increased from eight to nine it does re-emerge. In the version shown in the table it is still only a weak compensating component, along with wages, of the factor dominated by hours; but in the version omitting wages and hours it becomes a distinct factor, though more clearly dominated by Optional interaction than before.

The skill factor is rather less clear than before because Status level and Promotion time are now more closely related to it. We noted in relation to unweighted jobs that status within the firm and the associated success in the internal market entailed some opportunity for the workers to use their minds. This still holds when we look at the labour market through the weighted jobs, while the similar tendency with regard to skill, which was only weak at the level of individual jobs, now becomes equally clear. The importance of this will emerge more clearly in the following chapters.

The "skill" loadings are rather lower and that on Memory drops below the 0.2 level and is replaced by Learning, an equally relevant variable, since both feature in the constructed measure of skill.[13]

Table 3.4 Factor matrix (orthogonal) of Objective Job Scores, wages and hours: jobs weighted by number of incumbents

Variable	1	2	3	4	5	6	7	8	9
					Factor				
1. Outside	—	0.82	—	—	—	—	0.25	—	—
2. Exposure	—	0.82	—	0.23	—	—	—	—	—
3. Fumes, dirt, heat	−0.33	—	—	—	0.66	—	−0.21	—	—
4. Noise	—	−0.39	—	—	0.66	—	—	—	—
5. Danger	—	—	—	—	0.28	—	—	—	0.49
6. Effort: quantity	−0.21	—	0.22	0.62	0.21	—	—	—	—
7. Effort: pace	−0.34	−0.23	0.43	0.77	—	—	—	—	—
8. Manual dexterity	0.36	—	—	—	—	—	0.40	0.30	—
9. Work cycle length	0.47	0.65	—	—	0.33	—	—	—	—
10. Object variety	0.72	—	—	—	—	−0.22	—	—	—
11. Mathematical calculations	0.71	—	—	—	—	—	−0.21	—	—
12. Reading, writing	0.85	—	—	—	−0.21	—	—	—	—
13. Memory	0.84	0.21	0.33	—	—	—	0.27	—	—
14. Visualisation	0.65	0.25	0.48	−0.25	—	—	0.40	—	—
15. Concentration	0.26	−0.30	0.25	—	0.41	—	0.40	—	—
16. Complexity of decisions	0.77	—	—	—	—	—	0.23	—	—
17. Autonomy of decisions	0.54	0.60	—	—	—	—	—	0.25	—
18. Pace choice	—	0.76	—	−0.26	—	—	—	0.23	—
19. Responsibility	0.50	0.30	0.21	—	—	—	0.55	—	—
20. Supervision: absence of	—	0.83	—	—	—	—	—	—	—
21. Required interaction	—	—	−0.35	0.23	−0.30	—	—	0.32	0.53
22. Optional interaction	—	—	0.52	−0.21	—	0.29	−0.22	—	−0.27
23. Promotion time	0.55	—	−0.43	—	—	—	—	—	—
24. Promotion chances	—	—	—	—	—	—	—	—	—
25. Promotion from outside	—	—	—	—	—	−0.63	—	—	—

26. Learning	0.71	—	—	0.29	—	—	—	—	0.31
27. Qualification ties	—	—	—	—	—	—	-065	—	—
28. Hours: irregularity	—	—	—	—	—	0.76	—	—	—
29. Status in firm	0.57	—	—	0.72	—	0.22	—	—	—
30. Wages per week	—	-0.37	—	0.43	—	0.56	—	0.28	—
31. Hours: length	—	—	—	—	—	—	—	0.66	0.26

Number of different jobs = 275; weighting gives 949 cases
Rotation = varimax
Variance explained = 78 %
Loadings < 0.2 are omitted
Order of explained variance of factors is 1, 2, 6, 7, 5, 4, 3, 8, 9

Altogether the effect on this factor is again to make it rather more hierarchical.

The effort factor, with major loadings on quantity and pace of physical effort, was clearly hierarchical before and remains so.

Factor 5, however, has undergone something of a change, for taking account of the frequency of jobs splits it into two. In Table 3.2 we saw that the main variables related to this factor were the conditions of work, fumes and dirt, etc., and danger, with noise a little less related (and exposure not at all). Noise has become more important but danger is only weakly related and we have a new "danger" factor (9). Without wages and hours this shows up more clearly (Danger loading = 0.57). This is a predominantly hierarchical factor, but factor 5 has become rather less hierarchical than before.

Factor 6 remains essentially compensatory, with inconvenient hours set against promotion from within the firm to the grade above, and now good wages are more clearly a compensation for anti-social hours. There is some change in the other related variables, mainly in the direction of less variety and more status. Finally factor 7 is very little different, but marginally less hierarchical.

CONCLUSION

Whichever way we look at it, the general structure of the labour market is predominantly hierarchical. Jobs which are better than most on one characteristic tend to be better on others. The relations between individual job aspects are mostly hierarchical. When we explore the structure further by using factor analysis we see that the underlying factors are predominantly hierarchical. Thus, for example, the opportunities to use different sorts of mental ability tend to occur together, so that it is difficult to trade off one type for another. This provides the basis for the construction of factors for several types of rewards, and we see that the relations *between* these factors are also hierarchical. In the first place we analysed the relationships between individual jobs; then we took account of the actual availability of jobs in the market by weighting for frequency of occurrence. Both approaches give essentially the same result. In reality, therefore, the apparent wide variety of job types we observed at the start gives a much narrower basis for choice. However, we should not overstate this. In principle at least, real opportunities for choice remain within the generally hierarchical framework. Two, in particular, stand out – the possibility of obtaining short or regular hours of work by accepting unpleasantnesses elsewhere; and the possibility of obtaining considerable job autonomy (by working outside), with rather less cost, for those who don't mind being out in all weathers.

At this point we must consider the process by which workers arrive in jobs. Since the market is structured by firms, the initial step is normally an approach to a firm. We must now consider differences between firms.

4 Firms in the Labour Market

In the previous chapter we analysed the component parts of individual jobs. To make statements about the overall labour market, we simply summed up these jobs and concluded that a certain degree of hierarchy, combined with a few objective possibilities for choice, existed within the market. Yet that view of the market is not the worker's view. For him at least two basic component units of the market exist – the job and the firm. In this chapter we discuss the role of the latter unit. We begin by comparing the job variety offered by the firms as employing units to the total variety present in the market. This will enable us to see the extent to which the normal process of job application – to a firm – cuts down the potential choice available to the worker. Then we will discuss the further constraints introduced by the internal labour market and by the selection procedures of the firms.

INTER-FIRM DIFFERENCES

Let us look first at the differences between firms and relate them to differences within the firms. Previous research has shown considerable inter- and intra-plant variations in wages (Mackay, 1970; Robinson and Conboy, 1970). For certain restricted purposes it has attempted to separate the effects of the two. In the British engineering industry in Birmingham and Glasgow *increases* in earnings are more attributable to the firm than to the occupational group (Mackay *et al.*, 1971: 124–30). In Chicago, among selected manual occupations, factors connected with the type of employing organisation (industry, location) explain more of the total wages variance within each occupation than does seniority, which is an intra-firm variable (Rees and Shultz, 1970: Chapters 8–10). Obviously these are rather specific results. Only one study has attempted to compare directly inter- with intra-firm variation of wages at one point in time. In a study of a largely blue-collar sample in five firms in a New

England town, Marcia Freedman (1969: 58–83) found that significant variance was attributable to inter-firm differences. Her data consist of "wages per hour" and we have learned from the author that this means basic rate of pay per hour (and not gross wages divided by hours worked). To compare the differences between and within firms we have used the statistic E. The value of E^2 (which may be thought of as analogous to the squared correlation coefficient r^2) measures the proportion of total variance attributable to differences between firms, and so $1 - E^2$ measures the proportion of variance within firms. If we calculate E^2 from her data, we find it equal to 0.27, which means that 27 per cent of the variance is attributable to differences between firms – large, but less than the intra-firm variance. We should note that this says nothing about the reasons for the variation (which may be due to such things as the proportion of skilled jobs in each firm). We are only concerned at this stage with overall firm differences.

We have performed a similar analysis of variance on our data for wages and hours. In Table 4.1 this shows up a very clear pattern of differences between firms. The average wage per week ranged from £21.8 at Bettles to £31.4 at Perkins, while the "F" ratio (which relates inter- to intra-firm variance, giving the basis of a measure of significance for the corresponding E) has the very highly significant value of 67.6. $E^2 = 0.37$,

Table 4.1   Wages and hours: differences between firms

	Wages per week (£)		Hours		Wages per hour (pence)	
	Mean	Standard deviation	Mean	Standard deviation	Mean	Standard deviation
Baker Perkins	27.6	3.8	49.0	3.4	56.3	7.2
Bettles	21.8	2.4	52.1	2.5	41.8	3.5
British Rail	30.5	4.1	52.0	7.2	59.1	7.3
Combex	26.1	4.5	58.3	5.8	44.5	5.0
Farrow's	28.9	5.8	61.4	8.1	46.6	4.5
Horrell's	27.4	3.5	41.6	0.0*	65.8	8.6
London Brick	30.0	4.7	49.8	5.9	60.9	11.7
Perkins	31.4	2.2	43.8	2.3	71.7	2.9
Peterborough Corp.	22.4	3.6	51.0	6.9	44.0	4.4
Total	28.5	4.9	49.7	7.1	58.2	11.8
"F" ratio (8 and 933d.f)	67.6		70		187.8	
"E"	0.61		0.62		0.79	

* At Horrell's no estimate of the variance of hours is possible, since the figure for each man is an estimate of the average for all workers.

which means that inter-firm differences account for less than the variations within firms, although they do still account for a substantial part of the variance. This is a similar result to that obtained by Freedman. Clearly the firms are differentiated by wages, which means in this respect that they are ordered in attractiveness.

Similarly, the average hours ordered the firms. For a normal week they ranged from 41.6 for the milkmen of Horrell's[1] to 61.4 at Farrow's. Because of problems in arriving at "normal" hours the value of E and the "F" ratio can only be rough estimates. Nevertheless, the variance by firm is much the same as for wages, with E^2 about 0.38 and "F" about 70, giving another highly significant relationship. Thus the firms are again very clearly differentiated, though the ordering is different from that on wages. Comparing the ranks (in attractiveness) on wages and hours, we find that tau = 0.17, which is in the direction of a hierarchical relationship but far from significant.

The nature of the situation becomes clear when we combine wages and hours together in the rate per hour. This gives a range of 41.8 pence to 71.8 pence per hours, with the same two firms occupying the extremes as with weekly wages, but the value of E^2 has risen to 0.62 and significance has increased accordingly. This time the differences between firms are more than those within firms.

Not all variation within firms can be attributed to the systematic differences introduced by the internal labour market, especially with respect to weekly wages and hours. There will be substantial differences between men doing the same job because of different overtime work and different responses to piecework stimuli (cf. Robinson and Conboy, 1970: 250). Even the same man's earnings may vary considerably from week to week. Therefore the substantial and highly significant differences we found indicate the distinctive importance of the separate firms and, to some extent, a relative weakness of the internal labour market as a determinant of economic rewards. Especially is this so for wages per hour. This is what most strongly differentiates the firms along a dimension of economic attractiveness, although the differences are narrowed by a tendency in the low-paying firms to make up wages by working long hours. We noted this tendency in the previous chapter.

The overall pattern is unmistakably hierarchical. In spite of longer than average hours, Bettles pays the least per week and, with even longer hours, Combex remains one of the three worst-paying firms. At the other extreme the short hours of Perkins combine with a high rate to give the best weekly wages – clearly the most attractive firm on these two criteria. On the other hand, the variation in hours of work between companies does allow for some choice, most noticeably at Horrell's, where short hours combined with a high rate give a medium wage, and at British Rail and Farrow's where a high wage can be obtained by working long hours.

However, it is worth considering not only the length of hours, but also their regularity, and this is where the hierarchy weakens. The relatively attractive firms on wages and length of hours tend to have somewhat inconvenient or irregular hours. At Perkins, part of the price for an attractive economic return is the necessity to work alternate fortnights on day and night shifts; at British Rail, to work even more irregular shifts; at Horrell's, an early morning shift and weekend work. At the other extreme the two lowest-paying firms, Bettles and Peterborough Corporation, are among those which have essentially regular hours of work. If we consider wages, length of hours and convenience of hours, it seems possible to have two out of three as desirable, but not all three.

This tendency to equalisation of the advantages of employment is what neo-classical economists might expect, and they might point towards the usefulness of a compensatory view of the labour market. However, this situation is not altogether conducive to choice by the worker. To be sure, the firms do vary significantly in the weekly earnings available, allowing some scope for choice if the better-paying firms are not sought by all workers. But the high earnings are not generally an *alternative* to short hours (though they may be to other rewards). Rather, long hours serve to reduce inter-firm differences. The clear differentiation in hourly rates may be relevant to "alienated instrumentalism" where the aim is to minimise the time which has to be devoted to getting a reasonable wage. On the other hand, the essence of such an orientation is really to minimise the effect of work on non-work life, which entails not only the time spent but also the inconvenience of hours. In fact, the choice appears to a large extent to be between long and inconvenient hours – a choice which may not be seen as very significant. This does not, however, exclude the possibility of meaningful alternatives involving other rewards. To examine this we must look at the other advantages of employment measured by our Job Scores.

In considering these other job characteristics our five-point scores are not entirely satisfactory for a statistical analysis of variance, but they can be used as a rough guide. Accordingly, in Table 4.2 we list the E^2 values (all of which are significant) for the job characteristics considered previously.[2] Also in Table 4.2 we indicate the characteristics of each firm on which it differed markedly in attractiveness from the rest of the sample (*L* for exceptionally low attractiveness and *H* for exceptionally high). For this purpose we have added our estimate of the general level both of fringe benefits and of security. Where possible the data are presented at two levels of generality; the basic factors established in Chapter 3 show variations between firms in broad features, while the component variables provide more detail. We are concerned with differences which distinguish a firm's employment opportunities from those of other firms. Thus we are representing each firm by the scores of all its jobs, which means using job scores weighted by frequency of the job's occurrence. An extreme value indicates a high proportion of jobs scoring relatively low or high.

In order to examine extremes we considered separately the high and low scores on a characteristic for each firm. This we did by taking the mid-point of the scale as the zero point (i.e. subtracting 3 from all scores) and calculating positive and negative contributions to the mean. We modified this for one or two very skew distributions but the principle remains the same. In this way a firm can sometimes be above average at both extremes; for example, at Combex jobs tend to be rather heavy or fairly light, at London Brick the pace of work is often at one extreme or the other, and the relatively high number of jobs at Perkins involving quite complex decision-making is offset by even more than usual (50 per cent against 30 per cent) at the most elementary level. There are, in fact, quite a few instances of firms being above average in both directions, but in no case are the scores large enough to be taken as extreme. Usually the exceptional cases were obvious on inspection, but for consistency we used the formal criterion of scores 0.5 – that is 25 per cent of the possible range – more extreme than the mean in the relevant (+ or −) direction for all firms. However, since the actual value is arbitrary, for the two or three marginal cases we also examined the relationships of the firms' overall means. As we would expect, our method was entirely consistent in identifying firms with the highest and lowest overall means; its usefulness was in determining the cut-off points for classification as exceptional. For the factor measures of wages and hours a similar approach was used, with measurement from the mean, but then the outstanding cases were determined by inspection.[3] Similarly, the extremes on fringe benefits and security were determined from an inspection of the data. For wages and hours, it should be noted, because of the variations between men doing the same jobs, we used the amounts calculated for each individual rather than the weighted job averages. The latter would have underestimated the variations within firms and so given an exaggerated view of inter-firm differences.

The first point to note is that some of the job characteristics do

Table 4.2 Desirable job characteristics distinguishing firms

Characteristics	E^2	Baker-Perkins	Bettles	British Rail	Combex	Farrow's	Horrell's	London Brick	Perkins	Peterbro' Corpn.
Conditions (F)	0.26		L	H			H			
*Fumes, dirt, heat	0.30		L	H			H			
*Noise	0.22		H				H		L	
*Danger	0.20		L							
Exposure	0.67	H	L		H		L		H	L
Physical effort (F)	0.19	H	L							
*Quantity	0.18	H	L							
*Pace	0.18	H		H			L			
Skill (F)	0.06									
*Manual dexterity	0.05									H
Mental abilities (F)	0.28			H			H	L		
*Reading and writing	0.38						H	L		
†Visualisation	0.09		L							H
†Complexity of decisions	0.11						H			
Work cycle length	0.28								L	
Object variety	0.23	H						L		
Autonomy (F)	0.64		H				H	L		
*Decisions	0.27						H	L		
*Pace of work	0.45						H	L		
*Supervision	0.74		H				H		L	H
*Optional interaction	0.13						H			
Responsibility	0.25		L	H			H			
Hours: Regularity	0.65	H	H	L	H	H			L	H
Hours: length	0.38				L	L	H		H	
Wages per week	0.37		L						H	L
Fringe benefits	–	H					L			
Security	–					L	H			H
No. of H		5(7)	2(4)	3(5)	2(2)	1(1)	6(14)	0(0)	3(3)	2(5)
No. of L		0(0)	5(9)	1(1)	1(1)	2(2)	2(3)	2(3)	3(7)	2(2)

Note: the number in parentheses ( ) includes extremes on the component variables of the factors.

L = Exceptionally low desirability
H = Exceptionally high desirability
(F) = Factor
* A component of the factor under which it appears
† A component of both Skill and Mental abilities factors

differentiate the firms very clearly. That is to say, that in these respects there is only a limited amount of variation between jobs within firms compared with the differences between firms. Included here are Exposure, regularity of hours, and autonomy (although for the last-named the variance attributable to the firms in its component items ranges from 13 per cent for optional interaction to the high level of 74 per cent for interaction with supervision). For these job characteristics, the level tends to be set for the firm as a whole. On the other hand, there are some aspects of work, particularly skill and its different aspects such as manual dexterity, which are much the same anywhere, in the sense that internal differences are far more important than those between firms, apart from the odd exceptional firm. For the most part the inter-firm differences are highly significant and large enough to differentiate the firms, but variance within the firms is more important.

All the firms have some distinctive characteristics, and all but one (London Brick) have some relatively strong attraction. Baker-Perkins alone is distinguished only by attractive features (which is in keeping with its general reputation among our sample as a good firm). The others have a mixture of the unusually desirable and undesirable features, which means that their desirability as employers depends on the workers' priorities. We may see this most clearly in the contrast between Perkins and Peterborough Corporation. The former is out-standing for good economic rewards (as noted earlier) and protection from the weather, but is otherwise unfavourably distinguished. On the other hand, the local authority pays badly, for work which is frequently out in the cold and wet, but is otherwise distinguished by attractive characteristics.

It seems, therefore, that the firms can be regarded as offering distinctive employment opportunities. Of course, nine firms can offer only a limited set of alternatives – indeed, it is doubtful if all the firms in the area could offer anywhere near the total possible variation (except at the level of the individual jobs in the market). Nevertheless, they do provide the basis for real choices. However, we must not overlook the hierarchical element which also exists. Some firms emerge as more attractive than others, and this still holds when the less-distinctive features of the firms are taken into account; Baker-Perkins, British Rail and Horrell's are generally attractive, while Bettles, Farrow's, London Brick and Perkins are not. Of course it depends which job characteristics are considered, but the range covered is fairly comprehensive and the differences are quite clear. It is hard to see how Baker-Perkins would not, at the general level, emerge as more attractive than London Brick, although whether workers see it this way or whether they rate Peterborough Corporation above Perkins must depend on their preferences.

London Brick, Combex and Farrow's do not appear particularly distinctive, having few extreme features. All three come out below average on most aspects but not usually badly enough to be outstanding. At Combex and Farrow's there is a fairly consistent pattern of rather unattractive jobs, but at London Brick the position is more interesting. In this case the absence of extreme features does not reflect a preponderance of average or somewhat below average jobs but considerable internal variety. There are jobs with low effort and jobs where high effort brings in high pay; outdoor jobs with high autonomy and low noise, indoor jobs with excessive noise, and so on. For those entering this firm the possibilities of meaningful choice are greater than the summary data suggest. The possibilities are real in this case because of the job allocation policies of the firm which allow a fair measure of choice to the worker. On the other hand such choices (and those which may exist in other firms) are less likely to be visible to potential employees than are the extreme characteristics of firms as a whole. This raises the whole problem of the internal labour market and it is to this that we now turn.

THE INTERNAL LABOUR MARKET

We have found considerable variety between jobs within the same firm. This variety might be extremely complex in nature ot it might be simply and hierarchically organised, by an internal labour market. Are "better" and "worse" jobs within a firm equally available to potential employees or are the better jobs only allocated to existing employees? We attempted to collect systematic comparative data on internal promotion practices. In general terms we can identify the following "systems":

1. Direct recruitment to specialised jobs from outside. Most usual in the case of a generally recognised skill unrelated in nature to lower jobs in the firm, e.g. driving and building maintenance jobs in manufacturing firms.
2. Recruitment at the discretion of supervisors/personnel management, exercised according to "whoever is around", whether these are new recruits or established employees.
3. Promotions from within according to more or less rigid regulation.

Footplatemen on the railways adhere to the strictest system we found and in this case movement through the carriage cleaner → fireman → passed fireman (qualified to drive) → local driver → main-line driver hierarchy is entirely an internal process, spread over many years, where access to the top jobs is a matter of waiting for "dead men's shoes" (as they themselves expressed it).

However, the vast majority of appointing practices fall somewhere between these systems, being mixed and somewhat *ad hoc*. Especially confusing is the problem of where to locate the *boundaries* of any single promotion system. In some firms (notably British Rail and Peterborough Corporation) workers stayed within their particular departments, and promotion was almost exclusively confined within this area. But in most firms transfer was possible and frequent, though never the norm. Indeed, in general norms were ambiguous. In several firms management denied that there was an overall system in operation. This confirms the similar findings of Mackay *et al.* (1971: Chapter 11) for the engineering industry. Such ambiguity naturally lessens the predictability of internal job movement, and there are few cases where the worker would be able to calculate the likelihood of mobility.

Nevertheless, an internal hierarchy can still exist, even if the criteria for promotion are not clear. We tested for this with the aid of one of our job scores, the length of time normally taken to arrive at a particular job from entry to the firm. We will now compare those jobs open to short-service employees with those for which some seniority is necessary. We have taken our cut-off period as about six months. Jobs available within this period are likely to be seen as available by workers outside the firm, whether or not they can be entered immediately, and so may be regarded as in the external market. Table 4.3 shows the proportion of jobs available in this period within each firm. The figures for jobs investigated give an indication of the different types of work available and the weighted figures give the proportion of employment positions. The firms differ quite widely; at British Rail only a third of vacancies are available to newcomers, while at Combex, Horrell's and Peterborough Corporation the proportion is about three-quarters. Altogether just over half the jobs are "in the market" in this sense.

Table 4.4 gives the percentage "improvement" on various characteristics of the jobs requiring more than six months service over those more readily available. It is clear that longer service opens up the possibility of jobs which are more attractive in nearly all respects. Declines in attractiveness are tiny compared with the gains. The outstanding

Table 4.3 Jobs in labour market available within 6 months of entry to a firm, as % of all jobs

		Baker-Perkins	Bettles	British Rail	Combex	Farrow's	Horrell's	London Brick	Perkins	Peterboro' Corpn.	All
Jobs investigated	%	35	87	36	48	66	57	46	59	79	52
	N	86	8	42	27	35	7	61	39	63	368
Jobs weighted by no. of respondents	%	43	43	32	72	65	75	53	54	73	53
	N	157	16	155	36	52	32	180	189	124	941

Table 4.4   Difference between jobs requiring at least 6 months service in a firm and those more directly available: % increase in attractiveness.

Job characteristic	%	Job characteristic	%
Mathematical calculation	53	Physical effort: Pace	12
Complexity of decisions	52	Autonomy of decisions	11
Memory	52	Pace choice	10
Reading, writing	48	Fumes, Dirt, heat	10
Visualisation (of shapes		Physical effort: quantity	9
and relationships)	48	Exposure to weather	8
Object variety	47	Danger	1
Responsibility	34	Hours: length	0
Work cycle length	22	Supervision interaction	−2
Manual dexterity	20	Hours: irregularity	−4
Wages per hour	14	Noise	−5
Wagesper week	14	Optional interaction	−7

differences are in the various aspects of mental skill, with an average increase of 50 per cent. Next come variety, responsibility and manual dexterity, with substantial improvements. However, the "toughness" of jobs does not lessen much with seniority. There is little difference in working conditions, which is perhaps not surprising since the jobs are spread through the same environments, but there is only a modest lessening of the demand for physical effort. Also there is little improvement in autonomy, although this is made up of a modest gain in control over decisions and pace and a slight loss in the social aspects of autonomy.

Turning to the economic aspects, we see that hours are virtually unchanged with just a slight loss of convenience, while wages per week are only moderately (14 per cent) higher. This may seem rather surprising, as it is generally assumed that the jobs requiring some seniority for promotion receive better pay. This is usually though not always the case. The railways provide the extreme case where there is only a half per cent difference between the average weekly earnings of men on the two sets of jobs. Elsewhere the differences are usually clearer.

The point that emerges is that *it is skill rather than economic rewards which distinguishes those jobs directly in the market from those requiring seniority*. The variance of wages is higher for the jobs available at the point of entry, and this is due to more variation between firms. For both weekly and hourly wages the proportion of total variance explained by inter-firm differences is greater for these than for the longer-service jobs, to the extent that even for weekly wages it is almost half (values of E^2 are increased respectively to 0.46 and 0.68). The variance of hours is also greater but here it is due to greater variance within firms (E^2 is 0.30). The general picture is one where wages could be dominant in recruitment. Once in the firm, the rewards of staying rather than leaving are largely intrinsic.

The foregoing discussion suggests that to a large extent choices relating to job content will be made within a firm. If the more intrinsically attractive jobs depend on seniority and the intrinsic qualities vary more within firms than between them, then choices between firms are most likely in the negative form of leaving work that is disliked. Whether the workers have control of choice in the firm depends very much on the management policies, which may leave the worker feeling baffled and powerless. But in choosing firms preferences for job content are less likely to be in evidence. This, of course, is liable to support the employers' belief in the primacy of wages for recruitment.

In general, then, better jobs are gained through movement up the internal hierarchy, presenting a further limitation on choice, but a certain amount of scope remains. Some degree of trade-off is possible for all rewards, but particularly with respect to outside work, autonomy, hours and wages. The main weakness of these "compensatory" mechanisms is their failure to carry over into job content. With the exception of autonomy, differences in intrinsic job content — variety, manual skill and mental abilities — tend to lie within the internal labour market. Relatively skilful jobs are not readily available, even in return for sacrifices in other work aspects. Skilful jobs are obtained with seniority and are therefore accompanied by higher wages. As we have just noted, there are alternative routes to high wages but not to interesting, challenging work. Why is this? To answer this, we must first take a detour to look a little more closely at the nature of the more skilful jobs.

THE SKILLS NEEDED BY WORKERS

As we were conducting our job-scoring procedures in Peterborough, a rather curious impression began to strike us. We were consistently giving high scores on most of the job skill items to *driving* jobs. We paused to consider the implications of this, for here we were deviating from the job evaluation practices of industry itself which do not rate driving very highly. But in terms of the categories we were using, which are based on a strictly "technical" conception of skill, our scores seemed to us to be essentially correct. In terms of the fineness of hand-eye co-ordination (manual dexterity), of memory, of visualising the relationship between processes, of concentration, of complexity of decision-making involving the continuous re-assessment of interacting variables – in all of these, drivers were certainly toward the high-skill end of the jobs we considered. Now it is difficult to produce a composite measure of overall skill and to estimate the general skill level of drivers. A commonsensical measure would be the period it takes the average man to learn a job, and this would confirm our impression, as the time taken as a learner-driver is longer than is the learning period of nearly all our jobs. However, our factor analysis provides us with the most satisfactory measures of general technical skill which appear possible. From the derivation of the factors, as set out in Appendix III, it can be seen that factor 2 in Table AIII.1 is a direct measure of the skill of the job, as distinct from the need to use mental abilities (factor 1). Of course, the two are related but there are nevertheless two distinct factors. Now this "skill" factor would do very well, but it is better for present purposes to include "mental abilities" as well. Thus we use factor 8, labelled "General Abilities", which is the best summary measure of the components of the mental ability and skill factors. Drivers all scored above the mean. Fork-lift truck and most other internal works drivers scored only just above it, but outside road drivers and construction equipment drivers scored well above it. Taking the lowest-scored outside road driver (a chauffeur) as a reference point (1.3 points above the mean),[4] Table 4.5 contains a list of all the jobs scoring identically or higher, together with their number in the sample.[5]

The table shows how few workers actually exercise as much general skill as drivers – 13 per cent of the sample – while 87 per cent exercise less. Even the figure of 13 per cent may be misleadingly high because of our substantial coverage of railway-engine drivers, who account for over a third of the group. Note that apart from the (non-railway) drivers themselves, the highly skilled men are all at the top of the internal labour markets. Years of experience have apparently been a necessary precondition. Yet driving is not a skill in short supply (other than at the level of H.G.V. licences). Thus industry's job evaluation schemes downgrade it. It is nevertheless a fairly difficult skill, which takes some time to acquire. However, our society assumes that it is a skill which any normal adult can acquire, and this seems to be right. Though only a minority of manual workers actually drive their own cars, their failure rate in their first driving test (around 40 per cent) is the same as other socio-economic groups. (Sheppard, 1971: Table 2; Skelley *et al.*, 1972: Table 11). This

Table 4.5 Jobs and workers exercising comparable skill to the least skilful outside road driver (measured by the General Abilities Factor 8 in Table AIII.1)

Job Group		No. of Jobs Scored	No of Men
Skilled machinists (inc. dilutees)	(e.g. radial drillers, millers, tool grinders, tape drillers)	14	18
Metal workers	(blacksmith, electroplaters)	3	3
Furnace operators		2	10
Engine testers		4	17
Engine drivers and passed fireman (B.R.)		3	42
Gardeners/Groundsmen 1st class		2	10
Motor mechanics		1	0
	Sub-total	29	100
Drivers of outside road vehicles and earth-moving equipment		12	20
Lower skilled jobs		327	831
	Total	368	951

fact gives us a rare chance to comment on the *absolute* level of a work reward, and raises acutely the question of whether the ingenuity we have exercised in measuring job content is a methodological mouse, concerned with fine variations within a trivial range of job opportunities. Let us emphasise that this is not a study based on typical mass-production factories, like so much of the research produced in industrial sociology. Our sample has been deliberately widened, beyond even typicality, to produce as large a variation of job types as could be practically handled. And yet we still confirm the traditional picture of monotonous jobs, debased skills and under-use of human capacities. We must therefore conclude that this is indeed the objective situation of the majority of the manual working class. It is simply not possible for the worker to choose a skilled job, no matter how much he might be prepared to sacrifice in wages or other job rewards. On the other hand, some jobs are even less demanding and more monotonous than others. We have measured clearly discernible differences, which may be experienced as significant by workers, but are at a very low level.

In Chapter I we noted the traditional neo-classical way of handling skill, in terms of "human capital", "worker quality" and the "queue". The employer seeks more skilful workers for more critical jobs and he rewards them accordingly. Yet we have uncovered a situation where the vast majority of workers are capable of performing the vast majority of jobs. What then is "worker quality"? Perhaps the employers can answer.

EMPLOYERS' RECRUITMENT POLICIES AND "WORKER QUALITY"

The employers we studied all thought that they could distinguish between "better" and "worse" workers. Not all felt that they were able to secure "good" workers, who were considered to be in short supply in a tight labour market. Indeed, only Perkins said that they were entirely satisfied with the quantity or quality of workers, although in addition two others (British Rail and Horrell's) saw their problem as one of retaining rather than attracting good workers. So worker quality appears to be in short supply. Yet we have just seen that the vast majority of workers are capable of doing the vast majority of jobs. So what is the problem for the employers? To answer this we will use data we acquired through interviewing the managers and foremen responsible for recruitment in the nine firms. In all, about 25 persons gave us relevant information in unstructured interviews (although we took along with us an *aide-memoire* list of questions to ensure that, on certain crucial items, we obtained answers from all the firms).

Recruitment practices varied. Most firms advertised vacancies (we deal with the content of these advertisements in the next chapter) but also expected casual callers and those sent on by the local Employment Exchange. The callers might be interviewed by personnel managers, by production managers and foremen, or by both. The interview could last between a minute and half an hour, involving quite elaborate forms or no paperwork at all. One firm (Perkins) administered a formal test of literacy and basic mathematical ability, although several others required *ad hoc* evidence of literacy. All of the recruiters we talked to repeatedly said that they were looking for "quality" and that they could distinguish between "better" and "worse" workers. As one said, "I can get rid of at least 80 per cent after a five-minute interview just by looking and listening." Those recruiting for the firms at the bottom of the labour market naturally could not turn away 80 per cent of callers and they bemoaned the lack of "quality". What does "quality" mean? Bearing in mind the controversy between neo-classical and radical economists that we discussed in Chapter 1, is it closer to ability or stability, intelligence or co-operativeness? Let us start with ability, looking at the comments the recruiters made about physical and mental capacities.

Literacy in English was without question the most important formal requirement. Without the ability to read and write English, an applicant could work at only labouring and cleaning jobs at four of the nine firms (British Rail, Baker-Perkins, Horrell's and Perkins). And, as we have seen, these were generally the most attractive firms. Furthermore, no *responsible* jobs in any firm could be held by anyone who could not read and write English. Such a requirement did have some objective validity, given that in these jobs some written instructions were normally provided. Obviously this effectively excluded recent immigrants from non-English speaking countries, as well as native illiterates. We did not wish to question our respondents – all of whom, except some Italians, could naturally understand English – on the delicate subject of illiteracy, and we have no estimates of this among the sample.[6] Nationally, various estimates are available according to what measure of illiteracy is taken. The research has been summarised by the Bullock Report: *A Language for Life* (Dept. of Education and Science, 1975: 10–35). Relevant to our argument here are the results of a 1970–1 survey: at least 3 per cent of the 15-year-olds in England were either illiterate or "semi-literate", i.e. with a reading age of less than nine. These would be unable to read documents which touch ordinary adult life, like the Highway Code, a tax return, or a claim for industrial injuries. Naturally the proportion among manual workers is likely to be higher, although exact figures are not available. Whatever the precise figure it is clearly only a minority of workers, among whom foreign immigrants are dispropor- tionately concentrated, who are incapable of this kind of basic job skill. We might add that adult literacy courses are nowadays generally available. This skill is not beyond the reach of normal adults.

Yet this was the only formal qualification required by the firms (with the exception of Perkins's arithmetic test, compulsory only for pro- spective storemen). Level of educational attainment was not once mentioned by the recruiters – reasonably enough, since 95 per cent of our sample had left school without any qualifications. Nor were subsequent on-the-job training and qualifications referred to, though we should remind our readers that we had excluded from our study those jobs for which apprenticeship was the normal requirement. For most of the manual working class there are no such objective indicators of ability. So were the personnel recruiters engaging in subjective appraisal of intelligence? Apparently not, for, with two exceptions, they did not mention intelligence. The exceptions were at the opposite ends of the job hierarchy. At the top end, the recruiters at Baker-Perkins said that they were always on the lookout for workers of exceptional ability for eventual promotion into the dilutee craftsman grade. If one was spotted, he was put into the machine shop and advised to join the A.E.U.W. But such a man was rare, and he stood out from other applicants "like a sore thumb". At the lower end, several recruiters noted that some of their jobs were too undemanding for the worker of "normal ability". In fact, several said that they were looking for "normal ability", so that they appeared to be screening out unsuitables rather than positively selecting certain workers (this was also so with regard to physical strength, where apart from a few tough jobs, the recruiters' task was to exclude the relatively feeble). This left the lowest jobs for those excluded. In two firms general labourers were considered too unintelligent for pro- motion, and recruits from outside normally went straight into the next grade above.

Recruiters did not often mention intelligence, but they gave us many indications of something they did believe to be in short supply – "the good worker". One, bemoaning a decline in the quality of workers in recent years, said: "Lorry drivers have deteriorated most – the state of their vehicle maintenance has declined greatly and this is the crucial sign." Another, on the same theme of national decline, said: "We want responsible men who will work on their own, and we can't get them." A third agreed: "We can't be selective. They understand English, have two arms and two legs – then O.K. So our labour is getting worse. Foremen have to push more and more. Lots will stay only for a day or so. Too many are unwilling to work."

Another useful source was the reports written at Perkins on the two-week training period for machining jobs. Completion of this course was a requirement for most jobs in the company, including all of those with any significant measure of semi-skill. Only 1 in 300 failed, though rather more were considered unsuitable for machining work. Here is a typical report on an individual: "Should make an average operator with practice. Good solid worker but tends to watch the clock (too keen to terminate shift)." "Willingness to work" seems to be the crucial variable, in short supply and in national decline. Men who will work on their own, who do not need to be pushed, who are responsible.

For the most part, the recruiters relied on their subjective impressions of the likely co-operativeness of the applicant, measured, we suspect, by whether the worker listens in the interview. Nevertheless, for a minority they could use some of the "screening devices" we noted in Chapter 1. Two stood out here: family situation, and number of previous jobs held within the preceeding period. The ideal worker was considered to be married with small children. Thus he was likely to be about 30. Obviously this has little to do with intelligence and a lot to do with the employer's conception of "responsibility". The worker with dependents will do as he is told, not risk losing his job, be keen to do overtime, and show himself capable of promotion to a higher-paid job. Incidentally, although intelligence (as we have noted) was considered relevant for the lowest jobs of all, the recruiters used age as their first "screening device": workers of 50 or more were considered suitable for these jobs, not because of their low intelligence but because of their low aspirations and fear of unemployment. Similarly, there is no reason for believing that the worker who has had four jobs in the previous 18 months is of low intelligence, but his propensity for non-cooperation is clear. This is unfortunate in one respect, for, as we have noted, many job characteristics are not revealed to the worker until he tries the job. If he doesn't like them, he must chance his arm again by taking another job. It may take several moves to find a congenial job. Yet the more he moves, the more discriminated against he is. This is the "Catch 22" of the labour market, the equation of rationality with unreliability!

The other two screening devices of general importance (given that education cannot be used to discriminate between British workers) are sex and race. In Chapter 2 we noted that sex was a perfect discriminator in Peterborough, so much so that – as the jobs we were enquiring about were understood to be those of men – none of the recruiters even mentioned sex as a selection factor. We regret now that we did not raise the issue ourselves, for it seems clear that the division between men's and women's jobs was an unquestioned parameter of their recruitment policy.

Not surprisingly none of the recruiters admitted to discrimination on racial grounds, and the race stereotypes which emerged even varied within the same firm but on the whole were as likely to be favourable as unfavourable: coloured workers were more honest than whites, Pakistanis were reliable but they "need feeding up before they can do heavy work", Italians were "hard workers but a little reckless". These are slightly more favourable impressions than those held by the managers interviewed in Wright's study, where a majority believed coloured workers to be less skilled and less flexible than white workers (1968: Chapter 4). There is ample evidence elsewhere, of course, for the existence of discrimination in employment against immigrant workers (for a review, see Political and Economic Planning, 1976: Chapter 10). This was not an issue at the centre of our research and as we did not ask workers themselves about discrimination, this is an issue we must skirt, although we do find clear evidence of discrimination in the internal labour market (see Chapter 9). The literacy requirement does discriminate against most of the recent foreign immigrants, but it may be considered a defensible requirement. Beyond this, at the informal level, colour bars of a very traditional and tacit kind do still exist in at least two of our industries. Both Bettle's, the building firm, and Peterborough Corporation – who, it should be noted, do not run the local bus service – would be surprised if they received applications from coloured workers. It is believed locally that they do discriminate (in the case of Bettle's, because of the industry's rather than the firm's reputation), but this is not actually put to the test. As we shall see, immigrant workers are found in the better firms as well as the worse ones. Moreover, their wages are actually higher than are those of the native-born (see Chapter 9). For these reasons we doubt whether race is in fact used directly as a screening device throughout this labour market.

Nevertheless, in other respects, our findings clearly support the radical economists' view of the labour market, noted in Chapter 1. The "human capital" view of worker quality expressed by neo-classical economists is incorrect at the lower levels of the job hierarchy studied by us. Differentiation among the working class cannot be on the basis of degree of skill possessed by the worker, for the simple reason that nearly all of the jobs are within the skill capabilities of nearly all the workers.

However, managements were quite clear that most workers could not competently undertake the kind of job which we have observed is only equal in skill to the act of driving a car. Their fears were of two kinds.

Firstly, managements expressed worries about the cost of supervision of work that necessarily conferred a measure of autonomy on workers. Foremen and supervisors generally have two roles, that of organisational intermediary, ensuring that the correct flow of materials reaches their section, and that of coercive overseer, ensuring that the men actually do what they are supposed to. The costs of the latter function are galling to management, because – as we have noted – there is little objective difficulty in the tasks confronting their men. They should not *need* watching. Furthermore, many tasks cannot be closely watched, because of the geographical layout of the work situation. In our sample, workers like gardeners, groundsmen, many building and road workers, and lorry drivers are largely independent at work and the costs of effective overseeing would be very great. For example, we noted that our chats with groundsmen took place in comfortable chairs on pavilion verandahs from where we could see the arrival of the supervisor's van long before he could see us. If he wished, the groundsman could return to his work before the supervisor saw him. The supervisor was well aware of this; indeed, he joked about it. He had no real alternative to trusting the men and had largely to abandon the overseeing role. This situation requires a *responsible* worker who will work autonomously and conscientiously without being driven. As the job of groundsman is one of the most interesting, skilful and congenial in our whole sample, such men could be found to fill it. Yet the majority of autonomous jobs could not draw this level of commitment from their occupants and thus, to management, the responsible, self-motivated worker seemed in short supply.

Secondly, managements were concerned that many workers could not be safely entrusted with expensive machinery. In any co-ordinated system of machine production it is not merely that machine breakage is costly but also that erratic work on the part of one operator can interfere with the smooth flow of the whole. The assembly and machining lines at Perkins best exemplify this. The jobs on these lines are not technically difficult or even physically challenging, but they require concentration, steadiness and *discipline*. The ideal worker is essentially mediocre, working steadily at an average pace, accepting meekly the dictates of the technology.

Responsibility and discipline are thus the qualities valued by management and thought to be in short supply. They are thought to be revealed in a stable work history and induced by financial necessity. Hence the preference shown by recruiters for men with few previous employers and for those caught in "the life cycle squeeze". Yet even when accepted for employment, workers must still prove that they do possess responsibility and discipline. This is where we return to the internal labour market. We have already showed that the internal labour market stratified jobs more according to their intrinsic skill than to their wages, and most of all it distinguished levels of mental skills and of responsibility. Yet we have seen that these skills are not great and that most workers can easily do most jobs. Therefore, the question is not whether they could do the more mentally skilful jobs but whether they would. *The internal labour market is fundamentally an apprenticeship in co-operation.* Demonstrate discipline on routine jobs, and you may be rewarded! The essential point about jobs at the top of the hierarchy is not an unusual degree of skill, but the costliness to management of error and the likelihood of error being made.

This view of the internal labour market is at odds with traditional views in one important respect. It follows from our argument that management will not be opposed to seniority as a main criterion of promotion, because it is through length of service that responsibility and discipline are demonstrated. Yet labour relations theory has always taken the view that promotion policies at the manual level are characterised by a fundamental clash: while management favour "ability" as the criterion of promotion, workers and unions favour seniority. We are not totally rejecting this view, for – in Peterborugh as elsewhere – such tension is present. Management do emphasise ability, unions seniority. Yet the two are not in practice diametric opposites. This was particularly noticeable in those firms where management claimed they appointed entirely or largely by ability. These were (predictably) firms with weak unions – Horrell's, Combex and Farrow's. Yet what management meant was that they selected *from among the men on the next lower grade* on the basis of ability.[7] Thus seniority provides the framework within which management wishes to exercise its discretion.

This is of course a persistent grievance of unions – that promotion by "ability" means promotion of the foreman's friends. We think there is some truth in this allegation. We have already noted elsewhere (Blackburn and Mann, 1975) that our workers in better jobs tend to be rather more conservative and pro-management in their general attitudes than those in less skilled jobs.[8] We are not asserting that this correlation would hold up across the whole occupational hierarchy. But in the broad stratum of jobs we are studying, promotion is partly a managerial prerogative, and we do not find it surprising that a certain political bias should enter in through the managerial stress on co-operation. We conclude therefore that "ability" as conventionally understood is of little significance in determining the differential economic destinies of the bulk of the working class. Length of service and co-operative attitudes are more likely to be rewarded – eventually – with a more interesting and skilful job.

THE JOB ALTERNATIVES: A SUMMARY

We are now able to summarise the range of job alternatives "objectively" available to the workers, before, that is, we discuss either their own preferences or those of the employers, both of which may constrain choice in practice. We have so far in this chapter introduced two realistic constraints upon the wide range of jobs theoretically available: the fact that it is normally the firm that is the actual employing unit, and the fact that many of the jobs are filled only from within an internal labour market. Despite these constraints and those observed in the previous chapter, three main areas of potential choice still apparently remain.

Firstly, outdoor work, involving not only the pleasures of being in the fresh air of Peterborough but also considerable job autonomy, is available in exchange for relatively low wages and only moderate job skills. This is obviously a highly visible bundle of job attributes, for the presence or absence of a roof is apparent from afar! Of course it is not quite so simple as there are different degrees of exposure and opportunity to shelter, but there is no problem about where to look for such jobs. A somewhat different sort of Outside work is provided by driving jobs, which also are visible and offer high autonomy but combine this with relatively high skill.

Secondly, the length and regularity of hours tend to discriminate fairly clearly both between jobs and between firms. Short or regular hours are available and are potentially within the decision-making powers of the workers themselves. However, considerable sacrifices are involved in obtaining either benefit, for such jobs tend to be low-paid, environmentally unpleasant and not very skilful. A combination of relatively short and regular hours is possible but less open to choice by the workers, and the costs are even greater. One would have to be interested in work avoidance, in accordance with an "alienated instrumental" orientation, to choose this.

Thirdly, pay is clearly differentiated between firms, especially at point of entry jobs, so that to a considerable extent choice of firm will determine wage level. The internal labour market does not stratify wages to any marked extent and intra-firm differences in pay are not as great as are those in intrinsic job content such as the use of skills. However, this must be qualified, for we noted that the inter-firm differences in pay are greater for wages per hour than they are for wages per week, i.e. the low-paying firms make up some of their lag through working long hours. Furthermore, the high hourly rates tend to be associated with rotating or erratic shiftworking. Thus high wages of any sort tend to require *either* long *or* unsocial hours. Those high-paying jobs which are available to the outsider tend also to be rather low-skilled, while the top-paying jobs are also more interesting but available only through promotion.

Apart from these three main bundles of attributes we have also found that each firm tends to offer its own distinctive set of rewards and costs. Though some firms are generally "good" and others generally "bad", all but two (London Brick and Baker – Perkins) are distinguished by some desirable and some undesirable features. However, when a firm is not particularly attractive or unattractive in terms of a characteristic it is sometimes because the jobs within the firms differ widely in attractiveness. Furthermore, there is some difference between firms on all aspects. However, these differences are not great and, like the differences within firms, they are unlikely to be readily visible.

The area where choice is most difficult is the intrinsic quality of the job – the variety, skill and opportunity for a worker to use his mind. To get a truly interesting job is virtually impossible, as hardly any exist in this sector of employment. There are nevertheless significant differences even at the low level that is available, but choice of the better jobs is restricted by the fact that access is primarily through the internal market. There is little scope to make sacrifices on other aspects to gain these jobs since they tend to be better all round, with access dependent on seniority and approval of the employer. The best strategy is to sit tight, and if that doesn't work the only thing to do is to move to another firm and try again.

Employers make a direct contribution to market processes through their recruitment and promotion practices, although it would be a mistake to see them as controlling the situation. We have seen that they are concerned about not being able to get workers of the right "quality". However, the quality they seek is not ability – for which the demands are low – but co-operativeness. Thus the internal hierarchy gives them a chance to select those who have demonstrated their responsibility and discipline. Formal criteria have little relevance for either initial appointments or promotion. Employers depend on subjective assessments, aided by such rules-of-thumb as the disciplinary effects of family responsibilities. Thus the exercise of the employers' criteria not only reduces the workers' control of job selection but makes the situation uncertain.

5 Enter the Workers: Knowledge and Preferences in the Labour Market

In the two previous chapters we examined the range of job choices objectively available to the worker. Though we concluded that this range is severely restricted by hierarchical elements of the market outside of the worker's control, by low skill opportunities in general, by management behaviour, and by the sheer complexity of the market, nevertheless opportunities for choice exist. In this chapter we begin to look at the worker's response to this situation, using data from our interview survey. We shall first examine the extent of workers' knowledge of job alternatives and then move to the nature of their preferences. However, we shall also introduce a further component of the objective labour market, the information which employers make public about the jobs they offer. Obviously this is an important influence on workers' knowledge.

We begin by assessing the accuracy of workers' knowledge. As this chapter will show, our data are well suited to examine the overall extent of workers' knowledge, although less suited to testing the individual worker. We noted in Chapter 1 that there is some disagreement in the literature concerning the overall extent of workers' knowledge. The problem arose because traditional neo-classical theory assumed perfect knowledge of labour market conditions. A few labour market studies were sufficiently imbued with the neo-classical spirit to continue the emphasis on knowledge despite empirical difficulties. Yet most authors of empirical studies have interpreted their findings as a challenge to the neo-classical theory, emphasizing workers' ignorance and vagueness about job alternatives. Reynolds (1951: 84) concludes that workers "are poorly informed about job opportunities". Miernyk (1955: 28) says:

"The sample workers were rarely well informed about labor market conditions . . . only a few exhibited any real knowledge of the actual extent of local unemployment, the availability of jobs in the community, and the wages paid by and working conditions in industries or establishments other than those with which they were familiar through personal experience." Such conclusions are typical of research studies, as the two principal reviews of the literature note (Hunter and Reid, 1968: 115; Parnes, 1954: 165–90). However, both these reviewers have reservations. Hunter and Reid note that the evidence concerns situations of less than full employment (which is not true – Reynolds's study being the main exception) and is largely American (which is true). Thus worker ignorance has certainly not been well established in Europe. Parnes goes more deeply into methodological questions. His doubts seem to us to be more illuminating and we would like to expand on them.

The evidence for worker ignorance and vagueness is mostly rather impressionistic. Most studies do not *test* workers' knowledge. Instead, the author generally reports that it is his "impression" that, or "judging from the responses as a whole", workers seemed ignorant. If any direct question is put to workers, it is normally a rather general one of the kind: "When your job at Armour was terminated and you had to find another job, what possibilities were open to you?" (Wilcock and Franke, 1963: 95). Thus the worker is asked to *volunteer* information and to talk articulately about the labour market as a whole. Given the difficulties of communication between academic researcher and manual worker, such questions tell us more about the worker's self-confidence and articulateness than about the accuracy of his information. Moreover, the academic's assessment of what is accurate can be rather bizarre. We have already quoted Miernyk's confident conclusion that workers were "rarely well informed". The only evidence that Miernyk presents for this from his five case studies of plant closure in New England is from one case-study in which several workers are quoted as making rather simplistic statements about the decline of the textile industry and the growth of electronics in New England as a whole (1955: 50–3). According to this criterion, workers would have to read the business news before they could be well informed about local job opportunities! What we need are data, not on workers' generalisations about the level of business activity, but on their knowledge of the precise, actual job opportunities available to them. In all these studies, there are only two which begin to attempt this, those by Reynolds and by Myers and Schultz – both some 25 years old. As Reynolds firmly emphasises worker ignorance, while Myers and Schultz emphasize worker knowledge, we can see that the apparent consensus in the literature actually dissolves.

We will not dissect in detail the methods of these two studies in order to reconcile their differences. Parnes (1954: 165–90) has already done this quite adequately, and we shall merely repeat his conclusions. Firstly, Myers and Schultz's (1951) study was of a much smaller labour market, and its workers could be expected to have more complete knowledge of it. Indeed, a recent British study of unemployment in a small town asserts (without, however, presenting any supporting evidence) that workers were "fully aware of the major employers" because of the smallness of the labour market (Martin and Fryer, 1973: 146). Secondly, Reynolds asked employed workers about other jobs in the community, while Myers and Schultz asked currently unemployed workers how much they knew beforehand about jobs that they had previously taken. We would naturally expect the latter to have more knowledge – or, at least, to say that they had. As Reynolds himself argues, most of his employed sample are not in the labour market in any real sense. We shall shortly test this hypothesis with our own data. Thirdly, Myers and Schultz were clearly more generous than Reynolds in deciding whether a worker had specific knowledge of jobs. As Parnes notes, the former were willing to count statements such as "X is a good company" as knowledge, whereas Reynolds was not. It is difficult to decide who was correct without further analysis of what workers mean by such statements. They may indicate knowledge or they may not. It would need more probing than either set of authors provides to decide the issue. We attempt this in our own research, as will be seen below.

Of course, none of this enables us to decide on the *accuracy* of workers' knowledge. This may be precise but wrong. In the whole literature we can find only one study which attempts in a systematic way to compare workers' opinions about jobs with objective reality. Once again this is Reynolds's study, which found that the vast majority of workers thought their wages were fair in relation to those paid by other firms. No consistent relationship emerged between the proportion of a workforce being satisfied in this way with their wages, and actual wages. He concluded that workers had very little accurate knowledge of wage-rates (1951: 213–14). While these results are interesting, we do not feel they are conclusive. The question asked is one about "*satisfaction*" with wages, not about the believed *level* of wages. As with nearly all such questions the results reveal overwhelming satisfaction. The proportion satisfied varies only from 80 per cent to 100 per cent within each firm. Workers may have believed that *they* could not get better wages elsewhere. This is the thrust of Reynolds's own argument: that workers who move between firms stand to slip down the wage hierarchy. Thus the workers' replies *may* reveal accuracy of knowledge. Obviously this issue needs further testing.

We conclude that even the most thorough of the previous studies has failed to establish the degree and accuracy of workers' knowledge of labour market opportunities. The basic reason for this is that researchers have not *themselves* acquired such knowledge. Workers have been expected to volunteer information which, in an *ad hoc* way, the researchers then decide is precise or vague. This is an unsatisfactory methodology. As the last two chapters reveal, we have acquired considerable and systematic knowledge of the Peterborough labour market. Thus we were unusually well placed to judge the degree and accuracy of workers' knowledge. Making use of that strength, we asked our sample directly and systematically about those parts of the Peterborough labour market for which we had systematic knowledge.

The main evidence in this chapter derives from Question 22 in the interview survey, which asked about the workers' attitude to all of the nine firms sampled,[1] plus the major non-sampled firm in Peterborough, British Domestic Appliances Ltd. (part of G.E.C. – A.E.I., and known locally as "Hotpoint"), for which we had also been able to collect some basic information. This question was introduced by asking the worker to suppose that he had been away from Peterborough, and on return was looking for work. Where would he work – at Perkins? London Brick? etc. etc., until we had gone through the entire list. This was an extraordinarily successful question. Workers were ready to conceive of the hypothetical situation we asked about and they gave us much valuable information about their perceptions, knowledge and preferences.

KNOWLEDGE OF WAGES

We begin by looking at the answers to the last part of each section of the question: "Suppose you did go to (firm) to work? After about six months, what would be the total amount you'd be earning per week before tax and other deductions?" This gives us the worker's estimate of the wages paid for the kind of work he could expect to get at each firm, after he had had time to settle in. For nine firms we can compare such estimates with the actual wages paid to our samples in each firm to obtain some idea of accuracy. It would be extremely dangerous to use this comparison as a test of *individual* accuracy, for any guess falling within the total range of actual wages might be accurate. By aggregating, however, we can compare the average estimate with the actual average, and form an impression of the overall degree of knowledge of the workers. This we have done in Table 5.1.

The actual wages in this table are the mean weekly wages of our sample in each company for 12 weeks during February, June and October of 1970, including only those occupying jobs normally reached within three years of entry to the company, to correspond to the length of service in the estimates. This somewhat overestimates the contribution of jobs immediately available and jobs normally attained after six months to three years of service, but is the best compromise. The workers' estimates do not include those for their own companies, as these would probably overstate the accuracy for companies where we drew large samples.

An immediately striking trend of this table is that the estimates err on the low side for all companies. Peterborough employers pay about 25 per cent more than the workers think they do. Other surveys have shown that people generally underestimate the national level of wages (Cole and Utting, 1956; Abel-Smith and Townsend, 1956). This raises the question whether the workers underestimate because of actual ignorance, or because of a conservatism which induces them to name a level below which they know wages are unlikely to fall. By examining workers' estimates of their *own* employer's wages we can attempt to provide an answer on the assumption that workers are aware of the wages paid by their own employer. In fact, the employees are only very slightly more optimistic about the level of wages in their own firms than are non-employees. The average difference is only about £1 per week, and in three firms (Baker-Perkins, Bettles and British Rail) the employees are actually more pessimistic than the non-employees. Only in the case of Horrell's are employees very much closer to the actual level of wages. It is possible that the estimates, of both employees and non-employees, were pulled down by those with relatively high-paying jobs gained after long service overestimating their differential over men with only six months service.[2] Furthermore, the modal earnings are nearer than the means to the estimates. This indicates a degree of realism in the workers' pessimism since the most usual levels of earnings (i.e. the modal earnings) are towards the lower ends of the ranges. Although the number of cases in some firms is too low to place much reliability on the figures, the mode is below the mean for every firm.

From these results we would wish to attribute the low level of wage

Table 5.1 Mean gross weekly wages (£) and workers' estimates, by firms. Jobs available within 3 years of entry

	Baker-Perkins	Bettles	British Rail	Combex	Farrow's	Horrell's	London Brick	Perkins	Peterboro' Corp.	All
Actual	26.6	21.8	30.1	25.0	28.6	26.5	29.8	31.5	22.1	27.9
Rank	5	9	2	7	4	6	3	1	8	
Estimates	23.7	22.8	20.6	18.2	17.7	21.6	24.7	26.7	17.5	22.1
Rank	3	4	6	7	8	5	2	1	9	

estimates to caution and pessimism rather than to ignorance. As we shall show later, workers have a strong sense of the insecurities and impermanences of their position. A venture into the labour market is a risk and there is no point in *expecting* a good level of wages. Our figures for actual wages are based on full weeks, including overtime, but workers cannot expect this level all the time.

Yet the absolute level of the estimates is irrelevant to the problem of actual job choice, for which we need to know only the accuracy of the workers' comparisons between companies. For this, we look at the rankings and the actual wage differences between companies in Table 5.1. While some companies are accurately placed, three are way out. Bettles, British Rail and Farrow's account for all of the variation; without them the estimated ranking of the rest would be the same as the actual ranking. Even with the three exceptions on mean weekly wages, the product-moment correlation between the estimates and actual figures is 0.46. This is highly significant and reveals a degree of overall accuracy. Furthermore, all three notable mistakes are understandable. The ordering of the firms would have resembled our own before we actually collected the wages data, armed only with the knowledge of the industrial sociologist and a general familiarity with the industrial structure of Peterborough. We too would have assumed that building workers earned more.[3] We were not to know that the obsolete plant of a food company (which was shortly to close down) would pay high gross wages by offering an average working week of 60 hours. We would have shared, though not to the same extent, the general belief that railway workers were slipping down the wage hierarchy. The British Rail earnings were especially unexpected in that unskilled parcels-sorters working fairly long hours on rather generous group bonus schemes were able to earn almost as much as footplate staff.

Ideally, it might have been better to compare modes, which would have given quite similar results, but the estimates are in round figures and do not provide a suitable basis for relatively fine distinctions, while some of the actual figures are not very reliable, as we noted earlier. However, if we use the mode to indicate actual earnings the ordering is the same, except that Farrow's drops to ninth place, showing that as cautious judgments the estimates for this firm are quite accurate. Similarly, if we examine mean wages per hour, roughly the same result is found, with the Farrow's estimate noticeably more accurate. Hourly earnings are more closely related to what workers may regard as a "normal" working week than are our averages for full weeks. Thus, if our argument about low estimates being due to caution is correct, we would expect estimates to be closer to both the modes and the average wages per hour. This is indeed what we find, with the correlations rising to 0.65 and 0.74 respectively. Overall, then, we have established greater worker accuracy than previous research would have led us to believe.

We are not seeking to gloss over the inaccuracies which were revealed, but we are noting that workers' knowledge, where possessed, was that of an "informed outsider", and therefore liable to be upset by internal company policies, which management may not wish broadcast to the locality. After all, most companies are *private* institutions, while even public ones are responsible neither to their employees nor to potential employees. Their only direct channels of information to the locality on working conditions is through job advertisements and through details given to the local Employment Exchange. Few Peterborough employers advertised their level of wages to the public or to the Department of Employment. Only public employers, British Rail and Peterborough Corporation, consistently specified in their advertisements either average earnings or the basic rate of pay (though one local private employer not sampled – the bus company – also gave average earnings, and in 1972 London Brick advertised their rates for a time). Most of the private firms promised "good" or "excellent" wages, but gave no details. By contrast, almost all firms gave details of their fringe benefits, saying whether the pension and sickness schemes were contributory, mentioning canteens, and giving the length of their holidays. This is curious because almost all the management representatives we talked to claimed that wages dominated worker motivation. So why were they reluctant to give details of wages in public (for when workers actually arrived for interview they were told at length about the wages system)? Two factors were operating in management minds.

Firstly, they were reluctant to give workers "promises" about their likely earnings for which they might be later accountable. Wage systems are usually quite complex and it is actually quite difficult to predict a new recruit's future earnings. However, if some companies can specify averages, why can't all? This is especially puzzling in the case of those companies whose wages are pushed up by factors not readily visible to the community at large, like long hours, shifts or piecework schemes. In our sample both British Rail and Farrow's would surely benefit more by publicising their average earnings than they would lose by "broken promises" of doubtful status anyway.

Thus we feel the second reason to be decisive: the employers' reluctance to engage in public competition which might force up the level of wages. In a long-established industrial town like Peterborough, the broad outlines of the inter-firm wage hierarchy are generally known among employers. Perkins knew they were wage leaders, Baker-Perkins kept consciously just behind, Combex knew they were near the bottom. Several of the firms participated in local wage surveys, and informal contacts were also maintained between personnel managers. As one manager told us:

> I ring up my friends in all the larger companies in town and ask what they are paying a slinger, etc. A competitive rat-race doesn't pay in a tight labour market. We accept our relative position up the hierarchy and this stabilises wages. This is really why wage-rates are low in the town: we are isolated from other employers (in other towns), so we can control rates.

This is obviously collusion among employers to keep wage-rates down. Its effectiveness is limited by many factors. A rapidly expanding firm with an acute need for labour will tend to break such informal understandings and raise its wages, as Perkins had done in the previous decade. A militant group of workers will force the employer's hand, as Perkins workers did in the 1970s by demanding parity with Massey-Ferguson's other plants. Piecework systems and overtime notoriously escape managerial control. Some employers are tied to national or multi-plant agreements, as are the public employers in our study. Nevertheless, in Peterborough employer restrictions on competition are a factor in explaining wages structure and *the* factor in explaining the paucity of wages information. It is difficult to know how typical is Peterborough. American studies confirm this picture, emphasising the effectiveness of employer collaboration more than we do (Myers and MacLaurin, 1943: 40–5; Reynolds, 1951: 51–4; Sheppard and Belitsky, 1966: 192–3). The major previous study in Britain of the engineering industry doubts whether employers in large towns will have detailed knowledge of each other's wage-rates, and concludes that U.S. employers are more restrictive and collusive in recruiting than their British counterparts. But unfortunately it does not provide evidence directly on wage collusion. (Mackay *et al.*, 1971: 85–9). We suspect, therefore, that the Peterborough situation may be quite typical, certainly insofar as it restricts the information available on wage-rates.

This point can be generalised beyond wages for, like Reynolds (1951: 45–8), we found that information is even less about non-wage factors. With one or two exceptions, the local job advertisements did not seem to us to be designed to convey precise information to workers. The more informative ones generally contained three items: naming the vacant jobs, stating "good wages", and giving details of fringe benefits. Many advertisements contained a good deal less than this, including most of Perkins's, which would be regarded by the advertising profession as the "most sophisticated", and which resembled advertisements for consumer products. A carefully designed page or half-page in the local newspaper would trumpet a "theme" like "Perkins means power" or "Perkins respects individuality". In effect these advertisements are attempting to make as few public promises as possible. Fringe benefits are named because they are usually invariant, applying to all male manual employees. Where a job characteristic varies it is discussed only at the private employment interview. This makes understandable what amused some of the recruiting managers, that workers were often expecting to have to haggle about wages or hours in the interview itself. Historically, managements have generally resisted formalisation of conditions of employment. Even standardised wage-rates are largely the product of trade-union pressure over the years. If management both controls the sources of information, and is unwilling to standardise and publicise employment conditions, then we can hardly be surprised that workers fail to live up to the economists' model of "rational man".

It is also hardly surprising that formal recruiting channels are not of primary importance in attracting workers. We asked our sample what had made them come to their present employer (Question 12 of the interview survey). The largest group, 47 per cent, replied that friends or relations had suggested they come, followed by 25 per cent saying that they had "just turned up" or were attracted by the firm's "general reputation", compared with 13 per cent attracted by advertisements and 8 per cent from the Employment Exchange ($N = 949$). These results, stressing the worker's own informal channels of information, did not surprise us. They are in line with numerous previous studies of manual workers in Britain and the United States.[4]

Such a well-attested finding is usually given an existential status in the literature, and it is concluded that formal agencies, like the employer or employment exchanges, cannot hope to compete with the worker's own informal channels of information. But as they do not compete, this is an assumption not a verified hypothesis. At the moment, virtually all that a worker can learn from the employer or from the employment exchange is that a vacancy exists – the details must be supplied through his own grapevine. If employers did release details, much of the grapevine would be unnecessary. If they released them to employment exchanges then the latter could function properly, and eliminate most of the criticisms which workers now level at them (Daniel, 1974: 88–97; Hill *et al.*, 1973: 107–9; Parker *et al.*: 110–11, 183). At the moment, employers only notify employment exchanges of a small proportion of (principally unskilled) vacancies (Mackay *et al.*, 1971: 349–56), and even then only supply the barest details. Do employers really want a more "rational" market, in the sense of one that allows workers more choice? We will return to this in our concluding chapter.

With such sources of information, it is perhaps surprising that the workers' comparative wage estimates were as close to actuality as Table 5.1 suggests. Yet this table tells us only about the estimates that were made, and on a large number of occasions the workers refused to give any estimate at all. The average number of guesses per man was 4.2, out of a possible 10. Excluding their present firm reduces this to 3.3 out of 9, just over a third. As we would expect, they were more likely to guess at the larger companies, with the proportion of non-employees making guesses ranging from 58 per cent for Perkins to 20 per cent for Combex. In some cases, a refusal to guess was based not on ignorance of the firm but on knowledge of the complexity and uncertainties of its wage-rates. This is revealed by the fact that 11 per cent of workers refused to make an estimate for their own firm. We can presume that this line of reasoning would be more frequent for firms about which they knew less. And, of course, to the extent that actual wage structure is complex, employers would find it difficult to give accurate information about it to the outsider.

The knowledge of wage-rates obviously falls a long way short of the "rational worker" standards of the neo-classical economists' models of the labour market. The average worker is able to rank the wage-rates of only a minority of local firms, and, with *ad hoc* and outdated sources of information, is likely to make mistakes even with this minority. Furthermore, the *distribution* of knowledge among the workers may not be conducive to actual, informed job choice, because those with most knowledge may be those least likely to be looking for employment. We found a strong positive relationship between length of service and number of wage guesses,[5] and, of course, workers with high seniority are unlikely to change jobs voluntarily. At least there was no tendency for those who said they were actually thinking of changing jobs to give more wage estimates.

KNOWLEDGE OF OTHER CONDITIONS OF EMPLOYMENT

The "rational" model of choice needs knowledge of other conditions of employment besides wages. We can assume that virtually no one will choose lower wages in preference to higher wages; if a worker "chooses" lower wages it must be in return for some other benefit. It is rather more difficult to compare workers' estimates of conditions of employment with actual conditions when we move away from wages, for few of the others possess a commonly accepted scale of measurement. Even if measurement is objectively possible, as, for example, in the case of heat or noise at work, the worker will not be able to reply in terms of degrees or decibels if we ask him how hot or noisy is his work! So in these and other cases we have used a more indirect method to compare "subjective" and "objective". We asked for the reasons why the worker would, or would not, accept a job at each firm. Later on in this chapter we look at the overall nature of responses, but first we examine the responses by firms and pick those types of reasons on which a firm is thought by the sample as a whole to be either exceptionally desirable or exceptionally undesirable. The pattern of responses was too complex to do this by adopting a simple numerical rule. An item might be mentioned between 50 and 1,000 times, either as an advantage or a disadvantage, and the mentions might be confined to one or a few firms or spread across them all. Thus we counted a firm as extreme if the distribution of responses to it on any item differed markedly from the distribution of the responses to the other firms. Then we compared this classification of firms with the one based on our Objective Job Scores and the factors we derived from them contained in Table AIII.1. There, we were also looking for extreme scores within the firms. On both sides of the comparison, then, "extreme" means extreme in relation to the other firms and not to any absolute standard set by us or by the workers. We are aware that this type of classification by personal judgment can introduce many errors. Therefore we look only to the overall consistency of the results and not to individual inter-firm or inter-item differences. Are the firms picked out by the workers, as unusually good or bad on individual characteristics, also generally those we pick out? Or in the language of this table, does the letter B (for bad) generally go with the letter L (low) and G (good) with H (high)?

There are three main types of possible result contained in this table: cases of exact agreement where the firm appears as extreme in the same way to both workers and ourselves, cases only of mild agreement where one party considers it extreme, and cases of disagreement where both

Table 5.2 Desirable job characteristics distinguishing firms and workers' beliefs about these

	Baker-Perkins	Bettles	British Rail	Combex	Farrow's	Horrell's	London Brick	Perkins	Peterboro' Corpn.
Exposure	H G	L B		H G	G	L B		H G	L
Fumes, dirt, heat	G	L	H	B	B	H	B		
Noise		H				H		L B	
Danger		L B	B				B		
Physical effort (factor)	H	L B					B		
General interest* (factor)	G		H G		L B	H		B	H
Autonomy (factor)	H	H				H G	L B	L B	
Hours: convenience	H	H	L B	H	H	L B		L B	H
Hours: length				L	L B	H B		H	
Fringe benefits	H G		G		L	L			
Security	G	B				H			H G

Objective: Job characteristics
L = Exceptionally low desirability
H = Exceptionally high desirability

Subjective: Attitude of non-employees
B = Exceptionally bad
G = Exceptionally good

* It is doubtful if any firm can be regarded as really extreme on General Interest (E^2 is only 0.14) but those indicated are quite well differentiated. We may see in Table 4.2 that each of them is extreme on at least one component aspect. Also, we may note that of the other firms, those rated G or B score H or L respectively on one component.

consider it extreme but in opposite directions.[6] We find 19 cases of exact agreement, 33 cases of mild agreement, and only one case of disagreement (which has been ringed in the table). This is a striking pattern, and highly significant. As the errors of this method are large, mild agreement is not to be taken too seriously – it is to be expected that an item scoring extreme on one measure, will score in the middle on the other. But given these errors, it is impressive that the position of only one firm on one item is reversed. Though Horrell's had the shortest working hours of all the firms (41.6 hours compared to the sample average of 49.7), more of the sample picked Horrells out as having over-long hours than any other firm. Even so this is only 25 persons, and it is easy to explain *why* they did. Horrell's milkmen work *inconvenient* hours, from about 3.30 a.m. to about 10 a.m. They also work right through the week for five weeks, before having the sixth week off. No less than 317 workers mentioned the inconvenience of these hours, while only 25 got things slightly wrong by mentioning their length. The fact that the only case of disagreement is an understandable error reinforces what was said earlier about workers' knowledge of wages – this is the knowledge of an "informed outsider", liable to make mistakes in complex situations, but possessing knowledge of straightforward instances. Where knowledge of employment conditions other than wages is possessed, it is usually fairly accurate.

However, as we did with wages, we must consider not only the accuracy but also the frequency of knowledge. We cannot do this for individual items, for the data cannot be disaggregated, but we know how often the workers said they knew nothing at all about the firms. Exactly half the workers claimed some knowledge of all the firms, and only 3 per cent said they were ignorant of half or more of the firms. The highest level of ignorance was revealed in relation to Combex and Peterborough Corporation on which 29 per cent and 20 per cent respectively of workers were unable to provide any information. Apart from these two firms the level of total ignorance was negligible (in the range of 3–15 per cent).[7] Of course, this only means that the vast majority of workers thought that they knew *something* about almost all the firms. We have already shown that they were broadly accurate in their information, but how detailed or wide-ranging was this information? For this we must look more closely at the nature of their responses.

In Table 5.3 we have listed the main types of information given about the firms.

The table is based on an open-ended question, so the workers could reply as they wished. We first coded the responses to this (and similar questions) into 97 categories, and then condensed these as appropriate.

Table 5.3   Reasons for liking or disliking 10 Peterborough firms

| | All Workers | | | | | | Liked as % of all mentions | Employees' Likes only: % |
| | Like | | Dislike | | Total | | | |
	No.	%	No.	%	No.	%	%	%
Wages	647	14	779	13	1426	13	45	13
Hours and shifts	148	3	726	12	874	8	17	3
Fringe benefits	102	2	7	–	109	1	94	2
Security	212	5	436	7	648	6	33	7
Promotion	96	2	66	1	162	2	59	2
Outdoor or indoor work	1108	24	185	3	1293	12	86	5
Working conditions	167	4	970	16	1137	11	15	3
Job content	776	17	1031	17	1807	17	43	13
Type of work or industry	260	6	713	12	973	9	27	5
Management quality	494	11	301	5	795	7	62	15
Workpeople	138	3	260	4	398	4	3	7
Status	5	–	146	2	151	1	3	1
Personal suitability	476	10	377	6	853	8	56	22
Other explicit reasons	17	–	54	1	71	1	24	2
Total	4646	100	6051	100	10697	100	–	100
								(N = 1159)

We shall comment first on the overall magnitude of the reasons given, that is on the totals for all workers (column 5). Here the diversity of replies is at once evident, a diversity which has also appeared in previous studies (Parnes, 1954: 189). We have listed 13 different types of reason, each given at least 100 times, but none of which accounts separately for a fifth of the total. It will be noted that "job content", with 17 per cent of all responses, was most frequently mentioned. This is something of an artefact, for, as we shall see, it combines several rather different responses. Then followed "wages" (13 per cent), "outdoor" or "indoor" work (12 per cent) and "working conditions" i.e. the working environment (heat, dirt, etc.) (11 per cent). These were all mentioned over 1,000 times, an average of more than once per worker. As can be seen from the table, a further five types of reason were of importance, and several others were mentioned occasionally. So the first conclusion we are able to draw from this table is that, in a reasonably varied labour market such as Peterborough, workers will judge employment by a variety of factors. To some extent this reflects the manifold objective differences between the firms which we reported in Chapter 4.

However, we must add two qualifications to this picture of variety. Firstly, it appears that some of these reasons are somewhat vague and general in nature, and thus are not really *alternatives* to particular job characteristics like wages or hours but may, indeed, include them. Consider "type of work or industry". Here we were faced with workers who made such statements as this one, about Farrow's: "Oh no! I wouldn't work there – not in the food industry." We would then attempt to probe further, asking "Why not?" If a man explained in very specific terms that he didn't like the smell, or the low wages, or working with women, we were able to recode, so the "type of work or industry" reasons are· those that stayed at the vague or general level. The explanation given, in response to our prompt, might sometimes imply feelings about the content of the work (e.g. the type of product handled) but often might only be "Well, it's a pretty backward (rotten, inferior, etc) industry." Now obviously a backward, rotten or inferior industry will tend to have poor conditions of work in general, including, for example, low wages. Thus this type of response probably reflects the *hierarchical* elements of the labour market. Certainly the "type of work or industry" disliked were those represented by Farrow's, Combex and Bettles, all of which possessed simple technologies and (as we saw in Chapter 4) were not among the better Peterborough firms in terms of general employment conditions. Conversely, the two firms which called forth a positive "type of work or industry" response were the engineering firms Baker-Perkins and Perkins, two of the better firms. We can confirm this directly by looking at the proportions in the sample who said they would accept a job at each of the companies. These range from 50 per cent for Baker-Perkins and 40 per cent for both Perkins and British Rail to 13 per cent for both Combex and Farrow's.

Hierarchical elements appear to have penetrated other responses in Table 5.3. About 70 per cent of the "management quality" responses actually referred to the general reputation of a firm, especially to whether it was a "good firm". We noted earlier the controversy in the literature surrounding this type of response. Despite our persistent probing, workers remained vague. Many of the responses referred to Baker-Perkins, but the workers would not specify wherein lay its quality (and, of course, we avoided leading questions of the form, "Well, do you mean wages?"). But, as we saw in Chapter 4, this is a perfectly meaningful response because Baker-Perkins *is* a "good firm", being right at the top of the firm hierarchy in a number of respects. Thus we side with Myers and Schultz and against Reynolds in the dispute we mentioned at the beginning of this chapter: we have found that workers labelling firms as "good" are exhibiting broadly accurate knowledge.

Perhaps unexpectedly "workpeople" is also rather hierarchical. As can be seen from Table 5.3, two-thirds of these mentions were unfavourable. Most of the favourable mentions were made by employees to their present workmates. Of the unfavourable mentions, 40 per cent were of the form "I wouldn't work there – too many women", and 38 per cent wouldn't work with foreigners. We must grant that some of the white workers in our sample might have strong racial views, but are there really so many misogynists? Our female interviewers replied, definitely not! Yet without racism or misogynism, there are valid reasons why workers should avoid working alongside foreigners or women: the conditions of employment will be generally worse because these are the most exploited groups in the labour market (as we noted in Chapter 1). Thus any worker, male or female, black or white, would be well advised to use sex and race/nationality as *visible indicators* of generally "good" or "bad" employment. We will return in a moment to the importance of visible indicators in the labour market.

The final type of hierarchical response is "personal suitability". This was usually an explicit recognition by the worker that, regardless of what jobs were objectively available, only some were open to him. "They would accept me there" and "I know I can do that work" were rather doleful recognitions – usually by older workers and immigrants – that few employers would select them for employment.[8] Obviously it was the "better" firms that would not. This type of pessimism has been shown in previous American research to be prevalent among workers who are actually unemployed (Sheppard and Belitsky, 1966: 42, 60; Wilcock and Franke, 1962: 96–100).

Thus the "personal suitability" responses plus many of the "type of work or industry", "management", and "workmates" responses reflect the worker's perception of hierarchy in the labour market. They are not alternatives to specific job rewards like wages or working conditions, but may in fact include them. We cannot be exact, but such hierarchical responses may add up to as much as 25 per cent of the total.

The second qualification to the variety of reasons in Table 5.3 concerns two major types of reasons given which, though not obviously hierarchical, are similarly imprecise. These are "outdoor or indoor work" and some of the "job content" reasons. Eighty-seven per cent of the former responses indicated a preference for outdoor work. This is deceptively precise. As we saw in Chapter 3, outdoor work, as well as having obvious atmospheric components, is considerably more autonomous than work inside, giving relative freedom from the control of both technology and supervisors. This is obvious to the workers themselves – as many of them commented in their answers to these questions. So a preference for outdoor work might mean a desire for fresh air or for autonomy, or possibly a combination of both in a sense of freedom. Perhaps the worker has other job attributes in mind as well.

This is also so for some of the "job content" reasons. These were so internally varied that we have sub-divided them, in Table 5.4, presented later. One of the sub-types was the mentioning of a specific named job. There were 352 such responses, around 3.5 per cent of all reasons. Examples of this type of response are "I could be a fitter there" or "I would go there if I could get a driving job." While this is not perhaps as precise a response as we would wish for (why does he like driving work?) it does indicate that for some workers the labour market is made up not of firms but of *jobs*. The jobs named – lorry driving, building trades, gardening, machine maintenance trades – tended to be those with distinct occupational sub-cultures, which are found in most firms (though usually in small numbers). Men in these jobs might be expected to have a low attachment to their firm, as indeed a study of lorry drivers in Britain suggests (Hollowell, 1968). The attachment is to the job, and this might be for one of several reasons. Such workers generally use relatively high levels of skill, enjoy autonomy, possess a certain security of employment (though not necessarily in any particular firm), and wield a measure of occupational status. Which of these is being referred to by our workers? We do not know, but in the next chapter (see Table 6.3) we shall see they do tend to give high importance to interest and skill, autonomy and security in that order. We have no data on the importance of status, but the only other aspect they rate highly is promotion.

Thus about one-third of all responses are not in the form of preferences for precise and particular features of work but are "bundles" of preferences.

The reason is that the worker faces the same theoretical problem as the sociologist. The enormous complexity of the real world makes it impossible to develop a mental model of the labour market in its entirety. Theoretical simplifications are needed, and the worker faced with too much variation quickly simplifies by excluding a great deal of it on the basis of very general criteria. Luckily this often succeeds in giving a rough approximation of reality. Consider, for example, the preference for outside work. Some workers might really (according to the "rational-calculative" model) be making enquiries about the supervision practices of different firms; others about the level of fresh air, etc. Yet for all practical purposes they don't need to do this, for open-air work *is* a good guideline to these and other conditions. It is also highly public. Four of our nine employers offer factory employment, and their approximate level of supervision and fresh air is visible at roof-top level to most of Peterborough. Almost everyone by contrast knows that milkmen and builders usually work outside. Similarly with "type of work or industry", where a dislike for the food industry could indicate dislike for low pay, rather messy working conditions, low status, coloured workers or seasonal fluctuations. Dislike for women could also stand for most of the same bundle of characteristics. With all these indices the worker can dispense with a great deal of precise information about each firm. Why bother with finding out about Bettles if you already know it to be a building firm? Why bother with Farrow's or Combex's conditions of employment if you can see lots of women and Pakistanis emerging from its factory gates? Mistakes might be made using this rather indirect method (as we saw, Farrow's gross wages were rather higher than the workers realised), but it is generally quite accurate.

Yet there is a certain forced quality about most of these preference bundles. They do not necessarily consist of the worker's own desired combinations of rewards, but are forced on him by the exigencies of the labour market. Outdoor work, work in the engineering industry, driving work, work with male colleagues, offer a *given* combination of job features – you must take it or leave it. This one-third of responses reveals a necessary compromise forced upon the worker by the complexities of the labour market and by the fact that his preferences are not the decisive influence on its structure.

In view of this, relatively precise job features – wages, hours and the like – are probably more important to workers than Table 5.3 reveals. Discounting the bundles we have just discussed would increase their percentage contribution by over a third. In an ideal labour market this is what might occur. Let us turn to the major individual items named.

Table 5.4 gives further details of the job content reasons, which were the most numerous.

Table 5.4 Sub-divisions of 'job content' reasons for liking or disliking firms in Table 5.3 (all workers)

| Reason | All Workers | | | |
| | Like | Dislike | Total | |
	No.	No.	No.	%
Autonomy	80	162	242	13
Specific job named	309	43	352	19
Skill, interest, variety	328	464	792	44
Effort disliked	59	362	421	23
Total	776	1031	1807	100

We have already commented on the references to a specific named job. The separation of the "effort disliked" category is necessary because these reveal a rather different attitude to work than the other job content reasons. Whereas the others show a preference for demanding, challenging work of one kind or another, these preferred easy, undemanding routine. These workers tended to be older or in poor health, replying, in much the same vein as those mentioning "personal suitability", that they wanted a job they knew they could do. Apart from this group, the references to job content showed a consensus that a good job is varied, autonomous and is mentally rather than physically challenging. No one expressed a preference for work involving high physical effort.

Almost all of the wage mentions concerned their overall level. Neither piecework nor bonus schemes received many mentions, nor did the level of overtime worked. Hours and shifts were usually mentioned as a disadvantage of a firm, i.e. a firm was rarely picked out because of its short or convenient hours, but was often discarded because of length or inconvenience.

Working conditions are overwhelmingly considered as disadvantages. Though there were a few favourable references to clean work, the workers were mostly put off by dust, dirt, fumes, noise, excessive heat or cold, and the risk of accidents. The environmental conditions and hours of work are reasons for disliking but not for being committed to employment. They are considered as "normal" or "bad". In the present context we would expect them only to affect job choice negatively (in fact we find in Chapter 7 that they have little influence either way).

The low salience of fringe benefits is interesting in view of the publicity managements give to them as a recruiting device. But then, the real value of fringe benefits is low: in 1964 they amounted to about 4 per cent of total labour costs in British manufacturing industry (Department of Employment and Productivity, 1968: 5). When mentioned, they are almost entirely a reason for accepting a job, usually in public employment, with British Rail and Peterborough Corporation. Promotion is also negligible, though we would predict this on the basis of our findings on the objective labour market. Promotion practices are chaotic and thus not readily visible.

A third low-salience item is social relations at work. This is somewhat concealed by the table, for the apparently "relational" categories of "management quality" and "workpeople" in reality contain rather different responses, as we have already noted. Personal relations with managers, supervisors and co-workers only totalled under 3 per cent of responses. Again, however, we may doubt the visibility of these to outsiders.

For such low-salience items we thus have two alternative explanations: either they are unimportant to the workers or they are unknown to them. Promotion may be of great concern to the worker, but if he can obtain no information about a firm's practices, he will not mention it as an advantage or disadvantage of moving there. We can test for the knowledge hypothesis by comparing the responses of workers to their own firms with those of the sample as a whole. The employees' responses are contained in the last column of Table 5.3.

In the responses of employees two great changes are evident. The first is the move of "personal suitability or qualifications" into first position, with 22 per cent of all responses. This gives an indication of the conservatism of the workers in their attitudes towards the labour market. They are here, in effect, saying "I know I can do this work, and I know this firm will take me and keep me, so why should I risk another type of employment?" The second change is also a large increase in the importance of relations with workers and management. The references to workers (7 per cent) now all concern social relations. There are no mentions of the desirability or otherwise of women, blacks, etc. The references to management quality (considerably increased to 15 per cent) are more varied, about half concerning the firm's general ethos as good or bad (usually the former) and half concerning personal and industrial relations with management. Therefore we can deduce that workers *are* concerned about social and industrial relations, but that information available within the labour market does not enable them to choose employment on this basis. Nor is it easy to see how this information could be made available. Deciding whether one will get along with co-workers and with management must be very much on a "suck it and see" basis.

Among the factors which show a marked decline are the two environmental categories, "indoors/outdoors" and "working conditions", reduced from 14 per cent to 5 per cent and from 11 per cent to 3 per cent respectively. "Type of work or industry" is also halved in importance. These results confirm our earlier argument that workers seize upon "public" criteria like "outdoors" or "type of industry" in lieu of detailed knowledge, for employees – with greater knowledge of their own firms – are less likely to describe them in such terms. We may also note that "hours and shifts" declines from 7 per cent to 2 per cent of responses, largely because those actually working unusual hours are adjusted to them. Most remaining factors stay at about the same or slightly lower level of importance, and this includes the continuing insignificance of fringe benefits and promotion prospects. We must infer, therefore, that they are of negligible importance for workers within the context of the labour market. We shall return to this issue later.

Thus our data on employees responses to their own firms introduced one principal amendment: workers would like to base employment choice more upon relational criteria than they are able to. The most important positive attractions of a firm within the context of the Peterborough labour market are therefore the content of the job itself, the working environment, especially whether the work is inside or outside (which may be used principally as a guide to other factors), wages, and the relations with co-workers and with management. Security might seem important in a negative way, perhaps preventing but rarely inducing job change.

As yet, however, we cannot claim to have analysed workers' general, abstract preferences. Our questions are severely limited to the reality of the Peterborough market. We have argued that this is their very strength. We did also ask more abstract questions of the traditional "what are the most important aspects of work" form. We will report on these in the next chapter. But are such questions meaningful to the workers in the context of actual job evaluation? Our most important conclusion in this chapter so far is that abstract preferences are limited in two main ways in actual job evaluation and selection.

Firstly, some preferences cannot be made operative because of lack of knowledge. This is especially so with non-public job features like social relations and promotion practices, but it is bound to affect preferences as a whole because of the low level of information generally available to workers. It is a tribute to their rationality that their knowledge is as proximate to reality as we have discovered it to be. It is very incomplete, however. More evidence for this comes from our question asking workers what they had known about their present firm before they started working (Question 15b, Interview Survey). The answer was very little. Twenty-seven per cent said that they had had an idea of the wages, but the next most frequent responses indicated vagueness of one kind or another. Sixteen per cent had actually known nothing, 10 per cent said that it had been the only job available, 10 per cent mentioned the firm's general reputation, and 8 per cent that they had thought it was a secure firm in general. Only 4 per cent made any mention of job content. These findings are in line with our findings about the actual structure of the labour market. In Chapter 4 we noted that wage-rates did tend to differentiate the firms quite all well (gross wages rather less so), while general security is also a characteristic of a firm as a unit. By contrast, job content differences were greater within firms than between them, and very little precise information would be available to the outsider about job content. Previous research has found that, among workers who are actually in a position to turn down offers of employment, wage reasons tend to be dominant (Daniel, 1974: 76). At this stage, after a job interview, the worker has been given details of the wage-rate offered, but he still has only the barest idea of job content, working conditions, workmates, relations with supervisors and all of the other intrinsic aspects of work. Thus the dominance of wages over other job factors in actual job *selection*, may be less the result of preference than of the information available to him at that particular point in time.

Secondly, simplifications of the complexity of the labour market are often *given* to the worker rather than created by him. He will have to take the closest structural approximation to his preferences. This may be "the engineering industry", "outdoor work", "a good firm" and the life. The literature on worker preference tends to rate the importance of single, precise characteristics like "wages", "skill", "hours", etc. It had not prepared us for the reality of *bundles* of attributes like "working outdoors". Indeed, this factor alone accounted for 10 per cent of responses. Yet where has industrial sociology treated it? In short, we are claiming that our techniques have enabled us to capture more of the *reality* of the worker's position in the labour market. We can now move outwards to the more abstract issue of worker preferences with a secure base in that reality.

WORKER PREFERENCES

We have already referred to the workers' responses as "preferences" for particular job features, or in some cases as "bundles of preferences". In this chapter our use of the notion of preference is a little different from that in Chapter I, where it referred to desire for a particular type of work with relative priorities on all aspects (in keeping with the neo-classical model of rational choice). Here we are concerned with those aspects where the priority is sufficiently high to be decisive – or at least to be so presented in the worker's responses – in assessing employment in a particular firm. In the following chapters, on "orientations", we shall consider further what model is appropriate, but at this point we want to concentrate on the preferences expressed and the extent to which single aspects tend to dominate the worker's thinking in all situations.

We have argued that our questions about the Peterborough firms had the strength of realism, yet this also means that we have difficulty in generalising from them. As yet the evidence consists only of workers' attitudes to a particular set of employers. Thus although an element of choice is involved in the worker's selection of one item rather than another as worth mentioning to us, he may be largely constrained by reality. In the first place, the worker may be aware of a hierarchical competitive situation in which his market strength is limited, and may restrict his "preferences" accordingly. The "personal suitability" response seems a clear example, but an element of this self-evaluation may be contained in other responses. We shall consider these issues further in later chapters. Secondly, the factors mentioned might be less a reflection of the workers' preferences than a perception of what is actually offered by the Peterborough employers. At one extreme, if all employers offered the same level of reward on an item, either everyone or (more probably) no one might mention it. However, as we saw in Chapter 4, our employers offer a great variety of rewards. At the other extreme, if one employer offered extraordinary rewards of one kind, this would tend to dominate the responses to that firm and make a substantial contribution to the whole. We have two cases of this. The workers considered the hours of work at Horrell's so unreasonable that half of the "hours" responses refer to that firm. The effect is to so over-weight this item that we can deduce only that the sample dislike starting work at 3.30a.m and not that they attach a certain level of general importance to the convenience of their hours of work. Without the presence of Horrell's in our sample of firms, hours would have appeared unimportant. This is also so for "status", dominated by negative attitudes towards Peterborough Corporation and towards the refuse-collecting jobs which were often taken to be typical of employment there. However, there are no other reasons so dominated by one – or even two – companies. Our sampling aim was to include great variety on all major characteristics, and this has ensured that the peculiar characteristics of firms do not in general interfere with our interpretation.

Even so, our data confuse the characteristics of the firms with the preferences of the workers. To tap the latter, we must see the extent to which workers persisted in responding to different firms in the same way. In Table 5.5 we have examined the persistence with which the main job reasons are mentioned. If a worker mentioned an item four or more times we will term this a *persistent preference*. According to this formulation, just over 50 per cent of the sample possess a persistent preference (a few workers possess more than one, of course).

We have ordered the items in terms of persistence. This enables us to see clearly the relative persistence of a preference for outdoor work. Though fewer workers mention it than seven other items, they do so with greater persistence. Over 10 per cent of the sample mention it five or more times, double the proportion for any other reason, and 15 per cent mention it four times.[9] We certainly have a preliminary indication that a sub-group of "outdoor-type" workers exist in the labour market, with clearly definable preferences.

The next most persistent group are those mentioning wages, 12 per cent mentioning them four or more times. There is then a drop in frequency, with working conditions coming next. Remember that most such responses are *dislikes* of the working conditions of the Peterborough firms. Thus the 7 per cent of workers who mention this four or more times are virtually refusing to accept bad working conditions anywhere. After this rather small numbers of workers tend to persist

Table 5.5 Persistence of reasons for liking or disliking 10 Peterborough firms

Reason	Number of Workers Mentioning a Reason					% of sample mentioning item four times or more	Total (once or more)
	Once	Twice	Three times	Four times	Five or more		
1. Outdoors preference	133	70	49	37	102	15	391
2. Wages	244	145	104	68	55	13	616
3. Working conditions	268	171	71	41	28	7	579
4. Type of work or industry	296	137	59	29	20	5	541
5. Job content: skill, interest, variety	233	110	51	18	20	4	432
6. Personal suitability	340	107	47	17	17	4	528
7. Management quality	268	111	61	20	8	3	468
8. Hours and shifts	364	125	50	15	9	3	563
9. Security	217	103	45	13	7	2	385
10. Specific named job	161	59	11	6	3	1	240
11. Workpeople	229	57	10	5	1	—	302
12. Job content: effort disliked	238	62	14	3	1	—	318
13. Indoors preference	107	24	7	1	1	—	140
14. Job content: autonomy	131	39	7	3	0	—	180
15. Promotion	95	21	4	2	1	—	123
16. Status	108	13	4	0	1	—	126
17. Fringe benefits	74	14	1	1	0	—	90

with any item, and in any case several of those that follow are not single job features but, as we noted before, clusters of attributes which are not easy to interpret, or even to label as preferences. This is particularly so for the "personal suitability" responses which indicate the reverse of a preference — a sense of *constraint* rather than choice. Also, most of those stressing "workmates" and "management", as we have seen, are pointing to the *hierarchical* aspects of the labour market, whereby some jobs are not "different" but simply better on most dimensions. The "type of work or industry" is less a clear-cut preference than a bundle of given labour market characteristics. If we exclude these and add up the number of workers who persisted in mentioning one of the remaining reasons four or more times, we find that only about 45 per cent of the sample had a genuine persistent preference which governed their responses to a question about an actual labour market situation.

Before giving credence to this figure of 45 per cent as possessing a genuine, persistent preference however, we should consider whether it may be an artefact of the way we have classified our data. We have allowed 17 types of preference in Table 5.5. It is obvious that the more we allow, the more workers will fail to meet the criterion of four or more mentions. Had we grouped these 17 into a few, broader categories, perhaps nearly all the sample would have emerged with a persistent preference. But would these categories then have been meaningful? To test for this, we inter-correlated frequency of mention of the 17 items (using non-parametric coefficients) and then did several factor analyses. There is little need to present the results in detail, because — with one exception to which we shall return in a moment — the results were negative. The inter-item correlations were uniformly low (the highest, as we might expect, being a negative correlation between outdoor and indoor, with a Spearman coefficient of − 0.22) and generally without significance, and the factor analyses produced results which confirmed the independence of the items.[10] Throughout the factor analyses only two items generally behaved in a similar way and had overlapping meanings: job content and specific named job (although the correlation between the two was only 0.10). We therefore felt entitled to combine these responses into one "intrinsic job" preference, but retain all the other items unaltered.

CONCLUSION

We are somewhat reassured by the fact that the workers think they inhabit the same kind of world that we think they do. Their knowledge of the Peterborough labour market, where possessed, is in broad agreement with ours. We therefore think their knowledge to be generally not inaccurate! But we have seen that this knowledge is fragmentary and crude. This seems inevitable given the complexity of the labour market and the poor information services available. Managements do not help the worker by providing detailed information about only one aspect of work, fringe benefits, that workers actually find trivial.

Workers' sources of information are indirect and approximate. As labour market studies have traditionally found, workers obtain information through a network of family and friends that ultimately has its source in an actual employee of the company in question. But even this can only provide reliable information (perhaps slightly out-of-date) on job features that are relatively invariant within a company. We can guess, on the basis of our previous chapters, that this information source would be relatively strong on wage-rates (though not gross wages), hours and shifts, working conditions and – once again – fringe benefits. Information about job content – skill level, autonomy, etc. – from this source might be unreliable, given the high variability within each firm on these dimensions.

Secondly, workers derive information from what we have termed *visible indicators*. These are highly public guides to bundles of job attributes. Industry stereotypes are perhaps the most frequent – if you know that a firm is in engineering or food-processing you can predict certain of its job attributes, especially those concerned with job content (although internal variability will still exist), working conditions and perhaps wage-rates. The physical and geographical setting of a firm is also a guide: is it inside or outside work? is it enclosed within one factory? These are factors enabling us to predict job autonomy. The composition of the labour force is a third. Are women and immigrants streaming out of its gates? These are factors related to wage-rates and general conditions of employment. Such criteria are used extensively by workers, as our data on "persistent preferences" reveal. Some of these criteria are indicators of hierarchy in the labour market, others of compensatory processes. Thus engineering indicates generally better employment than food-processing, as does a largely male, all-white, British labour force, compared to a mixed one; but outdoor work is simply different from indoor work, preferred by some, abhorred by others. In this situation workers whose hierarchical position or preferences most closely resemble these bundles are singularly fortunate! They can choose employment relatively freely; others must "suck it and see". We will see later whether either of these strategies actually succeeds in bringing employment which is congruent with the worker's preferences.

In this chapter we have emphasised the rationality of the worker. Returning to the neo-classical model of the labour market, discussed in Chapter I, we have not found that workers contribute in any significant way to the imperfections of the "free" labour market. Their knowledge is greater than previous literature would have led us to believe, though it is of an approximate rather than a precise kind. Its imperfections are a reflection of the market itself. On the other hand, we have doubted whether employers are interested in a more rational market, and we would wish to attribute some of the market imperfections to their strategies of restricting information flow and collaborating to set wage-rates for the purpose of depressing general employment rewards.

6 Orientations to Work

In the previous chapter we noted that some workers evaluated employment opportunities in terms of persistent preference for one type of reward. We now ask whether such preferences are part of a wider mental set, conventionally termed an *orientation*. In Chapter 1 we defined an orientation as a central organizing principle which underlies people's attempts to make sense of their lives. With respect to the labour market, therefore, we ask whether the desires for particular types of work reward tend to determine the attitudes and behaviour of the workers. The central problem is that of *extent* and *stability*. The existence of orientations implies that workers have preferences which are substantially independent of immediate work experience, extending over different types of situation and relatively stable for a significant period of time. Whether or not orientations exist, in this sense, is crucial to experience and choice in the labour market.

In this and the two following chapters we will pursue three aspects of this problem:

1. We shall first examine the uniformity of workers' preferences and priorities across a variety of frames of reference. We shall be looking for coherence in attitudes which may be attributed to underlying orientations.
2. In the next chapter we shall consider how workers' orientations are related to job choice. Are workers in jobs which are congruent with their orientations, and if so, did they arrive there because of their orientations?
3. We shall also attempt to set orientations to work in a wider social context, to see how they influence and are influenced by both work and non-work factors. In particular, we shall aim to establish if there are stable influences shaping orientations to work which are outside the present work situation.

Although a major part of our purpose is to establish whether orientations, as defined, may be said to exist at all, we shall anticipate the conclusions by referring to the relevant measures as orientations from the start (as already done in 2 and 3 above). This greatly facilitates presentation, while turning the problem to the content of the orientations. Then we can see whether they conform to the character of "true orientations".

Although the ideas involved date back to such writers as Weber and W. I. Thomas, probably the most extensive, and earliest, discussion of the notion of orientations is that by Parsons and Shils (and colleagues), whose book *Toward a General Theory of Action* appeared in 1951. Their interest is primarily in "action", and "orientations" are first presented as descriptions of *action*:

> Action has an orientation when it is guided by the meaning which the actor attaches to it in its relationship to his goals and interests (1962 edn: 4).

However, in a different sense it is clear that it is the *actor* who has an orientation, which gives meaning to his experience and action, and together with "its attendant motivational processes" is said to make up his "personality" (1962: 7). Presumably, therefore, these orientations are relatively stable through time. Later, the individual is described as having a system of many orientations:

> Each of these "orientations of action" is a "conception" (explicit or implicit, conscious or unconscious) which the actor has of the situation in terms of what he wants, what he sees, and how he intends to get from the objects he sees the things he wants (1962: 54).

The "conception" entails not only wants, but also perceptions of the situation as it is, expectations and the possible choices. Parsons and Shils develop a detailed, abstract analysis containing many useful insights, but the scheme as a whole does not seem to have provided a suitable basis for later empirical research. More empirically grounded developments have included the concept of projects from Touraine and Ragazzi (1961). While strictly referring to a potential course of action, this involves two fundamental aspects of an orientation as set out by Parsons and Shils, *choice* and *expectancy* "in the sense that it is an orientation to the future situation as well as the present" (1962: 68). However, the work with the greatest recent impact in Britain has been *The Affluent Worker* by Goldthorpe *et al.*[1] There, the authors wholeheartedly adopt an orientation emphasis, stressing the coherence of workers' preferences, their relevance for job allocation, their influence on in-plant attitudes and behaviour, and the way they relate to non-work life. Their dominant theme is the importance of instrumental orientations, as may be seen in the following quotations (there are many similar ones throughout the three volumes):

> They have in effect *chosen* . . . in favour of work which enables them to achieve a higher level of economic return . . . a decision has been made to give more weight to the *instrumental* at the expense of the expressive aspects of work.

> Our ultimate argument will be that, in considering the attitudes and behaviour of the workers we studied – in relation to their work groups, their firms, their unions and their own economic future – themes and variations alike can best be explained in terms of the degree to which, in the different occupational groups, an instrumental orientation to work is approximated.

> (Goldthorpe *et al.*, 1968: 33; 41–2)

There has been, in such empirically based research, some development away from the earlier formulations. As will become evident, we have extended this development. One particular modification, at least in comparison with the usage of Goldthorpe *et al.*, should perhaps be made explicit here. In *The Affluent Worker* orientations are always considered as existing in relation to a concrete situation, and *manifest* in particular actions. Thus workers' orientations relate to present employment, and are "revealed preferences" expressed in taking and staying in their jobs.[2] Insofar as orientations are descriptions of actions, Parsons and Shils appear to have a similar approach. However, we do not think this position can usefully be maintained, and would suggest that our approach is at least implicit at many points in other works, including *The Affluent Worker*. For our part we regard them as relatively stable properties of people, treating them as underlying choice rather than as merely arising in the act of choosing[3] (which seems closer to Parsons and Shils when they regard them as components of personality). The main disadvantage of regarding orientations as existing only in their manifestations is that their explanatory value is severely limited. This is most evident in regard to choice, for either orientations exist which influence choice – as in our approach – or something else must exist prior to the choice to influence both the choice and the accompanying orientation.

There are also difficulties in explaining the source of orientations and their ability to explain change if they are too closely related to the specific situation. Of course, we do not disagree that orientations must relate to the actual situation, but this we see as a man's total environment, or at least the market rather than his present job, providing a basis for particular job choices.

All this presupposes the existence of orientations. However, none of the previous research has really been designed to test their existence. This is particularly true of *The Affluent Worker* study, as the authors themselves recognise, since the design of the study was directed to the different aim of testing the "embourgeoisement thesis". For all the stress on orientations, the influence attributed to them is more of a suggestion than a proof. While some other studies have come closer, none has attempted the systematic analysis which we now propose. To begin with we shall review some general problems that we raised in Chapter 1.

The orientations model implies choice, and insofar as workers are unable to exercise choice it is hard to see how orientations can develop. For choice to be possible it is necessary that not all workers have the same orientations, or the result is simple competition To appreciate the significance of this we must realise that most workers want the same rewards; good pay, convenient hours, interesting work, friendly work-mates and so on are attractions to virtually everyone. Thus orientations are not simply "wants" but entail priorities within the range of possible rewards. Furthermore, the possible levels of rewards are generally below what people would like in the abstract, in the sense that any increase would be an improvement. Their orientations are, therefore, in relation to what is available to them in the labour market, and require that on some aspect they see a significant range of variation.

The obverse of this is that workers are not likely to have orientations towards types of reward available in other sections of the labour market. Thus "bureacratic" and "solidaristic" orientations are not necessarily the alternatives to "instrumentalism" that Goldthorpe *et al.* (1968) suggest. As we suggested in Chapter 1, they seem to be characteristic of different social strata or occupational communities. Similarly, the convenient half-day and evening shifts, so valued by some family-centred married women (Beynon and Blackburn, 1972) are hardly relevant to the orientations of the men!

Given that workers have different priorities it does not follow that they can choose accordingly. First of all there must be a corresponding distribution of rewards. If, for example, there are not enough interesting jobs for those with this orientation then some will be frustrated. In general, the less the correspondence between the distributions of orientations and types of job, the less the scope for choice. This is further complicated by the fact that only a minority of jobs are vacant at any one time.

Quite apart from these logical possibilities is the question of how far workers can control their job placement. Goldthorpe *et al.* (1968) place a fairly strong emphasis on control and choice on the part of their affluent workers, and observe, "the present employment of these workers enables them to come close to achieving their present priorities in wants and expectations relative to work" (p. 80). Whether or not they were right·for their particular sample, our analysis so far indicates a sizeable degree of constraint in the market. Just how far workers do experience constraint or control in their job selection is likely to be of considerable importance.

At this point it is useful to introduce the distinction between what we term "strong" and "weak" orientations. For the most part the concept has been used in the strong sense. Here, concern with one type of work reward dominates, to the exclusion of all others, so that the worker may be characterised by his orientation, for example as an "instrumental" worker. This is particularly relevant at the lower end of the labour market where the attempt to gain a significant level of reward on one aspect may entail sacrificing all other potential sources of satisfaction.

There is, however, a weaker sense in which we may speak of workers having orientations. Rather than a single dominant concern, the worker may have a whole set of expectations and relative priorities. Such an orientation profile would rarely if ever be consciously expressed by the individual but would nevertheless underlie his actions and judgements about work life. In this sense it is still a "central organising principle", though a less-simple one.

This more complex version still allows for orientations to determine job choice, attitudes and so on, but only in the limiting case is the priority for one sort of work reward so great as to be completely dominant. More typically, job selection is a matter of balancing different combinations of rewards against the actor's relative preferences, and the optimal choice may not always be that maximising the top priority. For example, where money is the prime consideration a slightly lower wage may be preferred so as to avoid working inconvenient hours.

The strong form has an obvious advantage for the sociologist as it simplifies the explanatory model and allows the use of typologies. But this simplicity also has a substantive counterpart for the worker. If he has such an orientation it is also a simplifying principle for him, enabling him to evaluate and choose between jobs on the basis of fairly limited knowledge, and to consciously pursue the best jobs on his single criterion. Without such a clear-cut priority, a higher degree of knowledge is necessary. Now, a worker does have such knowledge for his present job, and either type of orientation may be essential to the way he experiences and evaluates it. However, the more complex is the worker's set of priorities, the more knowledge he needs to make rational prior choices, and so the more likely is choice to be limited to a "suck it and see" process of moving away from disliked jobs. Nevertheless, we should not underestimate the possibility of making prior choices on the basis of weak orientations. These are likely to be between a limited number of specific alternatives or simply whether or not to take particular jobs, with preferences coming into play as relevant. This may be a more restricted sort of choice than is entailed in the search for the highest reward in line with a dominant orientation. Certainly it is less active and more a matter of responding to situations, but it may be more relevant to the realities of the labour market.

The operation of the labour market depends not only on whether or not workers have orientations, but also on what type they have. If workers do have orientations in the strong sense of a dominant priority for a single reward it means that, potentially, they have more scope to make choices and exercise control over their job placement. We shall, therefore, be particularly concerned with evidence of such orientations, though our prime concern must be the existence and operation of orientations in either sense.

The essence of an orientation is that it is extensive, that it colours a worker's attitudes in general. Therefore, to unearth orientations we must ask a whole set of questions and see whether an individual responds in patterned ways. In the present study we do this in two ways. Firstly, we use the preference data, based on the evaluations of ten firms, which we discussed in the previous chapter. We take as a strong measure, four or more mentions of a particular aspect, which we have classed as a *persistent preference*. Although the questions were hypothetical we have good reason to believe they revealed "true" preferences. Certainly they minimise the likelihood of rationalisation that is liable to occur in reasons for attachment to the present job, which Goldthorpe and his associates were obliged to use,[4] and they avoid the additional problems of recall that arise in reasons for having taken the job. However, we also asked other questions using the same open-ended format as that underlying the preference data, and these results can be used to help establish the extent of orientations. Secondly, we asked workers what is salient to them in other frames of reference. We will concentrate on two of these, an abstract question about how important are certain factors in weighing up a job, and a question about job satisfaction. Both these were fixed-choice questions, that is, the workers were asked to evaluate a list of 12 specified aspects of work. As we used a different methodology to the preference data, a crucial question is, did they elicit similar results?

We begin by reviewing the preference data and exploring their implications for the orientations model. Then we add the open-ended questions with a similar format, before turning to the fixed-choice importance and satisfaction questions. This will complete the battery of attitudinal data on orientations. We can then turn, in the following chapters, to the further questions of whether workers with orientations have found congruent employment and what relationship their orientations have to their non-work lives.

PREFERENCES AND ORIENTATIONS

Our preference data provide several set-backs to the neo-classical, rational choice model, based on orientations to work, at least in their more usual strong form. Strong orientations, we have noted, both simplify job choice and reduce the knowledge needed for rational choice; the worker needs only information about his crude bundle of preferences. Yet half the sample were without any persistent preference; that is, their attitudes to the ten Peterborough firms did not concentrate on one (or more) type of reward, which would be indicative of a strong orientation. Furthermore, this is not because they possess greater knowledge on which to base more complex choices, since they tend to possess less than those who do have persistent preferences. Thus rational, informed choice must be severely limited for half the sample.

All the workers expressed some preferences – usually several – which is entirely compatible with the weak form of orientations. However, some of the preferences do not resemble very closely the ideal-typical "orientation". We noted that several of them represent compromises with existing reality, relating to *given* bundles of attributes as found, for example, in different industries – workers are not free to vary their preferences by fine shades but must choose one or the other. Several preferences revealed constraints of a *hierarchical* nature, being essentially preferences for *better* jobs, not different ones. Rather sadly, another "preference" was actually a resigned acceptance that the worker could not aspire to a better job, that is, the "personal suitability" response. As an "orientation" it may possibly be regarded as one of deference.

Nevertheless, we unearthed some preferences which are quite close to the ideal-typical "orientation". An obsession with wages (or *economism*) clearly emerged, just as previous literature has suggested. A concern to minimise unpleasant working conditions was also widespread. The most persistent preference of all was for outside work, a fairly clear desire for a combination of "fresh air and freedom". And small groups of workers were apparently dominated by the various other rewards listed in Table 5.5.

It is noticeable to us, however, that the other types of orientation suggested in the Affluent Worker study have not made much of an appearance in our data. The *bureaucratic* orientation sees work "as service to an organisation in return for steadily increasing income and social status and for long-term security – that is, in return for a career" (Goldthorpe *et al.*, 1968: 39). The rewards sought here are a combination of promotion, security and status. As we noted in Chapter 1, such are the characteristics of much white-collar work. We do not find among our sample of manual workers any significant appearance of such desired rewards – or rather, though they *might* ideally be desired, they cannot be influential in affecting evaluation of employment. Even totalling the number of workers who mention any of them four or more times, only gives us 24, i.e. 2 per cent of the sample.[5] The *solidaristic* orientation sees work "not simply as a means to an end but also as a group activity; the group being either the immediate work group or "shop", or possibly – say, in a small firm – the entire enterprise" (Goldthorpe *et al.*, 1968: 40). Again, we find that "social" responses are insignificant, and few of even the "management" or "workpeople" responses actually reveal social identification with these groups. However, this is not surprising, for the solidaristic attachment is more likely to be to one's *present* employment rather than to a variety of firms (which is the source of our persistent preference data). We have noted in previous chapters that social rewards at work are relatively invisible to the outsider, and cannot easily influence job choice.

The conclusion to be drawn about the non-applicability of these hypothesised orientations is simply, as we suggested earlier, that they are not usually *alternatives* for the same workers. The bureaucratic orientations may characterise a "higher" stratum of workers, i.e. white-collar workers; the solidaristic may characterise long-service workers in some firms, or more probably in occupational communities. Few manual workers can have one of these rather than an economistic orientation – in the way, for example, that we are beginning to suggest they *can* have an outdoors orientation.

The general distribution of preferences raises a significant point. The orientation which has received most attention in the past is economism. This is a straightforward orientation – a desire for high wages given priority over other rewards (although we shall see that this is not quite so straightforward as has commonly been supposed). Wage levels can easily be established and compared, and workers can always attempt to get higher levels. Thus it is an orientation which it is relatively easy for workers to adopt, and it is relatively easy to identify those who do. This is not so for many of the alternatives. It is difficult to concentrate on social rewards prior to entering a firm, but to some extent they can be obtained almost anywhere since they are largely created collectively by the workers. Working conditions can be bad but not really good – just "normal". Job content is heterogeneous, comprising such things as autonomy (itself somewhat varied, as Chapter 3 revealed), pace of work, and mental and manual skills. Furthermore, the intrinsic rewards tend to be found in "better" firms and in jobs at the top of the internal labour market. However, one reward which does offer a clear-cut choice is outdoor work, and this emerges as the most persistent preference in spite of its almost total neglect in previous work.[6] Now, outdoor work is not a simple reward but a collection of rewards, including autonomy – especially from supervision, which is readily identifiable and so can be sought directly. Similarly, because workers have difficulty operationalising orientations relating to particular features of work they resort to the rough-and-ready approximations offered by the other visible indicators of "type of work or industry" or "specific named job". It is worth noting that economism is not so different, either, since it may be regarded as a rough approximation for the non-work rewards the money makes possible, although in relation to work the concern is simply money.

In considering the possibilities of orientations in the strong or weak form, the frequency distributions of mentions on the separate preferences are instructive. In the first place, four mentions is the level where it becomes rare for an individual to have that number on more than one aspect. Thus it appears to be the appropirate cut-off for strong orientations. But if orientations are of this sort we would expect aspects to be mentioned this often or not at all, or at least for there to be a bimodal distribution. In fact, the general pattern is one of declining frequency as the number of mentions increases. In no case is the frequency of four mentions greater than that of three. However, there is an upturn at five on the outdoor preference, and the number mentioning it four or more times exceeds the frequency of two and three mentions added together and even the number with only one mention. There is also slight support for a strong wages orientation, in that the frequency of four or more mentions is greater than that for three mentions. For all other preferences the evidence can only be taken as suggesting the weak form. This cannot be regarded as conclusive, since the large numbers without a particular orientation may have a distribution which swamps any other trend, but it clearly lends support to the weak rather than the strong form.

FRAMES OF REFERENCE

So far we have been looking at the preference data in terms of their distribution and the type of orientation they might represent. However, we have yet to demonstrate their extensitivity, without which it is doubtful if we can regard them as indicators of orientations in any sense. All sociological measures are, to one degree or another, artefacts. Can we assume that these specific responses can stand for a much wider patterning of attitudes? We use two principal tests of this patterning: whether the sample as a whole mention the same kinds of factor in other frames of reference, and (where this is appropriate) whether the same persons mention the same factors in different frames of reference.

We begin with some *ad hoc* checks on the consistency of the individuals by relating general attitudes to work to some of the persistent preferences. The general attitudes were tapped by a question which contains a list of complaints about work. Workers were asked to agree or disagree by marking a cross on a 24-point scale.[7] Among the complaints are ones about wages, the intrinsic job, hours and security (which is a "trick" question, with the sense of the complaint reversed so that the workers are stated to have too much security). We should expect those who complain most (or least, in the case of security) to be more likely persistently to prefer this item. This is indeed what we find in all cases, with all differences significant at the 0.01 level.

Further checks are available for the wages preference. Those who persistently prefer wages are more likely to accept an hypothetical offer to change jobs for an extra 10/- (50p) a week; they are more likely (in Question 34) to rank "a really good wage" as a high priority in their lives in general; and they are more likely to have knowledge of the wage-rates of Peterborough firms. And those who persistently prefer "intrinsic job" rank "enjoyable work" more highly as a life-goal. All these differences are significant at the 0.01 level. These checks all confirm the usefulness of the persistent preference measures to tap actual preferences. They do not include several of the preferences, but it is difficult to see why these would be less effective measures. Therefore, we can proceed with the hypothesis that these preferences reflect attitudes of a rather general kind.

Next we examine the extent to which the sample as a whole mention the same kind of factor across different frames of reference. We start with one that is not dissimilar to the frame of the preference data in that it also concerns the labour market. This time, however, it is not hypothetical but actual behaviour, or at least the worker's account of his past behaviour in moving between firms. We sought to reconstruct the worker's entire job history, asking him to recount each of the jobs he had held, and why he had left each firm. As the average number of firms worked for was just over three, we were given well over 3,000 reasons (up to two reasons per move were coded – one for leaving and one for going to the new firm). Table 6.1 details the main type of reason given to us.

Because we are dealing with actual job movement rather than hypothetical preferences, this table includes reasons which have nothing to do with the worker's desires. The largest single category is "in-

Table 6.1 Job histories of respondents: reasons given for changing all previous firms

Reason	No. of mentions	%
Involuntary: dismissal, redundancy, conscripted, etc.	1,050	29
Wages	813	23
Location	336	9
Job content	181	5
Management relations	163	5
Promotion	153	4
Family reasons	143	4
Hours	138	4
Working conditions	120	3
Security	82	2
Indoor/Outdoor	60	2
Type of work or industry	52	1
Own business	45	1
Other reasons	237	6
Total	3,573	100

voluntary", of which just over two-thirds are layoffs and dismissals, with the remainder involving wartime conscription and direction of labour plus subsequent National Service.[8] Despite its size, this "involuntary" category is certainly an understatement of the number of enforced moves. Workers are somewhat reluctant to admit having lost their jobs in circumstances which might be thought to reflect discreditably upon them. Not a single worker confessed to having had a job history interrupted by the force of the law, yet – unless this is a totally atypical sample of manual workers – some must surely have been engaged in criminal activity and/or experienced prison. Of the 163 mentions of relations with management, 124 gave unsatisfactory personal relations with a boss as a reason for leaving. Some of those were dismissals, although it is not possible to draw a clear line between voluntary and involuntary movement of this nature, and in a previous study Daniel (1974: 56, 61) includes this in both categories. One of the liveliest of the men we interviewed said that he had left his first five firms after fighting with the boss, then left the sixth to *avoid* fighting with the boss. As he had been with his seventh firm for some time, it seemed that he had acquired prudence by degrees! Of course, interviewing in 1970–1 minimised the incidence of redundancy and unemployment in the workers' job histories, for this was the end of the longest boom in the entire history of capitalism. Earlier studies found a higher proportion of involuntary moves – sometimes up to 70 per cent – than we did (e.g. Myers and MacLaurin, 1943: 18). It is also worth recalling that we chose Peterborough partly for its low level of unemployment (increasing opportunities for job choice) so we might well expect higher proportions of involuntary moves elsewhere.

Turning to the more-or-less voluntary moves, the outstanding feature is the predominance of wages in affecting job movement. A quarter of all reasons, and a third of voluntary reasons, concerned wages. As in previous studies, pay was more important as an attraction of the new job than as a reason for leaving the old one (e.g. Daniel, 1974: 61, 98) although the distinction is not perhaps clear-cut. Of the other reasons, location is the only one to attain more than 5 per cent of responses. Location can be reduced, more or less, to two precise job features, wages and hours: one generally prefers employment near home, either to avoid travelling expenses (deductable from wages) or travelling time (which effectively adds to the length of the working day), although the unpleasantness (or even pleasantness) of the journey may also come into it. Where workers explained in detail what they meant by location, they usually referred to time. If we add the location responses to the "hours" category, this would amount to 13 per cent of all reasons, and to almost 20 per cent of voluntary reasons. Together, hours and wages form the crudest indicator of the work-effort bargain – maximising the wages while minimising the duration of the effort, although it should be borne in mind that the sacrifice in the "bargain" is not only in effort but also in loss or disruption of non-work life. It appears that about half of actual voluntary job movement – as remembered by workers – is explicable in these terms. Surprisingly few workers seem influenced by a more precise consideration of the work-effort bargain, involving the nature of the job content itself. Following closely behind job content reasons in importance among intrinsic considerations was relations with management. Relations with workmates was insignificant, another sign that this type of reward is not chosen by workers, but rather is acquired over a long period of time. We might add that the main pattern of these results – the importance of involuntary reasons, of wages, hours/location, and the scattering of other responses – is similar to that reported by Daniel (1974: 61, 98)

It is apparent that the distribution of these responses differs from that of the preference data. To some extent this is simply because we asked a different question. The preference data, being directly related to employment, do not allow workers to mention the lure of attempting one's own business: as Table 6.1 indicates, several workers have been attracted by this. Conversely, the outdoor-loving workers are not evident in this table, presumably because they have always worked outdoors, and so have never left in order to attain this. This table largely reflects the dissatisfactions of younger, short-service workers, for these are disproportionately the mobile. Among these workers the main interest affecting job change is the greater actual importance of wages and hours. Once again, we see the relative unimportance of the content of work activities and of relations with workmates in labour market behaviour. However, we suspect that the extreme dominance of wages in the recalled data is also due in part to a resort to a conventional response.

Both the preferences and the reasons for changing jobs reflect fairly realistic frames of reference. They are not necessarily statements about what the worker would ideally like, rather about what he thinks he can get and has got. But orientations also contain an ideal element. To be sure they must be relatively realistic, in the sense that they relate to what is possible, if they are to play a part in making sense of actual experience. On the other hand, if a worker is too realistic he simply accepts what is, and has no basis to seek to change the situation. So let us examine this further by looking at workers' frames of reference which might aim higher than their realistic expectations.

Table 6.2 contains the results of two open-ended questions, coded in the same way as the persistent preferences. The first column presents the results of the question, "Do you enjoy the time you spend at work, or don't you get much pleasure out of it? What do you particularly enjoy about it?" The second column is based on a question asking what the respondent liked most about the best job he ever had.

Table 6.2   Reasons given for enjoying present job and liking the best job experienced

Reason	Work as enjoyable (Q.20)		Reason for liking best job (Q.10)	
	No.	%	No.	%
Social relations at work	360	45	117	13
Intrinsic job activities	307	39	485	54
Wages	34	4	65	7
Working conditions	31	4	32	4
Outdoors/indoors	27	3	68	7
Other explicit reasons	37	5	128	14
All explicit reasons	796	100	895	100
No. of persons with enjoyable work	721	76		
No. not enjoying work	223	24		
Total persons	944	100		

Looking at the second column, we are struck immediately by the predominance of the intrinsic job aspects. Apparently, over half the workers remember their best job for the work they were asked to do. Of these, 144 remember its autonomy, 339 remember its interest, variety, skill or challenge, and a slightly out-of-key 32 remember its easiness. The next largest group recall social relations at work, and of these 57 enjoyed the company of their workmates, 47 enjoyed the chance to meet people (i.e. not workmates), and 13 liked foremen or managers. Together these two categories comprise over three-quarters of the responses. This is also so for the "enjoyable work" responses, although the importance of the two is reversed. Now, social relations are most important. The majority of these (260 out of the 360) concern workmates, followed by

75 meeting people on the job and 25 management. From the 307 job activity responses we must first perhaps discard the 50 somewhat negative responses that the work "keeps me busy" or "keeps me from idleness" and the six liking the easiness of the work, to arrive at 251 responses indicating enjoyment of the autonomy or some aspect of the skill or variety of the job.

These questions have elicited those very types of response which were strangely lacking from the more realistic views of the labour market. "Good feelings" about work, either remembering one's best job or enjoying one's present job, largely derive from the intrinsic activities and relationships of work. This is not surprising in the case of the present job in view of the wording of our question – here the interest lies in the predominance of social relations over other intrinsic work experiences. However, the things they liked about their best jobs are less restricted by the wording of the question and must be regarded as important potential rewards.

Here we have arrived at the major flaw in the orientations model, or indeed in any rationalistic model, of the labour market. It appears that, for the most part, workers are not able to choose employment according to some of their most important priorities. The most important element of work enjoyment is not even part of the employer's offer of work; it is largely created by the workers themselves and lies quite separately in the social relations among workers which must be experienced over a period of time. And the factors which induce positive feelings about work are not necessarily those factors which influence job choice. Now, we are not saying that these intrinsic aspects of work are of greatest *general* importance to the worker just because they are likely to induce "good feelings". Nor are we saying that they do not have a significant influence on labour market behaviour, particularly in decisions about staying or moving. Our argument is that different aspects can come into play with varying degrees of force in different situations. This does not mean that workers cannot have orientations where relative priorities are called up according to circumstances, but it casts doubt on the possibility of strong orientations, and on any model of the labour market solely in terms of workers' choice.

It only remains to determine whether, in spite of the different response distributions, there is any consistency between the preference scores and responses in these other frames of reference. As we would expect from the preceding discussion, relationships are not particularly strong but there is a general tendency to consistency, giving modest support to the notion of orientations.

One implication of the discussion in this section is that we cannot have a simple view of "importance". What is "important" to the workers depends on the frame of reference within which work is being considered. This should be borne in mind in the following sections where we consider importance as judged in a single, very general frame of reference.

IMPORTANCE, SATISFACTION AND ORIENTATIONS

We observed earlier that we also have two rather different ways of approaching the study of possible orientations. These are based on the satisfaction workers express with various aspects of the job and the importance they attribute to each aspect. It is convenient to introduce these together, although they involve different frames of reference. Satisfaction relates to the present situation and particularly to the details of the present job. Importance, on the other hand, is a more general and abstract question: it calls for a similar frame of reference to that of the preference measures, but at a more abstract level.

The job aspects were selected in advance, in the light of previous literature, and so do not correspond as closely as we might wish to those emphasised by the workers in the open-ended questions.

We asked respondents about the following 12 aspects of the job:

1. Their relations with management
2. Job security
3. How worthwhile the job was
4. The interest, skill and effort of the job
5. Fringe benefits, such as pensions, sick pay or social facilities
6. Trade-union strength
7. The friendliness of people they worked with
8. The hours of work, including the time spent travelling
9. The opportunity to get on with their work in their own way
10. Pay
11. Working conditions
12. Promotion chances

For satisfaction, respondents were first asked to say whether they were dissatisfied or satisfied with each item, and then to express the extent of this satisfaction or dissatisfaction by placing a mark at the appropriate point on one of two lines running from a neutral point to "completely satisfied" (or "dissatisfied"). They were then asked to "rate the same detailed things according to *how important you think they are in weighing up a job*". In the pilot study we had found a marked tendency to claim everything was extremely important, so respondents were asked to try to compare the items with each other so that some would be above and some below average. The items were then introduced with the phrase, "How important compared to other things is: . . ." This time, responses were recorded along a single line which ranged, in keeping with our attempt to discourage over-use of the extreme, from "Exceptionally low" to "Exceptionally high importance", with the mid-point labelled "Average importance". As we shall see, this strategy to spread responses was not entirely successful, the mean position on all items corresponding to considerably more than average importance.

Measuring responses in this way has considerable advantages over the conventional fixed-choice method. It allows compromise between points; it indicates equal intervals between cue points by visual presentation; it offers and creates an interval scale. However, it is not altogether satisfactory because of a tendency for answers to cluster at the cue points rather than being distributed regularly. This has little effect if each division of the scale for scoring purposes contains one, and only one, cue point, but finer divisions do create problems.[9]

We scored four divisions to each cue point (as marked on the lines). Thus satisfaction ranged from 0 to 16 and dissatisfaction from 0 to -16, the two being combined in one scale which we shall refer to as "satisfaction". Importance was similarly measured from 0 to 24. We may regard the scores on each item as belonging to an underlying normal distribution, but distorted by the tendency to cluster, or we may regard the cue points as distinct concepts to which people relate their views. We have in fact made use of both interpretations, and it seems that the notion of a continuous variable is theoretically justified (and is, of course, compatible with the second interpretation). Regarding the scores as belonging to a continuous distribution implies errors in the recorded values which reduce the variance and the correlation of these variables with each other and with other variables. This is important to bear in mind, since we shall be using forms of correlation analysis and dealing with quite small correlations.

IMPORTANCE

Salience is a basic aspect of orientations. Insofar as orientations to work

Examples of importance and satisfaction Scales

Importance

Exceptionally low importance	Well below average importance	Just below average importance	Average importance	Just above average importance	Well above average importance	Exceptionally high importance

Satisfaction

D.

Just dissatisfied	Moderately dissatisfied	Very dissatisfied	Completely dissatisfied

S.

Just satisfied	Moderately satisfied	Very satisfied	Completely satisfied

are a matter of priorities in rewards sought, they entail the relative importance of the various rewards. This is what our questions were designed to tap. We would not regard the scores as providing complete measures of orientations, however, quite apart from measurement deficiencies, because they do not take account of expectations. Nevertheless they are, on the face of it, direct measures of priorities which are independent of the specific context of work or even of the labour market.

An unavoidable drawback with the importance scores is that they may not be strictly comparable between individuals; the same scores may not mean exactly the same level of importance, even though the scale was designed to minimise this problem. This can be met by converting the scores to rank orders. Thus the most important is scored 1, and so on, regardless of the actual level of the original score. But this has the effect of over-compensating, providing the reverse problem of failing to distinguish real differences in the levels of importance for a given rank. For example, one man may rate two aspects very highly and a long way ahead of the rest, while another rates all aspects in a narrow range of moderate importance, yet the ranks are treated as equivalent for both men. Also, the ranking contracts the scale from 24 to 12 potential values. It seems the raw scores are probably a little better as continuous variables, while the rankings are useful for identifying the most important aspects. Neither measure is entirely satisfactory, but as they have different strengths and weaknesses we have made use of them both.[10]

The Strong Form

If workers have orientations of the strong form, with one or two clear-cut priorities, we might expect this to be reflected in the importance scores. It is not. We simply do not find responses indicating high importance for one or two aspects and medium or low importance for the others. This is in line with our observations of the distribution of frequencies in the preference data, providing further doubt about the existence of such clear-cut orientations.

However, it may well be a result of the form of the questions. It is to be expected that many things are judged important, particularly if people are asked about them directly, as our respondents were, while an orientation may be seen as a simplifying principle where only one, or a few aspects are involved. Even so, such orientations must be the most important aspects. Accordingly, we have taken as a provisional identification of strong orientations the aspects rated most important.

Because of the tendency for individuals to group their answers around cue points there were many ties for the most important aspect. Here we followed the strategy of allowing the possibility of two clear-cut orientations, so that where ties involved two aspects they were both allowed, and where more than two aspects were tied no orientation was allowed.

To give an overall picture of the importance attributed to various aspects, we give in Table 6.3, for each aspect, its mean score and the frequency with which it was rated the most important. For comparison we also include, where possible, the corresponding frequencies of persistent preferences, together with the overlap of the two orientations measures. In this and subsequent tables the aspects of work are numbered according to the order they were put to the respondent in Questions 28 and 30 of the interview survey, but abbreviated descriptions are used.

We see that, on the whole, the means fall within a fairly narrow range

Table 6.3   Importance and persistent preferences

Aspect of Work	Import-ance Mean	Most Important Frequency	Rank	Persistent Preference Frequency	Rank	Congruent cases
10 Pay	20.6	138	1	123	1	26
2 Security	19.5	63	2 =	20	6	1
7 Workmates	19.5	63	2 =	6	7	0
11 Working conditions	18.9	36	5 =	69	2	5
4 Intrinsic job	18.8	36	5 =	68	3	3
9 Autonomy	18.6	40	4	3	8 =	0
3 Worthwhileness	18.6	30	8	–	–	–
5 Fringe benefits	18.5	32	7	1	10	0
1 Management relations	17.2	23	10	28	4	0
8 Hours	17.0	18	12	24	5	0
12 Promotion chances	16.1	19	11	3	8 =	0
6 Trade union	15.6	25	9	–	–	–
Total	18.5	468*		345		35

* Excluding Worthwhileness and Trade union
Note: 37 respondents failed to score importance for one or more aspect and so cannot be included in the ranking. This includes 9 who had Persistent Preferences, as follows: Intrinsic Job 5, Pay 2, Working Conditions 1, Management Relations 1.

from "just above average" to "well above average" importance. A little above this range is pay, and this is followed by security and friendly workmates. Pay is also one of the main persistent preferences and is clearly ranked first among those included here, but the other two come just below half way in the preference data. Indeed, "workpeople" is a much wider category than "workmates" yet is the subject of very few persistent preferences. However, this is hardly surprising. The method of identifying preferences was unlikely to emphasise workmates because it is rarely possible to take them into account in choosing a job (as opposed to deciding whether to change a job), and we did find a much higher rate of references when workers were answering in relation to their present firms.

At the other extreme, trade-union strength is, on average, clearly the least important, followed by promotion chances and then hours of work and relations with management. Trade-union strength fits our previous finding of low importance, in that hardly a single preference answer made any reference to unions and there was no question of a persistent preference of this nature. Promotion chances came low on the preferences but hours and management relations were nearer the middle.

Turning to the aspects ranked most important, following our principle of allowing no more than two to be tied first, the pattern is quite similar to that of the means. The main changes are that autonomy and trade-union strength become relatively more important and hours less so. More interesting is to compare the ordering of both with that of the persistent preferences on the ten common items. If there are clear-cut, strong orientations, then we would expect both the persistent preferences and the most important aspects to tap them. Thus they should be well related, with a weaker relation between the former and the mean importance ranks. In fact, the results are rather different: the ordering of the aspects on preferences follows a somewhat similar pattern to that of the importance means, but its relation to the order of the most important aspects is much weaker – gamma = 0.40 and 0.22 respectively – and would disappear if it were not for pay coming first in both.

A more telling test than comparison of the general patterns of occurrence is to see whether the different measures of orientations identify the same people. Do those who persistently refer to a particular aspect also rate it most important? The final column of this table, referred to as "congruent cases", gives the number who were included in both measures. It is immediately apparent that the numbers are not great. Only in the case of pay is there a significant tendency for the same people to score on each measure, and even then it is a weak relationship.

As the frequencies on other aspects are fairly low for each measure, it requires quite a strong degree of congruence to produce a significant relation. We might reasonably expect such a level of congruence, but failing this we can overcome the problem of small numbers by considering all ten aspects together. Overall there are 35 congruent cases, roughly ten more than would be expected by chance,[11] which is barely significant. Once again, if pay is excluded there is no trend whatsoever.

Possibly the criterion of allowing no more than two to be tied as most important is too restrictive. Accordingly, we relaxed it to allow all cases where an item is rated as most important, regardless of how many other items tied with it. The pattern of congruent responses is much the same as before. The total is now 155, which is significantly more than the random expectation of 121, but hardly impressive, and once again the relation would disappear if pay were excluded. However, the trend to consistency with respect to pay is actually weaker, and somewhat stronger is a tendency to congruence on intrinsic job (33 congruent cases against an expectation of 23 for intrinsic job, and 79 against 71 for pay).

Looking at the problem a little differently, it might be argued that where a man rated an aspect as exceptionally high on importance it indicated an orientation, or at least that those with orientations would rate the relevant aspect as highly important. Accordingly, we repeated our test, only this time using a division between those scoring 24 on importance and the rest.[12] The results were much the same as before: a significant level of congruence on pay and intrinsic job, although the relationships were weak, and nothing on the others. At the opposite extreme was hours, with a total lack of congruence – not one of the 24 with a persistent preference among the 125 rating hours as highly important (nor even among the 78 scoring 23). Although it is not possible to estimate the expected overall frequency of congruent cases, since there is no way of establishing the degree of interdependence of importance scores, there seems to be a slightly stronger trend than we obtained from the ranks, but again it is not impressive and probably should not be regarded as significant if pay were excluded.

The evidence, then, lends little support for the strong sense of clear-cut orientations. There is some support for an economistic orientation, and possibly for one relating to intrinsic rewards, but that seems to be all. Of course, it may be objected that one, or both, of the measures is unsatisfactory, but this needs explaining in relation to the notion of orientations. If one of these measures is unsuitable to tap orientations, this has direct implications for the conceptualisation of orientations. A simpler variant of the point is that, because of the different and imperfect ways they identify orientations, they tend to pick out different people. Thus, rather than alternatives, the measures need to be combined for an adequate resultant measure. We shall return to these considerations presently.

The Weak Form

At this point we shall examine the possibility of orientations in the weaker sense, by relating preference frequencies to the full set of importance scores and ranks. Our aim is to see whether the frequencies with which workers refer to job aspects in the context of job choice are related to their more abstract judgments of importance. Firstly, we have made use of all the information and correlated the 12 importance scores with the preference frequencies. In addition to the faults we noted in the importance distributions the "preference" distributions are all quite heavily skewed, so we have preferred to use non-parametric correlation (Kendal's tau), although, apart from slightly lower coefficients, the results are little different from those using product moment correlation. In addition we have repeated the correlations, using rank orders of importance in place of the raw scores. Both sets of correlations are presented in Table 6.4, those for rankings being given in parentheses.

In view of the imperfections of the measures we might expect all correlations to be artificially low. However, it is quite striking to see just how low they are. With a few exceptions, one might believe these were carefully selected random data. In Table 6.4 "non-significant" results are excluded for the sake of clarity, apart from one or two given in italics when a significant result might have been expected. Since the two correlations are attempts to measure the same relationship, we have accepted a lower level of significance where they confirm each other. In this case both are significant at the 5 per cent level, though at least one is usually significant at a higher level. Otherwise, when only one coefficient is shown, the criterion is significance at the 1 per cent level. In the great majority of cases where no coefficient is shown the significance level was below 20 per cent. A one-tail test was used, which is appropriate in those cases when there is a clear hypothesis about the direction of the relationship — especially the diagonal cells — but may be regarded as over-estimating significance in some cases. It will be seen that, because of the large sample, these levels of significance only require quite small correlations; the relationships between significance and correlation are not perfect, but roughly the 5 per cent level corresponds to a tau of just under 0.05 and the 1 per cent to a tau just over 0.065. At a little over 0.08

Table 6.4 Correlations: importance scores (and ranks) with preferences

(The columns headed 8. Hours, 9. Autonomy and 10. Pay fall under the spanning label Importance*.)*

Preferences	1. Relations with Mgt.	2. Security	4. Interest skill, etc.	5. Fringe benefits	7. Workmates	8. Hours	9. Autonomy	10. Pay	11. Working conditions	12. Promotion	3. Worthwhile	6. Trade union
Management quality	**0.09(0.08)**		0.07(0.06)								0.07(0.05)	−0.04(−0.07)
Security		**0.10(0.05)**							**0.10(0.05)**			***(−0.10)***
Intrinsic job			**0.13(0.10)**	0.08(−0.07)		0.07	**0.08(0.08)**	*(−0.06)*		**0.08(0.06)**	0.07	**−0.05(−0.08)**
Fringe benefits				0.07(0.06)								
Work people					0.04 0.05	*0.02(0.03)*						
Hours						−0.06(−0.07)						
Autonomy						0.06(0.05)	0.05(0.09)		**0.07(0.10)**	−0.05(−0.08)	−0.07(−0.13)	
Wages								**0.13(0.12)**				
Working conditions				0.07(0.05)					*0.04(0.03)*			
Promotion										**0.10(0.10)**		
Status		0.08	0.07							**0.11(0.08)**	0.08	−0.06(−0.07)
Type of work/ind.			0.07(0.05)					−0.05(−0.05)			0.06(0.06)	0.06(0.07)
Effort not high			−0.06(−0.05)				−0.05(−0.05)				−0.05(−0.06)	
Indoors					*(0.07)*			−0.08(−0.06)			*(0.06)*	
Outdoors										−0.08(−0.07)		
Personal suitability			**0.08(0.07)**				**0.09(0.09)**	−0.05(0.08)				
Interest*										**0.08(0.07)**		
Specific job*		0.07	**0.12(0.07)**	*(−0.07)*						0.05(0.05)		*(−0.09)*

All correlations are Kendal's tau

Figures in parentheses ( ) are correlations between preferences and the ranking of individual importance scores.

Figures in italics are not significant, and are given for completeness only.

All others are significant at the 5% level ($p < 0.05$, one tail), including all cases where both coefficients are significant at this level and all remaining cases where one, as shown, is significant at the 1% level ($p < 0.01$).

Figures in bold type indicate highly significant coefficients ($p < 0.001$).

* These are the components of Intrinsic job.

the tau becomes significant at the 0.1 per cent level, and these highly significant results are indicated by bold type in the table.

Within this general context of low relationships[13] quite a clear pattern emerges. The ten aspects where there is a correspondence between the preference and importance measures are listed first, and we see a marked tendency for these to be positively related. Not only do the significant relations tend to lie on the diagonal, but these relations are generally higher than others. Pay, intrinsic job, promotion and management are outstanding, followed by security and autonomy, while fringe benefits is also significant at the 1 per cent level on each correlation. Workmates is significantly related (at the 5 per cent level) to workpeople only when measured by ranking, although the correlation using raw importance scores is barely below this level and all the forms of standardisation we tested would push it over the "significant" margin. In view of the difference in the content of the two variables this observed degree of association suggests that the data may conceal a more substantial relationship. The remaining two, working conditions and hours, are simply not significant, though even here all signs are as predicted.

Apart from the diagonal cells, the only outstanding relationship on both measures, in this part of the table, is between the importance of autonomy and the intrinsic job preference. However, we see this is something of an artefact, since autonomy is yet more strongly related to the specific job preference, which is one of the components, along with interest, of the intrinsic job measure.

None of the off-diagonal relationships appears symmetrically; that is, if a relationship is observed between a certain importance score and another preference score, there is never a relationship between the corresponding preference and importance items. The implication seems to be that the meaning of an item changes between contexts. Nevertheless, some of the relationships are readily interpretable, as for example the preference for security and the importance of fringe benefits, and the negative relations of intrinsic job with fringe benefits and pay.

Change of meaning from one context to another may be particularly relevant for the two aspects where the correlation between corresponding measures – the diagonal cells – is not significant. The importance of working conditions shows relatively strong relationships with expressed preferences concerning security and hours. This suggests that, despite the actual wording, this item was sometimes wrongly interpreted as "conditions of work", meaning conditions of employment, which would help to explain the low relationship with the preference variable. For hours also, some clue may be obtained from the relation of the importance measures to other preference items. Positive relations with wages and security as well as negative ones with autonomy, even though rather weak, do suggest an instrumental approach which might give priority to long overtime rather than short, convenient hours. Quite probably both sorts of considerations are involved in attributing importance, in the abstract, to hours.

Not surprisingly, in the more abstract context of the importance score promotion emerges as related to many aspects of preference. It is important in gaining a generally better job. Thus it is positively related to preferences involving status and intrinsic rewards, and negatively related to the "personal suitability" preference response, confirming the deferent nature of the latter. Less clear in this pattern is the negative relationship with the autonomy preference, but it is easy to see how it can come about.

The two importance aspects without corresponding preferences also entail a general reference to the job, both being related to a number of preferences. Worthwhileness tends to be regarded as of low salience by those with preferences for high pay or low effort, while high salience is associated with several other preferences. The importance of trade-union strength, on the other hand, is negatively related to a number of preferences, with positive relations confined to preferences for low effort and good working conditions but not extrinsic rewards. On the face of it, the salience attributed to these two aspects reflects commitment to and alienation from the job.[14]

Several of the preferences are related to importance judgments on a number of aspects, in keeping with our interpretation of them as standing for bundles of preferences. These include reference to a type of work or industry, management quality, status and security. Particularly noteworthy is reference to a specific job which, in terms of its relations with importance measures, seems to be a general "good job" preference with the emphasis on the job itself to the exclusion of extrinsic rewards. Our decision to treat it as a measure of intrinsic job preference and combine it with interest is justified by the higher correlation of the importance of interest, etc., with the intrinsic preferences than with either of its components separately. However, the reference to a specific job has a rather wider relevance than interest and skill, particularly by including autonomy in the job content. As we would expect, the intrinsic preference has a somewhat similar pattern of relations with priorities on the various aspects, the main change being – not unreasonably – that the relation with security is replaced by one with worthwhileness.

The outdoor/indoor preferences also relate to a number of priorities, but with a rather different pattern. On its own, neither is related to many priorities, but we see the shape of relations more clearly by considering them together. Thus the preference for work indoors is related to low salience of autonomy and interest, while the outdoor preference is associated with low salience of pay and high priorities concerning workmates and the worthwhileness of the job.[15]

In treating the salience and preference measures as continuous variables they are no longer nominal measures characterising different individuals: rather are they variable properties of each individual. The different aspects are to some extent still alternatives for each person, because of the methods used, but the result is a profile instead of a type. With this approach we formed a much clearer and more meaningful set of relationships between the two measures than was evident when we were concerned with orientations in the strong sense. The actual relationships are hardly impressive but there is definitely a pattern. In other words, there appear to be grounds for believing that there are orientations, in this weak sense, which persist across the different frames of reference. We noted that the preferences which related to importance on several aspects were of a rather general type. Also, the importance scores most related to preferences concerned promotion, worthwhileness and trade-union strength, which we suggest reflect general considerations of job quality. Promotion may be a particular priority, but the other two were virtually unmentioned as preferences, suggesting they are not so much orientations in themselves as assessments of importance reflecting other general attitudes. This seems to indicate weak orientations of a general nature in keeping with the worker's degree of knowledge. However, there is no escaping the fact that we have found only limited consistency from one frame of reference to another, whatever method we have used.

SATISFACTION

Another way in which we can approach the question of orientations is through a consideration of satisfaction with aspects of the job in relation to overall job satisfactions. There are a number of conceptual and theoretical difficulties associated with the idea of job satisfaction,[16] but these are somewhat reduced where workers share a similar experience of employment possibilities, and the procedure seems reasonable in the present case. In itself satisfaction is not, of course, a measure of orientation, but of attitude to a given level of rewards. However, if workers do have orientations which they bring to the work situation, these will influence the evaluations made. Thus we may be able to observe their effects in expressions of satisfaction or dissatisfaction.

There are two ways in which an orientation may affect satisfaction: through the level of expectation and through the salience of the desired reward. For example, an economistic orientation may entail both an expectation of a high level of wages and also the attachment of a high degree of importance to the extent to which this expectation is met. To some degree the two components of orientation vary together. It seems obvious that the more important money is to a worker the more he will want, but the relationship is not so simple. In the first place, there are some rewards such as money, but not outdoor work, which are wanted by everyone, and the more the better; so the level of expectation refers not to the level the individual would like but to the level at which he will be satisfied. Such a level, we believe, is a function of the worker's perceptions of what is possible rather than of his orientations. Indeed orientations, we have argued, are themselves confined to what is seen as possible and tend to give priority to those aspects of work where "reasonable" levels and significant variations in rewards seem possible. Satisfaction then depends on the relationship between orientations and actual experience within the frame of reference of what is perceived as possible.

We see from Table 6.5 that on the average respondents expressed satisfaction rather than dissatisfaction with aspects of their work and with work in general. This, of course, is in keeping with the findings of all studies of job satisfaction. It is worth noting, however, that in this case (probably because of the method used) the levels of satisfaction were not particularly high. Only with the friendliness of their workmates were respondents more than "moderately satisfied", while on promotion chances, trade-union strength, working conditions, fringe benefits and pay they ranged from barely satisfied at all to "just satisfied". We may recall that social relationships are the main source of enjoyment in their jobs.*

Where expectations are low, workers are more likely to feel satisfied with a given level of reward.[17] So we might expect levels of satisfaction on items to be inversely related to orientations, in the sense that those with the highest expectations are likely to be hardest to satisfy. When we look at the overall pattern, however, there is no relationship between the mean satisfaction scores and any other findings, such as mean importance or frequency of preferences. Satisfaction was at its lowest with promotion chances and trade-union strength, which have hardly

Table 6.5 Satisfaction with aspects of work: means, standard deviations, and contributions to general satisfaction

Aspect of Work	Mean	Std. devn.	Path to T	Path to X_1	Path to X_2	Path to T by X_1
1. Relations with management	22.9	7.5	0.090	0.246	0.257	0.152
2. Security	22.6	8.3	0.017	0.109	0.107	0.067
3. Worthwhileness	23.7	7.2	0.248	0.256	0.277	0.158
4. Interest, skill and effort	23.0	8.1	0.114	0.092	0.095	0.057
5. Fringe benefits	20.6	9.6	0.009	−0.009	−0.001	−0.006
6. Trade-union strength	18.2	9.9	0.042	0.014	−0.003	0.008
7. The friendliness of the people you work with	26.8	6.1	0.048	0.072	0.096	0.044
8. Hours of work	22.5	9.0	0.091	0.171	0.173	0.106
9. Autonomy	23.6	8.5	0.068	0.137	0.136	0.085
10. Pay	20.8	9.4	0.022	0.113	0.125	0.070
11. Working conditions	19.4	9.3	0.081	0.155	0.169	0.096
12. Promotion chances	17.2	9.5	0.156	0.237	0.241	0.147
T Work in general	23.1	8.0	–	0.619*	0.575*	
Residual path to T			0.776	0.786	0.784	0.786

X_1 Hypothetical overall satisfaction X_2 Hypothetical overall satisfaction with control for age
* Path to T from X_1 or X_2

emerged in our previous data as major orientations within the sample. Yet this should not be too surprising, as the actual level of rewards must also be taken into account. That an inverse relationship is not found may be because there are different levels of rewards on different aspects (which is hard to interpret precisely, but is not improbable), or because it is not equally easy to find jobs meeting expectations for all orientations, which is what we would expect from our data on the labour market.

A high standard deviation may indicate a high salience given to an item by the sample in general, so that small deviations from the expected level of rewards result in substantial variations in satisfaction. Alternatively, it may be due to substantial differences in expectations within the sample. This reasoning suggests that high variance in satisfaction occurs on items which feature importantly as orientations, either for the whole sample or a sub-section. On the other hand it may simply be due to substantial variation in the rewards received. When we look at the table we find another reason in our data. Because of the upper bound to the scale we see there is a strong inverse relationship between mean satisfaction and standard deviation – the nearer all workers are to being completely satisfied, the less the variations in responses ($r = -0.88$). This should not necessarily be seen as a statistical artefact, since an upper limit of complete satisfaction does have substantive meaning. Nevertheless, it does imply that if standard deviations are to give an indication of dominant orientations within the sample it should be on the basis of their size in excess of that expected in relation to the means. There are four partial exceptions to the general trend, with higher standard deviations than expected: fringe benefits, pay, hours and autonomy. Once again we find pay featuring as an important orientation, and if high variance on autonomy reflects the indoors/outdoors division we have found to be so important, this too is what we would expect. Not so the other two, however. We have not previously found any evidence for, and would hardly expect a major "fringe benefit" orientation, but evaluation of these rewards is likely to be based on other orientations, such as security (this is the item with which it has the largest correlation). Hours could well be the basis of a specific orientation, but in this case there is no reason to expect it to be widespread and so far there has been no evidence to suggest this.[18] Indeed, since our analysis of the objective labour market showed a relatively high degree of opportunity to choose between the length or convenience of hours and other job aspects, we might expect those with such an orientation to have found jobs to match it, so that if it were a common orientation we would expect a higher level of satisfaction. It seems more likely that the explanation lies in the actual variation in the length and inconvenience of hours worked. Insofar as the high variances on fringe benefits and hours relate to orientations, it seems most likely that, together with pay, they reflect a very general instrumental orientation.

Contributions to Overall Satisfaction

Another way to estimate the salience of the items is to examine their contributions to overall satisfaction with work. The more salient may be expected to make greater contributions. If, for example, a worker has an "intrinsic job" orientation we may expect his feelings about the "interest, skill and effort" of his job to play a predominant part in determining his attitude to the job in general. We cannot examine this in individual cases but, as before, we can look at the overall pattern.

Since the various items of satisfaction are more meaningfully regarded as causes than as indicators of the overall job satisfaction, the appropriate way to relate them is in a regression rather than a factor analytic type of model. There is a problem in that least squares regression entails the assumption of no idiosyncratic variation between individuals (see Birnbaum, 1977), which is not plausible here. Nevertheless, we should obtain a rough picture of the dominant trends.

In order to control for the effects of the different standard deviations we have preferred standardised regression or path coefficients. Essentially, we have used two approaches to assess the relative contributions of the items. The first is to take the responses to a single question on satisfaction with the job in general (measured in the same way as the other scores, and T in the table), and calculate coefficients for paths to this variable. The second approach uses the knowledge that job satisfaction is related to other variables to create an estimate. The model,[19] as shown in Figure 6.1, takes the 12 separate satisfaction items as independent variables determining a hypothetical overall variable, X_1. In turn, this determines four dependent variables, of which the single measure of job satisfaction is one, together with a similar measure of life satisfaction and constructed measures of ideology and generalised demands.[20] The value of X_1 is chosen so as to maximise the explained variance in the dependent variables. (In this case the canonical correlation = 0.73). Since age may be regarded as influencing all the variables concerned, the analysis was also performed with age as a control variable, giving the hypothetical variable X_2.

It will be seen from Table 6.5 that control for age makes little difference to the general pattern, and that the patterns are quite similar hether we use T or X as the measure of overall job satisfaction

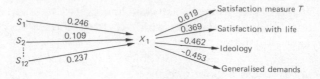

Figure 6.1   ($S_1 - S_{12}$ are the measures of satisfaction on the 12 items)

($r_{TX} = 0.75$ for both X_1 and X_2). This is confirmed by the values of the residual paths to T, which show that little explanation of T is lost by taking account of other variables and constraining the path through X_1. The last column of the table shows the coefficients of the constrained paths for comparison with the unconstrained paths to T. (They are the product of paths to X_1 and the path from X_1 to T (0.0619).)

Using X_1 or X_2 there is a very clear pattern. Three variables make major contributions to satisfaction with work: the worthwhileness of the job, relations with management and promotion chances. Some way behind come hours and working conditions, followed by autonomy, pay and security. At the other extreme, the contributions of fringe benefits and trade-union strength are negligible. Indeed, the path from fringe benefits is negative and so is that from trade union-strength when we control for age. There is no reason to attempt an interpretation of these negative values, which are so small; they should simply be regarded as indicating an absence of contribution. To omit these variables from the analysis makes very little difference.

How are we to interpret this pattern? In the first place, the low contributions of fringe benefits and trade-union strength are much as we would expect. In spite of the relatively high variance we noted on fringe benefits it would have been surprising, both intuitively and on the basis of our other data, if this variable had been of much significance (A lesson here for employers?). Similarly, we would not expect satisfaction with trade-union strength to have much influence for all but a small minority, though the actual strength may well lead to satisfaction on other items, through higher rewards.

The surprising results are the aspects which emerge as of greatest importance. First comes the "worthwhileness" of the job, yet many seem to have had a very narrow view of the relevance of this concept to their own situation. It is a concept which we confess now appears to have been unclear in our own minds when designing the questionnaire. We were probably referring to the (perhaps delusory) belief among middle-class people like ourselves that our jobs are "worthwhile", both for the common good and also for the fulfilment of our own potentialities. We did not expect non-skilled workers to share these delusions, at least not to the same extent. Perhaps these results indicate that they really do! But we think not, and have other evidence to suggest a rather different interpretation. Earlier in the interview we asked the workers, "Do you feel that your work is a worthwhile, valuable part of your life, or is it just something you have to do to earn a living?" If they replied that it was worthwhile and valuable, we asked in what way it was; and if they said that it was not worthwhile, we asked if anything could be done to make it more so. The overall results are presented in Table 6.6.

Table 6.6   The meanings of a "worthwhile" job

		No.	%
Worthwhile by our frame of reference (as well as the workers')	Functional (useful product, helping country)	104	11
	Personal satisfaction (challenging, interesting, social, healthy, etc)	144	16
Sub-total		248	27
Worthwhile by the workers' frame of reference	Keeps me from idleness	63	7
	Extrinsic status as wage earner, breadwinner	54	6
	No, or vague reason	30	3
Sub-total		147	16
Total responding "worthwhile"		395	43
Work not seen as worthwhile	Nothing can be done	346	37
	Improvements are possible	185	20
Sub-total		531	57
Total respondents		926	100

The majority did not think that their work was worthwhile and most of these thought that this was inevitable, that nothing could be done about it. On the other hand, 43 per cent of the workers replied that their work was worthwhile, which was appreciably higher than we had anticipated. Yet when they explained their reasons for this, an interesting discrepancy emerged between *their* and *our* definitions of "worthwhile". The first group of reasons in Table 6.6 contains our definitions: a job could be worthwhile because its activities helped to produce a socially useful result, because it developed one's abilities or health, or because it integrated the worker with his fellow-man. Only 27 per cent of the workers gave such definitions of their own work. But, in addition, 16 per cent thought their work was worthwhile in ways which we would not have included in this category. There were two principal reasons here; the "Protestant ethic" defence of work as opposed to idleness, with remarks such as, "It keeps me busy", and the usefulness of being a breadwinner providing a living for the respondent and his family. Our questions discouraged this latter type of answer by contrasting worthwhileness with earning a living, and elsewhere the workers seemed to make this contrast themselves; but here the emphasis was on the status of wage-earner with the reasonable insistence that being a breadwinner is a worthwhile part of their life. With both reasons of this second type, the work itself might be experienced as pure hell, leading to an utterly useless end result, yet it would still be worthwhile for extrinsic reasons. In this somewhat negative and pessimistic view of work itself they are not so different from those who felt it was inevitable that their work was not worthwhile.

It seems that the frame of reference within which judgments about worthwhileness are made is extremely narrow. To a large extent evaluations relate directly to the respondent's personal situation – this is true even of the majority of responses falling within our definitions – especially the content of the job. Thus the judgments of both importance and satisfaction concerning worthwhileness are most strongly related to the corresponding measures on interest, skill and effort. However, they are also likely to include most of the possible work rewards, including financial rewards, in the concept of worthwhileness, so that it cannot be clearly distinguished from them. This is in keeping with our findings in the previous section, where the importance of worthwhileness was seen to relate to several preferences. But there we noted a negative relation with the wages preference, and there is also a particularly low relation between the two importance measures, worthwhileness and pay. This would seem to support our earlier point that references to pay were concerned with being a wage-earner, that is having a wage, which follows from having a job, rather than with the level of pay. There are, then, two significant interpretations which we need to include in the meaning of a "worthwhile job". In the first, simply having a job rather than not having one is considered worthwhile. In the second sense, a worthwhile job is essentially a *better* one, further up the job hierarchy, particularly in terms of the immediate work situation. Both interpretations highlight a limitation of the "differential" orientations approach to workers' consciousness: workers may not regard wages, intrinsic job content, "worthwhileness", etc., as *salient alternatives* in job evaluation. On the other hand, we can now see why, in the situation of low expectations and the narrow context of evaluation, "worthwhileness" on either basis should make a major contribution to overall satisfaction.

Similar considerations are also relevant to the other two items which stand out as particularly important – promotion chances and relations with management. There is a distinctly *hierarchical* element to both. Promotion usually guarantees higher rewards on all dimensions – it is not generally an alternative to wages, security, interesting work and so on. Prospects are generally very limited; apart from an occasional appointment of a supervisor, promotion means moving up to a slightly better job within the limited range available. Thus within the narrow frame of reference of what is realistically possible, satisfaction with promotion prospects is in large measure satisfaction with the job in a future perspective. In looking to the future the constraints of realistic possibility are less restricting than in considering the present situation, so we find a greater tendency for expectations to outstrip reality, with a resultant lower level of satisfaction – the lowest average of all items. The low level of satisfaction and the high contribution to overall job satisfaction are thus related, but neither gives any real support to the idea of differential orientations.

We would attribute the surprising importance of relations with management to workers' consciousness of relative powerlessness in their employment. Since power rests with management, a good job *in all its aspects* depends on good management-labour relations. Even more than promotion and a "worthwhile" job, these may constitute a very diffuse attraction of work.

When we look at the paths to the direct measure of job satisfaction (T), we find a decline in the influence of relations with management, and also in the economic rewards, pay and security, which make only tiny contributions. At the same time, there is a relative increase in the contributions of the interest, skill and effort, and of trade-union strength, while worthwhileness is much more clearly the prime contributor. On the whole, with the possible exception of trade-union strength, this appears to represent a narrowing of the context to the actual performance of the job. In the light of our methods this is not surprising.

One thing is clear from this analysis of job satisfaction. Those aspects which have emerged as important bear little relation to the orientations we have found to be dominant in the earlier analysis. The importance and preference scores are well related for both promotion and relations with management, suggesting definite orientations, and we shall see that there are other ways in which promotion and worthwhileness are important. However, there is nothing to suggest that they are major overall influences, other than in the limited sense that the importance of worthwhileness and promotion are significantly related to several preferences. The conclusion which seems most justified is that orientations do not determine which features of a job contribute most of job satisfaction, at least not directly. It appears that the main contributions come from those aspects which, within the frame of reference in which they are interpreted, have a general "good job" quality.

However, we have been looking only at the overall pattern and attempting to infer which features are more salient for the population as a whole. To take account of individual variation we need to measure actual salience for each individual, and here we turn again to the importance scores. We would expect that weighting each worker's satisfaction scores by the importance he attributes to the corresponding items would give the contributions to his overall job satisfaction. On this basis we would expect the sum of the weighted scores for each individual to correlate better than the unweighted sum with overall satisfaction and the other indicators used previously.

In fact, the improvement is extremely slight and requires the inclusion of all aspects. When only a limited number are included, on the principle of taking account only of dominant orientations, such as those ranked most important, the correlation is lower. Alternatively, we may use the weighted scores in a new version of the path regression model discussed above, in which case we would expect the salience of the different job features to have been accounted for in the weighting, so that all path coefficients are roughly the same. Instead, we find the pattern of relative contributions remains much the same, and is only a little bit more even. However, there are considerable methodological problems involved in such an analysis, some of which tend to underestimate the effect of weighting. Yet when we take account of the problems, the explanatory effect of using the importance scores is very limited.[21]

This consideration of contributions to overall satisfaction has done little to support the notion of orientations. The model of satisfaction in which different aspects contribute according to their salience, as measured by evaluation of importance, has not worked. It appears to favour the weak rather than the strong sense of orientations, but in a rather negative way. To some extent we believe the results are due to deficiencies in measuring salience in terms of abstract importance; it can hardly be independent of work experience and might be better understood in terms of priorities for marginal improvements in actual or expected conditions.

Satisfaction and Orientations

Probably more important is the nature of the relations between satisfaction and orientations. On the face of it, it seems entirely reasonable that orientations, in combination with actual rewards, should determine satisfaction. Orientations define the levels of expectations and salience for the rewards on each job aspect, while satisfaction on each aspect is a function of the expectations and rewards, contributing according to its salience. The problem lies in the concept of expectations. It will be useful to distinguish between "reasonable expectations" and "desired expectations" or "wants". The two are not independent because both are constrained within the frame of reference of what seems possible. However, the first is what is reasonable in relation to the available possibilities, and so what is fair, while the latter may entail the maximum possible. Our evidence suggests that the two cannot be very different for non-skilled workers, but that they are not the same. This may be illustrated by the two forms of orientation placing high salience on wages: alienated instrumentalism seeking reasonable wages for short hours, where the "wants" are minimum time at work, and economism seeking to maximise wages – the "wants" being high wages.

The narrower the frame of reference, that is the more the present situation is seen as natural and inevitable, the less scope is there for "wants" to differ from "reasonable expectations". Satisfaction is concerned essentially with what may reasonably be expected, with fairness rather than pleasure, and fairness in the restrictive context of "the way things are". This being so, the weighted addition is not really appropriate.[22] Insofar as satisfaction is a measure of fairness, the aspects contributing most to the overall evaluation are likely to be those of greatest generality, as we saw with the initial path models of Table 6.5.

THE EVIDENCE SO FAR

In this chapter we have concentrated on workers' attitudes, analysing the extent to which they maintain the same type of preferences and priorities across different frames of reference. There is limited evidence to support the idea that workers do have orientations which come into play in understanding and evaluating work experience from different perspectives. On the other hand, it seems rather doubtful if these can be interpreted in what we have called the strong sense, where a worker can be characterised by his dominant orientation. Indeed, there seems to be reason to doubt whether orientations can play a dominant role, either in workers' consciousness or in their actual behaviour.

However, it would be premature to draw any firm conclusions at this stage. Our measures are by no means perfect but they do appear to tap real orientations. We can, therefore, relate them to various aspects of the workers lives, to investigate further the questions of their existence and their nature while examining the part they play. This is the problem we take up in the next two chapters.

7 Orientations and Job Experience

We turn now to a consideration of the relevance of orientations in the general experience and action of the workers, looking at their influence and the forces that influence them. This involves examining the relationships between orientations in terms of our measures of preferences and salience, and of other variables relevant to work and outside lives. The first step is to analyse the relations with job characteristics to see if workers with certain orientations are actually in jobs congruent with those orientations. We must also ask if the orientations really are substantially independent of the work situation, or solely a response to it and so not truly "orientations" at all. This question is then pursued further in the next chapter in an analysis of relations with background characteristics, which serves to shed light on the origins of orientations and generally set them in a full social context.

CONGRUENCE AND INCONGRUENCE: ALTERNATIVE MODELS

If the orientations thesis is correct we would expect to find that workers have chosen jobs which are congruent with their orientations. We have already indicated that there are many obstacles to this, such as lack of knowledge, selection controlled by employers and a lack of fit between supply and demand for different types of work. Nevertheless, the workers are not totally without opportunity to choose, so we should expect to find some tendency. On the other hand, without the influence of orientations on job choice we would expect our measures to be randomly distributed in relation to job characteristics. Unfortunately, although this is certainly true in principle, in practice the position is rather more complicated.

The major factor complicating the situation is the worker's reaction to the actual rewards received from his job. One form of response to the work situation is contained in the "socialisation" thesis,[1] which also

179

leads to the congruent empirical outcome. In this case workers adjust to the situation of limited rewards and come to value those that are available. For example, highly paid workers in boring jobs may have chosen and remained in the jobs because of an economistic orientation, or they may give primacy to economic rewards because they have adjusted to a situation where the money is the only good thing about the job. These two possibilities will require other evidence to distinguish them. The socialisation theory implies that congruence will increase with length of service in a job, but a similar outcome may be observed as a result of those who make wrong job choices moving to new jobs and those whose choices are congruent with their orientations staying put. We would expect an observable difference in the degree of congruence for those who have just entered a job, but as the two theses are not necessarily complete alternatives, this may not be clear. Ultimately we must extend the analysis beyond work, to bring in relations with individual background and social characteristics.

A quite different way in which the work environment may have influence is for workers to want improvement in the worst features of the job. Thus priorities are given to the aspects of the work situation which are most depriving. In itself this would lead to incongruence. However, this sort of influence is not so different from the ones already considered as it might appear, nor is the observable consequence so clear-cut.

If, for example, we start with a neo-classical "rational man" model of job choice, we can formulate the two rival sets of hypotheses, predicting congruence or incongruence. We might first expect that workers have been able to find jobs congruent with the preferences they now express. But, secondly, with a more dynamic conception of preferences, we might expect that, although workers did initially select employment according to their then preferences, they have subsequently amended their preferences and are now seeking different rewards, rewards that are precisely the ones denied to them by their present job. However, the situation of incongruence predicted by the second set of hypotheses might be further modified by workers changing jobs to avoid undesirable aspects. If present preferences and priorities are entirely due to the present work situation, then the prediction of incongruence is unaffected, but if present work experience only modifies previous "orientations", there will be a movement towards congruence over time.

At this point, it is important to recognise that there are no absolute standards of high and low rewards. Thus deprivation is relative to some desired or expected level. The simplest version of the argument is that both wants and expectations are the same for everyone,[2] while a more sophisticated modification is that they vary by class position and so are the same for those in the same labour market. In this case, it is as though there were absolute standards. All would seek the same rewards and be competing for the "better" jobs. Priorities would be determined by the lowest relative rewards of the actual job done (unless we assume actual levels of rewards have no influence at all). This would produce the incongruent situation we have considered.

Even if the workers' wants and expectations are the same, the choice of present job may be determined by differential salience of rewards due to non-work factors, but for all except the most favourably placed the actual distribution of rewards in the job will lead to a marked shift of priorities. This applies even more strongly to job choice based on priorities arising from the previous job, since they become largely irrelevant after the change, giving only limited scope for reduction of incongruence. The socialisation process cannot influence wants and expectations, since on this interpretation these are fixed. It may, nevertheless, modify the salience of rewards. This means that those which are felt to be best catered for become regarded as more important, while the salience of deprivation on other rewards is devalued. This would produce a progressive change towards congruence with length of service.

The model becomes more complicated if we allow differential wants and expectations as well as differential salience. Deprivation, and on one hypothesis salience, will still depend on the gap between the actual and the expected or desired level of reward. However, this is no longer perfectly correlated to the actual level; where expectations are high and rewards low, for example, the deprivation is more acute, but if both are low it is less acute. Thus high salience will tend to accompany high expectations and low rewards, heightening incongruence. On the other hand, the pressures towards finding congruent jobs and the possibilities of doing so will be increased. Also, the levels of wants and expectations may be modified by work experience, both immediately and more permanently. "Orientations" need not be seen as arising solely from non-work life, but may also develop through experience of work.

If we think of a worker having certain orientations when he enters a particular job, then the job may be regarded as producing both negative and positive feedback. Negative feedback tends to heighten the salience of depriving aspects, producing instability; positive feedback to reinforce all elements of orientations through what we have referred to as socialisation, an adjustment to the constraints or possibilities of the situation.

It is not necessary at this point to elaborate all the ramifications of the possible sets of hypotheses. Sufficient indication of the main elements has been given for us to interpret the observed data. It can be seen that the frame of reference in which judgments of preference and priority are made is important. Also, the extent of actual job choice possible will influence the outcome for "orientations" hypotheses. In general, however, we may summarise the component elements of the various hypotheses as follows.

Prior orientations lead to selection of jobs where rewards are congruent with the workers' orientations; absence or irrelevance of such orientations leads to random distribution of the "orientations measures". Similarly, socialisation leads to progressive increase in congruence as length of time in the job increases (starting from randomness, other things being equal), while its absence results in randomness. Reaction to deprivation produces incongruence, particularly in the frame of reference of the workers' present situation. This may be modified, at least in a more general frame of reference, by workers moving away from particularly depriving situations, and may be less for workers in better jobs. The alternative is again randomness. In each case randomness may be replaced by the operation of a different influence.

JOB CHARACTERISTICS AND ORIENTATIONS

For job characteristics we have used once again our Objective Job Scores and the factors we derived from these scores, together with data on individual earnings and hours. All were explained, it will be remembered, in Chapter 3.

We used nine different measures of orientations. Six were the measures we used earlier, based on preference and importance data. In the earlier discussion we suggested that a composite measure including both sorts of data might be better than either separately. Accordingly, we constructed three such measures. The first is a strong measure of orientation based on the measures used previously. It was obtained by taking, for each item, those who gave it an importance score higher than for other items (as before, allowing for an individual to tie two such items) which was also at the top of the range (23 or 24, exceptionally high importance) and combining them with those who expressed a persistent preference on the item (preference mentions of four or more). The second measure was of the weak sort, producing a score on each item for every person rather than characterising individuals as having or not having particular orientations.[3] This was constructed by simply adding half the importance score to the preference score. The result was a set of scales with roughly normal distributions. For the third measure this was then converted into a strong form by taking only the top part of the scale, values 14 and over. For convenience we have simply labelled these types of composite measure CA, Cb and CC respectively, the use of capitals A and C and lower-case b reflecting the difference between strong and weak measures. These new measures were created for the ten items common to preference and importance data.[4]

This gave us five strong measures and four weak ones for ten job aspects, while for other aspects we had either one or two of each as before. If any are to be regarded as measures of orientations they should be related to objective characteristics of the workers' jobs. Accordingly, we want to see which, if any, are better related, in order to judge which are the better measures of orientations. This provides a basis for choosing between strong and weak measures. Also, it may give guidance on the relevance of frames of reference. In particular, since the composite measures combine responses from different frames of reference, if they emerge as better it supports the notion of orientations which persist across frames of reference.

Statistical Difficulties

At this point we have to decide how to measure the relationships. This is a common problem in social research, yet the discussion of appropriate statistics in the literature tends to be very inadequate. Therefore, we give a short account of the relevant features of some measures, to bring out their limitations and advantages. We confine ourselves to statistics available in the S.P.S.S. programmes, since it was convenient to use these and we are not aware of any better ones, but also because these are the most commonly used and so best understood.

Unfortunately, there are no completely satisfactory statistics to measure the strength of relationships for this sort of data. In addition to the general problem, this does create a difficulty in our attempts to *compare* relationships on the different measures. Ordinary product-moment correlations would be ideal and are reasonably appropriate for some of the measures, but the distributions on other measures make them unsuitable. Thus rank correlations are called for. Spearman's is probably the nearest to a product-moment coefficient but not too good with many ties. In this case tau B (Kendal's tau) is regarded as better, although the two are very closely related with the tau coefficient having a slightly lower value.

The problem with tau *B* is that it is sensitive to the distribution of ties on the two variables (i.e. the marginal distributions of a table), and can only attain the maximum of 1 when these distributions are the same. It is usual in statistics to treat data as though they really were "given", but in sociology this is rarely true, especially with the marginal distributions of tables. In this case the distributions are undoubtedly artefacts of the ways we have measured orientations and job characteristics, although differences between distributions may also in part be due to a lack of fit between orientations and objective opportunity which genuinely reduces the strength of association.

Tau *C* is designed to overcome part of the problem, where the number of scores differs between the two measures, that is, where the matrix is not square but rectangular.[5] However, the value now depends on the marginal distribution of the variable with less values, a maximum of 1 only being possible if all these marginal totals are equal. The effect is not great in large tables, but can be crucial in small ones. Since our strong measures of orientations necessarily have only two values, with a minority holding the orientations and many more not doing so, the tau *C* statistic is completely useless. In this case it is not difficult to calculate a standardised coefficient = tau *C*/tau *C* max., tau C max. being the maximum possible for the given marginals on the variable with less values.[6]

This is, in fact the statistic Somers *D*, or more precisely one value of it (See Somers, 1962). Somers *D* is asymmetric, having two different values according to which variable is taken as "dependent", and in this case the "dependent" variable is the one with more values.[7]

As an asymmetric measure it is sometimes interpreted as indicating the extent to which one variable predicts, or even causes the other (e.g. Garson, 1971). However, the data do not, of course, indicate causal direction; the prediction is purely an activity of the researcher, and it is actually the order of pairs on the "dependent" variable which is predicted. It is asymmetric because the data are asymmetric. With the same marginal totals on the two variables the two values of *D* coincide,[8] but otherwise it is always easier to predict in one direction than the other. For these sorts of reasons a symmetric statistic is often preferred, and there is such a version of *D* derived by using the arithmetic mean of the denominators (the numerators are the same). However, we have preferred the alternative procedure of taking the geometric mean of the two *D* values, which turns out to be our old friend tau *B*.

At the same time it is useful to retain the asymmetric version of *D*, particularly the larger value. It is interpretable not only in terms of asymmetrical prediction, e.g. quality of work rewards predicted from our dichotomous orientation measures, but also as a general measure of association, especially for rectangular tables, with the variable which has more values taken as "dependent", incorporating an adjustment for an aspect of marginal distributions which can be a major cause of distortion. We can conceive of no situation where Somers D would not be preferable to tau C, although the two do converge for large tables. In spite of the adjustment, it does not necessarily mean that D has an attainable maximum of 1, as this still depends on the distribution of the other variable. The problem is essentially the same as for tau B in square tables, except that on the variable with more values it is groupings of marginals which must have the same distribution as the marginals of the variable with less values. Because groupings are involved, the match between the marginal distributions is likely to be better than with tau B, especially where there is a large difference in the number of values on the two variables – the more rectangular the table the better the match – so the upper limit of D tends to be nearer 1.

In many ways the best statistic is gamma, which represents the improvement on chance in the probability of accurately predicting order in pairs on one variable from knowledge of the distribution of the other.[9] It takes no account of the number of ties, one consequence of which is to give it a higher absolute value than the other statistics. More importantly, this makes it independent of the marginal distributions, in the sense that, whatever these distributions are, it can attain the values $+1$ at the limits. However, its value within this range does tend to vary inversely with the number of different values on each variable. Thus it overcomes many of the weaknesses of other statistics but instead has the drawback that it tends to be larger in smaller tables.

It has, therefore, been necessary to take account of a variety of measures of association.[10] The three main ones we have used are tau B, D and gamma. To summarise the various points we set out the important properties of each. Tau B is higher the squarer the table and also the more the distributions on the two variables are similar. D tends to be higher the more rectangular the table, with the larger number of values on the "dependent" variable (although it can attain unity for a symmetrical square table), and it depends on the correspondence between the two marginal distributions, although this has less effect than with tau B. Gamma is higher the smaller the table. Both gamma and D are useful for comparing tables entailing strong orientations. When the orientations are both related to the same job aspect variable, or ones with the same number of values, gamma is probably slightly better, but otherwise *D* has the advantage. This discussion should have demonstrated most forcefully that each single statistic has its own peculiar artefactual aspect. For general descriptive purposes one is often sufficient, when we usually prefer gamma.[11] However, to rely on any one for comparative purposes would be to court danger, as may be seen from Table 7.1. In general, with tables of different size and shape we can only argue a stronger relationship in one rather than the other if all these statistics are higher.

As can readily be imagined, we performed a great number of tests in analysing these data. Altogether we used measures of 44 job features and related them to up to nine different orientation measures on 19 different job aspects in a variety of ways. It would be incredibly tedious to report everything we did. Instead, we shall simply outline the results, with enough supporting evidence to indicate the general pattern of analysis. We begin by looking at each orientation and corresponding job aspect. As well as looking for congruence between orientation and job, we also look to see if those with an orientation tend to be in better jobs, particularly in terms of pay and intrinsic rewards.

Outdoors

Let us start with outdoor work, which appears as the most likely orientation in the preference data, and is also an aspect where choice is possible, which is most visible in the labour market. With no corresponding importance data we are limited to a strong and a weak measure on preference frequency. As can be seen from Tables 7.1 and 7.2, those who express a preference for outside work are considerably more likely to be working outside, both in the sense that they are more exposed to the weather and in the sense that their work-site is more independent of management.

In view of the imperfections of the measures used, these relationships may be regarded as impressively strong, particularly that involving working away from the central site, as may be seen from the values of gamma, *D* and tau. Since working Outside, away from the central control, is closely associated with exposure to the weather, there could be some spurious correlation. The relationship between an outdoor preference and Exposure could be a result of the relation between the preference and Outside work, together with that between outside work and exposure. Accordingly, we controlled for outside work, with the result that the gamma for the preference-exposure relationship fell from 0.49 to 0.26 in the full table and from 0.67 to 0.47 with the strong persistent preference measure. We would expect some decline, and

Table 7.1 Outdoor preference by outside work

Outdoor	Outside *(Job Score 1):* % in each situation				
Preference frequency	In factory	At works site	Away	Total	N
0	71	17	12	100	559
1	53	27	20	100	133
2	37	24	39	100	70
3	20	31	49	100	49
4	22	27	51	100	37
5+	15	24	62	100	102
All	55	21	24	100	950

Weak measure: (full table)	tau = 0.40 D = 0.40 gamma = 0.58	Strong measure: (frequencies grouped 0–3, 4+)	tau = 0.34 D = 0.53 gamma = 0.71

Table 7.2 Outdoor Preference by Exposure

	Exposure *(Job Score 2):* % in each situation						
Outdoor Preference frequency	Indoors	Good Shelter	Moderate Shelter	Mixed Exposure	High Exposure	Total	N
0	51	21	8	7	12	100	559
1	37	23	8	13	19	100	133
2	23	23	10	17	27	100	70
3	6	33	14	16	31	100	49
4	8	19	8	22	43	100	37
5+	3	21	9	13	55	100	102
All	38	22	9	10	21	100	950

Weak measure: (full table)	tau = 0.35 D = 0.39 gamma = 0.49	Strong measure: (frequencies grouped 0–3, 4+)	tau = 0.32 D = 0.56 gamma = 0.67

although this is quite large it still leaves a substantial relationship. It is just conceivable that this is due to not taking account of gradations within the categories of the control variable, but it seems much more likely that the relationship is genuine. It seems that some workers are able to satisfy a real liking for working in the wind and the rain, or perhaps they are just optimists hoping for the sun!

It can be seen from the tables that the trend is continuous; the more mentions of outside work, the more likely they are to have outside jobs. The trend is not quite consistent in the middle values of Table 7.2. There is some tendency for the second and fourth degrees of exposure to weather to be mixed, which may reflect the relation between exposure and site location (e.g. van drivers are rated 2 on exposure), but the overall trend is clear. On the other hand, when we consider the strong, persistent preference measure of four or more mentions against the rest, we observe substantial relationships with gamma and D both appreciably higher while tau B is moderately lower. It seems that the relationships are comparable in each case, in spite of the loss of information of a trend over 0 to 3 mentions in the persistent preference measure.

In these circumstances it is not appropriate to be considering a choice between strong and weak forms of orientation. It appears that in a sense the weak form is correct, yet the relationships with the strong form are more than just a result of the general trend. However, this is really what we would expect if the high degree of congruence is due to orientations of the weak type. Individuals may have them to varying degrees, but this does not necessarily mean that they seek varying degrees of reward, such as degrees of exposure, except insofar as it results from trade-off with other job aspects. As expectations vary, they may seek differing levels of reward, but to the extent that a higher level of orientation means a greater priority given to a reward, more effort will be made to see that it is obtained. Thus at the higher levels there is greater concentration in situations of congruent reward – in this case outside work. The implication is that orientations are of the weak type, but the effects of higher priority are such that they are, in a sense, qualitatively different at higher levels. However, before giving too much weight to differences at higher levels we must see the patterns for other job aspects.

The foregoing account seems reasonable but certainly is not the only possibility. In the first place, the congruence may be due to a socialisation effect, as discussed earlier. We shall return to this point later. Limiting ourselves to explanations in terms of orientations for the present, it is still possible that the observed results are due to orientations of the strong type. Bearing in mind that a preference score is only an indicator of an orientation and that rewards – insofar as they tend to be congruent – may also serve as an indicator, we may hypothesise two latent classes; one comprising those with the orientation, who tend to make frequent mentions of preference and also to have jobs with corresponding rewards, and the other comprising those without, who tend to make few or no mentions and not be in the high-reward jobs. Because of the probabilistic nature of the data the two classes will overlap independently on the preference and reward scales, producing the observed continuous relationship.

To examine this possibility further we have used latent structure analysis (see Lazarsfeld and Henry, 1968). In particular, we have used latent class analysis, in which the sample is divided into latent classes (not to be confused with social classes) comprising people of distinct types. The analysis is based on the idea that *within each class* everyone has the same basic probability of scoring positively on an indicator, so that there is no pattern of association between indicators. Extraneous influences produce actual differences, but the distribution for each indicator is random within a class. Between classes there are differences, however, which produce overall associations between indicators. For this purpose the variables used as indicators are dichotomised, thus dividing the sample into those who do and those who do not have a particular characteristic. We took being in a job which is Outside or involves high Exposure to weather as two indicators of wanting such work, i.e. having an outdoor orientation, together with the more direct indicator of having an outdoor persistent preference. All three are well related to each other, but if there is an "outdoor" latent class, then within it there is no association but each member has a high probability of being in Outside work, etc. In practice we cannot usually determine which class a person is in. What we are able to do is first to test whether it is possible for latent classes to exist, and if so, to determine their sizes, the probabilities of a class member giving a positive response on each indicator, and the probabilities of people with different response patterns belonging to each class. These probabilities enable us to see how clearly the respondents are differentiated, and which indicators are most important.

From the three indicators used here we were able to identify two clearly distinguishable latent classes, which we can take as an "outdoor" class and an "indoor" class. At the extremes the probability of being in the outdoor class is 0.995 for those scoring positively on all three items and 0.015 for those scoring positively on none. The division comes between those scoring positively on two or on one; the most marginal cases are those scoring on exposure and persistent preference with a probability of 0.88, and those scoring on outside work alone where the probability of being in the outdoor class is 0.30. However, this shows up an important point, for it is not the persistent preference but outside work which most strongly defines the class: the combination of two indicators giving the lowest probability of inclusion is that without outside work, while the highest probability for an indicator on its own goes to outside work. There is an extremely high probability (0.82) of those with persistent preferences being included in the outdoor class, but this is because they are relatively few and they make up less than half the class, while the proportion of the class in jobs with each of the objective features is over 70 per cent. This being so, we need to reconsider our interpretation. It seems that, rather than the Objective Job Scores serving as indicators of an orientation, the persistent preference may serve as an indicator of outdoor work, giving a rather meaningless class – a statistical artefact. Thus in spite of finding two distinct latent classes, the result is inconclusive. Failure to find classes would have been good evidence in the reverse direction, but of the classes we found we can only say they are consistent with, but not necessarily evidence of, strong orientations.

An important question is the extent to which a job satisfying an outdoor orientation involves a trade-off with other rewards, and how far it reflects the general hierarchical structure we have found to exist in the labour market. This is, of course, vital to the ability of workers to choose according to their orientations. At the individual level the analysis would be very difficult but fortunately is not really necessary. We have already seen the general pattern of relationships between objective features (see Tables 3.1 and 3.3) showing some basis for choice. What we need now is to see what happens to those with outdoor orientations: do they tend to have jobs which are relatively good or bad on other aspects?

The answer is somewhat mixed. There is a clear trend for wages and hours to be poor and also for effort to be high, although the degree of association is not remarkable. Most marked is wages per hour (gamma = 0.21 weak, 0.40 strong).

On the other hand, there is some tendency for such workers to be in jobs involving more interest and skill, particularly the use of mental abilities. Also, working conditions are apt to be better. This is not because they are in jobs with good conditions, as they may have to put up with quite a lot of dirt and mud, but they do escape the extremes of unpleasant factory conditions, such as fumes, heat and, above all, noise. The undesirable features are more strongly associated with the strong persistent preference, while the attractions are better related to the weak measures and for the most part the relations with the strong measure are not significant. This suggests the operation of two trends, the general hierarchical market structure and the trade-off necessary to get outdoor work, which is more marked among those with the strongest orientations.

Thus we see that there is a substantial degree of congruence between outdoor orientations and the corresponding work rewards. In the generally hierarchical market this probably reflects as great a degree of choice as we might expect. Trade-offs were made to achieve the desired type of work, especially by those with the strongest orientations. We have not been able to settle the question of whether the orientation is of the strong or weak type. However, our results suggest that the weak type exists, but at the higher levels it becomes qualitatively different in its effects, thus making it fruitful to use the notion of a strong orientations as well.

Autonomy

One of the main aspects of outside work is autonomy, especially from supervision. It may, therefore, be expected that this is a major component of the preference for outdoor work. In line with this we note that the outdoor preference is positively related to the autonomy preference, although this is at a fairly low level and it is unrelated to evaluations of the importance of autonomy. The result is more striking when we relate the outdoor preference to the aspects of autonomy in the job itself; we find that not only is the congruence substantial, but it is greater than that for the direct measure of autonomy orientation, with perhaps one exception.

In Table 7.3 we present the strongest relationships of the orientations measures to the autonomy factor. The other autonomy orientation measures give somewhat lower relationships than the weak preference score though they are generally significant.[12] The remarkable result is the strong orientation "CC", which, it will be recalled, is derived by taking the upper range of the composite score "Cb". A degree of caution is needed in considering this result, since only 11 people have this strong orientation. However, they did tend to be in the high-autonomy jobs, while the trend over the rest of the "Cb" scale is quite weak. All had jobs with more than average autonomy, considerably more in most cases.

Those with an autonomy orientation might be expected to choose outdoor work for the sake of the autonomy involved. There is, however, only a very limited trend discernible in our data. On the other hand, those giving top priority to autonomy tended to work nights or very erratic hours, which provides another situation where management are rarely present and supervision is less strict.

Table 7.3   Relations of outdoor and autonomy orientations to autonomy in the job

	Association with autonomy factor		
Orientation measure	*gamma*	*tau B*	*D*
Outdoor preference (weak)	0.46	0.32	0.36
Outdoor persistent preference (strong)	0.61	0.28	0.51
Autonomy preference (weak)	0.22	0.10	0.17
Autonomy orientation 'CC' (strong)	0.70	0.10	0.57

Among those who expressed a preference for working out of doors, insofar as this entailed a desire for autonomy it was clearly being met in many cases by outside work. To a large extent, the relationship we have observed between this preference and autonomy in the actual job may be explained in this way. Thus if we control for Outside work in the relation with the general autonomy factor we find gamma drops from 0.46 to 0.16 (0.61 to 0.27 for the persistent preference), a rather more marked drop than we observed in relation to exposure to the weather. However, once again this does not completely remove the relationship. This can be seen more clearly by considering freedom from supervision which, as we would expect, is the aspect of autonomy most closely related to the outdoor preference, with gamma = 0.5. Controlling for outside work has the expected effect but still leaves a gamma of 0.22, which is slightly higher than that for the relation between the autonomy preference and this aspect of autonomy. It seems that the outdoor preference does indeed entail a desire for autonomy in many cases, which can sometimes be met in other ways than working outside.

We tested for latent classes again, but here we were able to use as indicators two orientation measures and one objective measure, that is preference, importance and the autonomy factor. There were not enough cases to use our normal persistent preference cut-off, so we dichotomised at a lower point on the preference score. We tried ranking first and maximum score as the high-importance measures, and we varied the cut-off on the autonomy factor. In view of the results of Table 7.3 we might have expected a small latent class of autonomy-oriented workers, but none could be derived. This strongly suggests that autonomy orientations in the strong sense do not exist or are too rare to emerge in our analysis.

We also used the relation of the outdoor preference to autonomy to explore further the nature of an outdoor class. We added the autonomy factor to the two outdoor work indicators and the outdoor persistent preference to see if, and in what way, an outdoor-autonomy class emerged. The data fell quite well into two distinct classes, but even more clearly than before it was the objective indicators, especially Outside work, which defined the class.

Just as the autonomy orientation is less well related than the outdoor orientation to corresponding job characteristics, so the relations with other objective features are lower. There is again some tendency for the orientation to be associated with low pay. The position with regard to hours is less clear, however. Shifts involving limited contact with management are not quite the same as inconvenient hours, and we find that the salience of autonomy is associated with inconvenient and short hours while the preference score is associated with longer and more convenient hours. The pattern of the outdoor preference is repeated for interest and skill, with the opportunity for a worker to use his mind again providing the strongest association. On the other hand, we find here a contrast with regard to the effort of the job, the autonomy orientation being relatively well related to low effort. In general, there is again a mixture of hierarchy and trade-off, although the relations either way are quite small.

Indoors

Not many expressed a preference for indoor work, and only two did so often enough to be regarded as having a persistent preference. However, the overall pattern is much as we would expect from the previous discussion. There is a clear tendency (gamma = 0.56) for those mentioning it to work inside (i.e. a low score on Outside), with 80 per cent in completely indoor jobs, mostly in the four firms providing factory work. In keeping with this they tend to be in jobs allowing them only a low degree of autonomy (gamma = −0.35), but the relation disappears completely when we control for whether they work indoors or outside.

As with the outdoor preference, the relation with exposure to the weather is somewhat weaker (gamma = −0.39) than with Outside work, and even those working indoors are not all in heated buildings. Nor is there any relationship with good working conditions. This is rather surprising, since in this case lack of autonomy can hardly be an attraction, so we might expect the greater comfort of working inside to be the prime consideration. It seems that what is important is just being indoors and working in one place.

Status

The only other particularly high degree of association involving preference scores is between those valuing work status and the Status Level, within the firm, of the jobs held. The level of the gamma here is 0.44 (with the "position in hierarchy" factor, gamma = 0.41). There were very few expressed preferences for status, only 126 mentioning it at all and of these 108 mentioning it no more than once. Nevertheless, there is a continuous trend whereby the more workers mentioned status the more likely they are to be in high-status jobs; all five of those expressing a preference three or more times are in jobs at the highest level, the proportion declining with the number of mentions down to only 13 per cent of those not mentioning status having jobs at this level. As we shall see (Chapter 8 and Table AIV.1), there is also a strong relationship with the worker's occupational status in the wider society, although it is not quite so clear as that with status within the firm.

Specific Job, Type of Work or Industry and Effort

The remaining preference scores which are unmatched by importance scores (and so cannot be used in composite measures) are all weakly but significantly related to corresponding features of the objective job situation. The highest relationship is between reference to a specific job and factors involving interest and skill in the job, particularly the use of mental abilities (gamma = 0.22). However, it will be recalled from Chapter 5 that this preference has been combined with the one for interesting work to form an "intrinsic job" preference, and we shall return to relations with these objective features when we discuss that preference and associated measures. At this point it is worth noting, in view of our earlier discussion of the meaning of the specific job preference (in Chapter 6), that there is also a weak positive relation with autonomy in the job, suggesting a further element of congruence. Those making reference to the type of work or industry are also slightly more likely to be in interesting jobs. Those expressing dislike of effort are a little more likely to be in jobs demanding relatively low effort. When we consider the 49 mentioning the type of work or industry four or more times, we find the relation with interesting work is reduced. There is nothing here to suggest a persistent preference representing a strong orientation. For other aspects, as with the indoor and status preferences considered above, there is hardly anyone who could be classed as having a persistent preference, but there is nevertheless a trend over the range of frequencies, suggesting an element of weak orientation.

Personal Suitability
There is a general tendency for references to personal suitability to be associated with having jobs which entail less responsibility and are rather less desirable in terms of their content. At the extreme, the 34 classed as having a persistent preference by mentioning this consideration four or more times are highly clustered in the jobs with low Responsibility. All but one are in jobs at the two lowest levels, but as these levels account for over 70 per cent of the jobs anyway, the relationship is not remarkable (gamma = 0.47 but $D = 0.25$ and tau 0.08). Nevertheless, when this is taken together with a tendency towards having less-interesting jobs, these men do seem to have a distinctive outlook in keeping with their work.

Worthwhileness
Turning now to those aspects where we have measures based only on the importance scores, worthwhileness and trade-union strength, we recall our interpretation in the previous chapter that both have rather general meanings. A worthwhile job, we argued, more or less meant a good job, particularly in terms of job content. On this basis there is a clear congruence between judgments of importance and the actual rewards of the job. There is a significant relationship with most aspects, the strongest being with "position in the firm's hierarchy" – itself a measure of goodness of a job – where a gamma = 0.2, and with intrinsic job content, particularly the use of mental abilities (gamma = 0.21). The only job factor not significantly related is promotion prospects, but this is not really surprising because of the decline in promotion possibilities with status achieved. There is a low but significant relation between the importance given to worthwhileness and wages per hour (gamma = 0.08), which is what we might expect, although the relation with wages per week is not quite significant, even at the 5 per cent level, and there is no relation with hours of work.

Turning for the moment from the objective measures to the workers' own assessments of whether their present jobs are worthwhile, we find a congruent relationship with the orientation (gamma = 0.24). It is interesting to note that among those saying their jobs are worthwhile the degree of congruence varies according to the types of reason given. The main division is between those reasons falling within our own more conventional frame of reference – socially useful or self-fulfilling – and

those within the more private frame of reference of the workers –
extrinsic, "keeps me from idleness", etc. – (see Table 6.6). Thirty-five
percent of the first group are among those rating worthwhileness highly
important, compared to 27 per cent of the latter and 23 per cent of those
who feel their jobs are not worthwhile. This is in keeping with our earlier
suggestion that the second type of reason reflects a view not greatly
different from that of work as inevitably not worthwhile.

On the whole, the best-related orientation measure is the straightforward importance score, which is used for the values of gamma quoted
above.[13] The strong form of this, taking those scoring maximum
importance, gives relations at a level which is similar but probably a little
lower. At any rate, there is no basis for preferring the strong form.

Trade-Union Strength
Since trade-union strength emerged as the item with the lowest mean
importance, and also appeared to make little or no direct contribution to
the level of job satisfaction (in contrast to worthwhileness), we would
not expect it to show up strongly in the present analysis. Indeed, this is
what we find. The importance attributed to it is weakly related to
promotion prospects (gamma = 0.12), which tells us little, and to low
opportunity to use mental abilities, a "bad job" characteristic such as we
might expect. There is no relation with other job factors or with wages
and hours. The significant relationships were obtained using the
importance scale directly; none of the relationships using the strong
measures is significant.

A different sort of work reward which is relevant here is provided by
the trade union. Unions were generally available and the majority of
workers were members in most firms. Overall, 88 per cent were
members, but even so we find a clear trend towards congruence between
importance and membership (gamma = 0.52). Holding union office
may also be seen as a congruent reward for those with "trade-union"
orientations, and again we find a positive relationship, which is hardly
reduced if we consider only union members (gamma = 0.48 and 0.44
respectively). This time the strong measures also give significant
relationships, but for membership they are definitely lower and
probably can be regarded as lower for office-holding as well. Although
we have established definite relationships, they provide less evidence of
the influence of orientations than it might seem, because of the
qualitative difference of these rewards from others we are considering.
While it seems likely that the congruence is partly due to choice in
accordance with orientations, it simply is not plausible that such

involvement in trade unionism does not influence the orientation. We shall discuss this later on.

Wages

We come now to the remaining nine aspects for which we have the full range of orientation measures (autonomy was discussed earlier). On the whole, pay has probably shown up as the most likely of these to be the basis of an orientation, so we begin with economistic orientations.

There is a clear pattern, with congruent relationships on all measures of orientation. However, it is not clear which is the best single measure. We have chosen to use the composite measure "Cb" and the corresponding "CC" as the weak and strong forms, although there is very little to choose between these and the preference measures, while those using importance ratings are only marginally worse.[14] Once again it is impossible to make a clear choice between the strong and weak forms, although the former seems to have a slight edge, as may be seen from the first two columns of Table 7.4 below. This is further supported by the tendency for CC to be better related to other variables, both those in the table and others we shall consider, such as length of service.

As with outside work, it seems that there is a stronger congruent relationship at the upper levels of the orientation scale, or possibly there are two classes. The data are not completely suitable for latent structure analysis because, as we shall see, there are reasons why high wages go to those without a congruent orientation. However, by using importance and preference scores and wages per hour as the indicators we can explore the possible structures.

Two classes emerge, with about 80 workers belonging to an economistic class, but the classes are not particularly well distinguished. The combination of all three indicators gives a probability of 0.87, but there are only 18 workers with this response pattern. High wages and a persistent preference without high importance has a probability of 0.69, but again it is an unusual pattern with only 17 respondents. For the combination of the persistent preference and high importance, which we would expect to relate well to an economistic orientation as it contains the two direct indicators, the probability is down to a problematic 0.45. High wages and high importance in combination does not belong in the class, with a probability of 0.21, just below that of the persistent preference on its own. The remaining three response patterns are strong predictors of membership of the non-economistic class. Given that two classes can, in principle, be found, the result is rather as we might expect,

Table 7.4 Relations of wages orientations to job rewards

Orientation		Wages/ week	Wages/ hour	Hours: length	Hours: convenience (J.S. 30)	Autonomy (factor 3)	General interest (factor 9)	Physical effort (factor 5)	Working conditions (factor 4)	Promotion† time (J.S. 23)
Weak 'Cb'	gamma	0.14	0.20	−0.11	−0.11	−0.19	−0.06	0.06	−0.08	−0.11
	tau B	0.10	0.16	−0.09	−0.08	−0.15	−0.05	0.04	−0.06	−0.07
	r	0.15	0.22	−0.13	−0.08	−0.19	−0.06	0.05*	−0.07	
Strong 'CC'	gamma	0.19	0.27	−0.16	−0.14	−0.33	−0.12	0.13	−0.15	−0.19
(215 workers)	tau B	0.10	0.15	−0.08	−0.07	−0.18	−0.07	0.08	−0.07	−0.08

† dichotomised between jobs available in 6 months and those requiring longer service.
* not significant at 5% level

with the measures serving as rather poor indicators of the economistic orientation. We shall return to this point presently.

Turning to the relationships with different rewards, we see from Table 7.4 that there are congruent relations with wages per week and wages per hour and that the orientation is associated with short hours. In all other respects the jobs of those with economistic orientations tend to be unattractive. They are more likely to entail working shifts at hours inconvenient for normal social and family life, working in bad conditions, doing jobs demanding high effort with little interest or autonomy. Whether orientations led the workers to choose these jobs or the orientations arise from adjustment to them, it is quite clear that these workers are in situations where there is a trade-off between economic and other rewards.

It is interesting to relate these findings to the previous studies which have dealt with this sort of orientation, Goldthorpe *et al.* (1968) and Ingham (1970). It was also the argument of the "Affluent Worker" research team that relatively "instrumentally minded" workers had chosen high-paying but unpleasant employment. Yet their own results appear to contradict the argument. The two sub-groups of their sample which stand out as the most "instrumental" are also quite clearly the ones in which workers tend to get the lowest take-home pay (Goldthorpe *et al.*, 1968: 161, 187). We are not given any data on the relation between these variables at the individual level, which could still be positive, but the relation at the group level strongly suggests it is negative, and thus contrary to the authors' entire argument.

However, the argument is not so easily dismissed. In the first place, the Affluent Worker sample were all relatively well paid and the argument seems to be that all, or nearly all, were relatively instrumental. Thus the test needs to be carried out over a more diverse sample,[15] and here we find that, even if theirs do not, our data do support their argument. Similarly, Ingham found economistic workers had a higher take-home pay, although, as we shall see, his data have a rather different pattern.

A second, important point emerges when we consider not just the weekly earnings but the hourly rate of pay. The two most instrumental groups of "affluent workers" in the Goldthorpe *et al.* study worked less overtime. Far from working long hours in an attempt to push up their earnings, as we might expect, their extra hours were often minimal. What this does suggest is that their lower pay was due to shorter hours rather than lower basic rates. Indeed, on the basis of the available data it seems highly probable that, at least for the more economistic of the instrumental groups – the car assemblers[16]– the basic rates were higher.[17] This is in line with our data, which show orientations have a substantially stronger relation with wages per hour than wages per week, and a tendency to go with shorter hours. Bearing in mind that the premium rates for overtime tend to make both hourly and weekly rates vary together with length of hours, we would expect an even stronger relationship with basic hourly rates. Furthermore, the higher earnings of the more economistically oriented workers are entirely due to their higher hourly rates. Controlling for wages per hour, the correlation between orientation (Cb) and wages per week falls from $+0.15$ to -0.02. All this suggests a strong element of what we earlier termed "alienated instrumentalism", where the worker seeks to maximise his income at minimum cost in terms of time given to work. However, it seems the workers are prepared to suffer some extra cost to their non-work life in terms of the inconvenience of their hours.

If our findings are in line with the Affluent Worker data on this point, it is worth noting that the workers studied by Ingham show up quite differently. Once again we are obliged to infer the relation at the individual level from the characteristics of groups. The three groups with the most economistic workers also had the highest average pay, which might suggest a comparable situation to that we observed in Peterborough, but it is not so simple. Ingham's groups are defined primarily by firms, the three economistic groups being located in two large firms while the rest were in low-paying small firms. There is thus a clear division into two types of firm, which accounts for the relationship, though we would hesitate to attribute it simply to size. In our data the largest firm, Perkins, pays the highest wages and has the most economistically oriented staff. Apart from this, however, there is little or no relation between size and orientation, and only a modest relation between size and average earnings.[18] Therefore, to take the analysis a step further it is useful to look for divisions within the size groups of the firms studied by Ingham. The information is not available to do this for the small firms, but we can look more closely at the large ones. Here we find the most economistic were semi-skilled workers in a mass-production car-component factory, while the order of the other two groups depends on the measure of economism used. These were groups of skilled and semi-skilled workers in the other firm, with a unit or small-batch system of production. Perhaps not surprisingly, the skilled men had the highest basic wages and actual take-home pay. The most economistic workers had the lowest rate but were able to take home more than the other semi-skilled group by working longer hours.

Thus we find the expected relationship between orientation and income appears not to exist in the work of Goldthorpe and his colleagues, although there may well be a relation with rates of pay. In Ingham's study the contrast between large and small firms gives a relationship of orientations with both gross earnings and basic rates, but within the large firms such relationship as there is depends on the number of hours worked. Among our Peterborough workers the relationship exists, but this time the higher gross earnings are a result of higher hourly rates. On the other hand, if we consider the firm with the most economistic workers in each study, all have similar technologies and are large. This suggests a greater congruence of orientations with these features than with pay. This, in turn, seems to imply a process of socialisation rather than job choice determining the distribution of orientations. However, this is again too simple. We need to take account of the choices open to these and other workers. These firms are similar also, largely because of technology, in providing the trade-off noted earlier between pay and disagreeable work. For some they may provide the best possible economic return. In this connection we may note that the workers who were better paid and less instrumental were more skilled in the studies by both Goldthorpe *et al.* and Ingham. The reason why the relation between orientation and earnings shows up less problematically in our data may be our more homogeneous, non-skilled sample, although neither workers nor jobs should be regarded as uniform (see Chapter 3 and Chapter 9). At any rate, this analysis serves to emphasise the dangers of too simple an explanation without adequate considerations of the market forces which may be involved.

One point, which may be clearly seen from Table 7.4, is that although the congruent relationships are substantial they are far from impressive. The strength of association is appreciably lower than we found when considering the outdoor orientation, and perhaps rather less than we might have expected. One reason for this may be seen in the last column of the table, which shows a tendency for those with economistic orientations to be in jobs available to those with less than six months service in the firm. This tendency is clearer for the strong CC measure, and the same is true of the other relationships we are about to consider. Thus it is useful to identify a group of economistic workers, regardless of whether their difference is one of degree or kind, and this we have done in the following analysis.

This is further supported by a latent class analysis. We added to the three variables previously used a fourth indicator – whether or not the job was available in six months after entering the firm. This again produced two classes, but with notably better discrimination between them than previously. Even so, however, the relation between response patterns and latent class membership is not particularly good. It certainly seems useful to think in terms of a class of economistic workers, but we must bear in mind that they may be less different from the others and less homogeneous than the two latent class model suggests.

The tendency for the economistic workers to be in jobs which are available to those with less than six months service is not particularly marked, but it reflects a more distinctive pattern. In the first place, they are not disproportionately concentrated in jobs immediately available on entering a firm but in those which involve a move after, say, a few weeks. The former tend to be low-paying jobs and are held by all sorts of newly recruited workers as well as by those who have been doing them for some time, including some older workers who have, in effect, been demoted. The economistic workers tend to be in the better-paying jobs of those requiring a short period before promotion (gamma = 0.35). Of those who had moved on to jobs requiring about six months to three years before promotion the tendency to be receiving higher pay is even stronger (gamma = 0.59), although there are less of them. Relatively few had moved into jobs requiring more than three years' service in the firm and the tendency for them to be in higher-paying jobs than their less economistic colleagues is much less, since most of these jobs pay relatively well.

It seems clear that the economistic workers are seeking high wages in jobs that are seen as available. Those that are available within a short time of entering a firm are visible opportunities for workers outside the firm. After being there for a few months they may move on to a better-paying job if the chance arises, or else they are likely to go elsewhere. This is borne out by the fact that economistic workers tend to have shorter service in their present firms (gamma = 0.25). They also tend to have entered their current jobs more recently, although this is less marked (gamma = 0.16) since job changes within a firm are less in the control of the workers and cannot so easily be part of a strategy. In keeping with these findings we may also note that the economistic workers had made more moves between firms (gamma = 0.21). All of these variables are, of course, related to age, but between age ranges there are different patterns. All the relationships are much stronger at younger ages. For instance, there is an extremely clear tendency among those under the age of 25 for the economistic to have been in more firms (gamma = 0.61); from 25 to 30 the tendency is rather less (0.35), picks up slightly in the early and middle 30s (0.42), then falls right away (0.16) and finally changes sign (-0.09, not significant) among those over 50. Similar, if less clear, trends occur for economistic workers' length of service in firms and jobs, particularly the change in the late 30s to early 40s.

Everything points to a process where economistic workers move around to find higher-paying jobs. However, we have seen that such a strategy is ultimately self-defeating because the best-paying jobs tend to be those requiring promotion through the internal labour market. That is, high wages are often only available after considerable time in the firm. Some find opportunities to advance to better jobs within a firm, and then stay put. For others the strategy of moving for higher pay becomes increasingly difficult because of employers' reluctance to take on workers who have had "too many" jobs, so they too come to move around less often. The net result is that the degree of congruence is not particularly great; economistic workers tend to be in jobs which pay more than the average but are rarely in the best-paying jobs. They make sacrifices in terms of the non-economic aspects of the job to get their high pay, while the jobs paying most are often more attractive in other ways as well.

Intrinsic Job Quality
Following wages, the next most important job feature as a basis of orientation is the intrinsic job quality. Essentially, this means the interest of the job. In asking about importance we aimed for a more general aspect of job content by referring to "interest, skill and effort", which may have resulted in slightly higher relationships with actual skill and effort (negative), although interest is the dominant element. Similarly, our preference score is closely related to interest but has a rather wider meaning, especially as we added in the references to a specific job to form what we have called the "intrinsic job" preference.[19] Thus although the two types of measure have slightly different references, they can both be taken as indicators of intrinsic job quality, and they have very similar patterns of relationships with other variables.

As with wages and autonomy, we tested for latent classes using as indicators the importance and preference data together with a measure of actual rewards, which in this case was the opportunity to use mental abilities (see below). It emerged that there are no latent classes which these data can fit. This then must be taken as a powerful indication that there is no strong "intrinsic" orientation.

In line with this we find that the best single orientation measure is the composite weak form Cb, which, it will be recalled, is a weighted sum of the importance and preference scores. Of the strong forms, the high-importance and persistent preference measures are each better than their composite, with the former having a slight edge. Table 7.5 shows relationships with selected variables.

The strongest relationship is with the extent to which the job gives a worker an opportunity to use his mind. This is closely followed by the general interest of the job, as represented by our summary factor covering mental abilities, skill and variety. We might have expected this general factor to be better related, as it corresponds most closely to the content of the orientations (and its components all relate positively to the orientations), but it seems that the mental aspects of the job are crucial. The skill involved is less-well related, although the general-abilities factor, encompassing mental components as well, is almost as well related as the general-interest factor. The variety of parts, tools, controls and so on which are used in the job is quite well related, and length of work cycle (not shown) is also related, although at a rather lower level (gamma = 0.15 weak; 0.09 strong, which is not significant at the 5 per cent level). However, whatever the levels, all of these associations are congruent.

It is notable that the orientation is associated only with desirable job characteristics. In addition to the corresponding features which we have already discussed, we see from Table 7.5 that there is also an association with autonomy, low effort, good conditions and the general "good job" feature of hierarchical position. Also, there are relations with high hourly wages and short hours, although they are only significant when orientations are measured by preference scores. This is probably not an indication that we are dealing with a "good job" orientation, but rather a reflection of the hierarchical nature of the market. Those jobs with higher intrinsic quality are also likely to be more attractive in other respects. So if a worker is in a job in keeping with a desire for interest and so on, it is likely to be a good job generally. This, in turn, makes it difficult for a worker to have and act on a strong intrinsic job orientation.

One of the major obstacles to acting on this orientation is the existence of the internal labour market. We saw in Chapter 4 that jobs in the internal market, as defined by requiring at least six months service in the firm, are very much more attractive in terms of intrinsic quality. Thus, if workers are seeking this sort of reward they must stay put, and this is the strategy most had followed, so that they tended to be in the jobs requiring longer service in the firm. They had not worked for a significantly lower number of firms however, which suggests that they move between firms until an opening presents itself. In keeping with this,

Table 7.5 Relations of intrinsic job orientations to job rewards

Orientation		Mental abilities (factor 1)	Skill (factor 2)	Object variety (J.S. 10)	General interest (factor 9)	Autonomy (factor 3)	Effort (factor 5)	Working conditions (factor 4)	Position in hierarchy (factor 6)
Weak: Cb	gamma	0.24	0.17	0.22	0.24	0.11	−0.14	0.14	0.19
	tau B	0.20	0.13	0.17	0.19	0.09	−0.11	0.11	0.15
	r	0.26	0.15	0.20	0.23	0.11	−0.13	0.11	0.18
Strong: importance	gamma	0.26	0.16	0.23	0.24	0.10*	−0.11	0.20	0.22
(156 workers)	tau B	0.13	0.08	0.11	0.11	0.05*	−0.05	0.09	0.10

* Not significant at the 5% level.

we find a clear tendency for those with stronger intrinsic orientations who are in jobs requiring six months' to three years' service (as well as those requiring less time) to be in the more intrinsically rewarding jobs. There is no such tendency among those in the jobs which are only attainable after more than three years in a firm, but these are nearly all among the most desirable jobs. Workers achieve jobs congruent with their orientations both by making choices in the early period with a firm and also by staying on. However, the competition for the generally more desirable jobs, coupled with the fact that movement in the internal market is essentially controlled by the employer, puts a considerable limitation on the workers' ability to find jobs with relatively high intrinsic rewards.

We took the length of service necessary to obtain the job currently held as another indicator of an intrinsic quality orientation, and again looked for latent classes. This time, with suitably chosen cutting points, we did find two classes, although they were not well distinguished and seemed to reflect the fact that more intrinsically rewarding jobs require longer service, rather than the existence of strong orientations. While compatible with a number of workers having strong orientations, we would not regard it is persuasive evidence.

Promotion

It will be recalled that the possibility of promotion is more or less restricted to quite small improvements within the range of non-skilled work. Not surprisingly, few people mentioned promotion prospects or rated them as highly salient, and in this sense it is not an important orientation. On the other hand, we have found some reason to believe it may be important for a small number of workers, or it may have influence at a fairly low level for many workers. In the latter case, and possibly in the former as well, it is likely to be a "good job" orientation, based on the logic that promotion tends to increase all rewards.

In testing for congruence we have two different types of rewards, promotion prospects and promotion attained, as reflected by "hierarchical position". The latter is congruent at a moderate level, correlation with the weak-orientation "Cb" form giving $r = 0.18$, while the strong and weak importance measures give slightly higher relations. The relation with "promotion opportunities" is also in the congruent direction, but on most measures is too low to be significant.

We have noted before that, because of the limited chances of promotion out of the range of jobs covered, prospects and attainment are negatively related. Accordingly, we controlled for each when examining the relation of the other to orientations. In the case of promotion opportunities the control for hierarchical position had a modest effect in the expected direction, producing low but significant relationships. For instance, the correlation with "Cb" increased from the non-significant $r = 0.05$ to $r = 0.07$, which is significant. Thus allowing for the effects of past promotion produces a congruent association between orientations and promotion opportunities. The position is not so clear for attainment with control for prospects; the partial correlation is very slightly higher but the partial gammas tend to be lower, although the relationship remains significant. In any case, it is reasonable to think of hierarchical position determining promotion chances and not vice versa, so if we assume a model where orientations lead to attainment and prospects, it is only meaningful to control for hierarchical position.

Since age is closely related to promotion we also controlled for its effect. In keeping with the foregoing analysis we found that the relation between promotion orientation and level attained increased strongly with age, while the relation with promotion opportunities was stronger in the younger age groups, particularly among those in their early 30s. Not surprisingly, the orientation itself tends to decline with age, so that controlling for age increased the relation with attainment and decreased the relation with prospects. It seems that concern with promotion varies with the chances available but also leads to its attainment.

There are too few cases of people classed as having strong orientations to allow a comparison between strong and weak measures. However, we were able to carry out two latent class analyses, using the preference and importance data as usual (using a dichotomy on the preference data between those who mentioned promotion at all and those who did not) and the two objective indicators, prospects and attainment. For promotion prospects we identified a small class of about 18 people, confined essentially to those scoring positively on all three indicators. There do appear to be a few workers with a positive concern about promotion prospects. On the other hand, we could not identify a class when we used hierarchical position. It seems that the congruent relation here is with a weak orientation, which probably reflects the desire for a "good job".

Since hierarchical position is itself an indicator of other desirable job features, we would expect these features to be positively related to the promotion orientation. This is roughly what we find, although the interest and skill aspects are more strongly related than we would expect on the basis of the hierarchical relation alone. This is particularly so for the opportunity for a worker to use his mind ($r = 0.22$), which was also the aspect most closely associated with the intrinsic job orientation. Wages and good working conditions are also positively related, but there is a slight tendency towards low autonomy.

The overall picture is not entirely clear but is probably best summarised as follows. At any one time a small section of workers (under 2 per cent in our estimate) are positively concerned about promotion. These are men at a stage when some degree of promotion is a significant possibility. More generally, and especially for those who have attained the desired promotion, the orientation becomes a concern for a relatively good job.

Working Conditions

In terms of the frequency of preference mentions, working conditions appeared as an important potential orientation, but we found no significant relationship with the salience measure to support this. The relations with objective job features tend to confirm the pattern. Neither the importance- nor the preference-based measures show any relationship with the working-conditions job factor. This is clearly the most relevant variable for testing congruence, and reveals neither congruence nor incongruence on any measure.

The preference measures are not related to anything, except for a weak positive relation (gamma $= 0.18$, tau $B = 0.06$) between the strong persistent preference and exposure to the weather, which may be regarded as a second aspect of conditions (unrelated to the working-conditions factor). In fact, the relation is curvilinear, with the 69 who expressed such a persistent preference being in jobs with either low or high exposure, but primarily high. This incongruent relation is matched by congruent ones of similar low degree for the importance measures. It seemed that this result might be the effect of outdoor preferences, but control for this tended to increase the contrast slightly. Thus it is difficult to interpret the positive relationship between preferences and exposure. Are the men wanting healthy open-air work, or are they reacting against more exposure than they want?

The importance scores also relate positively to the "good job" characteristics. There are associations in the desirable direction, albeit at a low level, with the various interest and skill factors, wages per week and (more clearly) per hour, hours and position in the firm's hierarchy. In addition, as we have just seen, these orientation measures have the same sort of association with exposure.

In view of the foregoing results it is not surprising that there is no latent class. We used the conditions factor and exposure to the weather, separately and in combination, together with the two direct measures of orientation (including the ranking of importance), but to no avail. There is no basis for supposing strong orientations and very little to suggest weak ones. It seems that the frequency with which workers refer to working conditions in weighing up jobs in different firms bears no relation to the importance they attach to conditions in a more general frame of reference, and neither bears much relation to the actual conditions of the job they are in.

Hours

It will be recalled that, as with working conditions, we found no relation between the salience and preference measures of orientations concerning hours. This shows up again in the relations with actual job characteristics, but here there is a definite element of congruence. Those making frequent references to hours in relation to the hypothetical job choices (preference data) are in jobs with relatively convenient hours, mostly working days, but there is no tendency for them to work shorter hours. On the other hand, those rating hours as highly important tend to work shorter hours, but not more convenient ones. It is not clear why the questions, employing different methods and entailing different frames of reference, should tap orientations of the two distinct types, but this appears to be what has happened.

In both cases it is the strong measure which is best related to the corresponding aspect of hours. In view of the low levels of relationship, however, it may simply be that only at the extremes is any effect going to be apparent. Indeed, this is strongly supported by the absence of a latent class, whether we use length and convenience separately or in the same analysis.[20]

Once again we found the orientations are rather better related to "good job" characteristics. The importance measures are significantly though weakly related to hierarchical position, wages and intrinsic job aspects. The one exception is a slight tendency for autonomy to be low. This "good job" relationship is somewhat surprising, since hours of work was not found to be a particularly hierarchical job reward, i.e. short hours are not generally associated with other desirable features.

Management quality

We come now to a number of orientations which do not have directly corresponding job characteristics, or at least not ones which we were able to measure. On the whole, they relate to firms rather than jobs, allowing us far less scope for comparisons. Consequently, our judgments of congruence are rather imprecise and impressionistic.

We start with management quality, based on the importance of "how you get on with management" and references in the preference data to the firm in general, labour relations or relations with management. The best weak measure is the composite Cb, but it is not clear which is the best strong form. Nor is it clear whether a strong or weak form is preferable, and there is no way to explore this through latent classes.

The only job characteristic we measured which might be thought of as entailing relations with management is closeness of supervision, and we find a slight tendency for the orientations to be associated with low supervisory contact. However, this may be just an aspect of autonomy in general, which tends to be a little better related. The orientation is also associated, at a low level, with other job content rewards, especially the chance to use one's mind, and with good working conditions, low effort and high status. There is, however, no tendency towards better pay or hours. Thus there is a small tendency towards a good job in terms of the job itself, although not in terms of economic rewards, which may be regarded as a sort of congruence.

It is not possible to measure the quality of management in the different firms, but we can devise a rough order by taking account of such things as security, fringe benefits, notably good or poor labour relations, and general reputation among workers. On this basis there is a rough sort of congruence between the extent of orientations in the firms and the ordering of firms, although it is certainly not perfect.

Security

As we might expect, the security orientation tends to be associated with having a good job, which it is probably fair to regard as a sort of congruence. Status in the firm, wages and hours, effort and skill all fit this pattern. This time the general-interest factor is better related than the use of mental abilities, unlike orientations considered previously. Relations are low, the correlation between the Cb measure and the "position in hierarchy" factor being $r = 0.17$, with slightly lower levels for other aspects, but the association seems to be with good job features in a very general way.

We also find a tendency for the security-minded to be further removed from the labour market in that they are more often in jobs which require longer previous service in the firm. While representing a form of congruence itself, this also raises the question of whether their higher attainment is really a result of their age and length of service.

We examined this, using hierarchical position and wages per hour as the measures of good jobs, together with the length of service needed to attain the job. Both orientations and rewards tend to increase and then decline with age, and both tend to increase progressively with length of service. Nevertheless, controlling for age and length of service has very little effect; the congruent relationships are not dependent on these variables.

We attempted to rank the firms by security on the basis of the data collected in the first stage of the research, prior to the interviews. We used information on redundancy, short-time working, policy on keeping workers on the payroll when ill, and so on. This should have given us a better basis for judgment than is readily available to the workers. Subsequent experience showed us to be moderately accurate, but there were some developments which neither we nor the workers could easily have predicted. Accordingly, it seems more meaningful to use our original assessment as the "objective" base, rather than to be wise after the event, and it probably does relate better to the workers' orientations.

There is a rough degree of congruence. In each firm there are some with a high level of concern for security, but they do tend to be in the firms offering greater security. In the two firms we rated lowest on security – the building firm and the food firm which subsequently closed down – the level of security-mindedness was especially low. At higher levels there is one particular exception. The local authority, which on our estimates offered most security, was fairly low in terms of the proportion with a security orientation. Overall, the evidence points to a modest tendency for workers with stronger security orientations to be in more secure employment.

Fringe Benefits
Fringe benefits were mentioned by few people in the preference data, and they emerged as being of low importance in the analysis of the last chapter, but there is at least a significant association between the preference and importance measures. It is not surprising, therefore, that we find some association with the objective situation but of a fairly limited sort.

With so few mentioning fringe benefits our measures do not allow an effective comparison between strong and weak orientations. There are enough scoring the maximum on importance, but the importance measures are the least related to job features. On the other hand, the best version of a strong orientation is the *CC* measure which identifies a mere six men, although they do all seem to have a definite interest in fringe benefits. Perhaps the situation is best summed up by the fact that instead of the usual persistent preferences, we divided the preference data to obtain a group of 16 men who mentioned fringe benefits more than once, and this gave quite good relationships. Mentioning an aspect of work more than once can hardly be regarded as defining a strong orientation! Rather, it seems to be a matter of identifying those for whom fringe benefits are relatively important.

Fringe benefit orientations are significantly associated with the good job features of "hierarchical position", "general interest" and autonomy. The six workers identified on the CC measure tend to be top on these variables (gamma = 0.55, 0.71, 0.79 respectively), while the preference scores relate equally well on the last two and also go with low effort (gamma = 0.56). In addition, there is a slight tendency to shorter hours (significant only on weak measures) but wages appear to be slightly lower.

The crucial question, however, is how the orientations are distributed between firms. Here we find a definite trend for those scoring highly on the various orientation measures to be in firms offering better fringe benefits. In general, there is a clear if hardly outstanding element of congruence.

Workpeople
Finally, we come to orientations concerning other people encountered at work. It will be recalled that the friendliness of other workers was rated the most satisfactory job aspect. It was also rated highly on importance, but workpeople were not mentioned particularly often in the hypothetical job choices, and the relation between the two measures is barely significant. This is not surprising, as workmates may be relevant in considering leaving a job but can hardly contribute towards the choice of a new one, and where workpeople were mentioned in the preference data it tended to be with unfavourable reference to types of workers (e.g. women, coloured) who might serve as a guide to job quality.

We find a slight tendency for both types of measure (and the composites) to be associated with the good job features of status, interest and working conditions. However, only the importance measures are related to earnings, and the relation is negative.

The one job feature which might be regarded as corresponding to the orientation is the freedom to interact with other people while at work. There is a tendency for this to be a feature of the job for those who ranked workmates first on importance, but there is no relation with any other measure. However, if relations with other people at work are a reason for job attachment rather than job choice, we would expect a positive relation with length of service, which we do find at a very low level. Thus there is some evidence of congruence, but the relationships are not adequate to make useful comparisons between the various measures of orientation.

LENGTH OF SERVICE

We have already looked at the influence of length of service in examining some of the items. We now want to consider it directly for the light it can throw on the meaning of the congruent relations we have found. The basic question is whether the congruence is due to orientations operating through job choice or what we have termed socialisation – the adjustment of "orientations" to match what is available.

We begin with a consideration of the outdoor preference, which provides the highest level of congruence. Whether we use congruence with outside work or with exposure to the weather the result is much the same. Congruence starts at a fairly high level, increases slightly for those with a year or two's service, and then falls off somewhat among long-service workers. For example, in the relation with outside work gamma = 0.57 for those with less than a year in the firm, rises to over 0.60 and fluctuates a little, with a highest value of 0.68, then falls after 12 years service, down to a gamma of only 0.15 for those who have been in the firm more than 24 years. For exposure the decline is less marked, the initial, peak and long-service gammas being 0.49, 0.66, 0.21, respectively. The only differences when the degrees of congruence are related to service in the particular job rather than the firm is that the congruence starts a little lower and declines rather less with longer service. This suggests that workers choose and change jobs on the basis of congruence; there appears to be a fair measure of congruence when workers enter jobs, which increases as the dissatisfied leave. The decline with longer service is not compatible with a socialisation effect. Rather it suggests that jobs have been changed because of promotion or of lower resistance to bad weather with increasing age, or alternatively that the workers would now like to be able to change jobs but have not been able to do so. The decline with long service in the job also suggests a change of orientation over time.

Another way of looking at the problem is to compare the degrees of congruence for a short period in the firm and for the same period in a particular job. Within, say, 18 months of joining the firm quite a few change jobs, while many of those who have been in their present jobs for less than 18 months have been rather longer in the firm. Thus for a given period in the firm, compared with that period in the present job, we would expect lower average time in the job, and therefore less time for adjustment to influences from the job or from the firm. Therefore, according to the socialisation hypothesis we would expect lower congruence. On the other hand, if job choice increases congruence, the more recent changes of job, and especially the recent changes of firm in which workers have more control than in changes within firms, would lead us to predict higher congruence. This is what we do find. For example, gamma = 0.62 and 0.51 for the relation with outside work among those with less than 18 months service in the firm and the job, respectively. For shorter service the difference appears rather more marked (0.71 and 0.47 for less than six months),[21] in keeping with the hypothesis of choice based on orientations.

The other job aspect with a sufficiently clear and common orientation to allow us to undertake this sort of analysis with some confidence is wages. When we turn to this aspect we find essentially the same pattern. Congruence starts at about the average level, first increases with service and then falls back among long-service workers.[22] This drop in congruence – down, in fact, to zero – is more than we found for the outdoor orientation, but need not surprise us; it is largely due to the effects of age in relation to both family commitments and the internal labour market. Again, we find higher congruence for a short period in the firm than for the same period in the job. While the data on other aspects of the job are less reliable for analysis which breaks the sample down in this way, they do lend support to the argument.

JOB ATTACHMENT

As a final check we looked at the relation between attachment to present job and congruence of orientations with rewards. Attachment was measured in reverse by responses to the question, "Are you thinking of changing your job in the near future?" We have used two levels of positive response: "weighing it up" and some positive action taken such as a visit to the employment exchange or an actual application for another job. At the other extreme we took a definite "no" as showing greater attachment to the present job than a "don't know" response. However, it is not certain that this is correct, as a definite answer may imply some serious consideration, and thus less attachment, than the response of the man who has just not thought about it. We shall see that the latter interpretation does seem to fit our data better.

In Table 7.6 we present the coefficients of association (gamma) between selected orientations and the corresponding rewards, for those giving each type of response. Since over 80 per cent answered "no" the numbers giving each of the other responses are quite small, creating some problem of the reliability of the coefficients; it will be seen that even with the more common orientations presented here the coefficients are not always significant, although the general pattern is clear enough. We have chosen to use strong measures of orientations where they are appropriate, as they show the trends a little more clearly, but in all cases both sorts of measure give very similar patterns. For the intrinsic job orientations the weak measure is more reliable, but it should be recalled that the gamma coefficients are artifically low relative to those for strong measures (an increase of a little over 20 per cent would make the overall figure comparable).

Table 7.6 Congruence† between orientations and rewards by attachment to present job

Orientation and reward	Thinking of chang-ing job No	Don't Know	Weighing up	Action taken	Total sample
Outdoor (strong)					
– outside work	0.75	0.90	0.54	0.17*	0.71
Economism (strong)					
– wages/hour	0.32	0.10*	0.12*	0.04*	0.28
Intrinsic (weak)					
– mental abilities	0.24	0.37	0.23	0.06*	0.23
Promotion (strong)					
– status	0.32	0.88	– 0.68	0.01*	0.25
Promotion (strong)					
– prospects	0.02*	0.33*	0.21*	0.83	0.07*
N	766	54	63	63	946

† Congruence is measured by conditional gamma coefficients
* Not significant at 5 % level.

To begin with let us consider only the first four rows of the table, as the fifth is quite different. The most striking thing is the extremely low level of coefficients among those who have taken some sort of action towards changing jobs. In two cases the association is negative, and would also be negative for the intrinsic orientation if we used the strong measure; all are too low to be significant.

At the other end of the attachment scale, the congruence among those who said they were not thinking of changing their jobs is higher than for the whole sample (the differences are only small because the group is most of the sample). In three cases the congruence is higher still among those answering "don't know". The exception is the non-significant low coefficient for economism which breaks the general pattern. It might be that with a larger sample the first two columns would converge, but on the face of it the "don't know" response seems to have the highest congruence. Those weighing up the prospect of a job change have lower congruence, remarkably so on promotion.

Ideally it might have been better to reverse the approach and look at attachment for different degrees of congruence, but that would have entailed excessive technical difficulties. As it is, we have quite a clear pattern of congruence varying inversely with attachment. Those thinking most seriously of leaving showed least congruence. However, we should note that it is not simply a case of incongruence providing the impetus. Essentially, the relations of orientations to rewards are random for this group, suggesting there are also other factors at work. It could be argued that among those who are not inclined to move the congruence is a result of rationalisation, but it seems more likely that the attachment is due to orientations being met.

What then are we to make of the deviant fifth row of Table 7.6? Although the figures are not particularly reliable they do appear to follow exactly the reverse of the main pattern we have found. Congruence is high among those who had taken some action, more or less zero among those answering "no" (which may be regarded as a reliable estimate, the lack of significance simply reflecting lack of association) and negative for the "don't know" group. The other four rows, including promotion and status, related to congruence between orientations and rewards attained. This is rather different as the prospects refer to a possible change of job – rewards to come in the future. Those with promotion orientations tend to show less attachment than the rest. It seems, then, likely that the job changes considered by those with positive orientations and good prospects are actually promotions. Indeed, while no other explanation suggests itself, this makes good sense when we consider together the two types of rewards, status and prospects, relevant to a promotion orientation. It gives further support to the argument that orientations in conjunction with the actual rewards tend to determine the degree of attachment to the job.

ORIENTATIONS AND JOBS

Our analysis of congruence between the orientations measures and job characteristics has produced the strongest support so far for the existence of orientations which influence job choice. In all cases but one we found some degree of congruence and no evidence of incongruence. Thus with considerable confidence we can reject the hypothesis that preferences and priorities are a response to the depriving aspects of the worker's present situation. The choice between the socialisation and orientations hypotheses is less clear-cut, as both predict congruence. However, although we cannot completely reject the former as having no influence, the weight of evidence indicates not only that orientations exist but also that they have greater influence. Since our preference measures are based not on attitudes to the present firm but to other firms, this is what we might expect once we had established that they were meaningful measures. Nevertheless, it is important to see that the explanations in terms of orientations make sense of many details of the relationships of the preference and salience measures with the objective job features.

In many cases the composite measures are better related to work features than their components, suggesting that orientations do carry across different frames of reference. This gives further support, then, to the notion of orientations which are in some degree independent of the present work situation.

There was more support than in any of our earlier analysis for the idea of strong orientations, which are dominant and so characterise individuals. We found three latent classes (or just possibly four) which might be groups of workers distinguished from the rest by possession of orientations in this sense, two of them involving the two clearest orientations — outdoors and wages. However, the evidence is not conclusive, while for most aspects no latent classes are identifiable. Similarly, there are several aspects where the strong form seemed to give better relationships with the actual job characteristics, but most are unclear and in a few cases the weak form seems better. We suggest the correct interpretation is that orientations are essentially of the weak form, which individuals may hold in varying degrees. However, as the degree increases it becomes more dominant in relation to other orientations and other factors, so that its influence increases disproportionately. In this sense it may be useful to distinguish people at the upper levels, as though they had orientations of the strong type.

In spite of the evidence to show that orientations are relevant, we cannot get away from the fact that in general the levels of congruence are low. We have been able to see to some extent why this is. There are other influences which tend to limit the extent to which workers are located in jobs which meet their expectations and priorities. Indeed, it would be rather surprising if we found notably higher levels of association in view of all the inherent difficulties arising from the structure of the market, which we have previously noted. It is significant that we do find this element of positive choice, although the increase of congruence over time among the younger workers suggests that the choice is exercised quite considerably by a trial-and-error process.

8 Orientations and Social Background

So far we have established the existence of orientations, and argued that they are not just a product of experience in the present job. The question which now arises is, "Where do the orientations come from?" The answer to this question may be sought in the social backgrounds of the workers. If it can be shown that orientations are influenced by aspects of an individual's social background, we may conclude with considerable confidence that they do have an existence transcending the immediate situation, and so can have a real influence on job choice.

There is, of course, no neat division between work and non-work life; they are both part of the totality of a person's social experience. In particular, work and market situations are fundamental aspects of location in the class structure, and so basic to life chances and the whole of social experience. It would, therefore, be quite extraordinary if work did not have a bearing on the development of orientations. Accordingly, our notion of social background embraces both work and non-work characteristics.

There are a great many potentially relevant variables to consider, and of those we covered almost all are significantly related to several orientations. Because there are many background factors related to each orientation, we would not expect the degree of association of any one to be particularly high, and for the most part this is the case. However, we cannot simply assume the effects are additive, since the background factors are themselves interrelated, so their influences overlap. If an interval level of measurement were available some form of multiple regression, such as path analysis, would be useful, but as it is we can only take variables separately (or with control for a second) and look for patterns. It means that we cannot make any estimate of the adequacy of the complete explanation but only of the relevance of the separate variables. However, this is less of a drawback then it might appear, as our primary concern is not so much to look at prior (non-work) causes as to identify patterns of social and individual characteristics associated with the different orientations.

In Table A IV.1 of Appendix IV we present a summary of the different characteristics associated with each orientation. This provides, in a compact form, a great deal of detailed information about the orientations, which we shall not repeat in the text, apart from drawing out one or two points. We shall then go on to discuss the various background factors to identify their patterns of influence. This does, of course, use the same information as is contained in Table A IV.1, but the structure of presentation is quite different.

There are a substantial number of factors associated with each orientation. While they do not form neatly coherent and distinct clusters there are some discernible trends. Thus different sets of factors are related to the outdoor and indoor orientations. On the other hand, there is a fair degree of similarity between the non-work factors associated with the outdoor and autonomy orientations, as we would expect. These two orientations differ in that workers with the latter orientation are more urban and their social life centres around friends and clubs rather than relatives, while the relationships with work factors are quite different. Those with intrinsic job quality orientations tend to have similar backgrounds to those seeking autonomy, including urban origins and work history, but are definitely of higher status* (perhaps due to success in finding congruent work). Most similar to the men with intrinsic orientations are those giving priority to the worthwhileness of the job. They are again of relatively high status but rather older, and in this case it has meant moving up in relation to their extended families, although they have maintained contact with them. The orientations classified as "type of work or industry" are broadly similar in relations with background factors, to those involving worthwhileness, intrinsic job quality, autonomy and, rather less clearly, outdoor work.

In contrast to all the foregoing orientations, which are concerned in one way or another with job content, is economism — both as a type of orientation and in its relations with background factors. It differs most from the outdoor orientation, in terms of the number and strength of opposite relationships with background factors, but it is quite distinct from all of them. The most important influence is the "life cycle squeeze", as may be seen from the age and family commitments of men

---

* Throughout this chapter "status" refers to status in the community (not Status Level in the firm) and is measured by a seven-point job stratification scale. For details see Chapter 9, pp. 270–1.

with this orientation. Also, the tendency to go out with the family more than most suggests an element of family-centredness to make them feel the squeeze more. The high frequency of feeling reluctant to go to work, coupled with the degree of absence and the unwillingness to think about work outside working hours, supports our earlier suggestion of a strong element of alienated instrumentalism. The exceptional extent of radical ideology seems to indicate this is not a form of apathy. The ideology measure is composed of attitudes towards industrial relations, and we see that their view of work as an undesirable means of earning the necessary money is combined with a marked hostility to the system.

We may note that, contrary to the hypothesis and tentative findings of Goldthorpe *et al.* (1968: 164–7), there is no relationship between economism and downward mobility. We looked at mobility in many different ways and found only one relationship that fits the hypothesis at all: those with *orderly* downward careers, in the sense that most of their job moves were downward, are slightly more economistic. On the other hand, those who had previously held white-collar jobs are less economistic. This is the measure of downward career mobility used by Goldthorpe and his colleagues, who fail to find a significant relationship, although Ingham (1970: 134) subsequently reported a positive relation, i.e. the opposite of our finding. Ingham differs further from Goldthorpe *et al.* in finding no other relationship between mobility and economism. The overall pattern from our more extensive data, which is not really changed if we add the data of both Goldthorpe *et al.* and of Ingham, is an absence of relationship. On the other hand, as we shall see, social mobility is related to most other orientations.

There are a number of other readily intelligible relationships. A concern to avoid excessive physical effort arises from poor health or disablement, and it is fairly clear why it should not be so important to those with occupational qualifications. Those with "trade union" orientations come from trade union family backgrounds and, very clearly, have high union involvement. The involvement is doubtless due to the orientation, but also must tend to reinforce it. Probably as part of a similar feedback process they also have a marked tendency to radical ideology. In contrast, those with a "management"orientation are unusually conservative and also tend to have a qualification (again, in contrast to those with "trade union" orientations) and to be in higher status jobs. Both the promotion and the status orientations are strongly related to present status but in this case it is not clear how far this is a cause and how far an effect. They are distinguished by the promotion orientation being associated with upward mobility relative to first job and to fathers and friends, while the status orientation is more closely associated with present high status. Also, men with the promotion orientation are younger, with most of their careers ahead of them, and perhaps as an aspect of their youth they appear to lead more active social lives.

Two orientations for which our measures have not really proved satisfactory up to now are hours and working conditions. For these we have used the importance and preference data separately and again arrived at different patterns of relationships. However, for hours they do seem to complement each other to some extent. Between them they cover a wide range of family and social commitments which we might expect to produce a concern with working hours. Thus the preference score relates to club membership, while importance relates to frequent attendance; the preference relates to visiting the pub and the importance to visiting and going out with relatives. On the whole, the importance data fit the pattern better. There is, however, a clear divergence on mobility: those rating hours important have been upwardly mobile, while those mentioning them most in the preference data have had a career with a high proportion of downward moves. For working conditions the contrasts predominate. The importance score relates to what, as we shall see, may almost be regarded as the standard characteristics of workers with any orientation; native-born, urban, Protestant, in good health, high status, having been upwardly mobile. The preference scores have a more distinctive pattern of associations; ex-farm-workers, of rural origin, in poor health, from low-status backgrounds, although they too have moved up. Bearing in mind that this was one of the most common preferences it is somewhat surprising that this measure is not better related to the characteristics of the men's work, although we can see why the importance score is not well related to it or to work characteristics.

To examine the influence of social background in more detail we shall look at it from the standpoint of the different factors, to see which are more important and what sort of influence they have on orientations. The following discussion is intended to complement the listing of influences on individual orientations presented in the table of Appendix IV, and to elaborate on their meaning. It is useful to divide the background factors into three types: non-work, present employment and work history. All are part of an individual's biography and the division is somewhat arbitrary, with some aspects which do not fall clearly within one type. However, it is simpler to consider the separate aspects within this framework.

NON-WORK

This is itself a very wide area, including pre-work history such as education and family background, present life cycle position, community attachment and personal characteristics such as health. We have identified many significant influences within this area.

The single most important background influence derives from where a worker was born. This has some bearing on every orientation except "effort". The main division is between overseas immigrants and British-born workers, but there are also differences among the immigrants. It will be recalled that these immigrants had come mainly from Italy, eastern Europe and Pakistan (then undivided). Although workers from each region are extreme on some orientation measures this is so most often for the Pakistanis, closely followed by the Italians, while those from eastern Europe are usually less clearly distinguished from the native-born.[1] Also, the notion of immigration has to be applied on a finer scale in some cases to include movement to the Peterborough area from other parts of Britain; roughly, the relationship with the orientation varies with distance from Peterborough. Almost invariably the relationship with orientations is negative, that is, immigrants are less likely to have most types of orientations. The main exception is "personal suitability" which is itself a sort of negative orientation and so fits the same pattern. In addition, the European immigrants, especially the Italians, but not immigrants from Pakistan, tend to have economistic orientations; the Pakistanis, and to a lesser extent the Italians, are more likely to have a preference for indoor work (with corresponding extreme absence of outdoor orientations); and the Italians are alone in giving priority to a strong trade union.

This particular variable illustrates well the way in which work and non-work experience are interrelated. In itself, where a person is born is unquestionably a non-work characteristic but, as we shall see in the next chapter, it is related to the opportunity to exercise job choice. Immigrants are regarded by employers as less desirable employees and have difficulty in getting the better jobs, although they do a little better on gross wages per week and it seems probable that those wanting it could get indoor work. Thus market experience appears to play a large part in shaping the orientations, with a predominant tendency for the very limited scope for meaningful choice by immigrants to lead to an absence of orientations, other than to find a job where they will be accepted.

Market forces, however, cannot account for all the differences stemming from the workers' birthplaces. For instance, they do not account for the differences between the eastern Europeans and the Italians – particularly the Italian commitment to trade unionism. The further influences may come from cultural differences in the countries or regions of origin or in communities they have established within the Peterborough area. The Italians maintain a consciousness of their national identity to the extent of employing someone to teach Italian to their children, while the Pakistanis are united by religion and are subject to greater discrimination. Those from eastern Europe have little likelihood of visiting their old countries and generally less reason to maintain a separate identity (they come from several different countries anyway), so they are less distinguishable from the native population in terms of their orientations. On the other hand, birthplace is related to other background variables and we cannot be sure how the net effects are produced.

Another aspect of one's birthplace is the size of the town or village. Turner and Lawrence (1965), analysing their North American data, argue that living in a small town or village provides a cultural context which encourages orientations seeking intrinsic rewards and autonomy, and perhaps worthwhileness, although they are less explicit on this. It seems reasonable to suppose that the cultural context of early life would have a similar influence carrying over to the present, but when we look at our British data we find exactly the reverse. All three orientations (intrinsic quality, autonomy and worthwhileness) are positively related to the size of town, as are the desires for fringe benefits, promotion and security. The only orientation clearly associated with coming from a village or small town is the deferent concern with personal suitability.

We cannot really apply the same test to present residence as all live in the same broad area, but we used a more suitable, related measure – the rurality of residence, as measured by the proportion of jobs in agricultire in their census enumeration district. This gives a similar result for autonomy – urban dwellers are more concerned to have autonomy – and also for fringe benefits, but no significant relationships on the other variables noted above. However, those living in the country are more likely to be concerned about the type of work or industry and the hours of work, while dislike of high effort and commitment to a strong union are more usual among those living in the town.

The other background variable considered by Turner and Lawrence is religion, which they used as characterising areas to make a division almost coinciding with the city – small town division; the areas were classed as Roman Catholic, or Protestant and Jewish, or a mixure of both.[2] Our data are at the individual level using acknowledged religious affiliations. Nearly 16 per cent have no religion, just over 4 per cent are Moslems and there are no Jews. Neverthless, the Catholic–Protestant divison among the 755 Christians turns out to be important, and this time is more in line with the Turner and Lawrence hypothesis. There are quite strong tendencies for Protestants to give priority to intrinsic job quality and worthwhileness. Since the largest group of Protestant workers, the Anglicans, are barely more likely than Catholics to have an autonomy orientation, the general Protestant – Catholic difference is not significant in this respect. However, Catholics are significantly less likely than members of Protestant sects to have this orientation and are also less likely than those with no religious affiliation. Furthermore, there is a distinct tendency for those with outdoor orientations – which involve an element of autonomy – to be Protestants. We also find, in keeping with Turner and Lawrence, and other American studies (see Lenski, 1963: 91–2), that Catholics are more likely to have economistic orientations, although they found the trend confined to younger workers, whereas we find it is only among the older ones, while the Protestants are if anything the more economistic of the young men. In addition, Protestants are more likely to have orientations involving promotion, workpeople, working conditions and hours, while Catholics are more likely to value a strong trade union – which was also the case in Lenski's study of Detroit (1963: 98–102).

At this point we should note that the Protestants are almost all native-born while most of the Catholics are immigrants. Controlling for immigration, the relationships (as measured by partial gammas) almost all disappear or become insignificant. Only the trade-union orientation of Catholics remains barely affected, although we do see that this relationship is much stronger among immigrants – it will be recalled that the orientation is relatively common among Italians. Also, the tendencies for Protestants to want worthwhile work and for Catholics to want high wages are only moderately reduced, although the latter was never very strong. The relationships between Protestantism and orientations relating to workpeople and working conditions are actually confined to immigrants, and with control for birthplace they are, if anything, reversed. Clearly the relationship between birthplace and religion is important, and this is further supported by a tendency for Moslem immigrants to resemble the Catholics more than the Protestants. However, we should not be too ready to dismiss the effects of religion as spurious. Even where there is complete overlap of effects from religion and ethnic group it may be cultural factors, including religion, which differentiate the workers with respect to some orientations, rather than just the fact of being or not being an immigrant. In this connection, it is worth noting that the similar findings of Turner and Lawrence were also based on groups with different national origins, though few are likely to have been first-generation immigrants.

Another background variable related to immigration is type of house tenure. As an aspect of where people live we might expect it to have an influence on orientations, but it is probably more significant as a consequence of other aspects of social experience. In this, competition for better housing is, we believe, the most important, with immigrants losing out in the allocation of council housing. (See Rex and Moore, 1967; Prandy, 1979a). This has a rather unexpected result, for immigrants are very much more likely to be buying their own homes. In Peterborough the Italians and eastern Europeans have the highest proportions of owner-occupiers, with 87 per cent and 61 per cent respectively, while hardly any are renting from private landlords. These are people who have been here some time and have probably moved out of privately rented accommodation, but even among the more recently arrived Pakistanis 53 per cent are buying compared with only 33 per cent of those born locally (see also the national study by P.E.P., 1976). This suggests that home ownership may be seen as largely a second-best to renting from the council for this section of the working class. It is a strategy forced on them by their failure in the competition for council housing, but they can only afford to buy low-quality houses. However, private renting is less desirable and, as we would expect, is most common among those who have most recently arrived and have great "ethnic distance" from the native British, the Pakistanis (Prandy, 1979a).

Thus we can rank the type of housing tenure by its desirability: council housing is the most sought-after, while private renting is the least satisfactory. (For this purpose we ignore living with parents, etc., since it cannot meaningfully be ranked.) Ordering types of tenure in this way gives a regular pattern of association with several orientations – the better the housing the stronger the orientations, except for the usual reversal with "personal suitability", with the biggest difference being between those in council housing and the rest. As we would expect, this is partly, although not entirely, an effect of (or at least coincident with) immigration. Control for this effect still leaves some relationship between the desirability of type of tenure and orientations concerning security, outdoor work and working conditions, while the relation with trade-union strength actually increases to a significant level. In the last case the high union orientation of the home-owning Italians is a major consideration.

We might expect to find the responsibility of home purchase leading to a concern with income and security, but this is not so. If anything, there is a slight tendency among both immigrants and native-born for those buying their homes to be less economistic, while we have already seen it is council tenants who are most likely to seek security, although the orientation is stronger than the usual trend would suggest among native-born house buyers. On a rather different approach we might expect those buying their homes to be men with middle-class aspirations who would also stress promotion and status, but it is not so. The only trend is for the promotion orientation to be relatively rare among buyers, but in this case it is also rare among council tenants and most usual among those renting privately.

Another important area of influences is life cycle and family position (see Shimmin, 1962). As we noted earlier, the "life cycle squeeze" leads to an economistic orientation. The typical worker who gives priority to monetary rewards is in his middle to late 30s, married, with at least two dependents. As can be seen from Table 8.1, they are much more likely to have dependent children and to have more of them than other workers. Of those without dependent children the young married men are just as likely to be economistic as other workers, presumably in anticipation of future responsibilities. In addition to children they are more likely than not to have another dependent. Nearly half the wives are without paid jobs, mainly because of the ages of their children, and a fair number have other dependents, although in this they are little different from the rest.

Table 8.1   Number of dependent children by economistic orientation

Economistic orientation (c.c.)	Number of dependent children (% with)					
	None	1	2	3 or more	Total	N
No	59	16	14	11	100	718
Yes	40	16	24	20	100	215
All	55	16	17	13	100	933

(gamma = 0.31, D = 0.21)

Looking back to our finding that Catholics are more likely to be economistic, it seems we now have a partial explanation. Catholics tend to have more children, and when account is taken of this the relation with economism is reduced. However, it does not entirely disappear, suggesting some influence from culture or ethnic relations.

The security orientation is similarly related to life cycle position, except that, rather surprisingly, there is no significant relation with the number of dependent children or with all dependents. There is, however, a somewhat greater tendency for workers with this orientation to be married – all but one of the 20 who might be classed as having a strong orientation are married and living with their wives. Also, the concern with security reaches its peak in the late 30s and then declines. On the whole, the security-minded are a little older than the economistic workers, but the decline among the older workers is still rather surprising.

A similar life cycle influence operates on the status orientation, except that the number of dependents is important while there is no relation with being married. The age pattern is similar to that for the wages orientation, with the peak in the late 30s and a general tendency to be younger.

Family situation, although perhaps less so life cycle position, is a significant influence on the importance accorded to hours of work. Although there is no relation with age, both being married and having dependent children lead to a greater concern with the hours devoted to work.

Exactly the opposite sort of life cycle trend occurs for those with the outdoor orientation. They tend to be single, without dependents, and generally older, although least likely to be in the middle or late 30s. Perhaps this reflects an absence of family commitments which would create other priorities.

Workpeople, autonomy, intrinsic job quality, worthwhileness and type of work/industry are all orientations related to an absence of dependents, although with different patterns of relationship to the other life cycle variables. Only the last relates to being single. In all other cases the relationship of the orientation is to not having dependent children rather than dependents in general (indeed, the relation with worthwhileness is not otherwise significant). The emphasis on workpeople is also related to age, being quite high among young workers, then declining gradually to about 50 when there is a sudden increase, so that it is highest among the older men. It seems that there are two patterns of response here, reflecting the social interests of the young people and perhaps a greater attachment to workmates on the part of the older men. Among the younger men the orientation is more likely to be associated with participation in leisure organisations, visiting and going out with friends than it is among the older men.

Autonomy and intrinsic quality orientations are not related to marital status or age, while the orientation in terms of worthwhileness links them, and those considered above, with a different life cycle influence. This is an influence involving the older, married workers, who are most likely to be concerned with personal suitability, relations with management and the worthwhileness of the job, in that order. At the other extreme, it is the young workers, regardless of family situation, who are most likely to stress promotion.

The importance of the family in shaping certain orientations is further borne out when we look at leisure activities. All but two (status and personal suitability) of the orientations which are positively related to family position – being married and/or having dependent children – are also related to the frequency with which a man goes out with his immediate family. Having a family to go out with does help, of course, but most of the men are married, and it is easier for husband and wife to go out together where there are no dependent children. It seems, therefore, that these are the orientations of family-centred men, at least where there are children.

The extended family also appears to have some influence. Visiting, going out with and working at the same firm as relatives may all be taken as indicators of the strength of extended family relationships. Each relates to several orientations, with a tendency for them to relate to the same ones. This is particularly so for the outdoor and security orientations to which all three are related.

However, seeing relatives or working in the same firm depends on the relatives being available and this is affected by geographical mobility. Quite simply, we would expect contacts to be highest among those born locally and to decline with distance from the person's birthplace. This is indeed what we find, apart from two exceptions. Those born in Peterborough itself go out with and visit relatives less than we would expect. On the other hand, the Italians are more likely than other immigrants to have relatives in the same firm and many see their relatives outside work quite often. Most visit them sometimes, even if it means a return to Italy, and those with relatives living locally seem to maintain close contacts.

This brings out cultural differences relevant to our earlier discussion. Also, it illustrates the point that we should not be too ready to dismiss the relevance of extended family connections just because of the overlap with birthplace. Not only are there variations in the effort and apparent desire to maintain contact, but the contact itself is socially relevant and part of the consequence of staying put or being geographically mobile.

In particular, regular contact with extended kin is an aspect of social integration in a community. In this way it is important in itself and may also be part of a wider integration. This may be seen with respect to the security orientation which is positively related to almost every indicator of social integration. The promotion orientation is also strongly related to the social integration measures, including visiting and going out with relatives.

The integration measures can be divided into several different types. First, there is involvement in churches and clubs, where the important thing seems to be membership rather than the actual frequency of attendance. Such involvement is positively related to many orientations, but especially to security. On the other hand, there is only one negative relation, those with outdoor orientations being less likely to join clubs or churches. Then there are visits to friends and relations, going to the pub, going out with the family, relatives and friends, and going out alone. The last, measured in reverse, is possibly the best single indicator of social integration and we find those holding most types of orientation rarely go out alone – the only exception being that those who do make solitary outings tend to want a strong trade union. The same applies to the frequency of visiting or going out with friends, and so on. The relationships are all positive – apart from those who stress workpeople tending not to visit friends, and those concerned with personal suitability visiting neither friends nor the pub. Working with friends and having relatives in the firm are perhaps less good indicators but they give the same pattern.

Finally, a rather different sort of integration measure is trade-union connections, as evidenced in the union membership of close relatives and the individual's own involvement. Again, the relations are predominantly positive, both occurring with security, hours, conditions and trade-union strength. Of course, trade-union involvement (membership and office-holding) is more of a work-related characteristic and it is not altogether clear how far it is a cause and how far an effect, as exemplified by the strong relation with the trade-union orientation (gamma = 0.49) compared with the relatively weak association between the orientation and family unionism (gamma = 0.09). Nevertheless, it is a form of social integration and it fits the general pattern. The only negative relationships entail union involvement associated with the outdoor orientation, which is largely due to the isolated work of many with this orientation and provides the familiar contrast to the positively related economism, and once again with the deferent "personal suitability" orientation. Those with this last orientation are the ones with the lowest level of integration. It seems that social integration in the local community promotes the holding of orientations of any non-deferent sort, but especially one concerning security.

On the general point we would suggest that integration gives a sense of competence and thus a greater sense of ability to make relevant demands. A similar line of reasoning may be applied to the tendencies noted earlier for immigrants and those who have not succeeded in getting council houses to have less, or weaker orientations. Also, the pattern may be seen in a tendency for the degree of satisfaction with life in general to be positively related to many orientations.

Turning again to the influences of early life, in addition to when a person was born two major considerations are the father's occupation, giving an indication of class background, and education. In fact, neither appears to have a great deal of influence, largely because of the limited amount of variation in these two features. Almost all fathers were manual workers, but there were differences in occupational status which are significantly associated with some orientations. A higher-status background is associated with orientations concerning intrinsic job quality and promotion, while lower levels tend to go with trade-union strength, indoor work and working conditions.

Nearly all had been to elementary or secondary modern schools (or foreign equivalents) and left without any formal qualification. This leaves the age of leaving school (which is closely related to qualifications) as the best single indicator of differences in full-time education. Because of changes in leaving ages over time it is necessary to control for age to avoid confusion with other age-related effects, although this still leaves some distortion due to the practices of different countries. Nevertheless, we can discern positive relations between the extent of education and orientations involving intrinsic quality and promotion, while less education is associated with trade-union and security orientations.

In addition to the 4 per cent who had attained some sort of qualification at school a further 11 per cent had acquired a qualification at work, although usually at a low level. This provides little basis to differentiate the labour force and the effects are small, but we do find a tendency for the qualified to be more concerned with management characteristics and less with trade-union strength. Also, those with qualifications gained while working are more concerned with the intrinsic quality and worthwhileness of the job, and less with the degree of effort. Like the leaving age, qualifications are related to generation, being more common nowadays, but there is little trend in our data, so the relationships are virtually unaffected by control for age.

Qualifications may be seen as a property of the individual which relates directly to his market position, in that employers may use them as criteria for selection. The remaining non-work characteristics to be discussed are also of this type.[3] This is not to argue that their market relevance is the only influence on orientations; on the contrary we would expect each to have its own type of influence, but it is reasonable to suppose it has some bearing.

The rating by interviewers, which we suggest is not unlike the assessment of ability and co-operativeness made in an employment interview, is only related to two orientations: positively to the status orientation and negatively to the concern with trade-union strength. The degree of radicalism, which may be regarded as a negative qualification insofar as it is taken into account by employers, is much more important. The more radical are, as we would expect, more pro-trade-union and more likely to look for good wages, hours, fringe benefits and working conditions. On the other hand, the more conservative want indoor work and good relations with management. Health is a rather different variable of this sort. Most clearly and understandably those with health problems want jobs which do not entail excessive physical effort. They also tend to want autonomy and not to seek promotion, status or security. In addition, they say good working conditions are of low importance but mention them often in the preference data. While we might explain the first three of the aspects they tend not to want on the grounds that they would probably be unattainable, we cannot imagine why those in poor health should be significantly less likely to want to work in reasonable conditions, while we can understand the reverse, and so would place more weight on the preference measure of this orientation. Finally, we should note that ethnic differences and life-cycle position, which have already discussed, also belong in this group of characteristics affecting attractiveness to employers.

Present Employment

Moving to aspects of the worker's present employment, we continue with features relating to employers' views of the workers, namely the frequency of being late or absent from work. They may be seen as indicators of low commitment to work or at least to the present job, although we should not overlook the fact that they may be consequences of general poor health, the type of work done or even the practices for recording the statistics. The latter considerations seem particularly relevant to lateness, which is related to several orientations without any clear pattern. For instance, it seems likely that the tendency for those with outdoor orientations to be rarely recorded as late, in contrast to those with indoor orientations, may be an indirect consequence of the different work locations of those whose orientations are met. On the other hand, a low rate of absence does seem to reflect some degree of commitment (c.f. Ingham 1970). Those rarely absent are concerned with promotion, the nature of the job or its worthwhileness, while higher absence rates go with economism, interest in fringe benefits and working conditions, and a desire for strong unions. Furthermore, the intrinsic quality orientation is the only one to be associated with being rarely absent or late, while the working conditions orientation goes with high frequency on both. Autonomy is the only other orientation associated with high frequency on both absence and lateness (trade union strength and promotion are actually reversed), but this is also associated with poor health.

We included two measures which Kornhauser (1965) takes as indicators of the worker's "mental health", but here a more directly literal interpretation seems appropriate. Responses to the question, "When you start off for work, how often, if at all, do you find yourself thinking 'I don't want to go in today'?" may be taken as having both interpretations, reflecting an attitude of reluctance to work similar to that we hoped to tap through absences and lateness. In fact, such reluctance is, like at least one of absence and lateness, related positively to economism and conditions, and negatively to outdoor orientations. In addition, the feeling of reluctance to go to work is associated with high concern about hours and low concern over personal suitability, while low reluctance goes with either high or low levels of security orientation.

The second of these measures relates to the extent to which work problems spill over into non-work life: "If a problem comes up in your work which isn't settled when you go home, how often, if at all, do you find yourself thinking about it after work?" Such spill-over might be taken as an indicator of mental stress, but on the basis of its relation with orientations it seems to be more an indicator of commitment to work. It is associated positively with orientations involving worthwhileness, type of work and management quality, and negatively with economism. A positive relation with the security orientation may be given either interpretation, while the negative relation with the outdoor orientation, in view of the latter's association with infrequent lateness and rare reluctance to go to work, may possibly be a reflection of low stress.

Probably the most important aspect of present employment is occupational status. We do not wish to discuss here the meaning of "occupational status", which is too important and controversial for a brief digression.[4] For present purposes we are concerned only with the relationship between stratification, as commonly conceived, and orientations. Similarly, our discussion of status differences and mobility will be in terms of a rough, conventional stratification hierarchy (see Chapter 9, pp. 270–1) without making any specific theoretical claims about its nature.

The relevance of present occupational status in relation to the total stratification structure of the society hardly needs mentioning, as it is fundamental to the context of this study, but even within the narrow range we encompass it is of considerable influence. Present job level is related to most orientations, usually in a positive direction; in 12 cases high status is associated with an orientation while low status tends to accompany only economism and concern with personal suitability.

At first sight it is not clear if the relationships are due to the effects of status or whether the orientations have led to occupations at higher levels. However, the former interpretation is borne out when we consider interactional measures. The best such measure is based on the occupations of friends, since friends are freely chosen and the relationship is reciprocal (see Stewart *et al.*, 1973, forthcoming). We find the pattern of relationships between orientations and the mean occupational level of friends is very similar to that for the respondent's own job level. To a lesser extent the mean occupational level of close relatives (father, father-in-law and brothers) also follows the pattern. An individual's orientations are not going to affect the occupations of other people, although they may well affect choice of friends, particularly through effects on status. Therefore, it seems that we should regard the occupational level and orientations as tending to exist together, with at least some effect from status to orientations.

The strongest relationship is with the status orientation, which serves well to illustrate the foregoing point. There is a positive relation with the status of relatives, which must be causally prior to the orientation. However, as we have argued earlier, the orientation does tend to lead to congruent employment situations, which means relatively high-status jobs. Thus there is a stronger relationship between the orientation and present job status. As we would expect, the relation with status measured by the levels of friends' jobs comes in between.

Other orientations strongly related to status, as measured by the levels of both the individual's job and his friends' jobs, concern security, worthwhileness and job content, although only the last is related to the status of relatives. Orientations involving promotion and management quality are also significantly associated with all three measures, the relation of the former with the individual's own job being quite strong.

More generally, the tendency for orientations to be stronger among those of higher status is another example of a sense of competence to control one's fate, here arising from occupational success, leading to belief in the possibility of making significant choices within the labour market. This is further borne out when we consider the occupational levels of friends and relatives, not as indicators of status but as providing frames of reference against which the worker evaluates his own position. Several orientations are stronger where the man's status is higher, mainly in relation to relatives, while none – apart from the deferent "personal suitability" – is associated with lower status. Form and Geschwender (1962) show that such favourable comparisons lead to a greater sense of satisfaction. Now, satisfaction depends on job rewards meeting expectations which are "realistically" limited to the levels attainable (Stewart and Blackburn, 1975). In the same way their comparisons encourage them to feel they can successfully make worthwhile demands within the narrow range of available possibilities.

Work History

The comparison between the individual's present occupation and those of significant others naturally leads on to the subject of mobility, and it is here that we begin our considerations of work history. We have a number of ways of looking at this. First, there is the conventional intergenerational mobility as measured by the difference between the respondent's job and his father's job at the time he left school. As an intergenerational measure this is far from satisfactory, as has often been pointed out, not least because the fathers' occupations all relate to an age of about 40 while the sons' are spread through the whole range of working life. However, it is much more use as a measure of the individual's mobility from the status level of his early, pre-work life to the present. This is still affected by the man's age, although less so for our non-skilled sample than it would be for a sample of the whole working population. In fact, we do find variations by age in the relationship between mobility and orientations, but the numbers in each age group are insufficient for detailed analysis and controlling for age has hardly any overall effect. The second interpretation, in terms of mobility in the individual's work life, is supported by the very similar pattern of associations for career mobility, as measured by the difference between first and present jobs. Both show positive relationships between upward mobility and a number of orientations, but no negative ones. The main differences are that only mobility from father's occupation is associated with indoor and trade-union orientations, while mobility from first job relates to orientations involving workpeople and job content and is also more strongly related to the one involving worthwhileness. In addition to worthwhileness, both relate to orientations involving security, hours and conditions.

These measures of mobility span the whole of a man's work life. However, if the career has not been continuously up or down, the experience of the more recent direction of mobility may be important. In this respect the highest job level previously attained is likely to be particularly relevant. Accordingly, we used the difference between this and the present level. Downward mobility is only related to the personal suitability orientation, while there are four positive relations between upward mobility and orientations, including security and hours, which are also related to both measures of work-life mobility, and trade-union strength, which is related to the one from father's occupation. At the general level we find again, in all three measures, the pattern of a sense of competence – here engendered by individual achievement – positively associated with orientations.

Pursuing the idea of movement up and down within a man's work life, we looked at the proportions of moves which were in upward and downward directions. Relatively high proportions tend to indicate orderly careers (Wilensky, 1961) up or down. The outdoor orientation is associated with low proportions in both directions, but especially down. This may be interpreted as a tendency for those with the orientations to have stayed at one level but to be more likely to have moved up than down. Apart from this, a low proportion of upward moves is not associated with any orientation, while a high proportion is associated with several, in keeping with the sort of pattern noted above. Also within this pattern, a low proportion of downward moves goes with a trade-union orientation while a high proportion goes with "personal suitability". However, there are also exceptions, as a high proportion of downward moves relates to orientations concerning indoor work, wages and hours.

Instead of looking back to the highest-level job we can take the level of the one the worker has liked best of all his jobs, including the present one, and the gap between that and the present job. The first point to note is that mobility is not relevant here, its relations with orientations being weak reflections of the effect of the "best job". Those whose choice of their best job was a relatively high-status job tend to have stronger orientations on a number of aspects, especially intrinsic quality, worthwhileness, security, promotion and status. On the other hand, those who specified lower-status jobs as the ones they had liked best are generally less likely to have orientations, although they are a little more likely to have the outdoor, wages or trade-union ones.

Turning to the type of work done previously, it is useful to make the conventional distinction between manual and non-manual jobs. As well as entailing different work experience it may serve as an indicator of status. Self-employment may be regarded in a somewhat similar way, although it is less common and less well related to orientations. A high proportion of non-manual jobs in the past goes with orientations concerning status, promotion and intrinsic quality. In addition, both non-manual and self-employment are associated with concern about personal suitability. Low proportions of jobs in self-employment and non-manual occupations – which for the most part means always being employed as a manual worker – are associated with orientations involving trade unionism, outdoor work and wages. Additionally, being employed relates to concern with the type of work or industry, and manual work relates to concern with conditions and hours.

A different aspect of the type of previous work is the sector of employment. Here we may pick out work in agriculture and in manufacturing industry as being of potential relevance. Working conditions is the only subject of an orientation positively associated with work in agriculture, and it also goes with few jobs in manufacturing. Unlike Touraine and Ragazzi (1961) we find no relationship between economism and agricultural work or the other indicators of rural background discussed earlier. Little or no work in agriculture is linked with orientations involving autonomy, intrinsic quality, security and fringe benefits, all of which are associated with being born in a large town, and the first also with urban residence. These would seem to be "urban" orientations. Status and promotion orientations are also negatively associated with the extent of past work in agriculture, although not with other urban-rural indicators, and it seems possible that not working on the land was a consequence rather than a cause of the orientations. Similarly, the combination of few jobs in manufacturing with the outdoor orientation and of a high proportion of such jobs with the indoor and wages orientations may be largely the effects of the orientations.

A rather different aspect of work history which we thought might be important is the experience of unemployment and involuntary job moves (redundancy, dismissal, etc.). Nearly half the sample had some experience of involuntary moves, even when we exclude military conscription and wartime direction of labour. Also, over a quarter had been unemployed at least once for more than a few days, mostly for at least three months. Yet these do not emerge as important influences. Apart from a tendency for those who had spent a longer time unemployed to seek easier work, orientations are related to the more favourable experience. Those with little or no experience of redundancy or other involuntary job changes are more likely to have orientations involving status, worthwhileness and fringe benefits. Low unemployment, in terms of the amount of time and frequency, is associated with the promotion orientation. Somewhat paradoxically, those who have been unemployed more often are less likely to give priority to security, possibly because they have come to accept insecurity. Also those with experience of more than three months unemployment, particularly if it has been recent, are less likely to have outdoor orientations.

The impact of unemployment tends to be reduced by different influences depending on when it occurred. Thus the more time a man has spent unemployed since the Second World War, the less likely he is to have an orientation of worthwhileness, but there is no trend for unemployment in the Depression. For other orientations it is not possible to establish trends, but in some other cases there appear to be stronger relationships for more recent unemployment. Whether this is due to unemployment having different meanings to the unemployed at different times, or whether it is that the effects of the experience fade with time we cannot say.

The final aspect of work experience to be considered is the number of firms worked for. We have already seen that this is partly a consequence of movement in an attempt to satisfy orientations and that it is a criterion employers use in assessing workers. Thus the relationships with orientations are the outcome of a variety of influences. The more firms worked for, the greater is the concern with personal suitability, which seems to reflect an awareness of employers' attitudes. Also, working for many firms is associated with the quest for high earnings, as we saw earlier, but interestingly with no other orientation. On the other hand, there are negative relations with several orientations, particularly trade union strength, but also type of work, promotion, status, intrinsic quality, outdoors and autonomy. The last two may reflect the ease of identifying firms providing these rewards. The others may stem from the confidence of those in stronger market positions, or it may be that experience of employment in several firms makes aspirations in these directions seem irrelevant.

We have seen that there are a great many relationships between background variables and orientations. These cannot be interpreted solely as indications of causal influence from the background factors, but to a substantial degree this does seem to be the case. In principle, background characteristics could influence the present job through mechanisms other than the worker's choice, and the job could then determine orientations. In fact, some characteristics do have a bearing on job placement, through employers' recruitment policies, but it is hard to see how they could all have such effects, and relationships with job characteristics are limited. In any case, there is no evident way in which control for the job would remove the relationships between orientations and background characteristics, while control for orientations does tend to eliminate the association between background and present job. Thus we conclude that the various aspects of experience do contribute to shaping orientations. Some of the influences are readily intelligible but for others there is no clear theoretical explanation available at present. Most background factors influence several orientations, so we have different combinations associated with each.

The clearest result to emerge, however, does not concern the influences on specific orientations but the kind of people who are likely to have orientations, or to have stronger ones (apart from the deferent "personal suitability"). These are definitely not immigrants or older workers. They are people who are generally satisfied with their lives, well integrated socially in their family and the community, with relatively good jobs and successful careers. They are people whose experience leads them to believe that they can make effective choices and exercise some control over their lives.[5] The extent of alternatives open to them in the market is, as we have shown, severely limited, but they regard them as significant.

ORIENTATIONS IN PERSPECTIVE

In this and the two previous chapters we have been examining the existence and nature of orientations to work. Our basic interest is in their relevance to job choice and so to the operation of the labour market, but we have also been concerned to develop a more adequate understanding of orientations themselves.

We started by defining orientations as general organising principles underlying the way people make sense of their lives, or at least attempt to do so. By "making sense" we refer not only to the interpretation of experience in a diversity of situations, but also to a sense of purpose and control over their own situations. Orientations serve to give coherence and direction to their lives. They must, therefore, have a permanence between different situations and over time.

Thus a fundamental question is whether orientations in this sense exist. In other words, is the theoretical approach in terms of orientations as we have conceived them – or indeed in any other sense – justified? In the specific context of this research the problem is the relevance of orientations to job choice. For workers to exercise choice they must have preferences which are substantially independent of immediate work experience. Orientations, in so far as they exist, provide the basis of such preferences.

Accordingly, an initial question that we considered was simply whether orientations to work actually exist to any significant extent, or whether attitudes and behaviour are to be understood in terms of response to the work situation. In a more sophisticated form of the latter argument it is allowed that different orientations exist for non-competing sections of the labour force but that there is no variation within each relatively self-contained section. Consequently all are in competition for the jobs which are "best" on the basis of the common orientation. A particular version of this relevant to the non-skilled sector is that all the rewards available, apart from the money, since that is necessary, are at such a low level that differences between them are of no significance. This would not be distinguishable from the monetary model of the market, where income is treated as the only reward at any level to be set against the cost of having to work, which not only implies the absence of orientations but also a high degree of alienation.

A second problem concerns the actual nature of orientations. In the strong form, concern with a particular type of work reward dominates, so that other rewards become relatively insignificant, and the worker himself can be characterised by his orientation, for example he is economistic or has a promotion orientation. This simplifies the problem of job choice for the worker but also increases the chances of frustration, particularly as the distributions of orientations and rewards are unlikely to match each other, so it would be impossible for all to be satisfied. In the weak form of orientations the individual is not characterisable by any one, but rather has a profile of varying degrees of orientation on several aspects. Work experience is integrated in their lives through such orientations, which operate as they are called up by circumstances. Job choice is less clear, in that it operates not through the pursuit of specific rewards but by making decisions between more limited and concrete alternatives. Perhaps the simplest case is the decision to change jobs as an escape from the present one to something which might be less unpleasant. Such orientations make it harder for workers to maximise the congruence between their actual and "ideal" jobs (ideal within the limits of their sector of the market), but easier to find a job providing a modest degree of such congruence.

To measure possible orientations we used ratings of importance and preference scores. The latter entail the frequency of mentioning different work aspects in open-ended questions relating to a hypothetical set of job choices, and we used a similar approach, incorporating the same classification of "preferences" for other questions, to explore different contexts. We also looked at influences on job satisfaction, taken as a consequence of how work is experienced. On the basis of direct consideration of these measures, the evidence for the existence of orientations with an element of permanence across contexts was rather thin. This was so whether we considered the different types of measures separately or related them together. In particular, there was hardly any support for the notion of strong orientations, although there were appreciably more grounds for accepting the existence of the weak form. Probably the most important evidence at this stage in favour of orientations was the set of significant relationships between the importance and preference scores, with both in their weak forms.

However, when we looked at the relations between orientations and job characteristics the picture was rather different. Here we found a clear, persistent element of congruence between the rewards sought and obtained. In principle, such congruence might be the result of socialisation rather than orientations, but all the evidence suggests that it is predominantly the latter.

The extensive pattern of relationships between background characteristics and orientations would seem to clinch the matter. It appears that they do not arise through the job as an intervening variable, and it is not plausible that such relationships would exist if the "orientations" were mere products of experience in the present job. Furthermore, the orientations are related to many aspects of individual biographies which have greater permanence than the immediate present, such as place of birth, number of dependents and experience of mobility. Thus the orientations must also have a degree of permanence, an existence transcending present experience.

As we have defined them, orientations relate to all aspects of people's lives, and we have seen how orientations to work are enmeshed in the totality of social experience, both at work and outside. A view of them as something brought into the work situation from outside is too static and fragmentary. Not only are they influenced by experience of work and market processes, but through their influence on job rewards they influence non-work life. This effect on life outside work is most obvious for such job aspects as status, security, pay and hours, but all aspects are relevant to a person's life experience as a whole.

The conclusion from our analysis must be that workers do have orientations to work. These are influenced by their social characteristics and experience in all areas of life, and tend to lead them into congruent job situations. However, they are quite limited in their effects. The orientations are of the weak form, but occasionally one may be held to such a degree as to dominate job choice, so that it may be regarded as being of the strong form.

The clearest orientation, and the one where there is most justification for seeing some workers as having strong orientations, concerns a preference for outdoor work. There is a high degree of congruence between this orientation and the work situation. This is a significant finding, which can serve to illustrate a general point. The orientation appears to be a basic liking for outdoor life which contains (but is more than) a substantial element of desire for autonomy. Knowledge of which jobs are outside is easily come by, and the jobs are usually accessible without moving through the internal labour market. Furthermore, not everyone wants outdoor work, particularly as wages tend to be a little lower, so competition for the jobs is reduced. With regard to autonomy, it will be recalled that one of the two main possible trade-offs was the hardship of working outside in all weathers in exchange for autonomy. Thus by far the easiest way to meet the desire for autonomy is through outside work. Indeed, this is the one area where workers have a considerable opportunity to exercise choice, and also where choice tends to be successfully made on the basis of definite orientations.

We observed earlier that wages are less dependent on the internal labour market than many rewards, and knowledge is fairly accurate, so we would expect a reasonable element of choice to be possible here. In fact, wages are the second-clearest orientation, again providing some grounds for regarding some workers as having orientations in the strong sense, and there is a modest degree of congruence with actual wages. The attempts to exercise choice are greater than the congruence might suggest, as workers with an economistic orientation tend to move around to find the better-paying jobs among those more immediately available (needing less than six months service). This keeps them from the best-paying jobs, which can usually be attained only by promotion within the firms and are unlikely to be offered, as employers are wary of men who have changed jobs too often.

In passing, we may note that the congruence is primarily with wages per hour rather than gross weekly wages, and hours tend to be relatively short, suggesting an orientation of "alienated instrumentalism" where the concern is to minimise the cost, in terms of the time that has to be sacrificed, to obtain a reasonable wage. This is in keeping with the tendency for those with the orientation to be family-centred, although not privatised.

The orientation concerning intrinsic job quality also emerges as important. On the whole it seems to come a little below economism, although it is marginally better related to the corresponding job rewards. Since we found that the aspects involving intrinsic interest (particularly using one's mind) clearly differentiate jobs, we would expect workers with this orientation to be relatively successful in obtaining congruent jobs. On the other hand, access to the more intrinsically attractive jobs is virtually dependent on promotion in the internal labour market, and we find those with this orientation do tend to be in jobs requiring longer service with the firm. Indeed, when we use being in such "internal" jobs as an additional indicator, we find some grounds, although perhaps not particularly good ones, for regarding a number of workers as having strong orientations.

In general, the opportunities to choose other rewards are more restricted, orientations are less clear and congruence is lower. However, a number of orientations stand out as important in one way or another. Of particular note are those relating to security, worthwhileness, trade-union strength, promotion, status and personal suitability. This is not to say they are important in terms of the numbers holding them to a high degree. For example, promotion is the only other orientation for which there is any evidence that it may usefully be regarded as existing in the strong form, yet only a handful of workers could possibly be characterised as having this as a dominant orientation. Even the orientations we have not named all have something to distinguish them. Furthermore, as we have seen, there is an element of congruence throughout, to the extent that the existence of orientations is most evident in their influence on job choice, in spite of its limited extent.

Overall, we have seen that there are very considerable constraints on the exercise of job choice. Under these circumstances we would not expect to find well-developed orientations, and we do not. Orientations can only flourish where there is some realistic possibility of their being relevant to the individual's life. In the labour market the scope for their relevance is small but variable, and the development of orientations reflects this. In view of the obstacles to rational job choice, even the limited degree of congruence between orientations and rewards is not unimpressive. Clearly the workers do their best to exercise some control over their fate in the labour market under very difficult circumstances.

Those who have the strongest orientations are those with most reason to believe they can make effective choices. They are those with relatively high status who are well integrated in the community, successful in their work careers and in relatively strong market positions – just the opposite of the workers with the deferent "personal suitability" orientation. On the one hand they have a sense of competence; on the other they accept their situations, in that their orientations relate to the non-skilled labour market and they regard the limited possibilities within it as significant.

9 Stratification Within the Manual Working Class

In the last three chapters we have concentrated on the problem of the worker's degree of choice in the labour market. We found that despite the many constraints we traced in earlier chapters, certain restricted yet real choices were being made by many workers. Around half, in fact, possessed the essential elements of "orientations", which some were able to put into effect in selecting the type of work they preferred. However, we also found that such workers tended to be in better jobs than workers without orientations, and we began to speculate whether they might constitute something of an élite within the manual working class, more confident of the control they could exercise in the labour market and actually rewarded with better jobs.

This brings the employer back into the picture. In Chapter 4 we noted the employer's concern to recruit "better" workers, in the sense of more co-operative, responsible and self-motivated workers. Perhaps the findings of the last chapter indicate that they are successful, for workers with orientations are relatively confident of their ability to control within the system given to them, and therefore to be co-operative. This would of course *stratify* the labour market into hierarchical levels, differentially rewarded by the employer. Is this what is actually happening? And if so, is the employer able to do this on the basis of real differences in terms of abilities and social background among the workers, or is the causation the other way around? After all, we doubted in earlier chapters whether the employer could really tell workers apart in terms of their abilities. Perhaps co-operativeness, confidence, and self-motivation are the *result* of being rewarded comparatively highly and not its cause. We shall see. It will be remembered that the neo-classical, dual, and radical models of the economists all presupposed a high degree of selection by the employer of "better" and "worse" workers (although the radicals have a somewhat jaundiced view of what constitutes "better"). We have presented an array of evidence concerning job structures which lends some preliminary support to their view. That is, hierarchical features of the labour market produce "better" and "worse" jobs. The question is, are these jobs filled by different kinds of worker? The three models all answer affirmatively, although they present varying hypotheses about the nature of such differences. They are:

1. *Neo-classical* Better jobs are filled by more *able* workers – more intelligent, more adaptable, more skilful, stronger.
2. *Dual* Better and worse jobs tend to polarise into two sub-markets, the primary and secondary markets. As the employer has no obvious way of distinguishing the abilities of the workers, the primary sector employer uses crude "screening devices" and discriminates against women, youths, and exploited racial and ethnic groups. Thus the better jobs will be filled by *adult, native-born, white males*.
3. *Radical* Better and worse jobs need not be so sharply polarised, although race, sex, etc., will be used as part of the employer's strategy to fill better jobs with more *co-operative* workers. The emphasis in this model is on the divisiveness of the employer's policies.

These are the descriptive hypotheses of the three models. We have collected data relevant to all three. We cannot examine sex differences within the framework of our sample, but its ethnic diversity is quite large. From a consideration of ethnic differences we shall proceed to other social characteristics of the worker, seeing whether those in better jobs are – from the viewpoint of the employer – distinctively "better" in their characteristics. Our aim is to present a full description of the degree of internal hierarchical differentiation within that segment of the working class covered by our study. We can then move in the last chapter to more theoretical conclusions concerning the nature of class.

ETHNIC STRATIFICATION

Our sample of 951 respondents contains 199 persons (21 per cent) born outside the British Isles. Rather unusually for British labour markets, the majority of these are not from the British Commonwealth but from Europe. The only large single national group are Italians. The others are more conveniently grouped by region: central and eastern Europeans (Poles, Czechs, Germans, Ukrainians and other Soviet minorities), and workers from the Indian sub-continent (Indians and Pakistanis – remembering that we interviewed before Bangladesh broke away).

There are only two West Indians and no Africans in the sample.

Obviously this is an unusual collection of immigrants, contributed principally by the brick industry, which (as in its other main centre, Bedford) recruited extensively among prisoners-of-war and European Voluntary Workers at the end of the Second World War. When this source of labour dried up, the brick companies, especially London Brick, started recruiting directly in Italy and the tradition, although declining since 1960, has continued. We find Italians and other Europeans in seven of our nine companies, although 89 out of the 146 are at London Brick and almost all have worked there at some time in the past. The Indians and Pakistanis are more widely dispersed, again in seven of our companies, but with no company contributing more than the 30 per cent of Farrow's. So in this case "immigration" is not co-terminous with "colour". We are dealing more with ethnic than racial divisions, as these terms are conventionally understood. We believe, however, that these are rather similar phenomena within the labour market. The recruiting activities of London Brick among Italians are parallel to those of major textile and rubber firms among Pakistanis. And all the groups in our sample share one problem, usually absent with West Indians in Britain, a linguistic barrier between themselves and the host-nation. Furthermore, we could find few relevant differences between the main immigrant groups in our sample. The Asians were slightly younger than the Europeans, and in terms of the job characteristics we discuss in this chapter, we will mention the few differences as we go along. As we found few significant differences within the British Isles group, i.e. no difference between English, Welsh, Scots, Irish (of whom we have very few, however), our analysis will proceed by simply contrasting British (i.e. British-Isles born) with immigrants.[1]

We will present data on wages, hours and various intrinsic job aspects (with data derived from the factor analysis of Chapter 3). Are the conditions of employment of immigrants significantly different from those of natives? However, the answer to this question is on its own insufficient to test the dualist hypotheis. Even if we demonstrate that the conditions of immigrants do differ, this might be due not to their essential "foreign-ness" but to some other, coincidental feature of the immigrant group. This is especially likely in the case of the manual labour market, given the findings we have already presented. The importance of the internal labour market, and of seniority as a criterion of promotion within it, ensure that better jobs are often filled by older workers. We will examine this in detail later in the chapter. But as immigrants are usually relatively young, they may have worse jobs for this reason alone. Thus we have controlled for age, and also for length of service and works status, in this analysis. First, then, we examine whether the immigrants do differ on these characteristics.

Table 9.1   British-born and immigrants by age, length of service and works status

Percentage in age group	− 25	25−35	36−43	44−51	52−59	60+	Total	N.
British	10	23	22	16	15	15	100	746
Immigrant	6	24	26	34	8	3	100	198

Length of service	− 1 yr	1−3 yrs	3−6 yrs	6−12 yrs	12−24 yrs	24+ yrs		
British	16	16	15	18	18	17	100	743
Immigrant	15	15	25	17	28	0	100	196

Works status	Lowest	Level 2	Level 3	Level 4	Highest			
British	10	15	36	22	18		100	746
Immigrant	16	22	35	23	4		100	198

Table 9.1 shows the expected. Immigrants are slightly younger, of slightly less seniority, and of lower works status. But the details of the table are worth close examination. It is not that the immigrants are especially youthful, but rather that they contain more of the middle-aged and fewer of the oldest workers. Only 10 per cent of them are 52 +, compared to 30 per cent of the British-born. Perhaps as a consequence, their seniority is similarly concentrated in the middle ranges, and none has worked with their present employer for 24 years or more, compared to 17 per cent of the British. But this pattern is not carried over to works status, where the difference is now at the extremes: only 4 per cent of immigrants, compared to 18 per cent of the British, are in the highest status level, while far more are in the two lowest levels (38 per cent compared to 24 per cent). Here, indeed, we have the first sign of actual ethnic difference. The low attainment of immigrants – which we can, perhaps safely, predict – is not merely a question of lack of seniority. Even when they possess seniority, it does not apparently transfer into promotion. Let us now turn to the details and mechanisms of discrimination.

First we examine the most obvious job characteristic, wages. The first

Table 9.2   British-born and immigrants — work rewards by works status level

All Workers	Mean wage per week (£)	Mean hours per week	Wage per hour (pence)	Mean Job Factor Scores*				
				Mental abilities	Skill	Autonomy	Effort	Working conditions
A British-born	27.9	48.7	58.2	0.25	0.10	-0.00	-0.03	0.18
B Immigrants	30.9	53.8	58.3	-0.60	-0.31	-0.40	-0.30	-0.13
C Difference expressed in standardised units†	0.61	0.72	0.02	0.80	0.42	0.37	0.31	0.40
D Eta value	0.25	0.29	0.00	0.33	0.19	0.15	0.12	0.20
E Differences — by status levels between British and immigrants‡								
Within lowest level	-4.3	3.4	-4.9	0.16	0.05	0.63	-0.21	0.42
Level 2	-5.7	4.8	-5.9	0.29	-0.02	0.23	0.00	0.01
Level 3	-3.6	4.1	-2.8	0.53	0.22	0.37	0.27	0.29
Level 4	-2.7	6.0	1.5	1.28	0.38	0.33	0.52	0.45
Highest level	-2.6	4.4	0.9	0.73	0.30	0.71	0.70	0.90

* For Job Factor Scores see Appendix III. The mean of these scores approximates to zero, and one standard deviation to 1.00. A positive score indicates a relatively desirable level of reward on that factor, a negative score a relatively undesirable one. This assumes consensus about the characteristics of a "desirable" job. Remember that we discovered in Chapter 5 that our sample considered the high expenditure of physical effort to be undesirable — as low opportunity to use mental abilities, skills, autonomy, and as are noisy, dirty or dangerous working conditions. Thus "effort" in this table alone is scored in reverse order to that normally used in this work.

† As a decimal proportion of 1 standard deviation from the mean of each item.

‡ A minus score indicates that British workers do less well than immigrants.

· Only 8 immigrant workers are in this category, making comparisons rather risky.

three columns of Table 9.2 contain details of wages per week, hours, and wages per hour (i.e. wages per week/hours).

We cannot pretend to have expected such results! The immigrants receive higher weekly wages than British-born workers. Nor is the difference trivial: the immigrant figure of £30.9 per week is 11 per cent higher than the £27.9 of the British. Controlling for age, length of service and status does not alter this, for the differences persist within almost all the sub-groups. There is a slight decline in the difference if we control for age – for the fact that more immigrants are prime-age males earning higher wages – but it is still there. There is, however, a very simple explanation, which the rest of the table reveals. It is that the immigrants work longer hours, 11 per cent longer to be exact, and so the wages per hour of the two groups are almost identical. Of course, as their wages contain substantial overtime premiums, their basic rate of pay must be lower than that of the natives. Within the immigrant group we find a difference here, as the non-Europeans work significantly longer hours than the Europeans. Indeed 47 per cent of them actually work 60 hours or more per week, compared to 13 per cent of the Europeans and only 5 per cent of the British. These are very large differences. But the Europeans make them up somewhat on another aspect of the wage-effort bargain: more work on piecework (55 per cent of the Europeans, 47 per cent of non--Europeans, and 40 per cent of British). These findings make clear our overall interpretation: that immigrants must work harder, either for longer hours or on piecework, in order to reach the same wage. In the last chapter we noted that immigrants from Europe, but not from Asia, were rather more "economistic" than the native-born. Thus they, at least, are highly motivated to work harder for these wages. Actually, the wages can be looked at in two ways: we can choose to emphasise the higher weekly wages of the immigrants, or we can stress the fact that immigrants must work harder for the same wage-rate. The first emphasis minimises discrimination (indeed, it reverses it), the latter maximises it. Of course, if longer hours are not available – as they would not be during a period of recession – the immigrants will do relatively less well. Nevertheless, at least in a period of high employment, wage discrimination is not high.

How do these surprising results fit in with those of other surveys? The presupposition is surely that they do not, for discrimination against immigrants is generally believed to be widespread. Indeed, several pieces of careful research conducted by P.E.P. have thoroughly documented a high level of discrimination, although the latest study showed a welcome decline in such practices (1976: Chapter 10). However, such difficulties are experienced by immigrants in job selection, not in wages. Wages *per se* do not seem to differ as much as might be expected. As we noted in Chapter 1, average differences in the wages of native and immigrant workers are in the region of 10–30 per cent. Before interpreting this, however, two controls are necessary, for job level and for age. Controlling for job level – i.e. for the depressing effect on immigrants' wages that their predominantly low-skill level produces – can sometimes *reverse* the difference. The most comprehensive recent study is that conducted in 1974 by P. E. P., to which we have just referred. That also found that the wages of the Asian and West Indian semi-skilled and unskilled men were actually *higher* than those of white men in these categories, while those of the skilled Asians and West Indians were only about 4 per cent lower than those of their white counterparts. Our results are not out of line with these. However, when P. E. P. introduced the second control and looked only at prime-age males aged 25–54, the differences at the semi- and unskilled levels disappeared entirely, and at the skilled level the white men now earned rather more (11 per cent more) than the Asians and West Indians. There were not additional differences in hours worked, but the Asians and West Indians were considerably more likely to be working on shifts, as they were also in the Department of Employment study (1976: 44–9). On both these specific points our own findings diverge from that of the P. E. P. study, but the more general point remains: that near wage-equality may be the product of greater *effort* on the part of immigrants, through longer hours, piecework or shiftwork.[2] Yet even if we take note of this, the data of the P. E. P. study do not really support the conclusion of its author, that for men "there are substantial inequalities of earnings between the minorities and whites" (1976: 84–8). The differences among manual workers are actually quite small and disappear altogether at the lower strata.

So our findings, although slightly inflating immigrants' wages, are not very atypical of the British employment scene. Also, the slight deviation is readily explicable in terms of the biases of our sample. We have not sampled thoroughly what dualists term the secondary sector of the economy. True, we have three firms located in *secondary* industries, i.e. these termed secondary by American dual theorists: Bettles, in the building industry, Combex, in low-quality plastics and chemicals, and Farrow's, in simple food-processing. But in Britain, in general, immigrants, apart from West Indians, do not work in building firms (unless one counts the Irish as immigrants). As for Farrow's, this is the main firm at which extremely long hours push up wage-rates. But excluded from our sample are the two sectors which in Britain probably pay the lowest wages (outside agriculture) and which employ large numbers of immigrants: personal services (restaurants, shops, etc.), and textiles and similar industries organised into domestic out-work and "back-street sweat shops". Compared to their comrades in these industries, our immigrants are undoubtedly privileged. Secondly, as we noted in Chapter 2, our immigrant sample is biased towards those who speak adequate English – with the exception of Italians, whom we interviewed in their own language but who are white. This naturally gave us relatively privileged immigrants. P.E.P. discovered that earnings level was strongly and positively related to fluency in English (1976: 86–7). Wherever we went we could not fail to notice that among the Asians it was the fettlers and not the foundry labourers, the machinists and not the sweepers-up, who made the language grade and were interviewed. This helps to explain the wage level of our immigrants. The rather more surprising results that now follow should be regarded as appertaining to relatively well-placed immigrants and not to the immigrant communities as a whole.

Our main contribution to the debate about immigrants in the labour market lies in our analysis not of wages – which have been documented in earlier studies – but of the intrinsic nature of the job. Here we can use our Job Scores, and the factors derived therefrom, to give a detailed picture of the jobs which this immigrant élite is asked to perform. The last five colums of Table 9.2 present these data, broken down by *works status*, one of our Job Scores measures, which divides each firm's jobs into five hierarchical levels.

We should note, therefore, that jobs of equivalent status level in different firms are *only* similar in this single aspect – their ranking *within* their firms. They may be very differently ranked in terms of overall wages and conditions. Thus this table enables us to separate two aspects of occupational achievement: the works status measure gives us relative achievement within the internal labour market, the job factor scores measure achievement within the labour market as a whole. Separating these two aspects produces rather remarkable results.

The overall finding of this table is absolutely clear: that immigrants have worse jobs: they expend more effort but use fewer manual and mental skills, they are less autonomous in their work, and their working conditions are more unpleasant. The largest difference concerns the opportunity to use mental abilities, as can be seen in Table 9.2 from row C which standardises the differences. The next largest differential is in terms of hours, followed by wages. All the differences are significant. The difference in effort was already prefigured by our wages and hours data, and confirms that to obtain equivalent wages immigrants must work harder or longer, or both. We should note that the mental abilities factor does include ability to read instructions in English, which might be thought to have a significant effect on the overall result. However, almost all the non-Italian immigrants in the sample were able to read basic English, and as there was no overall difference between the scores of the Italians and the other immigrants, we can discount this objection. The mental abilities scores are also backed up by the results for skill and autonomy. Finally, the working conditions of the immigrants are significantly worse.

So we arrive at a rather interesting finding. White and English-speaking immigrants can rival the wages of native British workers – but only at very significant costs in terms of the intrinsic nature of the job. The most frequent working-class trade-off – wages in return for unpleasant effort – is worsened even for relatively privileged immigrants.

So far, we have examined average differences between immigrants and native-born workers. But, as we noted in Chapter 1, arguments about "dual" and "segmented" labour markets should centre on actual *segregation* between the jobs and job rewards of the two groups. In a moment we shall look at job segregation itself – whether immigrants are working side-by-side with the natives. But first we can see whether the job rewards are segregated. This we have done with an analysis of variance, calculating the eta values in Table 9.2.

Eta may be taken as a measure of association between ethnicity and work rewards. As there are only two ethnic groups in question, it is analogous to a dichotomous correlation coefficient. As can be seen, except for wages per hour, the correlations are all clear, and all are significant at the 0.001 level. Now, if we square these correlations, we obtain the proportion of total variance attributable to differences between native and immigrant workers. As the correlations are not high, the values of E^2 are not very impressive. Mental abilities produces the highest figure for E^2 of 0.11, which means that ethnicity accounts for 11 per cent of the differences in the use of mental abilities within the Peterborough labour market. Hours is next with 9 per cent followed by wages – 6 per cent. This means that the degree of *segregation* between the ethnic groups is not great. Although immigrants receive less on average, their conditions overlap very considerably with those of native British workers. As we have already remarked, our sample of immigrants is to be regarded as relatively privileged, and the degree of overlap between immigrant and native workforces in Britain as a whole is perhaps a little less than this. However, the situation would have to be extraordinarily different to produce actual segregation.

Now let us see what happens in Table 9.2 when we control for works status. With one or two small exceptions, the results are uniform. Immigrants have worse jobs partly because their status is lower. But controlling for this still leaves differences which widen with higher status. This means that "status" is for immigrants somewhat deceptive, applying only to the internal labour market and not to the market as a whole. They may rise up a firm's hierarchy but this does not lead to a good job. Controlling for length of service produces almost identical results (not shown here). Thus the relative position of immigrants worsens with years of experience. As this is also true of their wages, we can see that it is a general feature of their market position. They do not seem to benefit from the internal labour market. We have two possible interpretations: either the immigrants are in the worse firms, or they are more subtly discriminated against within the higher status levels of each firm. Let us examine which.

The immigrants tend to be concentrated in a few of the firms. Almost half are in London Brick and 86 per cent are in four of the nine firms (London Brick, Baker-Perkins, British Rail and Farrow's). Our sample understates the degree of concentration. In no firm did immigrants compose more than 52 per cent of the sample (the London Brick figure). Yet we should also take account of the number of the immigrants whom we could not interview because of language difficulties. If we return to the original sampling frame, then around three-quarters of the labour force of three firms (London Brick, Combex and Farrow's) is composed of immigrants. Are these the firms that also provide the worst jobs? A negative answer is suggested by the lack of significant correlation between a firm's overall ranking on the job factor scores and the ranking of the firms according to the proportion of immigrants in their labour forces (details not given here). However, this could be because of the crudity of the comparison. In the case of the worse firms we need to know whether immigrants are doing its worst jobs. So we will look in a little more detail at the jobs being done by immigrants, and see whether they are also performed by natives. This is also the best measure of actual job segregation.

Our basic data here are the detailed job titles used by the companies and further sub-divided by us so as to enumerate separately every job whose tasks differed significantly from those of other jobs. For example, our list of job titles enumerates separately among the engine testers at Perkins "Marine Engines Tester, Rate 1", "Quality Control Tester, Rate 1", "Other Rate 1 Tester", "Long Tester, Rate 2", "No. 1 Tester,

Rate 3", and "No. 2 Tester, Rate 5", while machine operators usually have such specific titles as "Machine Operator, Base Trays: Farrow's, Preserves Department". This wealth of detail gives us much finer classification than do census data concerning ethnic segregation in the labour market. Perhaps the classification is too fine, because we are left with a number of jobs performed by only one man! If we exclude these cases, then we find that 28 per cent of the remaining immigrants do not share a job with a native British worker (25 per cent among the European immigrants and 38 per cent among the Asians). These figures are significantly higher than random allocation would produce, and so there is a measure of ethnic segregation in the labour market, but nevertheless the majority of immigrants are sharing jobs with the native-born. Except for quite trivial merit bonuses paid to the individual in one of the firms, the conditions of employment are identical within these job titles. Therefore the majority of immigrants are enjoying equality of formal treatment with at least one native-born worker. We cannot quite say that they are also working *alongside* a native-born worker, because we have no data on the physical proximity of co-workers of different ethnic groups. But workers in most of these jobs are indeed working relatively close to each other. Thus the level of occupational segregation is not high by this measure.

The next step is to examine the characteristics of those jobs which are performed by immigrants. Are they the worst of jobs? By and large the answer is positive. Virtually all the exclusively immigrant jobs (excluding the solitaries) are in the lowest two of the five status levels of their firms. Even the exceptions on the higher status levels are distinctively "immigrant jobs" in some way – they are either jobs as chargehands in command of other immigrants, or jobs involving quite complex machinery in unpleasant working conditions (e.g. as furnace operators). The distinctively immigrant jobs are spread throughout the labour market – they are in five of our nine firms – but they are at the lower levels. By contrast, the jobs shared by immigrants and native-born tend to occur at all status levels, as indeed do the all-native jobs.

Thus, among our relatively privileged working-class immigrants we find that, although the majority are integrated in formal ways into the native job structure, a minority of just under a third (and just over a third in the case of the coloured Asians) are occupying clearly segregated, low-level jobs.

These are obviously "intermediate" results in terms of the theories of the labour market we are examining. Both in terms of the jobs they do and in terms of the work rewards they receive, immigrants are not homogeneous. The degree of overlap between them and native British workers is considerable, although that is more because we find the natives at every level and in almost every job than because immigrants are similarly dispersed. As the immigrant's work life lengthens, the differences between himself and native workers widen. This parallels the findings of Parnes *et al.* (1970, Vol 1: 116–28) that occupational differences between U.S. blacks and whites are greater in their current jobs than in their first jobs. The opportunities for advancement for immigrants and ethnic minorities are extremely restricted, and there can be no doubt on our data that illegitimate discrimination against them occurs. Our Asians and most of our Europeans can speak and understand English. Our immigrants as a whole are slightly healthier than our U.K. workers. Thus most higher-level jobs in our sample are objectively within their competence, as they are within the competence of almost all workers. Yet they rarely reach them. On the other hand, there are no such obstacles to wage-earning capacity. The cross-cutting effects of these three processes – little wage discrimination, substantial discrimination in terms of other work rewards, and only partial segregation – produce a mixed situation to which immigrant organisations will have difficulty responding. Across-the-board discrimination and segregation would obviously call forth a strong anti-racist reaction of protest. But when the employment situation of immigrants is not homogeneous, industrial and political action is likely to be muted by the satisfaction of many with their wages and by the satisfaction of a few with their employment in general. Now that Britain's apparatus of immigration legislation adds only a trickle of new immigrants, we would not expect nationally any very dramatic occurrences in the sphere of race relations in industry. Overt race conflict is more likely to be found in the housing and educational spheres, where segregation is considerably greater, than in industry.

EXTREMES OF WORKER "QUALITY" – HEALTH AND QUALIFICATIONS

In this section we deal with two supposedly extreme cases of worker quality, as perceived by employers. At the lower levels are those who for reasons of ill-health simply cannot perform relatively demanding jobs. We asked workers, "Have you any injuries or health problems which limit the type of work you can do?" If the response seemed to justify a further probe, we then asked if he were a registered disabled person (Question 33). Though some workers may have wished to conceal their health limitations from us, we can safely assume that the minority who did respond positively were in fact of "low quality" from the employer's point of view. At the opposite end of the spectrum, supposedly, lie workers who possess qualifications, certificates of particular abilities valued by employers. Only a small minority of the workers did possess any such qualifications. Thus before turning to the question of "worker quality" in general, we are dealing with two small sub-samples whose attributes might seem to set them apart.

Out of 948 workers responding on this item, 136 considered that they had health limitations, and of these 26 were registered disabled. It is worth remarking this large proportion: 14 per cent of workers consider themselves handicapped in their work. Almost all the handicaps were clearly diagnosable as physical ill-health (i.e. very few explained that their problem was "nerves" or the like). The range of illness and injury was large, with back injuries, which restricted movement, especially lifting weights, as the most common disabilities. The unhealthy were somewhat older than the sample average. Of the Registered Disabled Persons (R.D.P.s) 69 per cent were aged 44 or more, as were 64 per cent of the less impaired, although this age group constituted only 46 per cent of the sample. Looked at differently and perhaps more significantly, 20 per cent of these older workers felt themselves to be in restricted physical condition. We can compare these figures to a national sample enquiry conducted by O.P.C.S. at about the same time. In response to the question, "Do you suffer from any long-standing illness, disability or infirmity which limits your activities when compared with most people of your own age?", a rather higher proportion of the older workers than in our study replied that they did. Among the age group 45–64, 24 per cent of the skilled, 34 per cent of the semi-skilled and 42 per cent of the unskilled felt limited by ill-health, as compared with 10 per cent, 11 per cent and 18 per cent respectively among the age group 15–44 (O.P.C.S., 1973: 272–80). The responses indicate only a subjective state of mind, and in any case the two studies use slightly different questions, but these results indicate that many manual workers do feel afflicted by poor health. As they grow older, illness and accidents become a substantial, even a normal, hazard.

Table 9.3 shows that the unhealthy had very different job rewards. Their wages are considerably lower (as was also the case in other British and American research, reported respectively by O.P.C.S., 1973:288, and by Parnes *et al.*, 1970, Vol. 1: 48–50), their opportunity to use skills and mental abilities is much less. On the other hand, their expenditure of effort is rather less and their degree of autonomy is greater. On all

Table 9.3 Work rewards by health

Qualification	Mean wage per week (£)	Mean hours per week	Wage per hour (pence)	Mean Job Factor Scores					N
				Mental abilities	Skill	Autonomy	Effort	Working conditions	
Normal health	28.9	49.7	59.1	0.12	0.06	-0.12	0.13	-0.12	812
Significant impairment	26.7	49.6	54.2	-0.18	-0.20	0.07	-0.10	0.02	109
Registered disabled	23.2	50.8	45.5	-0.35	-0.75	0.45	-0.31	-0.32	26
Sample average	28.5	49.7	58.2	0.08	0.01	-0.08	0.09	-0.11	947
Eta	0.23*	0.03	0.22*	0.11*	0.14*	0.10*	0.11*	0.07	

* Significant at the 0.05 level.

these items the R.D.P.s are at one extreme, with the less impaired in the middle. All the etas for these items are significant. The pattern of these very clear-cut results encourages us to believe in the utility of the self-reported measure of impairment. They are all readily interpretable: we would expect the unhealthy to be given, or only to accept, easier, less demanding jobs, and these tend to be somewhat autonomous in most employment situations. Note, however, that health only explains a small part of the average variation. The highest eta value, that for wages per week, still only explains 5 per cent of the variance. So again we see that the unhealthy, although worse off, are hardly segregated from other workers in terms of their work rewards. One of the reasons for this is that the *firm* operates as an intervening statistical variable. The unhealthy and disabled are not simply concentrated in the worst firms. Their concentration appears to be partly a product of "social conscience", operating either among management alone or in joint management-union negotiation. Baker-Perkins and Peterborough Corporation both employed more R.D.P.s than they were legally obliged to do, while London Brick had a disproportionate number of the less-seriously impaired. These firms appeared to recognise a duty to keep in employment those workers who had been damaged by the heavy work imposed on them there. And the first two of these firms were among the better employers on several dimensions.

We do not have large numbers of the unhealthy and we have little knowledge of the causes of their ailments, so we cannot come to very firm conclusions about their life histories. Most illnesses and injuries described did not seem congenital, but the result of long manual labour, poor working environment and industrial accidents themselves. Yet we did not collect systematic data on this point. What we can do, however, is to assess the stability of their deprivation, to see whether their lowly situation in the labour market was broadly predictable from knowledge of their and their family's past, or whether ill-health and disability are a potential and unpredictable outcome for most workers. We examined both the level of their first job and that of their father (see below, for an explanation of the precise methods used here). There was a very slight tendency (significant at the 0.05 level) for the unhealthy to have had fathers with lower job levels, but the degree of association was weak: gamma was 0.13. There was no relationship at all between level of first job and health. We thus conclude that the degree of inheritance and life-time stability of generalised deprivation was very limited. The unhealthy are not a stable quasi-*lumpenproletariat*.

At the other end of the spectrum are surely workers with

qualifications. As we noted in Chapter 1, these are an important part of the human-capital theory of neo-classical economics. Employers wish to fill their better jobs with better workers and are thought in this model to use educational or job training qualifications as indicators of the quality of a worker. However, we noted two problems confronting the model. Firstly, there is some doubt at the manual level whether jobs are sufficiently skilled to require an unusual degree of worker abilities. Our own data have emphatically supported this objection. Secondly, with regard to Britain, very few manual workers have proper qualifications anyway. This is true within our own sample where only 4 per cent have any educational qualification (to the level of C.S.E. or G.C.E. "O" level), only 5 per cent have completed an apprenticeship or obtained an O.N.C. or City and Guilds qualification, and a further 5 per cent have obtained lesser work qualifications (such as completing an army training scheme).[3] However, we must consider whether this minority are somewhat differentiated from the rest of the sample.

Table 9.4 compares the average level of attainment of the qualified vs the non-qualified in a way that by now will be familiar. We have separated the qualified into those with either completed apprenticeships or lesser job training qualifications and those who have educational qualifications (and who, in addition, may have passed through job training). Only the briefest comment is necessary on a table which finds virtually no difference. Only the eta value for the use of mental abilities attains a significant level, and it is interesting that this is due to the better jobs of those whose qualifications were obtained at work rather than in the classroom. Within this stratum of the working class, therefore, formal qualifications appear to count for little. (For rather different U.S. findings, see Parnes *et al.*, 1970, Vol. 1: 50–3.)[4]

WORKER QUALITY IN THE MASS

We have so far found two sub-groups in the male manual workforce. Both immigrants and the infirm tend to be in less-favoured categories, their mobility and their work rewards restricted. If we turn to the mass of workers, do we find further stratification within it? Are there clearly differentiated strata in terms of market position and job content? We will answer this at first with respect to the *employer's* attempt to stratify. In Chapter 4 we noted the way in which employers try to distinguish between what they consider to be better and worse prospective

Table 9.4   Work rewards by qualifications

Qualifications	Mean wage per week (£)	Mean hours per hour	Wage per hour (pence)	Mean Job Factor Scores					N
				Mental abilities	Skill	Autonomy	Effort	Working conditions	
None	28.5	49.8	58.1	0.03	−0.02	−0.09	0.10	−0.11	802
Job only	28.3	48.9	58.8	0.44	0.16	−0.01	−0.02	−0.10	101
Educational or job + educational	29.3	50.5	58.9	0.11	0.11	−0.11	0.17	−0.19	40
Sample average	28.5	49.7	58.2	0.08	0.01	−0.09	0.09	−0.11	943
Eta	0.03	0.05	0.02	0.12*	0.06	0.02	0.05	0.02	

* Significant at the 0.05 level

employees. If they are actually able to allocate workers to jobs according to such criteria, we would expect to find better workers (from their perspective) to be in better jobs. Let us see whether this is so.

When we examine the employers' preferences, however, a problem arises. For some of those preferences are not for workers of a kind different from others, but for workers at a different point of their life cycle. The preference shown towards married men with small children, usually around the age of 30, if successfully determining job allocation, cannot stratify the working class (in the conventionally understood sense of that term) because we can presume that most workers will go through this stage. Accordingly, for the moment we will leave aside lifecycle factors, or we will control for their effects, and concentrate on those employer strategies which might conceivably stratify within the working class. The following analysis concerns only native-born British and Irish workers who consider themselves to be in good health; it therefore excludes the confusing effects of the two sub-markets we have discussed.

The worker characteristics which might stratify are all equal-interval continuous variables and so we have used product-moment correlations to relate them to work rewards. This is not ideal in the case of one of the variables, however. "Number of times unemployed" does not have a normal distribution, as two-thirds of the sample have never been unemployed.[5] As the job rewards all have normal distributions, their correlations with this item are artificially reduced. Thus we will also use non-parametric statistics to establish their association.

The variables in Table 9.5 fall into three groups. First come those which represent the employer's view of worker quality (bearing in mind that we have already shown that worker qualifications are of negligible importance). It will be remembered that, at the end of the interview, our interviewers were asked to assess the worker's ability to comprehend and respond meaningfully to the questions. This was done on a 16-point scale. Naturally we do not claim this interviewer rating to be an objective measure of "ability". The worker's responsiveness is a mixture of at least three important ingredients whose individual contributions are unknown: co-operativeness, intelligence, and fluency in English (or Italian). Yet these are precisely the qualities that the employer is seeking – not intelligence or ability *per se*, but a willingness to comply with instructions as well as to understand them. We discussed this at length in Chapter 4, and it seems to us that our rating procedure is a slightly more systematic version of the employer's own assessment techniques (more systematic, because based on a three-quarter hour

Table 9.5 Correlation matrix of employers' measures of worker quality, actual work rewards and control variables (healthy U.K. workers only).

	1	2	3	4	5	6	7	8	9	10	11	12	13	14	15
Worker Quality															
1. Interviewer Rating															
2. No of firms	-0.09														
3. No. times unemployed	-0.02	0.23													
4. Degree of radicalism	-0.04	-0.05	0.00												
Work Rewards															
5. Wages per week	0.16	-0.21	-0.14	0.06											
6. Hours	-0.08	-0.02	0.00	-0.06	0.05										
7. Wages per hour	0.18	-0.15	-0.12	0.09	0.78	-0.57									
8. Use of mental abilities	0.21	-0.13	-0.12	-0.13	0.18	-0.02	0.15								
9. Use of skills	0.14	-0.12	-0.07	0.02	0.18	0.06	0.11	0.66							
10. Autonomy	0.04	-0.03	0.03	-0.14	-0.32	0.33	-0.48	0.46	0.30						
11. Effort	-0.11	0.16	0.04	0.13	-0.03	-0.07	0.04	-0.42	-0.21	-0.25					
12. Working conditions	-0.08	0.13	0.08	0.10	0.04	-0.05	0.07	-0.33	0.05	-0.29	0.34				
13. General interest	0.20	-0.14	-0.10	-0.08	0.18	0.05	0.11	0.92	0.86	0.44	-0.42	-0.15			
Controls															
14. Age	-0.15	0.10	0.08	-0.27	0.00	0.17	-0.12	0.09	0.03	0.24	-0.14	-0.05	0.07		
15. Length of service	0.04	-0.35	0.00	-0.04	0.26	0.06	0.16	0.30	0.23	0.25	-0.26	-0.16	0.30	0.52	

Minimum number = 602
Maximum number = 640
Significance: All correlations of 0.06 or more significant at 5% level

interview instead of a 10 minute one). Therefore, we use Interviewer Rating as an indicator of the employer's assessment of quality, not quality *per se*. This naturally applies to the other indicators as well. We noted in Chapter 4 that the employer considers frequent changing of jobs and unemployment as evidence of undesirable instability. Indeed, we hypothesised that overall the employer is more interested in reliability and co-operativeness than in "native abilities". We have pushed this hypothesis to its extreme in predicting a (negative) relationship between radicalism and job rewards. The indicator of radicalism is the first factor derived from an analysis of responses to the nine-part Question 17 of the interview survey.[6]

The work reward variables should be familiar to the reader by now. For the first time in this chapter we have added the summary job factor of "General Interest", which combines all the indicators of the intrinsic attractiveness of a job. Finally, we have introduced as controls, age and length of service.

Let us note firstly that the four indicators of the employer's assessment of worker quality are all associated in the predicted way with major work rewards. Those rated more highly by the interviewer have better jobs in the sense that they are likely to be using more mental and manual skills, to have better working conditions, to have work that is less physically tiring, to work shorter hours but at a higher rate of pay (none of this information was available to interviewers at the time, so a "halo effect" cannot have been operating). Only autonomy is not significantly related to the interviewer rating. Secondly, the number of previous employers is significantly related, as predicted, to all the rewards except hours and autonomy. Thirdly, the number of times unemployed is related, as predicted, to all rewards except hours, autonomy and effort. If we trichotomise this variable into those never unemployed, those unemployed once, and those unemployed more than once, and then do an analysis of variance, w largely confirm these findings: the eta values are significant for wages (both measures) and mental and manual skill, but not for working conditions. Finally, radicalism is more weakly related to most of the intrinsic job rewards, but its relationship to wages is in the opposite direction to that predicted. This is the only significant relationship existing in the opposite direction. Although the general level of correlation is not high, the pattern of results is consistent and significant. Stability and co-operativeness are apparently rewarded, although more in terms of the job content than of wages.

Yet nterpretation must await further analysis. The control variables appear to be intervening in various ways. Length of service is related to all the work rewards, demonstrating the importance of the internal labour market in bringing a better job to the worker. Yet it is naturally strongly and negatively related to number of previous employers. Age is also related to some of the work rewards, but is positively related to previous employers and unemployment, and negatively to radicalism. Quite clearly we must sort out the confusing effects of these variables. Moreover, they also affect any causal argument we might make – a co-operative set of attitudes might be the result of high job rewards rather than the cause of them. Length of service is the key here, and we need to add the further control of length of service in *present job*. In Table 9.6 we give the partial correlations between the indicators of worker quality and work rewards, with age, length of service in present employment and length of service in present job simultaneously controlled for.

Table 9.6 Partial correlation coefficients between employers' measures of worker quality and work rewards. Age, length of service in firm and length of service in job controlled for (healthy U.K. workers only).

	Interviewer rating	No. of firms	No. of times unemployed	Radicalism
Wages per week	0.12	−0.07	−0.14	0.02
Hours	−0.05	−0.07	−0.01	−0.01
Wages per hour	0.13	−0.01	−0.11	−0.03
Use of mental abilities	0.19	0.01	−0.13	−0.16
Use of skills	0.12	−0.01	−0.08	−0.00
Autonomy	−0.05	0.02	0.01	−0.10
Effort	−0.10	0.08	0.05	0.12
Working conditions	−0.06	0.07	0.08	0.10
General interest	0.19	0.00	−0.11	−0.11

Maximum N = 631
Minimum N = 617
All correlations of 0.07 or more are significant at 5 % level.

The effect of the controls is to reduce the degree of association found in Table 9.5. The interviewer's rating is now more weakly related to the work rewards, and indeed it is no longer significantly related to either the length of hours or working conditions. Yet those regarded by our interviewers as intelligent/co-operative are still more likely to have higher wages, more skilled jobs (both in the manual and mental sense) and to work at a more moderate pace. The worker's radicalism is also less of a predictor, except in the case of the use of mental abilities (where the relationship is now stronger). The greatest decline occurs in the case of the number of previous firms worked for, and the remaining associations (wages, hours, effort and working conditions) are barely significant. Age and length of service clearly account for most of the apparent relationship here. Finally, however, the number of times unemployed is unaffected by the controls. Those previously unemployed remain significantly more likely to receive lower wages, lower-skill jobs and worse working conditions.

To control for variables is not, however, to discount them. Age and length of service both have interesting independent effects upon work rewards, as can be seen from Table 9.5. Length of service is quite strongly related to work rewards and it is largely a linear relationship: the greater the seniority, the higher the rewards. There is thus no tendency at the longest-serving levels for a slight decline, with fading strength. The latter undoubtedly occurs, but the worker with seniority is protected from it. Once again the importance of the internal labour market is highlighted. For native-born British workers the best way to get ahead is to stay with the same employer. By contrast, age – although obviously related to seniority – is less clearly associated with work rewards. Older workers have two distinct advantages, greater autonomy and less effort. But in return for this they have slightly lower wages and longer hours.

Yet these correlations conceal almost as much as they reveal, for the effect of age is not linear. Indeed, four of the work rewards, the two measures of wages, mental abilities, and skills, have a clear curvilinear relationship with age. We show three of these (omitting wages per hour) in Figure 9.1, along with their relationship to length of service. These work rewards rise to a peak between the ages of 31 and 40, then drop down to just above the level from which the worker started. When we look at length of service an interesting contrast emerges. Wages are still distributed in a curvilinear fashion, peaking at between 10 and 15 years service, and then dropping slightly. But the drop is much less and the final wages earned are considerably higher than starting wages. These findings are almost identical to a U.S. study of white workers (apparently at all occupational levels) among whom earnings – peaking slightly later, at the age of 44, than in our sample – drop off with advancing years much more markedly than at the highest levels of seniority (Alexander, 1974: 78). When we turn to job skills in our sample, we find no deterioration at all with the highest seniority levels – indeed, these are the workers with the most mentally and manually skilled jobs. So these core rewards of wages and skill are apparently conferred by seniority much more than by age, and indeed the seniority

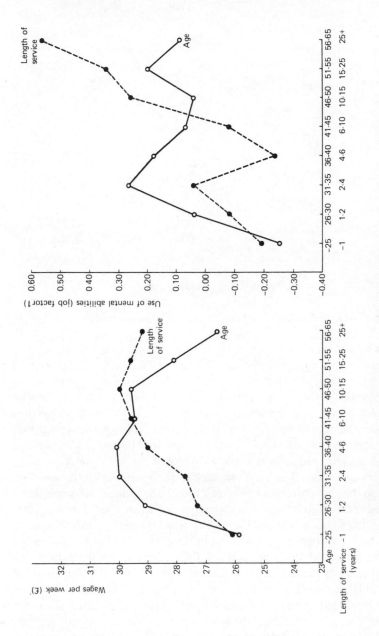

Figure 9.1 Wages per week and use of mental ability and skill by age and seniority (whole sample)

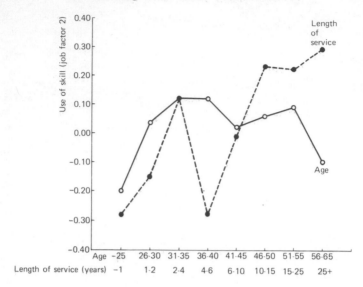

Figure 9.1:   (continued)

required for significant improvement is considerable – around 10 years.[7]

Obviously there are two contrasting mechanisms at work, one connected with ageing, the other with seniority. The latter can protect the worker from the effects of the former. This is so even if age brings ill-health with it, for – if we control for age – there is no relationship between health and length of service, i.e. the unhealthy are not discharged if they have seniority. But without seniority the worker will experience a cycle of rising rewards until middle age and a decline thereafter. With wages there is also evidence of the "life cycle squeeze" – workers with dependent children *need* money more. Both the age data and also the high correlation between wages and numbers of dependents (partial correlation between wages per week and number of dependents, controlling for length of service in firm, is 0.29) reveal that they actually get it. Life cycle processes could not in themselves produce *stable* stratification within the working class, for they merely divide workers at different points in their life. But the intervention of seniority, that is, of the internal labour market, could stratify, especially among older workers. Those protected by an internal labour market in late middle age are in a very different situation from those who are unprotected. Moreover, this division seems reinforced by employer preferences. Those who stay put are cumulatively rewarded, while those who move are cumulatively punished. Workers defined by management as less able and co-operative, and who are more radical, will be unable to attain seniority and will experience greater unemployment and job mobility. This, in turn, will lower their quality in management eyes.

All managements are not equal, however. As we saw in earlier chapters, some firms are distinctly better than others and are recognised as such by many workers. The better firms are more popular and recruit more easily and selectively. We might ask, therefore, whether there are significant association between the quality of work *forces* and the level of reward offered by the firms. Unfortunately, our sample is not well suited to this form of analysis. We have only nine firms in our sample, which is a very small number on which to perform statistical operations. In particular, we are unlikely to reach acceptable significance levels unless we find almost perfect association. We computed Spearman rank correlations between four measures of the average level of "quality" of workforces and the average level of rewards in each firm, and although some of the associations seemed quite strong, none was significant. The highest associations involved the proportion of each firm's total manual workforce with poor command of English and the average previous job level of the sample in each firm.[8] For example, the rank correlation between the former and each firm's average weekly wages was 0.40, while that between the previous job level and each firm's average 'general interest' factor score was 0.45. These were the highest correlations, but even these were not significant. In general, the correlations were in the expected direction, so that 'better' workers were in better firms, but we must regard this result as tentative rather than demonstrated.

A certain consistency has emerged in our findings so far. Quality, as defined by management, is rewarded. However, the tendencies are not overwhelming in their effects. It may be doubted whether they are sufficiently strong, stable or predictable to stratify workers in any enduring manner. The most impressive evidence for the stability of stratification would be if hierarchical differences were transmitted intergenerationally. How similar are the jobs of our sample to those of their fathers?

THE STABILITY OF DIFFERENTIALS

We do not intend to delve deeply into the fast-growing "social mobility industry" within academic sociology. We shall confine ourselves to making a few limited comparisions. Yet in one respect our mobility data are quite rich. Our intensive study of job characteristics has enabled us, within the occupational field of our sample, to validate more fully than most sociological studies the occupational hierarchy with which we operate.[9] Our hierarchy is composed, not of groups defined according to the extraordinarily vague concept of "prestige" or "social standing" (as is usual in mobility studies) but in terms of job characteristics that are recognisable and meaningful to workers themselves. Now, the existence of a hierarchy cannot be assumed: it has to be demonstrated. Chapters 3 and 4 made clear that a hierarchy among manual occupations exists but is far from perfect. Our indicator of hierarchy is imperfect, not primarily because of measurement error but rather because *reality* is not quite so hierarchical. Yet, additionally, as soon as we compare our respondents' present jobs with any others they may previously have held in other firms, or which other family members might have held, we are bound to introduce measurement errors. For such occupations we do not have precise objective data. Therefore, our methodology in studying mobility has been to attempt to fit occupational titles not in our sample into their equivalent level within the sample. We derived five broad strata within our occupational range, not by statistical means but in terms of descriptive categories based on our knowledge of labour markets in general and a preliminary inspection of the raw job scores: They are:

3. *Skilled* Not the Registrar General's Social Class III, Manual, but a more restrictive category including only those jobs for which an apprentice training or its equivalent is available (although this need not be the normal requirement), e.g. fitters, turners, carpenters, bricklayers, grade I or II gardeners and groundsmen, railway-engine crews.

4. *High semi-skilled* Highly specialist work without formal training but requiring a lengthy learning period and considerable knowledge of routines, e.g. engine testers, furnace operators, storekeepers.

5. *Medium semi-skilled* Jobs requiring some measure of both precision and knowledge, which can yet be picked up fairly quickly, e.g. complex machining, drivers, storemen with clerical duties.

6. *Low semi-skilled* Jobs requiring precision of movement but a negligible learning period, e.g. mates, assemblers, routine machining, specialised labouring.

7. *Unskilled* Neither accuracy nor knowledge required, e.g. machine-minders, cleaners, labourers, warehousemen.

We have numbered from 3, because for certain purposes we shall insert above these categories two non-manual ones:

1. Registrar General's Social Class I or II.
2. Registrar General's Social Class III, Non-manual (i.e. lower manual).

We have no empirical validation from within our study for the hierarchical position of these two categories. In Table 9.7 can be found the validation for the ordering of categories 3 to 7.

Table 9.7 Correlations between job level and work rewards (whole sample)

	Job Level
Wages per week	0.19
Wages per hour	0.19
Hours	0.04
Mental abilities	0.73
Skill	0.74
Autonomy	0.26
Effort	−0.33
Working conditions	−0.15
Position in hierarchy	0.71
General interest	0.83

Our main descriptive criterion was skill, and it can be seen that this proved to be extraordinarily accurate. The correlation of the ordering with the general interest factor is 0.83, a remarkably high figure (and one that staggered us!)[10] Component parts of this factor, mental abilities and skill, are naturally also highly correlated with level, as (reassuringly) is poition in the firm's hierarchy. All the factors except hours are strongly and significantly correlated. Let us emphasise that there is no "absolute" validation of a constructed ordering such as this. We have simply produced an ordering that is a very good predictor of attractiveness, particularly in terms of job skills and to a lesser extent in terms of other real and important work rewards.

With this in mind we can relate present occupation to father's occupation. For this, two controls were absolutely necessary. In the first place the fathers of the immigrants often had inadequately described or pre-industrial occupations which were not strictly comparable with ours. Therefore, we have excluded immigrants from our mobility calculations. Secondly, although our sample's own jobs had to come from levels 3 to 7, those of their fathers could also be in 1 or 2. Thus to test statistically the degree of association between the two generations' occupations we had to exclude all workers whose fathers' occupations were in levels 1 or 2. Thus although Table 9.8 contains those with non-manual fathers, it only gives statistics appertaining to those with fathers in levels 3 to 7. Before interpreting the results, one caution is necessary. Ideally, intergenerational mobility data should compare fathers and children at similar points in their life cycle/work career. We have not done this; father's occupation was asked for at the time that the respondent left school, while occupation of respondent is measured at whatever point in his career the worker had reached in 1970. Thus our data probably underestimate slightly the degree of occupational stability, although very much less than if orderly career patterns of the type found in non-manual jobs existed among manual workers.

There is no significant relationship, if we exclude those with non-manual fathers, between own job level and the father's.[11] That is to say, there is no significant tendency for those with higher-level fathers to hold higher-level jobs themselves. This summary statistic is composed of two main elements. Firstly, there is no substantial amount of inheritance of exact occupational level; although the skilled and unskilled tend to inherit, the other levels do not. Secondly, there is no tendency for a normal distribution to form around the inheritance cases (which we have boxed in the table). There seems to be a high degree of random intergenerational mobility within our sample. This impression is confirmed if we compute the associations between both present and father's level, on the one hand, with an occupational level which is intermediate in time, that of the respondent's own first job.

present job and first job—tau $b = 0.08$, gamma $= 0.10$ (N$=485$)
father's job and first job—tau $b = 0.13$, gamma $= 0.18$ (N$=367$)[12]

Both taus are significant at the 5 per cent level, although they are still very low. Jobs that are relatively close together in the worker's life history share some similarity, but the longer the time scale the weaker the link.

Table 9.8 Present job level by job level of father (healthy U.K. workers only)

	Higher non-manual	*Lower non-manual*	*Skilled*	*High semi-skilled*	*Medium semi-skilled*	*Low semi-skilled*	*Unskilled*	*N*
				Father's Job				
Skilled	8	12	33	6	15	10	15	99
High semi-skilled	7	10	6	4	14	8	14	63
Medium semi-skilled	15	23	45	20	36	26	52	217
Low semi-skilled	13	13	31	16	26	8	38	145
Unskilled	5	2	6	13	13	5	16	60
N	48	60	121	59	104	57	135	584

Statistics (excluding non-manual fathers): tau *b* = 0.06 not significant at 0.05 level
gamma = 0.07 (N = 476)

Similar results occur if we look at other qualities of the worker which are predictors of his level of job reward. Seniority and number of times unemployed are unrelated to level of first job or father's job. Health – as we noted earlier – was weakly related to father's job but unrelated to own first job. On the other hand, as we have seen, these qualities are all related to present job level, and – we might add – are rather more weakly related to the worker's previous job. Long-term continuity of experience seems lacking, and we are unable to predict the worker's hierarchical destination in terms of his hierarchical beginnings.

Another way of examining the degree of stratification within our sample is to look at the pattern of social relationships. Here we used a measure of class status which employs multi-dimensional scaling of the occupations of respondents and their friends (for an explanation of this technique, see Stewart *et al.*, 1973). This method examines the relationship between the respondent's own occupation and those of the four closest friends whose occupations were named in response to Question 40. It is an example of "social distance" approaches to the study of stratification. Naturally, social distance between friends is minimal! But the interesting question is whether *occupations* tend to be close to each other. If a clear-cut hierarchy of occupations existed within our sample, we might expect this to be revealed in friendship patterns. This technique first establishes the "distance" in terms of friendship choices, between each occupation, and all the others, and then enables us to see whether a good "one-dimensional solution" to the distances exists – can the occupations be placed on a graph and their positions fitted by a single line? Finally, if this were so, we can deduce that this dimension is a hierarchy if, say, the occupations at one extreme resemble labouring jobs while those at the other are craft positions – this, of course, is not a statistical operation but an act of the sociological imagination! The technique has been recently applied to a large sample of non-manual workers (by one of the present authors, together with collaborators), and a clear one-dimensional solution emerged which was obviously hierarchical. Therefore, non-manual workers' interaction patterns are internally stratified (Stewart *et al.*, 1973). Yet within our sample no clear one-dimensional solution was revealed. Friendships were predominantly within the occupational stratum we investigated, and such differentiation as occured within this reflected residence and place of work rather than internal stratification. Indeed, an attempt at a two-dimensional solution revealed a map of occupational distributions which bore some resemblance to an actual map of Peterborough. The lack of interaction between certain occupations could be explained by our drawing the River Nene – a real geographical barrier within the town – across the two-dimensional solution!

CONCLUSIONS

With two exceptions we have not found any marked degree of internal stratification in the labour market chances of our sample. Those exceptions are health and ethnic identity, both of which tend towards the segregation of a minority of the workforce. Nationally, all immigrants (excluding the Irish) constitute around 4 per cent of the workforce. If our data are representative, a rather larger proportion – perhaps 15 per cent of manual workers – suffer from health problems which limit their labour market opportunities. They are, disproportionately, older workers. For the rest of our sample the only other substantial differentiator was also the ageing process, or, to be more precise, the related process of *work-life*. Seniority is the major systematic determinant of differential opportunities within that large segment of the working class which we have studied. As the discrimination against immigrants was more marked among longer-service workers, all our findings point in the same direction. Hierarchical differentiation separates workers at different points in their *career cycle*. It is a *temporary* phenomenon, repeated anew by each generation of workers. It does not lead to the development of segregated strata within the manual working class. This is partly because the process seems largely unpredictable. With the exception of the ascriptive identity conferred by ethnic groups, we have not found clear predictors of success at attaining seniority. Some attain it, some do not. Managerial selection policies affect attainment slightly, and workers with the "right" qualities and attitudes are marginally more likely to be rewarded.

Of course, as we showed in the last chapter, other social characteristics of the workers are related to the type of job they hold. In general, however, this does not have the effect of stratifying the workers, for two reasons. Firstly, some of the most important characteristics – as we have noted – concern the temporary stages of the life cycle. Married workers use more mental abilities and skills and earn more money than single, widowed, or divorced workers, but this difference disappears if we control for age. Workers with more dependents are less autonomous, put in more effort, and earn more, and these differences remain even if we control for age. These are hardly ways in which stable stratification could emerge. Secondly, some of the characteristics are associated rather with "different" than with "better" jobs, as we have just seen is the case with number of dependents. Workers who live in rural areas also differ somewhat; they are less autonomous, work harder, have worse working conditions, but work shorter hours and receive higher wages per hour. The only clear-cut hierarchical differences are found among those who were born in Peterborough (who have slightly better jobs than the rest of the British) and those who have worked previously in agriculture (who have slightly worse jobs). These differences are not particularly impressive. However, most of the selection criteria used by managers are either totally out of the worker's power to manipulate (like race) or partially unintelligible to him (like an assessment of co-operativeness). Overall, the market seems sufficiently chaotic to allow circumstances a very powerful role. If the worker finds himself in a progressive internal labour market, then provided his firm does not go bankrupt, and he keeps his health, he will be relatively advantaged. But his initial allocation to that position seems to us to be largely random, and his advantage cannot be transferred to his children. Thus, although the market contains strong hierarchical elements, and although hierarchical selection procedures operate, the *stability* of the hierarchy is but weakly developed. For this reason the term "stratification" seems wholly inappropriate as a way of describing differentiation within our sample. We withhold final comment on theories of class and of the labour market until the next chapter, but it is clear from this discussion that in many respects the workers share a common situation.

10 Conclusions

We began the account of our research in Chapter 2, relating the population from which we sampled – male manual workers whose jobs did not require them to be qualified by apprentice training – to the other major manual working groups. Virtually complete segregation exists in the manual labour market between men and women, who are almost never in competition as individuals. In contrast, no such clear-cut gap exists between "skilled" and semi- or unskilled workers. Using a broad definition such as that of the O.P.C.S. (Registrar General), most skilled workers have not served an apprenticeship or its equivalent, and their differentiation from workers beneath them is precarious. Even in those jobs normally performed by qualified craftsmen there are many unqualified workers. However, the possession of qualifications derived from formal apprenticeship does set some craftsmen apart from other "skilled" workers, by enhancing their market capacity and thus their independence of the employer. We will comment on this later. Our study concerns male manual workers who do not have nationally-recognised credentials for their work – perhaps three-quarters or even four-fifths of male manual workers.

In Chapter 2 we also explained our choice of the research setting and sampling procedure. To start with, we needed to find a relatively self-contained labour market, with a variety of different types of manual employment and a relatively low rate of unemployment, so that there could be a real possibility of job choice, rather than of just working or not working. This led us to Peterborough, a medium-sized town on the fringe of East Anglia, with an ancient tradition of brick manufacture and a rather more recent one as a railway centre. Despite the general decline of the railways both industries are still important in the town today. More recently Peterborough has developed as an engineering centre and, not surprisingly in view of the rich agricultural hinterland, food-processing has become important. This combination of major industries in a town of modest size has given Peterborough an unusual variety and volume of employment. We were able to sample a great variety of jobs in nine firms of widely different type and size, both in manufacturing industry and outside of it, and to examine the ethnic diversity now characteristic of many British labour markets. We will discuss the "typicality" of our sample later on.

The next stage, reported in Chapter 3, was to study the jobs. We looked at several hundred different jobs and their location in the work process. On 368 of these we carried out a detailed "job scoring" analysis, rating them on 31 different aspects of work, covering diverse features of working conditions, mental and manual skills, autonomy, social interaction, status, shifts, and promotion practices. Of these jobs, 275 were held by workers in our samples, for whom we collected details of wages and hours. Thus we were also able to estimate average wages and hours for these 275 jobs. We first asked a simple question: "Do high rewards on one aspect tend to be accompanied by high rewards on all aspects?" We concluded that on balance they do, and therefore that the overall structure of the market is *hierarchical* rather than compensatory. Within this structure, however, several compensatory possibilities – i.e. possibilities for worker choice – exist. Since all the relationships are only tendencies, an element of possible choice exists throughout, but beyond this there are a few distinct possibilities – at least in principle.

Firstly, workers can obtain short or regular hours of work in return for generally low rewards on other dimensions, including wages. Secondly, high job autonomy in outside work can be obtained by those who are prepared to put up with the discomforts of cold or wet weather in jobs that are apt to be rather poorly paid and lacking in other attractions. Finally, wage levels (which have naturally tended to dominate the economists' view of the labour market) cannot be simply fitted into either a hierarchical or a compensatory model; high wages are associated with some other high rewards, as well as with some other low ones. The explanation may be seen in the results of our analysis in Chapter 4 (as we shall explain in a moment).

In exploring the relationships between job aspects we carried out a factor analysis which revealed that the structure is not only hierarchical but has a distinct pattern. Rewards cluster into different types which vary together. For example, all aspects relating to the use of mental abilities are positively related, which means that a worker cannot normally choose a job allowing him to use his mind in one way rather than another. This fact gave us the opportunity to create several general factors to measure job characteristics, which we used in subsequent analysis. From the point of view of job choice, there are two consequences. On the one hand, it is not generally possible to sacrifice one aspect of a given sort of reward in order to gain another. On the other, this simplifies the structure of alternatives, and to this extent makes choice easier, especially for workers with limited knowledge. However, against this is the fact that the relations between the factors are essentially hierarchical.

Chapter 3 was somewhat abstract, taking no account of the fact that jobs in a labour market are actually grouped into firms, with their own internal labour markets. In Chapter 4, therefore, we undertook an analysis to examine the relative contributions of internal and external markets. The intra-firm variations on all items is largely contributed by the internal labour market; with seniority the worker may be promoted to jobs that tend to be better in all respects. Thus there are actually two alternative routes to higher wages; either one takes high-paying but intrinsically unpleasant jobs, which are more readily available with some of the firms, or one stays with virtually any firm hoping for promotion to generally better jobs. This accounts for the confused results concerning wages in Chapter 3. Yet the internal market distributes wages less than it does other job rewards. Inter-firm differences are preponderantly for hourly wage rates, and although the low-paying firms tend to make up some of the leeway in actual earnings by offering very long hours at overtime rates, the differences within firms are only partly due to the internal market. On the other hand, intra-firm differences dominated several aspects of job content. Differences between firms are usually sufficient to allow the possibility of choice but, particularly for those characteristics affecting the interest of the job, most of the variance is within firms and is largely related to the internal promotion hierarchy.

We then asked whether internal labour markets are uniform and predictable and concluded that in general they are not. Most promotion practices are unclear and so the entering worker can rarely be in a position to predict his "career" within the firm. Thus the internal market reduces the possibilities for choice. However, the possibilities we unearthed in Chapter 3 are not lost, and we can now add a precise choice with regard to wages. The other possibilities indicate that higher wages go with bad hours and low autonomy; to this we can add the chance of moderately high wages in return for intrinsic unpleasantness. The attractive combination of high wages *and* a better job is possible, through internal promotion, but is not within the worker's control.

Looking closely at the intrinsic quality of the jobs revealed a significant point. For, no matter that job skills differed relatively to one's position in the internal market, the *absolute* level of skill of all but the very highest jobs is – to say the least – minimal. Eighty-seven per cent of our workers exercise less skill at work than they would if they drove to work. Indeed, most of them expend more mental effort and resourcefulness in getting to work than in doing their jobs. From this remarkable result flow two important consequences. In the first place, nobody can choose a challengingly skilled job, no matter how much he is prepared to sacrifice in terms of wages and other work rewards. The most effective way to intrinsically attractive manual jobs is through a craft apprenticeship. For unqualified workers, the only such jobs, few as they are, exist at the top of the internal labour market, necessitating years of seniority and bringing higher wages as well. For the most part the jobs differ in this respect only: they involve different levels of human debasement. Secondly, it follows that most workers are objectively capable of acquiring the skills necessary for most jobs; we estimate that 85 per cent of workers can do 95 per cent of jobs. Management would disagree with us; they are very concerned – as neo-classical economists would expect – with a shortage of "worker quality". However, when we investigated what they meant by this, we found that they were worried, not about intelligence or manual dexterity, but about *worker co-operation*. Responsibility, stability, trustworthiness – such are the qualities by which (reasonably enough) they wish to select and promote. From the employer's point of view, the internal labour market allows workers to demonstrate these qualities (if they have them) over a number of years before they reach jobs where mistakes would matter. It should be noted that all this is very much in accord with the radical political economists' view of the internal labour market which we discussed in Chapter 1. By contrast, little support could be given to the *human capital*, neo-classical view of "worker quality" in the labour market.

In Chapter 5 we switched to the workers' subjective experience of the labour market. We found that they had about as much knowledge of the market as we could reasonably expect them to have, considering its complexity. We also noted that their sources of information must of necessity be informal and poor, as employers reveal virtually nothing to prospective employees. When workers felt able to rank firms according to their wage level, they did so with reasonable accuracy, and when they claimed knowledge about other work rewards, this too was not inaccurate. However, most workers possessed little knowledge *in toto* or in detail, and they were heavily dependent either on general public stereotypes or on supposed "visible indicators" of a firm's exact conditions. Thus, for example, the presence of large numbers of woman or immigrant workers would be used as an indication of poor wage-rates and working conditions – and, more often than not, this would be a correct inference.

In Chapters 6 to 8 we examined the question of orientations to work. Given that there does exist a limited amount of opportunity for choice in the structure of job rewards and that workers do have enough knowledge, it still does not follow that choices are made. For this the workers must have preferences which are substantially independent of immediate work experience, which means that they have "orientations". Thus their existence and nature is central to the operation of the labour market – not just for the neo-classical model to which they are essential, but for the whole question of choice and control. Assuming they exist, a particular issue is whether orientations are of the strong form, where an individual may be characterised by a dominant concern for one type of reward, or the weak form, where he has a set of varying degrees of orientation covering all job aspects. The strong form, which has been predominant in previous literature, simplifies the problem of job choice for the worker. With the weak form job choice is less clear, in that it calls for more complex knowledge, so that it has to operate not through the pursuit of specific rewards but by making decisions between more limited and concrete alternatives.

In Chapter 6 we took a general look at this problem and explored the persistence of orientations across different frames of reference. The notion of strong orientations received a considerable set-back, with scarcely any evidence to support it. In fact, the support for the existence of orientations of any sort was not impressive, although the evidence was more favourable to the weak form. This rather uncertain outcome is not altogether surprising; if the objective labour market severely limits the choices available to workers, there can be little scope for orientations to develop.

However, the situation became clearer in Chapter 7. When we related orientations to actual job rewards we found a pervasive tendency to congruence. Workers are likely to be in jobs where the rewards meet the priorities in their orientations, at least to some extent. Since the congruence appears to be the result of job choice rather than "socialisation", this provides much stronger grounds for the existence of orientations. Also, it means that a considerable amount of choice is exercised in relation to the limited opportunities.

To some extent orientations are clearest where there is most scope for choice, but this is not entirely so. The two clearest concern outdoor work and wages, and for both of these it is possible to apply the idea of strong orientations. These fit the pattern. On the other hand, hours of work provide the basis of a very ill-defined orientation, while intrinsic job quality is one of the most clear, with a relatively high degree of congruence in spite of the importance of the internal labour market. The hierarchical nature of the market produces a general tendency for those who have jobs congruent with their orientations to be in better jobs on other aspects as well, although to a lesser extent.

On the nature of orientations we concluded that they do exist in the weak form, and influence job choice. However, this does not completely rule out orientations in the strong sense. For a minority of workers one particular aspect may dominate their orientations to such a degree as to produce a qualitatively different effect, so that we may usefully characterise them as having a strong orientation.

In Chapter 8 we set the orientations to work in a wider social context and found an extensive pattern of relationships. Clearly the orientations must be seen as an element of the workers' whole lives, and not just as a response to work experience or to prior non-work influences. In particular, this supports the findings of the previous chapter on their relevance for job choice.

Also, we found that the workers tend to be differentiated by the strength of their orientations perhaps more significantly than by the content. Those with the strongest orientations are the ones with successful work careers and high status who are well integrated in their families and the community. Thus they have most reason to have a sense of competence to control their lives. Yet, at the same time, they are the ones who most fully accept their situation. They have the clearest orientations, but all orientations are confined within the limits of the labour market. They, and probably nearly all workers, give significance to the small variations in the low levels of available rewards and do their best to exercise choice within a situation of considerable constraint.

In Chapter 9 we examined *stratification* within our sample. Are better jobs filled by distinctive workers? In particular, are they filled with those whom employers would regard as "better" workers? We found clear differences by ethnic group. Immigrants are not discriminated against in terms of wages, but on all intrinsic job aspects they do distinctly worse, and the superiority of the native-born U.K. workers increases with seniority. Thus immigrants are only minimally able to take advantage of the internal labour market.[1] Secondly, health distinguishes between workers. As might be expected, the minority (about 15 per cent) of workers with poor health have considerably worse jobs. Thirdly, a slight tendency exists for workers with many previous employers, a history of unemployment, or a less co-operative set of attitudes to have worse jobs. These are all criteria used by employers to identify "undesirables", although we cannot say how far the attitudes are a cause or a consequence of treatment by management. Fourthly, seniority in the firm is a near-guarantee of relatively good employment conditions (except for immigrants). Whereas age is generally associated in a curvilinear way with job quality (i.e. the best job being held in middle age), seniority is related more linearly (i.e. the greater the length of service, the better the job). Thus the internal labour market clearly distinguishes between older workers.

Yet although the structure of the labour market is stably hierarchical, the processing of workers through it is not very predictable. With the exception of ethnicity (with which one is born) neither these worker "qualities" nor the quality of the job held seem predictable in the long run. Virtually no occupational inheritance occurred and very little long-run occupational stability. From the point of view of the worker, career processes are hazardous. Thus we do not believe that, with the exception of ethnicity, any significant degree of internal stratification exists within our segment of the working class. Furthermore, even the ethnic differentiation is not *segregation*. The degree of overlap between the occupations of our immigrants and native-born workers is far greater than that found in the residential or educational spheres of British society. We doubt whether on the basis of *employment*, ethnic stratification of a very clear-cut form could develop.

THE TYPICALITY OF OUR SAMPLE

To what extent can these findings be regarded as typical of the manual working class today? After all, our study concerned only male, non-apprenticed manual workers in the town of Peterborough in the years 1969–72. We must consider three hazards to generalisation of our findings: our occupational, geographical and temporal coverage.

Occupationally, it may be claimed that our study has covered only the "middle stratum" of the manual working class, for we have excluded both women's jobs and jobs requiring apprenticeship. As we noted in Chapters 1 and 2, these are omissions of a different order.

Female manual workers are fairly clearly segregated in both production and the labour market from male workers: they are almost never interchangeable, and the employment conditions of women are considerably worse—although they are perhaps improving. In many countries recent legislation has formally outlawed unequal pay for equal jobs and discrimination against women in recruitment. Furthermore, the worldwide recession has had rather odd effects on employment levels. For the first time in a recession, female employment levels in the period have not decreased faster than those of men—indeed, they were still increasing. This is due entirely to women's over-representation in the service sector, which has been less hard-hit than manufacturing (O.E.C.D., 1976). Yet discrimination still exists, even if it is lessening. Women use even more debased job "skills", receive lower wages, are largely denied access to internal labour markets—they are less in control of their own job allocation and less able to make choices. And whatever the justice of the claim that such treatment is not experienced as hardship where women are only secondary wage earners in their households, we should point out that around 20 per cent of women workers are in fact the principal wage earners in their household.

However, the segregation between men and women does lead us to modify our conclusions concerning stratification within the working class. Women manual workers, unlike any of the male groups we have considered, are probably a "secondary" labour force in the sense of the dual and radical labour market theories. The internal labour market and other defences against insecurity exist on the backs of a secondary labour force, and in this country, that means largely on the backs of women.

The relationship between our sample and that stratum of manual workers that lies above it would seem to be rather different. Apprenticed skilled workers possess a marketable qualification which distinguishes them alike from the unskilled, semi-skilled and skilled workers in our sample. Our workers could take to another employer, at most, experience and a recommendation from their present employer. Very few manual workers are sufficiently confident of the marketability of these qualifications to attempt such a move voluntarily. We will expand on this difference between the fully skilled worker and the rest of the manual working class a little later in this chapter. For the moment, we note merely that members of one stratum of workers are in a better, more controlling, situation in the labour market. Bear in mind, however, that this is a small stratum, as we demonstrated in Chapter 2.

We turn now to geography and to the "typicality" of Peterborough. We should emphasise that our sampling procedure, described in Chapter 2, was not random. We chose Peterborough for its peculiarities (especially its employment variety) rather than for any supposed representativeness it might possess. Within Peterborough we sampled both firms and jobs for theoretical reasons and not simply randomly. With such a stratified sample, at the least, if we wished to generalise about "the Peterborough working class", we should first go through an elaborate weighting of the responses of the different occupational groups in our sample according to their distributions in the local population. But then our interest does not lie in generalising about Peterborough workers. Rather we are interested in a full description of a section of a labour market whose parameters are specified: full (or nearly full) employment and great employment variety. In *that* setting our main findings of confused and somewhat unpredictable homogeneity and relatively weak internal stratification and differentiation apply. We must now ask whether there are other settings where different results would probably be obtained. Naturally there are. For example, in a company town, employment opportunities are likely to be more restricted and (probably) predictable. If the dominant company is stable and capital-intensive (e.g. a steel company), greater internal stratification by seniority is to be expected. In a metropolis like London we would be likely to find more labour market segmentation into primary and secondary sectors because of the importance of a relatively exploited labour force in the service sector (supporting evidence for this can be found in Department of Employment, 1977). Such peculiarities of place could be extended. However, one result does not seem possible, that a labour market could be found with rather more real choice available for workers. In this town of great employment variety, only limited choices are actually present. Why should it be different elsewhere in Britain, or indeed in any capitalist nation?

This raises the problem of generalising outside of Britain. Many of the labour market features we have described are well-nigh universal to capitalism, at least in the developed nations. The relationship between internal and external labour markets, the low level of job skills, the limited role of job choice, the difficulties confronting employer assessment of "worker quality" – most of our findings either reinforce or extend those of previous studies in various countries. We have been fairly indiscriminate about whether a particular piece of previous research was conducted in Britain or in the other major English-speaking industrial nation, the United States. Yet on one point we must proceed with caution. If we emphasise working-class homogeneity, might this not be a reflection of the well-known cultural and class homogeneity of this country? From America, the British social landscape seems uniform, especially in the relative absence of ethnic divisions. Apart from the Irish we have no history of immigration, and although the 1960s seemed at first to herald the arrival of very large Asian, West Indian and Mediterranean minorities, the flow was reduced to a trickle by racist legislation. Perhaps Enoch Powell was responsible for the relative absence of a dual labour market in Britain! Dual and radical theories alike seem more appropriate in their homeland, the United States of America, and nothing is gained by their mechanical application to other countries. Although some of the processes specified by these theories are inherent in capitalism itself, others are not. The dynamic uncertainties of capitalist development do lead employers to seek a regulation of the volume of labour supply, but whether one is found depends, among other things, on existing and potential stratification among the population. The universal subordination of women provides one potentiality everywhere; but ethnic diversity is a variable.

Finally, we must consider the period in time at which we conducted our enquiry. This was right at the end of the largest continuous period of expansion in the history of capitalism. Apart from rather minor recessions, economic growth and a rise in general living standards had been general in this country and in capitalism as a whole from 1945 to around 1970, when we began our interviews. Subsequently, of course, we have witnessed a severe and long-lived recession, worse in this country than in almost any other advanced capitalist nation, but nevertheless general to capitalism as a whole. Are not our results peculiar to that first period and thus out of date?

Our reply is essentially the same as it was when we considered the sex bias of our study: that the inclusion of the present economic situation, like that of women, could only make our pessimistic picture gloomier. We considered the careers of our workers to have been somewhat unpredictable, and yet only just over a quarter of them had ever been unemployed for longer than a few days (although most of these experiences had lasted over three months) and a little under a half had experienced an involuntary job change (excluding all cases of conscription and direction of labour). How much more faltering has their subsequent progress been in the transformed economic climate? Let us consider in detail the progress of our nine firms. One, Farrow's, has closed down, making redundant all but a few key workers, transferred to the parent company in Norwich. In such an eventuality the internal labour market and seniority give only the limited protection of a larger redundancy payment. Two more firms also found themselves compelled to discharge large numbers of workers. One of these cases, that of Perkins, was perhaps predictable, as its employment level has always been sensitive to the business cycle; the other, Baker-Perkins, renowned as a highly stable employer, came as a bombshell to the locality. Two more, London Brick and British Rail, were already involved in a steady process of labour-shedding, which was merely speeded by the recession. In all four of these cases seniority within a department was the main criterion for escaping redundancy, but the departments were not evenly hit, thereby making prediction of his future difficult for the worker. On the other side of the coin, a rather surprising firm, Combex, weathered the storm most successfully, actually expanding and improving employment conditions throughout the subsequent period. Windfall or bombshell, such processes are not within the worker's control.

Thus we feel able to approach the wider theoretical implications of our findings with relatively few reservations about our ability to generalise.

THEORETICAL IMPLICATIONS

Choice and Constraint
At the beginning of this monograph we formulated a simple two-part question: "Does the labour market objectively allow to the worker a significant measure of choice over his economic life? Does he subjectively perceive this as choice?" Our answer is perhaps paradoxically best summed up as "no" and "yes" respectively. Very little choice is objectively available "on the ground" and workers do not delude themselves that more exists, but they still take seriously such choice as is available. There are two sorts of limitation on significant choice. In the first place, the wide range of different jobs provides only a narrow range of differences in work rewards. As we have seen, one job is much the same as another in this section of the market, and even among the best jobs there are few that can be regarded as positively attractive. Secondly, the structure of the market presents many obstacles to choice, both because of its general hierarchical form and because the major systematic source of variation in work rewards is the internal labour market, which is largely out of the worker's control. Thus the context of choice is narrow and the possibilities are limited.

Nevertheless, this is not felt by the workers as constraint, in the sense of an active and alien force imposing itself in their lives. They have internalised the constraint and identify it as reality itself. One of us in previous research has noted this as characteristic of manual workers' employment experience in general (Mann, 1970, 1973a). Now, after systematic research, we reinforce the argument with respect to the labour market.

The workers accept their market situation in the sense that it is part of the normal reality of their lives. The jobs they see as ones they might possibly do are all in the "unqualified" sector. Their expectations with regard to earnings are not only realistic but a little pessimistic. Their orientations exist in relation to the unqualified manual market, and they try to treat it as a "true" market where they have some choice over the sale of their labour power and what they get in return. The most frequently suited are those liking outdoor employment, but attempts to satisfy most preferences meet with a modicum of success. Their behaviour may be seen as rational in the sense of making the best of a bad job. They recognise the limits of their situation and do their best to exercise choice within it. Therefore, although the context of choice is narrow, this does not confirm what we have termed the "alienation hypothesis". It seems that no matter how restricted the choice, they treat it as real.

It might be objected that we exaggerate the degree of constraint, since the workers are not confined to the sort of jobs we have considered. Although they cannot move to skilled jobs requiring formal apprenticeship, they can and sometimes do move into white-collar employment. But there are no identifiable regular procedures for promotion into the non-manual stratum, other than into a few foreman positions. Any worker who *counted* upon such promotion would be deluding himself. Other research has shown that when unqualified manual workers are "promoted" into white-collar jobs, they are often older men, and they actually move into comparably non-skilled work with no better pay and usually no more chance of further promotion (Stewart *et al.*, forthcoming). Such moves have the character of an unexpected "windfall". Unpredictable moves are an important aspect of the non-skilled labour market, but usually they are unwanted, with redundancy the most common cause. Altogether about one-fifth of all job changes by workers in the sample were involuntary, and this does not include military conscription. For the individual worker the market has a strong element of uncertainty.

Just because workers lack control, except within a narrow area, this does not mean that control rests directly with the employer. Obviously the employer is able to exercise some choice over recruitment and promotion practices, but he is also confronted by processes emanating from the economy as a whole over which he has little control. In any case, there is a certain "cancelling out" effect of the various local actors involved – workers, unions, employers – and of the internal and external labour markets, so that the overall market appears random or at least uncontrollable to the participants. Indeed, it is our major criticism of all three economic models of the labour market that we have considered – neo-classical, dual, and radical – that all over-emphasise the *orderliness* of labour market processes. We hesitate to go so far as to summarise our findings as random,[2] but the Peterborough labour market (and, we believe, manual labour markets in general) is far less orderly and rational than any of the economists would have us believe.

So, can it be made more rational? It is difficult to answer that without considering "rational for whom?". Market processes are not such as to give a high degree of control to workers or employers. However, it certainly does not follow that increasing control for one side will be seen as an advantage for the other. Furthermore, it is doubtful if significant improvements can be made from either point of view without a radical change in the organisation of production.

To illustrate the limitations on moves towards rationality, take, for example, the very poor state of information services in the labour market. The prospective employee will know that vacancies of x type exist; he may additionally know the wage-rate (though not actual earnings), and perhaps something about shifts and fringe benefits. The probability is that he will learn nothing about the content of the job, its working conditions, the social relations on the job, the actual wages and hours, the promotion prospects, or the degree of autonomy, until he starts to work there. It would not be difficult to provide some public information about some of these things. Equally, it would be possible to frame legislation making it compulsory for employers to do this for their vacancies – through the Employment Exchange services. This would provide a more rational basis for job selection, but it is not clear that employers would regard this as being in their best interests, or that workers' ability to choose would really be extended. Public knowledge would lead to a more competitive situation. In Chapter 5 we suggested that employers think they gain from the restriction of competition in the labour market. It could also make the market more hierarchical, restricting even more the objective scope for choice of the worker (although this might improve the employer's selection efficiency, and help the better employers).

There is, however, a more important objection to our suggested improvement – it would be largely irrelevant. For the most part it would be facilitating choice between more or less unpleasant jobs, demanding little or no skill. Since the jobs are generally mindless, from the employers' standpoint the workers are merely undifferentiated and interchangeable labour power. So what is the point of a more competitive market? Of course, employers do have ideas of worker "quality", but as we have seen these either tend to be irrational (e.g. ethnicity or sex), or are difficult to take account of in the process of actual recruitment. The main element of such "quality" is co-operativeness, and the fact that this is a problem at all relates to a further aspect of irrelevance in the suggested change.

We do not want to suggest that the choices involved are unimportant to the workers; minimising unpleasantness can be just as significant as maximising attractions, and just because the scope for either is limited does not mean that the difference does not matter. The point is, that the levels of all intrinsic rewards tend to be well below the levels available outside work, so that differences have low relevance for their life as a whole. The main area of exception concerns social relationships, but these are not included in the suggested change since their quality cannot be defined in advance – it is created by the workers themselves.

One particular choice, that of relatively high wages in return for unpleasantness, has tended to dominate previous research. This is especially true of the more recent sociological research, in which the "economistic" or "instrumental" worker has figured prominently. Economists have concentrated more broadly on the movement of workers after higher wages, without considering what "costs" might also be involved for the workers. The importance of wages cannot be denied. Money is a necessary return from work for non-work life. Consequently it is always sought, and insofar as there is little scope to choose other rewards it may seem to dominate, but to divorce the desire for money from other possibilities and the context of constraint which brings it to the fore, is quite misleading. The idea of economistic orientations is more satisfactory in that it refers to a particularly strong concern with wages, thereby implying the possibility of other orientations, though the emphasis on economism has led to the neglect of such possibilities. Yet the different types of concern with wages have not been properly understood. In particular, we may distinguish "alienated instrumentalism", where other rewards are not seen as significant and the aim is to make enough money at minimum cost in interference with non-work life, and the direct concern with high wages, usually the outcome of financial need which is often a temporary phase due to "life cycle squeeze". In either case the choice is somewhat constrained. Thus, paradoxically, the neo-classical theory of the labour market has some validity, because constraint facilitates "choice".

For there to be more significant choices, more challenging, less debased jobs must needs exist. There is no way round this. Most workers are alienated from their work, and to remedy this would involve major structural changes in the process of production. General recognition of this simple truth began to grow in most advanced capitalist countries in the late 1960s at the tail-end of the boom period, when the "stick" of unemployment no longer seemed real enough to motivate workers in a climate of intensifying international competition (although sociologists had been making the point for some time). Managerial concern about the low level of genuine co-operation from their workforce was evident in Peterborough. Rather more importantly, both the British and United States governments produced research reports full of concern about "the quality of work life" and "worker motivation" (Department of Employment, 1973; Special Task Force Report to the Secretary of Health, Education and Welfare, 1973).

From this period date the popularity of Herzberg and other management consultants advocating job enrichment, job enlargement, job rotation, participative management styles and the like. From this period, also, dates an upsurge in worker activism and militancy which saw worker militants, shop stewards and union leaders thrust into greater prominence in many countries. These currents for reform (and in some cases for revolution) have various causes, and they differ greatly among themselves and between countries. The advocates of reform fall into two main groups: those interested in shop-floor improvements (job enlargement, etc.) and those – usually more radical – interested in worker control of higher-level decision-making within the firm. In Britain the recent Bullock Report, for example, concludes that shop-floor reforms are on their own inadequate: ". . . the area of decision-making in which they allow employee participation is extremely narrow" (Department of Trade, 1977: 46). Accordingly, the report recommends the adoption of a co-determination scheme with an equal number of workers and employer representatives at board level. We hesitate to enter into this debate, both because it is largely outside the terms of reference we have set ourselves and also because we feel guilty about spreading our pessimism to such well-intentioned and progressive reformers. However, we have our reservations about whether *either* sets of reforms would do much to alleviate the situation we have been describing.

Our reservations stem largely from our reformulation of the meaning of *skill* in the manual working class. The dominant view of skill in industry today is what we would term a "technicist" one: that is, it sees skill as technique, a combination of manual and mental capacities for manipulating objects and tools. This view informs both the sphere of production and that of the market. In production, it underlies job evaluation and work study procedures which differentiate jobs by the technical complexity of their tasks (as well as by other characteristics, of course). In the market, it underlies the neo-classical theories of "human capital", "the queue" and "worker quality", as well as the more commonsensical lament among managements of the shortage of skilled and competent workers. The managerial and trade-union reformers to whom we have just referred go a step further, for they believe that more interested, more skilful workers would appear if only we could devise work routines that would challenge them. Thus their concept of skill is also technicist: increased skill would consist of increasing work variety and the complexity of decision-making.

It is this technicist view we wish to challenge, for we believe that it grossly neglects the social and political (in the sense of "power") aspects of skill. Let us recall some of our findings. Our own technicist measure of job skills (the Job Scores) unearthed the fact that complex technical skills are rarely encountered among manual workers except at the top of the internal labour market and among qualified craftsmen. Even there we discovered that management required a high level of co-operation and responsibility rather than complex hand-eye co-ordination or an unusual variety of techniques. A relatively skilled position was one of *trust*, where the worker was granted a sphere of competence within which decisions, whether routine or complex, could be taken by the worker himself. This "guaranteed autonomy" is the essence of the traditional craft occupation within which the workers themselves control their productive process (and often their market allocation, too). Psychologically, it is an encouragement to self-direction. As Marsden has expressed it, ". . . the individual seeks his own salvation . . . He is invited to be ambitious, trusting, optimistic, loyal and honest" (Marsden and Duff, 1975: 234). That, we think, sums up what management means by the "good worker". It is social, not technical. The centre of the technique is not complexity, but autonomy and freedom.

Thus if we are to improve worker skills, we are talking about increasing the worker's control over an area of undisputed competence. This is the very opposite of some of the reformers' schemes which seek to *merge* workers till further into the structure of the firm. These schemes are, in one sense, an accompaniment of the debasement of worker skills during this century rather than an attempt to resist it. Taylorism, scientific management, the assembly line and all other technological innovations have sought a greater *integration* of the factory. All have had the effect of threatening occupational and departmental autonomy, and therefore of debasing skills. Some were accompanied by an unpleasant ideology which viewed human beings as automata or mere adjuncts of the machine, and contemporary reforming schemes for "co-determination", "partnership", etc. are a welcome reaction against that ideology. However, these schemes also attempt to integrate, that is, to reduce autonomy. We must therefore stress that they point in the opposite direction to the traditional reality of skilled work, which is towards autonomy and decentralisation.

Whether skill could be changed from "autonomy from" to a "merging into" depends on the wider framework of control to which the worker is subject.

Alienation is the result of loss of control. The worker's labour power is controlled directly and superficially by machines and supervisors but this is within the double framework laid down by the bureaucratic hierarchy of the firm and the dictates of the capitalist market. Job rotation and enlargement and the like will certainly change the relationship of the worker to machines and supervisors, but will not alter this framework. Co-determination is rather different, for it does provide a second channel of decision-making to the formal chain of managerial, bureaucratic hierarchy, but despite the claims made by its proponents it is a *second* channel. It does not replace the hierarchy. Nor does it alter anything in the market. Worker-directors will continue to accept market principles if they wish their firm to stay in business, and if they accept higher rates of reward for trained managerial personnel, the going rate of return for investors, plant closures and the like, it is difficult to see how the system is fundamentally changed.

Reforms along such lines encounter an additional problem. Workers accommodate themselves to harsh realities by digging into defensive positions from which they are reluctant to move. Partly it is their understanding of the way things have to be, and partly an avoidance of risk. This is especially so in terms of their reactions to the ever-present threat of economic insecurity. We will illustrate this with the cautionary tale of red-bearded Fred.

At one of the firms we studied, the stratification between management and men is given very apt physical expression. Management offices are situated above the shop floor and are connected by a cat-walk from which one can look down upon the workers. On numerous occasions we were escorted along the cat-walk by managers, and several times they stopped and pointed out Fred (an alias) to us. Fred's flaming red hair and beard, right beneath us, tended to dominate the view anyway, but his behaviour also concerned liberal-minded managers. Fred was a machine operator. His work cycle was less than 10 seconds, his movements within that time were simple, undemanding, repetitive (unless the machine proved faulty). Managers were concerned that anyone in their firm should be asked to perform such sub-human tasks, and they had apparently proposed to Fred various schemes of job enlargement and job rotation. Fred had rejected these, saying that this was his job, he didn't want to move and he didn't want to share it with anyone. "How can you reform industry with workers like that?" reasonably asked one manager. What he and the other managers correctly perceived was that Fred was giving about as much of himself (i.e. virtually nil) to this firm as he wanted to. Nobody was going to persuade him into higher levels of commitment and co-operation. What was not fully realised, however, was Fred's reasoning. For Fred's machine was a very tangible sign of his job security and his job property rights. As long as that machine was needed, so would he be. Making him interchangeable with other workers in a more interesting, even participatory structure would reduce his security. He felt himself protected and given a work identity to some degree by an internal labour market which marks out specific job titles with wholly artificial lines of demarcation from other jobs. Labour actually *is* interchangeable, objectively, but Fred and workers like him would resist such a notion. Fred had made a fairly typical defensive compromise with capitalism, digging his heels into an artificial job structure, keeping his head down, and surviving.

It is obvious that we would have difficulty persuading workers like Fred that shop-floor reforms would constitute an improvement. More demanding work in return for less apparent job security – you must be joking! But worker-directors would make little difference either, nor would even complete worker control within the firm, as long as the fear of insecurity remained. We do not believe that alienation can be removed merely by reforms, even compulsory ones, located within the firm. Political reforms would also be necessary, principal among which would be the guarantee of economic security to every citizen whether he was in employment or not. That, of course, means the abolition of wage labour, and of capitalism itself. To most of our readers that must seem a chiliastic and perhaps chilling solution. But the harsh reality of the present system must be squarely faced.

Stratification Within the Working Class
Our emphasis on constraint rather than choice, although it will be

politically unacceptable to many, is in itself fairly traditional. It will surprise neither radicals, whether Marxist or not, nor industrial sociologists. In a sense, what we have done in this respect is to join together and confirm some of the arguments of the radical political economists concerning the labour market and those of the industrial sociologists on alienation. However, our analysis of the relationship between choice and constraint does have some important implications for the understanding of stratification. Indeed, our findings on stratification and differentiation part company with all previous orthodoxies. We can identify three main traditional viewpoints, although they are not entirely homogeneous or distinct.

The first tradition may be labelled Weberian, in that Max Weber gave to it the most comprehensive theoretical treatment. In defining a class as (mainly) a group with common *market capacities*, he opened the way to the possibility of identifying many social classes, if skills, goods and other capacities are diversely distributed. Indeed, a tradition of analysis has grown up in which the population is divided into many classes or strata, each composed of one or more occupational titles. However, the direct influence of this tradition has been considerably less than might be expected. While it has been quite usual to refer to the market, in practice it has been largely neglected and different criteria of stratification have been used – particularly "prestige" which we shall discuss presently. Nevertheless, market factors have been incorporated, at least implicitly, particularly in terms of skill and income. This may be seen in the five "social classes" of the British O.P.C.S. classification. Although formally defined as reflecting "general standing within the community", the divisions among manual workers correspond to three levels of skill. This scheme was not devised by sociologists but it has, nevertheless, been extensively used by them. Similar grading schemes exist in other countries. In all these conceptions the population is differentiated in a hierarchy of several occupational strata, with all divisions between strata accorded equivalent theoretical status except, perhaps, for a split between manual and non-manual workers. The manual workers are divided into at least two strata, and usually more.

Our results demonstrate a certain lack of realism in this sort of approach. Formally qualified craftsmen do have a different market situation from all other manual workers, but they are usually included in a wider "skilled" stratum. Among the unqualified, clear-cut hierarchical divisions do not exist, either in the market or in relation to the process of production. Certainly there are differences between workers, most notably in terms of sex, race and health, but none of these provides a basis for class stratification. Nearly all manual workers constitute relatively homogeneous, interchangeable labour power. They have the same market capacities, the same lifechances; they are members of the same class.

This last sentence contains a nice irony, in that looking at stratification from a Weberian perspective we have arrived at a quasi-Marxist conclusion. At the beginning of this work we announced that we were departing from current orthodoxies concerning class in one important respect. We have abandoned any distinction between the production process and the market in our analysis of class. This was for two reasons, one theoretical and one empirical. The very definition of capitalism as a productive process involves a double separation between capital and labour and between different branches of production among whom commodity exchange takes place. Thus capitalism presupposes markets, one of which is a labour market. Furthermore, we argued that empirically a worker's location in production corresponds to that in the labour market: workers interchangeable in one sphere are interchangeable in the other. Previous theory has tended to separate these two spheres and to emphasise the primacy of one or the other – Marxian theory emphasising production, Weberian theory the market. It has been generally assumed that the varying emphases would lead to varying results. We dispute that. Indeed, in case any Marxist critics feel like attacking us because – superficially, anyway – we have concentrated on labour market processes, let us repeat that this method has *not* led to the expected Weberian conclusion, namely, that if one defines classes in terms of the goods they bring to the market, many classes will emerge. We have been looking only at one part of the labour market, but a very substantial part, including the majority of male manual workers, where we have found an essentially interchangeable mass of workers selling only simple labourpower. This is not to deny the heterogeneity of manual jobs, but we have shown that, for two reasons, this is no basis for stable stratification. Firstly, much allocation of workers to jobs is unpredictable. Secondly, the main predictable criterion is seniority. Thus each worker has a reasonable chance of experiencing that heterogeneity within his own workcareer. Manual workers are thus homogeneous in their experience of heterogeneity!

The second tradition from which we diverge may be identified as *voluntarism*, and is also influenced by Weber. There are many strands to this tradition but all concern the moral involvement of workers in the structure of inequality. The commonest form is stratification based on consensus, and measured by status, prestige or social standing. The notion of status gives a further link with Weber, although this has not been particularly in evidence. This approach has been dominant in North American sociology, which in turn has had considerable influence throughout the world. As we have just seen, it is not entirely distinct, empirically or conceptually, from "market" stratification. This may be illustrated with Duncan's (1961) "socio-economic index of occupations", which is a weighted sum of education (an indicator of market capacity) and income (an indicator of market success); but the weightings of the components and the validation of the resulting scale are derived from the N.O.R.C. scale of occupational status. To some extent these scales based on evaluations are open to the same objections as those based on market considerations, in that they identify many strata within the manual workforce which have little significance in terms of class.

However, we did identify meaningful hierarchies of jobs, both within firms and in the market as a whole. These might be thought to confer correspondingly different levels of prestige on incumbents, and so create a prestige hierarchy among manual workers. We did not examine this directly but the following considerations seem sufficient to settle the issue. Other studies have not found the consensus of evaluations necessary to establish a prestige hierarchy. Indeed, such attempts to measure stratification have demonstrated beyond question the unsoundness of their theoretical foundations. Yet the scales obtained show a high degree of similarity and are meaningfully related to other variables, so if they are not based on subjective evaluations of prestige they must be taken as reflecting perceptions of an objective structure (see Stewart and Blackburn, 1975: 485–94). This structure may entail class differences, taking us back to the earlier discussion, and/or differences in the "goodness" of the jobs themselves. Goldthorpe and Hope (1972: 38) have argued for the latter interpretation for all occupations and used it as the criterion for their own scale construction (1974). We find that among the manual workers we studied few evaluated jobs in terms of "status" and that when they did it usually meant that they wanted better jobs or to avoid the most degrading, rather than a concern with the evaluations of others. There seem little grounds for identifying status strata among unqualified manual workers.

There is a further problem with voluntarism itself, which applies not only to consensus theory but also to much Marxist and other radical writing involving such ideas as "false consciousness" or "ideological hegemony". In general, workers do not wrongly evaluate or reluctantly decide to put up with constraints. For the most part the constraints are not subject to evaluation – they are the "given" context of action. The prime exception is when the constraint is due to the competent action of others, such as managers, which may be judged and challenged. We see this in their trade unionism, concerned with collective bargaining over pay and immediate problems of worker-management relations but rarely over the wider issues that underlie the problems; we see it in their many specific criticisms of industrial relations, coupled with an absence of a strong or salient radical ideology; and in those orientations to work concerned with "management quality".

A rather different form of voluntarism is involved in the notion of *orientations* to work. A labour market working through the "free" preferences of workers, on the neo-classical model, would imply a legitimacy for stratification in the sense that all got what they wanted (or perhaps it might be supposed to incorporate an element of competition, taking the best men to the top). However, although we find orientations differentiate between workers, this is over a narrow range of choice within parameters of constraint. Interestingly, we found that a major form of differentiation is by the strength of orientations held. Those with more positive orientations, being more confident, with a greater sense of ability to control their lives, might be thought most capable of initiating change. Indeed, they do tend to be trade unionists and in keeping with this, slightly more radical in their general attitudes. However, their consciousness shows no belief in class action because, we suggest, the possibility of effecting change is not visible to them. The experience which engenders their sense of competence comes from greater social integration and occupational success within the present arrangements.

In one important respect they differ markedly from apprentice-trained craftsmen. To a large extent the successful workers among our sample owe their success, and the sense of confidence we have seen it engenders, to the internal labour market of the individual firm. By contrast, the fully qualified craftsman's success is independent of the firm and is marketable. Together, these workers form the top stratum of the manual working class, the stratum from which action to change the situation might come. Yet one group's confidence is *dependent* on, the other's *collectively autonomous* of, the employer. This is an important division, considerably reducing the homogeneity and class solidarity of manual workers.

Apart from this, however, we have emphasised homogeneity. It is true that we have found that the market is hierarchical, in the sense that desirable job features tend to vary together and there are significant job hierarchies both within firms and in the market as a whole. This does mean that some workers are better off. But there are no stable, predictable patterns. Individual experience may differentiate by being more or less rewarding, but it is all within a common market situation of uncertainty. In the preceding discussion we have, for the sake of clarity, somewhat overstated the degree of homogeneity of class situations (early chapters present fuller details), but this is the most salient feature.

Our emphasis on homogeneity might seem more congenial to the third traditional approach, that of Marxism and of its offshoot among economists, "radical political economy". We have already noted our basic agreement with this position *vis-à-vis* the descriptive issue of the predominance of constraint. Yet as we noted in Chapter 1, contemporary Marxists have often also accepted the basic descriptive postulate of Weberians, namely, that the working class is divided into stable, often conflicting, fractions. We must add in their defence that most of these writers are writing about the United States, in which an emphasis on working-class disunity is much more plausible than it is in Europe. We shall leave aside this simple descriptive issue for the moment and return to it by way of our disagreement with the most popular contemporary Marxist *explanation* for supposed disunity.

This is a fairly simple explanation: disunity is the result of the cunning of the capitalist. This is really another element of voluntarism, this time on the part of the capitalists. An example of such an approach is the influential work of Katharine Stone. In an analysis of the history of the United States steel industry, she argues that the internal labour market, embodying promotion by seniority, was specifically and consciously designed by employers to divide a working class which was becoming a threat to them (1975: 27–84). We hesitate to comment on her conclusions in view of our ignorance of that industry. However, we would like to make two critical comments. In the first place, that would be an erroneous interpretation of the development of similar practices in the British steel industry. There the replacement of the old contracting system by elaborated internal promotion lines was a compromise between three main groups, the employers, unskilled underhands, and the craftsmen-contractors (Wilkinson, 1977). This raises the second point. To many Marxists, the potential existence of a united, homogeneous working class seems "natural" and its actual emergence is thwarted only by employee-divisive strategies. In their accounts equally "natural" sectionalism among workers is consequently ignored.

This point can be expanded if we consider the common quality of many types of worker-sectionalism found within capitalism: the conflict between aristocracies of labour and unskilled workers (as in the above example), the division between male and female, between native-born and immigrants, between ethnic groups, between young, middle-aged and old, and between those privileged by an internal labour market and those not so privileged. The essence of the division is the same: it is between established and new workers, that is between those already established in the process of production and those recently brought into it by the expansion of capitalism. As we noted in Chapter 1, as capitalism has revolutionised the forces of production, it has brought new groups into the industrial labour force. If the expansion had proceeded evenly across all branches of industry and through time, the conflict of interest between established and new workers would have been less. However, there is also competition between established groups, particularly over demarcation but also more generally over differentials. This was not particularly in evidence in the workers we studied, who are relatively interchangeable between occupations, but is more common with occupational communities, especially when there is a formal qualification. If we include non-manual workers, we see that professionals are by far the most vigorous pursuers of sectional interest as they have more to protect, but our primary concern is with divisions among the less privileged sections of the labour force.

Because capitalism is competitive and unpredictable, no one's place is secure. Firms rise and fall; so do national economies. Thus established workers universally seek to protect themselves against another, and potentially surplus, labour supply. Trade unions are the inevitable protective organisations, for by their very nature they collectively organise workers "already there". Intra-class conflict is thus the historical norm within capitalism; and its incidence is to be explained in terms of the relative balance of the supply of and demand for labour, not in terms of class-conscious employers. To this we must add the workers' definitions of the situation in terms of given economic forces. If they could see how they might exercise control, individually or collectively, there would be no need for sectional conflict. It is because they "know" there are immutable economic "laws", in the face of which their position is vulnerable, that they are driven to defensive sectionalism.

Where workers have separate occupational identities, that is, they have reason to protect and further the interests of their present occupation rather than move to a more attractive one, and they are organised in separate unions, there will inevitably be divergent interests. However, it is only in situations of direct competition for employment that conflict is acute. The resolution of such conflict depends either on the establishment of equality, or on one group accepting its subordination, as most newcomers have done during an initial period in which their reference point is the pre-industrial reward structure. Women, usually sharing a household, and therefore part of their identity, with male workers, have internalised the legitimacy of their economic subordination over a much longer period. Frequently, the internal labour market can provide a basis for equality, protecting the rights of the established workers while providing a route for new entrants to move to more secure and rewarding positions, so that their interests are focused on individual promotion instead of collective improvement of the present occupation. In the example of the British steel industry just quoted, that is precisely what happened. Such an outcome is based on several conditions. Capitalism must continue to expand fairly evenly across the main branches of the economy, otherwise the newcomers will not gain seniority (as, it is argued, has occurred in the "secondary" sector of the U.S. economy). Also, the technological development must not be such as to concentrate expansion at the bottom of the internal market. This is what has happened in office work, creating the "secondary" market for women, but is unlikely in the manual sector. Exclusive educational qualifications may be introduced to restrict entry to the better jobs, as happens with professions and quasi-professions, but there is little basis for this, and it is against the trend, in manual work. Finally, hereditary, ascriptive criteria must not be applied to prevent equality. However, the historical trend within most capitalist nation-states may possibly be towards sexual equality (at least, it seems unlikely to be the reverse) and appears undoubtedly to be towards racial equality in employment. The complete maintenance of racial inequality, as in South Africa, appears to need a large, directly repressive apparatus. Thus the long-term expansion of capitalism appears to generate a continuous process of intra-working-class division and reconstitution, a process which could only stop with the integration of the world's population into the labour force of capitalism.

Now – without, we hope, too much of a sense of anticlimax – we can return to the parish of Peterborough and (for we are prepared to generalise) to contemporary Britain. The oldest industrial nation, ethnically homogeneous, with severe restrictions on immigration, Britain is obviously not a major candidate for a divided manual working class. Our analysis shows that only sex is a major, stable division, and because of the existence of the family that does not divide the class. We find, therefore, that – sex apart – the major divisions form around the internal labour market. Yet it not only brings unity to the potential conflict-groups among the workers; it also benefits the employer. As we saw in Chapter 4, the employer welcomes seniority as a promotion criterion, provided he still retains some discretionary power, for the combination ensures co-operative workers. Thus the manual working class, though homogeneous and united in work experience, is also *compromised*. Here, too, our interpretation differs from that of most Marxists, for whom unity equals strength. Most workers have a fair chance of achieving a tolerable job. It is guaranteed for virtually no one, but is made more likely by stability and co-operativeness. The growth of internal labour markets has been described by one of us in previous research as the growth of *mutual dependence* between employer and worker (Mann, 1973b). At that time, Mann was ambiguous about the effects of such dependence on class conflict, unsure whether dependence might intensify the salience of disputes between employer and worker. Now we see it as reducing the *class* nature of the conflict, by isolating workers in one firm from those in another. (Though contrary influences may also be at work, for example the growing role of the state in industrial relations.)

Thus the manual working class *is* divided, not into stable, quasi-hereditary strata, but into two non-stable groupings: employment organisations and age-seniority cohorts. Both divert potential class action, the first into "free collective bargaining" which can only reinforce the market nature of capitalism, the second into an essentially conservative posture of sitting tight and quiet, waiting for promotion. Neither can be seen plausibly as an alternative source of group solidarity, of genuine "community", to class.

The two types of division are in one respect very different. The age differences appear as unshakeable, permanent. The characteristic ageing process appears to have been dominant for very many years now; young workers are discontented and militant, family responsibilities and the experience of constraint teach them to comply in early middle age, stability earns a tolerable job in middle age, fear takes over later.[3] Young workers are too ill-organised and inexperienced to press their interests against the older workers, before they too are drawn in and moved to the next stage, while employers have an interest in continuing to reward co-operation.

By contrast the inter-firm differences are dependent on a pre-condition which seems more problematic, the continuance of market competition. State intervention, incomes policies, "social contracts", all threaten the bargaining system whereby individual employers or industries can agree conditions of employment with their own workforces. Social democracy has also made some gains in reducing the threat of economic insecurity in the market, although naturally the contribution made by unemployment insurance schemes, redundancy payments, pensions, etc, is somewhat limited. All such developments reduce the dependence of the worker on his own employer – though they have been paralleled by the extension of private fringe benefits which have the contrary effect. At least the enumeration of such trends shows that this type of intra-class division is a *variable*, its future somewhat uncertain. This can be seen in the confused and rather unpredictable reactions in the British trade-union movement in 1977 to the rival policies of a "social contract" and "free collective bargaining". We are not crystal-gazers and we have no intention of making rash predictions about the outcome.

However, we do claim to have investigated the reproduction of the class structure. We have documented the way in which manual workers are constrained to come to terms with industrial capitalism, principally by participating in internal labour markets and by bargaining within the structure of the external labour market. As we have emphasised elsewhere (Blackburn and Mann, 1975; Mann 1973a), this is no "sell-out" by their leaders – it is the obvious, rational solution directly available to them all. We have argued that workers do not generally challenge the existence of the market or its structure of constraint, but only the actions of employers or workers within it. The constraints of the market are matters of cognition rather than evaluation, taken for granted as part of their conceptualisation of society or learnt from experience.

While such acceptance of their market situation means that the workers try to act rationally in pursuit of their interests within their section of the labour market, the resultant experience is one of constraint and uncertainty. Their powerlessness in the face of a harsh unpredictable reality is continually in evidence.

We have seen that unqualified manual workers share a common class position, characterised by powerlessness and uncertainty. Yet their experience of the market is such as to inhibit consciousness of a common identity, let alone provide an impetus for change. Far more important, however, is that, in the context of their ordinary experience, the possibility of successful action to transcend the limits of their situation and so transform it is so remote as to be irrelevant. It is not that they dismiss the possibility, but that it does not normally enter their consciousness. Other factors may promote change and make the present structure problematic in the worker's consciousness. The forces of a crisis could well do this by leading to a redefinition of "reality" However, processes within the market are essentially operating to maintain a stable structure of social inequality.

Naturally, our research does not cover all aspects of the reproduction of class structure. We have examined only the direct production and market experience of a section of the manual workforce. To comment fully on the position of the working class in the contemporary economic system would require analysis of other factors – the relationship of our workers to non-manual workers, macro-processes in the economy, the processing of conflict, especially in times of crisis, and many other aspects of contemporary capitalism. This is not merely an "empirical" problem, for it involves considerable work of conceptual clarification, especially over the troubled notion of "the working class" itself (see Carchedi, 1975, Poulantzas, 1975, and Wright, 1976, for recent contributions to this problem). Our kind of research is complementary and not antithetical to such work. For in the area of the labour market we have replaced speculation by systematic analysis. The reader has had to bear with us, perhaps painfully, through a massive statistical exercise. But at the end of that painstaking progress we are able to make statements with a greater degree of confidence than has hitherto been possible. We have been able to evaluate some alternative theories, and to develop a clearer, more adequate understanding of the overall structure and internal processes of the labour market. And, at last, we are able to emerge from behind our statistical tables and methodological appendices with a certain degree of emotion. The human reality of the labour market has been distorted for long enough. It is not rational; it wastes human resources; it stunts, alienates and dehumanises – all in the good times of full employment!

Appendix I
Interview Survey
Questionnaire

1 Could you tell me first what is your normal job at present?

2 Later on I want to ask you more questions about your present work, but first could we fill in some background details of your life up to now? We might as well start at the beginning and work up to the present.
So firstly, when were you born?

3 Where did you live for most of your childhood? Did you actually live in . . .? Whereabouts is . . .?
Actually lived in . . . Lived near . . . Region/Area/County

4 How old were you when you left full-time education?

5 What type of school did you last attend full time?
  a. Secondary Modern   e. Grammar
     Elementary   Direct Grant
     Senior   Senior Secondary (Scot.)
     Junior Secondary (Scot.) f. Public
  b. Central   Private
     Intermediate   g. Foreign
  c. Technical   h. Other
  d. Comprehensive

6 While at school, did you obtain any formal qualifications, like, for example, G.C.E., School Certificate, or C.S.E.?
  a. None b. G.C.E., S.C., C.S.E. c. Higher qualification

7 Have you ever attended any educational or training courses since

leaving school which lasted longer than six months?
What kind of course? Did it get you any qualifications? Which?
a. None, or none relevant to work
b. Started Apprenticeship or O.N.C. or City and Guilds, but didn't finish
c. Other work-related course, no qualifications
d. Minor qualifications
e. Finished apprenticeship or obtained O.N.C., City and Guilds

8 At the time you left school, what was your father's job? Whom did he work for?
(Please ensure respondent is as specific as possible. If several occupations, ask about main one; if during wartime (or father retired or dead) record and ask for former occupation. If self-employed, note this down under job title, and also record industry.)

9 Now I'd like to know about the main jobs you have had so far. Let's start with the first job you had and then work up to the present. We'll include any army service you might have had.
a. What was the first firm you worked for?
b. Whereabouts was that?
c. Did you move house when you got that job? (If yes) did you move house *for* that job?
d. How long did you work there?
e. Why did you leave?
f. What were the main jobs you held there?
[Repeated for all subsequent jobs]

10 Casting your mind back on all the jobs you have ever had, *including your present one*, which have you liked the best?
Best
What did you most like about this job?

11 Have you ever been unemployed for longer than a few days at a time?
Yes   No
(If yes:) How many times? About how much time altogether? How long ago was the last time?

12 What made you think of coming here for a job?
a. Agency:
     i friends/Relations already working in the firm
     ii friends/Relations elsewhere

   iii general reputation of the firm, hearsay
   iv 'just turned up'
   v advertisements
   vi labour exchange
   vii company recruiting agent
   viii other
  b. Information obtained, i.e. how did you know there was a job here?

13 In your experience, what do you think is the best way to get on to a better job? Is it to stay with the same firm a long time or is it to move around a lot between firms?
  a. Stay with firm   c. Move around
  b. Mixed   d. Don't know

14 Are you thinking of changing your job in the near future?
  Yes No Don't know
  (If yes:) Have you done anything about it yet, or are you still weighing it up?
      Done something Weighing up
  (If has done something:) a. What have you done? b. Why are you thinking of leaving your job?

15 What do you expect your job will be five years from now?
  Job title a. Will it be the same job?
        b. Will it be with the same firm?
        c. Will it be the same line of work?

16 What would you *like* your job to be five years from now, if things went really well for you?
  Job title a. Same job
        b. Same firm
        c. Same line of work

17 Now I would like your opinion on some general industrial questions. I will read out some statements about industry today and I want you to say whether you agree or disagree with them, and how strongly you feel about them.
I'd like you to do this by making crosses on these lines.
(Hand him check-list and pencil. Explain to him what he should do, with the help of the examples, p. 1 of the check-list. Then go over the

example question. It is essential to stress that: (a) the line is a measure of how strongly he feels; (b) he can put his cross anywhere, so that normally his crosses would not be right over the words. The following wording is a guide – pointing to the lines as appropriate:) Each line is a measure of agreement or disagreement and of how strongly you feel. They run from "very strongly disagree" at this end to "very strongly agree" at this end. Only use these ends if you feel very strongly about something. The middle is marked "half-and-half": the further you go on this side, the more strongly you agree, and the further on this side, the more strongly you disagree. We have put crosses on this first page to show you what we mean; for example, this cross on line 1 would mean fairly strong disagreement – between mild and strong disagreement. The next one is only very mild agreement – not quite coming up to the mild point. You can see that most of the crosses are in the spaces between the words because anywhere along the line can be used.

(Example: Will you say whether you agree or disagree with this statement, and how strongly you feel about it?

Automation is supposed to benefit everybody, but the worker generally loses out when you put in new machinery.)

(Now continue on p. 2, reading out the statements one at a time.)

a. Most decisions taken by foremen and supervisors would be better if they were taken by the workers themselves.

b. Most managements have the welfare of their workers at heart.

c. Full teamwork in firms is impossible because workers and management are really on opposite sides.

d. Managers know what's best for the firm, and workers should do just what they're told.

e. Most major conflicts between managements and workers are caused by agitators and extremists.

f. All managements will try to put one over on the workers if they get the chance.

g. Giving workers more say in running their firms would only make things worse.

h. Industry should pay its profits to workers and not to shareholders.

i. The worker should always be loyal to his firm even if this means putting himself out quite a bit.

18. Now I'd like to ask you a few questions about whether you think people like you get a fair deal at work. By "people like you" I mean

similar people in the country as a whole. We'll do it in the same way
as the last questions, so will you mark your agreement or disagreement with the statements I read out.

(Turn to Page 3 and read out statements one at a time.)

a. In this country there is not enough opportunity for people like me
   to get promoted and get ahead.
b. There's a lot of talk about fair wages, but nobody pays a fair wage
   for people like me.
c. Workers like me need stronger trade unions to fight for their
   interests.
d. Managements should let people like me organise our work in our
   own way.
e. People like me have no opportunity to use their real abilities at
   work.
f. To get a decent wage you have to ruin your social life by working
   much too long on overtime or shifts.
g. I think workers have too much security nowadays – we should
   learn to stand more on our own two feet.
h. Nowadays managements treat people like me just as numbers and
   never as human beings.
i. Workers like me are never treated with anything like the respect
   they deserve.

19 Do you feel that your work is a worthwhile, valuable part of your
   life, or is it just something you have to do to earn a living?
   Worthwhile   Not sure   Earn a living
   (If not sure or "to earn a living":)
   a. do you dislike this, or have you grown used to it?
   Dislike   Grown used to
   b. Could anything be done to make it more worthwhile and
   valuable?
   Yes No Don't know
   (If yes:) What?
   (If worthwhile:) In what way is it worthwhile and valuable?

20 Do you enjoy the time you spend at work, or don't you get much
   pleasure out of it?
   Enjoy   Not sure   Not pleasurable
   (If not sure or "not pleasurable":)
   a. Do you actually dislike it, or have you grown used to it?
      Dislike   Grown used to

    b. Could anything be done to make it more enjoyable?

    Yes No Don't know

    (If "enjoy":) What do you particularly enjoy about it?

21 Now I'd like to get some idea of how you rate the firms in the Peterborough district as places to work. Let's do it by supposing that you had been working away from home for a spell and then wanted a job back in Peterborough.

    a. If you went straight to one firm in the Peterborough district for a job, which one would you go to first?

    b. Why this one?

    c. Suppose you did go there to work. After about six months, what would be the total amount you'd be earning per week before tax and other deductions?

22 Suppose now that you didn't get a job there, but that several other local firms were offering jobs to people like you. If I read out the names of several local firms, will you tell me whether you would be interested in getting a job there?

    a. The first firm is Perkins – Perkins Diesel Engines. Would you be interested in getting a job there?

    Yes Not sure No Don't know Conditional answer, e.g. 'If . . .' 'Unless . . .'

    (If don't know:) Leave and go on to next firm.

    (If yes:) What would be the main attraction of working there?

    (If no:) What would be the main disadvantage of working there?

    (If not sure:) Why aren't you sure?

    (If conditional:) Ask, if the condition were met/not met as they wished, what would be the main attraction/disadvantage? (as above).

    All except don't knows: Suppose you did go to Perkins to work? After about six months, what would be the total amount you'd be earning per week before tax and other deductions?

    (Repeat with other firms. Probe behind vague "good" and "bad" reasons. Make a note if his first response is vague.)

    b. British Domestic Appliances, that is, the Hotpoint factory.

    c. Peterborough Corporation, that is, working for the local authority.

    d. Farrow's, the food company.

    e. The London Brick Company.

    f. Combex, the small plastics firm.

    g. British Rail, Peterborough.

  h. Bettles, the building firm.

  i. Baker-Perkins.

  j. Horrell's Dairies, the milk people.

23 Supposing you were offered a job at about the same level as your present one somewhere else in Peterborough district, but at 10/- a week more than you get here. Would you accept it?

Yes No Don't know

(If no or don't know:) If it was at 30/- a week more, would you take it then?

Yes No Don't know

(If not or don't know:) If it was at £3 a week more, would you take it then? This is my final offer!

Yes No Don't know

(If no or don't know:) Why would you prefer to stay and lose £3?

24 If you could start your working life over again would you choose this kind of job?

Yes No Don't know

25 If a problem comes up in your work which isn't settled when you go home, how often, if it all, do you find yourself thinking about it after work?

Often Sometimes Rarely Never

26 When you start off for work, how often, if at all, do you find yourself thinking, "I don't want to go in today"?

Often Sometimes Rarely Never

27 Are you a member of a trade union?

(If yes:) Do you hold any official position in the union?

a. Not a member b. Member c. Official

28 Now I'd like to get an idea of how satisfied or dissatisfied you are with various things about your present job. I'll read out a list of these things and I want you first of all to say whether you are satisfied or dissatisfied with each one and then to show me how strongly satisfied or dissatisfied you feel by marking a cross on a line again.

(Turn to p. 4 of the check-list, and point:)

So for each of the things I read out, you will mark a cross on either the satisfied line or the dissatisfied line. To give you an idea of the kinds of things I will be asking about, here are three of them: pay, trade-union strength, and working conditions. We'll do them one at a time.

(Now read out list one at a time. Always establish first whether he is satisfied or dissatisfied and then make sure he marks the right line. If he is neither satisfied or dissatisfied write in a large nought between the two lines. Stress again that he can put his cross anywhere along the line.)

a. How you get on with management.
b. Job security.
c. How worthwhile the job is.
d. The interest, skill and effort in your job.
e. Fringe benefits, like the pension, sick pay or the social facilities.
f. Trade-union strength.
g. The friendliness of the people you work with.
h. The hours of work, including the time spent travelling.
i. The opportunity to get on with your own work in your own way.
j. Pay.
k. Working conditions.
l. Promotion chances.

29 Now I'd like you to think of your job as a whole. On the next page could you mark how satisfied or dissatisfied you feel about your job in general, all things considered?
(Turn to p. 7 of the check-list.)

30 Now I'd like you to rate the same detailed things according to how important you think they are in weighing up a job. (Explain markings on line. Stress that he can put his cross anywhere.) Try and compare them as you do it, so that some are above average importance and some below average. This time there is just one line per thing. How important compared to other things is:
a. How you get on with management.
b. Job security.
c. How worthwhile the job is.
d. The interest, skill and effort in your job.
e. Fringe benefits like the pension, sick pay or the social facilities.
f. Trade-union strength.
g. The friendliness of the people you work with.
h. The hours of work, including the time spent travelling.
i. The opportunity to get on with your own work in your own way.

   j. Pay.

   k. Working conditions.

   l. Promotion chances.

31 No one has a perfect job, and almost everyone could think of ways in which his job could be improved. If it were possible for you to have a small improvement in any one thing, which one would you choose? And which would be your second choice?

32 Is there any other job in (name of present firm) which you would rather do than your own?
Yes No Don't know
(If yes:) What job?
(Allow foreman/supervisor but not any higher position. If one given, probe for another at lower level.)

33 Have you any injuries or health problems which limit the type of work you can do?
Yes No
(If yes, establish nature of problem, write it in, and if relevant ask:)
Are you a Registered Disabled Person?
Yes No

34 Now I'd like to turn to more general things.
This is a very general question. Here are six cards with things on them that people usually want in life. (give him cards in any order and read each one out.) I want to know the order in which you want them. (Read out again.) To begin with which do you think you want the most, which would you place first?
Enjoyable work
A happy social life with good friends
A nice home to live in
To get on in life and be respected
A good family life at home
A really good wage

35 Thinking about your life as a whole are you satisfied or dissatisfied about the way it has been working out? Could you mark how satisfied or dissatisfied you feel on the last of the lines.
(Turn to Page 10 of the check-list.)

36 We are coming to the last section now. Can I have some details of your life outside work? Firstly, what is your present address?

37 Thinking of your house or flat, are you:
   a. buying it?
   b. renting from the council?
   c. renting it from a private landlord?
   d. or are you living with parents or someone else who is responsible for it and paying the rent/mortgage, etc?

38 Are you married (have you ever been married)?
   a. Single b. Married c. Other
   (If married:) Does your wife have a job?
   a. No b. Part-time c. Full-time
   What type of job is it?
   a. Agricultural job   c. Other manual job
   b. Factory job   d. Office and non-manual
   About how much does she take home a week?
   (If not single:)
   Do you have any children? How many?
   How many of these are living at home?
   How many of those living at home are working?

39 Is there anyone else living in your household?
   (If yes:) Do they work or are they dependent on you?
   Number of workers:
   Number of dependents:

40 Can you think of four men with whom you are friendly, and tell me what jobs they have? You can include relations, workmates, neighbours or anyone else with whom you are friendly.
   (For each one named:) Is he a relative? What relative?
   (If same firm:) Does he actually work with you?

41 Can you give me some details of the types of job held by your close relatives? First, I'd like to know about your father. What job does he do? (Then brothers and father-in-law. Take note of don't knows. If anyone is deceased, retired or is unemployed ask of last normal job,)
   Do you actually work with him? (If same firm).
   Is he (was he) a trade union member?

42 Do you belong to any churches or clubs or associations? We'll start with churches:
   (If has religion:) a. What is your religion, if any?
                      b. About how frequently do you attend?
                      c. Do you hold any official position in it?
   Now any clubs or associations of which you are a member – any social clubs, sports clubs, works clubs, anything political, or any organised group. (For each, repeat questions (b) and (c) above.)

43 Thinking of your other social activities, how often do you:
   a. go out visiting relatives, or receive visits from relatives?
   b. go out visiting, or receive visits from other friends?
   c. go out to a pub for a drink?

44 Thinking of all the times you go out anywhere in your leisure time, how often do you go out:
   a. with your wife and/or other members of your household?
   b. with or meet up with other relatives?
   c. with or meet up with other friends?
   d. on your own?

45 How long on average does it take you to get to work?
   Number of minutes:

46 Finally, suppose someone you hadn't met before asked you "What do you do for a living?" What would you say?
   (If he is baffled by this question, prompt with, " . . . say, the brother of a friend?" No other prompting, but note whether he mentions occupation, industry or firm.)

After the interview is finished will you rate the man's intelligence by putting a cross *anywhere* along the line below. Pay particular attention to his ability to answer the general attitude questions in a meaningful and intelligent way.

Exceptionally low ability	Worse than most	About average	Better than most	Exceptionally high ability

Appendix II   Job Scores: Master Guide

Although most jobs can be scored fairly easily, a few are extremely difficult, and the following convention has been adopted to deal with the most problematic group. Some men have more than one job to do, and in some cases (e.g. building workers) the proportion of time allocated to each is unpredictable and variable. In such cases, unless otherwise stated, the final score given to the man is a compromise between the various scores given to his sub-jobs. All scores are in the range 1–5 except for no. 35 which also has a 0. Some scores have no values of 2 or 4.

	1	2	3	4	5
1. *Outside* (2 and 4 are blank)	In factory or in one building all the time, e.g. storemen.		At works: i.e. reporting and working in same perimeter with management present		At site or away, e.g. exterior or ferry driving, pit worker.
2. *Exposure* N.B. Frequency of time outside will slightly raise score.	Indoors (heated, etc.)	Fairly well sheltered, e.g. cab with heating, good hut.	Moderate shelter, e.g. unheated cab, exposed shelter.	Mixed indoors and outdoors, with possibility of normally sheltering, e.g. groundsman.	Often forcibly exposed, e.g. gardener, building labourer.

	1	2	3	4	5
3. *Either fumes or dirt* or excessive *heat* or refrigerated *cold*. Count the highest of the three, except where two of the three would score 4, – then score 5. If highest score is marginal choose lower one of marginals. Rapid changes, e.g. in heat increase score.	Consistently normal all the time.	Occasionally high (up to 25% of the time; *or* always medium)	Consistently fairly high or high, 25–50% of the time	High, 50–90% or always fairly high	Consistently high, 90%+.
4. *Noise*	Ditto	Ditto	Ditto, i.e. difficult but possible *for us* to talk	Ditto: shouting necessary *by us*.	Ditto: impossible *for us* to talk or understand.
5. *Danger.* N.B. look for protective headgear in particular. (2 and 4 are blank)	Normal, e.g. most jobs.		Dangerous, e.g. shunter, foundry worker, driver of very heavy load, building worker, (not painters or carpenters), spotters, slingers, some fork-lift drivers.		Very dangerous, e.g. knockout labourers.

Factor					
6. *Quantity of Physical Effort.* Compensate weights and degree of body movements, taking especial note of higher factor. Score highest normal activity where daily rotation of duties.	Low, e.g. machine watching, sitting, stores work.	Fairly low: walking or standing about, moving light weights, operating light drill, e.g. brick watchers, most drivers.	Medium exercise and weights, e.g. lifting and swinging medium weights (10–30 lbs). Heavy drill, considerable walking, e.g. tractor drivers.	High activity, e.g. stretching with medium weights (10–30 lbs).	High whole body exertion, e.g. lifting and moving weights of 40 lbs+. Heavy labouring.
7. *Pace of Physical Effort.* Compromise where daily rotation of duties (e.g. building labourers).	Easy pace, no pressure e.g. machine watching, rare action.	Fairly easy, e.g. lorry drivers doing no loading.	Medium pace.	Fairly intensive pace and effort.	Continuous effort.
8. *Manual Dexterity.* Physical + hand-eye coordination.	Intermittent simple movement, e.g. cleaners.	Continuous simple manipulation; or between 1 and 3.	Manual movements of fair precision. Complicated sequential co-ordination of mind, eye and limb.	Manual movements of high precision or great variety of movement; or between 3 and 5: Fitters.	Simultaneous co-ordination of mind, eye and limb, e.g. road drivers.

	1	2	3	4	5
9. *Length of overall work cycle, variations within cycle, and determinacy of cycle.*	Well-defined short cycle (− 5 mins); or medium (5–15 mins) cycle but repetitive within cycle; or normally inactive with short or medium action cycles.	Well-defined medium *or* fairly long (15–60 mins) but repetitive within. *Or* fairly short ill-defined cycle (e.g. material handler). *Or* normally inactive with fairly long action cycles, e.g. storemen.	Well-defined fairly long; or long but lightly repetitive within cycle; or medium ill-defined. Well-defined long (60 mins+) or fairly long ill-defined.	Sequence of cycles largely indeterminate but within cycles some repetition, e.g. most labourers, shunters, drivers.	Sequence and content of cycles indeterminate, e.g. self-organising chargehands, drivers.
10. *Object Variety* Types of parts, tools and controls and dial, to be learned.	1-4 e.g. cleaners	5–12	13–28 normal drivers	29–60	60+ stores work
11. *Mathematical calculations* (no 2 or 4)	None		Addition, subtraction		Areas, volumes, pressures, complex calculations, slide rules.
12. *Reading, writing and understanding English.*	Minimal understanding: neither reading nor writing.	Some understanding, minimal reading, no writing.	Moderate reading: fairly repetitive but detailed instructions. Minimal writing: simple recording in categories.	Write short structured reports *or* read varied reports and instructions.	Complete ability, e.g. reading and writing letters.

	Low	Fairly low / intermittent	Medium	Fairly high	High
13. *Memory for instructions, rules, routines.*	Low: e.g. simple response to machine-paced work, e.g. belt watcher.	Fairly low, e.g. craftsman's mate, simple internal driving.	Medium, e.g. storeman.	Fairly high, e.g. non-apprenticed craftsman, storekeeper	High: learning of rule books, varied schedules, etc., e.g. drivers with routes.
14. *Visualising shapes and relationships, processing consequences of process.*	Low	Fairly low	Medium, e.g. craftsmen, internal drivers.	Good working grasp of complex machinery, e.g. train driver, transfer operators.	High, e.g. road drivers.
15. *Concentration*	Low	Fairly low or intermittent	Medium, e.g. Perkins track operator, train driver.	Fairly high: driving in traffic.	High: mind absorbing, e.g. fettler.
16. *Complexity of decision-making (i.e. mental demands)*	Low: simple choice between few specified alternatives, e.g. Perkins track, cleaning, labouring.	Fairly low: simple choice between many specified alternatives. High tolerance of error. Simple use of judgment for specific objectives.	Medium: simple static choice between many variables. Low or medium tolerance of error.	Fairly high: feedback effects for further decisions. Medium error tolerance (i.e. important but little pressure), e.g. burner, furnace ops., maintenance mechanic, chargehand.	High: continuous reassessment of variables interacting, low tolerance of error (i.e. some pressure), e.g. drivers in traffic, skilled machinist.

	1	2	3	4	5
17. *Autonomy of decision-making* (autonomy in tasks more important than in methods).	Low: entirely determined, e.g. Perkins track, setters, Combex moulders. There may be informal rotation of these jobs.	Fairly low: peripheral method decisions, e.g. 2nd man, mate; *or* simple rearrangement of schedules, e.g. small batch machinery, material handling; *or* between 1 and 3, e.g. hand-drawing.	Medium: routines laid down. Standard decisions made within routine on central methods, many alternatives, standardised but varied feedback, e.g. Perkins testers, transfer ops., storeman, cleaner, routine driver.	Fairly high: general problem laid down and worker translates this into operations, making central decisions in the process. Method has feedback, e.g. drivers, guard, night-watchman, planned maintenance, most changehands.	High: worker determines task or problem, e.g. breakdown mechanic, groundsman.
18. *Pace Choice* Includes both proportion of time and tightness of schedule.	Mechanically, or system determined at least 90% of time to rigid time schedule.	Largely mechanically, or system determined with a little schedule flexibility, e.g. typical machine operator, railways parcel-handling, mate.	M or S determined 40–60% of time, or manually determined with moderate flexibility, e.g. transfer machine, short-haul drivers.	Own pace for most of time, e.g. material handler, carriage and wagon, most maintenance work, storeman, cleaner.	Can set own pace at least 90% of time, e.g. groundsman, callow dragline.

19. *Responsibility for men and materials* (probably not a scale as relationship between 3 and 4 uncertain).	Negligible, e.g. driller, most labourers.	Small responsibility which could be emphasised by worker, e.g. Perkins tester, 2nd man, storekeeper.	Responsibility for large and expensive equipment and goods, e.g. transfer op., watchman, chargehand.	Some responsibility for human life, e.g. slingers, crane drivers, some internal drivers.	High responsibility for human life, e.g. all public drivers (except milk floats).
20. *Frequency of interaction with supervision.*	Constantly observed or frequently inspected, e.g. typical factory assembly line.	Supervision constantly around, frequently observes, sometimes inspects.	Supervision frequently around and never far away, occasionally observes, e.g. material handler.	Supervision normally some distance away but on site. Left to get on with job but regularly visits, e.g. chargehand.	90% unsupervised, geographically separated from supervision, e.g. groundsman, outside driver.
21. *Required interaction with other workers.*	Normally works independently of others except for receiving inputs and giving outputs.	Work-flow close contact only, sequential dependence, e.g. next worker previously works on component, e.g. assembly line.	Intermittent teamwork with other(s).	Normal teamwork with one other or frequently with others.	Normal teamwork with others.
22. *Optional interaction with other people.*	Impossible: worker must concentrate on own job, or no one in area.	Discussion possible but difficult, e.g. noise or distance is barrier, e.g. Perkins tester.	Normal discussion with few possible.	Normal discussion possible with many in area, i.e. limited movement.	More freedom of movement to talk over wider area, e.g. material handler, milkman.

	1	2	3	4	5
23. *Promotion time* shortest length of time between entering present employment and arriving at present job. (High scores may be reduced if there are significant exceptions.)	None: immediate entry from outside normally possible, *or* demotion job for old and infirm.	–6 months	6 months – 3 years	3–10 years	10+ years, e.g. train drivers.
24. Our estimate of *future promotion chances of the present group of men in this job* (excluding questions of their "ability", age, etc.) and of the *modal average length of time between entering this job and promotion from it* for those who do get promoted.	Negligible 1 in 10 or more *and* more than 10 years.	Poor (a) 1 in 10 or more *and* less than 10 years. (b) 1 in 5–10 *and* more than 3 years. (c) 1 in 2–5 *and* more than 10 years.	Medium (a) 1 in 5–10 *and* less than 3 years. (b) 1 in 2–5 *and* 1–10 years. (c) Better than even *and* more than 3 years. (d) Near certainty *and* more than 10 years.	Good (a) 1 in 2–5 *and* less than 1 year. (b) Better than even *and* less than 3 years. (c) Near certainty *and* 1–10 years.	Very Good Near certainty and less than 1 year.

25. *Proportion of next grade above this one promoted from outside (2 and 4 are blank).*	Normally recruited from below.		Mixture		Normally recruited from outside.
26.: *Learning period before normal performance, i.e. training may be as previous job if specific.*	–1 week	1–4 weeks	1–3 months	3–6 months	Longer
27. *Qualification Ties* Previous experience normally required outside the organisation on auxiliary jobs (2 and 4 are blank)	Formal training, e.g. driving licence.		None or negligible		Apprenticeship
28. Type of pay system *normally* worked (if mixed score as 0).	Daywork with fixed rates for the *job*.	Individual merit system, i.e. rating the *man*.	Individual incentive system	Small group incentives	Large group incentive

	1	2	3	4	5
29. Incentive philosophy* where applicable (2 and 4 are blank).	Not applicable		Regulative		Incentive
30. *Irregularity of Hours*	Days	Other fixed hours	Regular rotating shifts with regular weekends.	Irregular rotation, or "on call" frequently.	Wholly variable hours
31. *Position up pay-status hier-archy of organisation* 1 = Lowest 5 = Highest	Each organisation divided into *five* hierarchical strata, principally by pay, making use of organisation's own pay-grade system. Where pay grades do not split into five, introduce status/power, etc. as discriminant, e.g. Farrow's has only 4 grades, so reserve the score 5 for chargehands. If only 4 categories can be filled, leave blank the biggest jump in status.				

* See M. Bolle de Bal (1969).

Appendix III
Construction of
Factors to Measure
Job Characteristics

Nine new measures of job characteristics were created, by factor analysis, from the Objective Job Scores. These are presented in Table A III.1. Under each measure the table sets out the component variables with the factor loadings, or pattern, and the factor score coefficients. The latter are the weights applied to the variables, in standardised form, which are then summed to create the new measure. The loadings give the proportion of each variable directly explained by the factor. Where there is a single factor this is the correlation between factor and variable. In general, this is so for any number of orthogonal factors, but the only analysis where we extract more than one factor is for factors 1 and 2 which are not orthogonal; in this case the loadings exclude that part of the correlation due to the other factor. The loadings, then, may be seen as providing a guide to the adequacy of the new measures. The higher the loadings the more sense it makes to represent the variables by a common factor; or looking at it the other way, the better the variables are as indicators of any underlying factor, the higher are the loadings. For the factors constructed here the loadings were judged to be satisfactory.

We may note that where there are only two job score variables the factor analysis is not really necessary since they contribute equally, but for comparability they have been treated and presented here with the others. In particular, the loadings give comparable information on the adequacy of the resultant measure.

At this stage our aim was solely to construct these measures, which were already conceptualised. Thus only variables selected for their relevance were included in the analysis for each measure. However, we had already conducted an exploratory analysis which enabled us to

Table A III.1   Job Factor Measures

1. Mental abilities / 2. Skill

Variables	1. Mental abilities Loadings	Scores	2. Skill Loadings	Scores
Manual dexterity	-0.04	–	0.90	0.48
Mathematical calculation	0.77	0.15	-0.12	–
Reading, writing	0.93	0.44	-0.13	–
Memory	0.72	0.30	0.35	0.09
Visualisation	0.40	0.04	0.62	0.18
Concentration	-0.05	–	0.76	0.17
Complexity of decisions	0.51	0.15	0.55	0.24
Learning time	0.59	0.10	0.24	0.03

Factors 1 and 2 are correlated 0.34

3. Autonomy

Variables	Loadings	Scores
Outside	0.64	0.19
Autonomy of decisions	0.72	0.28
Pace choice	0.72	0.29
Supervision: absence of	0.76	0.35
Optional interaction	0.27	0.06

4. Working conditions

Variables	Loadings	Scores
Fumes, dirt, heat	0.81	0.68
Noise	0.44	0.15
Danger	0.51	0.19

5. Physical effort

Variables	Loadings	Scores
Effort: Quantity	0.74	0.48
Effort: Pace	0.74	0.48

6. Position in hierarchy

	Loadings	Scores
Promotion time	0.82	0.49
Status level	0.82	0.49

7. Promotion opportunities

	Loadings	Scores
Promotion chances	0.62	0.45
Promotion from outside	-0.62	-0.45

8. General abilities (Mental abilities + skill)

	Loadings	Scores
Manual dexterity	0.69	0.15
Mathematical calculation	0.60	0.13
Reading, writing	0.71	0.16
Memory	0.89	0.20
Visualisation	0.85	0.19
Concentration	0.59	0.13
Complexity of decisions	0.88	0.20
Learning time	0.75	0.17

9. General interest (Mental abilities + skill + variety)

	Loadings	Scores
Manual dexterity	0.62	0.12
Mathematical calculation	0.62	0.12
Reading, writing	0.73	0.14
Memory	0.89	0.17
Visualisation	0.83	0.16
Concentration	0.53	0.10
Complexity of decisions	0.86	0.17
Learning time	0.77	0.15
Work cycle length	0.44	0.08
Object variety	0.77	0.15

check if the variables selected *a priori* would combine well together.[1] This they did in all cases but one, the exception being exposure to the weather, which is not positively related to the job aspects making up the working conditions factor and is therefore treated as a separate variable.

We had two types of reason for combining groups of job scores into new measures. The first was to summarise sets of job score variables in single summary measures; the second, and generally more important, was to create new, theoretically meaningful variables. These are not independent aims so much as different aspects of the same thing. "Theoretical" concern requires that the variables should all be indicators of an underlying factor, while "summary" calls for a factor which explains most variance in a given set of variables, and provided it does make sense to represent them by a single measure even a fairly disparate set may be so summarised. Both considerations are always relevant, but differences of emphasis are possible, and these led to two sorts of measure with slightly different methods of construction.

The new "mental abilities" variable may be taken to illustrate the "theoretical" type. Here our intention was clearly to combine the several job scores. However, the crucial point is that in doing so we were treating them as indicators of a single theoretical variable. The resultant measure represents a relatively homogeneous and distinct aspect of a job, which is broader than the components but, for some purposes at least, is a more appropriate variable. On the other hand, the "general interest" measure is a summary of four related but theoretically separate job aspects: mental abilities, skill, work cycle length and variety in the materials and controls used. The summary measure may be taken as representing the attractiveness of the intrinsic job, which is useful to relate to some of our subjective data, but we are not regarding it as a particularly homogeneous or precise characteristic. It will be seen that the distinction is only one of degree, but it is related to the theoretical context of the research. In a different context, for example, the distinction between verbal and mathematical ability might be as significant as that between skill and length of work cycle, but not, we would argue, in the framework of this study. The empirical data tend to bear this out.

In terms of actual measurement we have used "principal factor" and "principal component" analysis for the "theoretical" and "summary" types respectively.[2] In principal factor analysis the rationale is that there is an underlying theoretical variable(s) accounting for common variance in the component job scores but not totally defining them. That is, each job score may be seen as having a unique part and a part relating it to the other job scores through the underlying theoretical variable(s), which is created to reproduce maximally the correlations between the indicators (i.e. job scores). In the method of principal components the factors completely define the variables – in this case the job scores. The first unrotated factor (first component) is then the best single summary measure, being the linear combination of the job scores which makes a maximum contribution to their total variance.

In Table A III.1, factors 8 and 9 are of the "summary" type. In each case there are two significant factors, showing the lack of homogeneity, but we are only interested in the first. The remaining seven factors in the table are of the "theoretical" type. Factors 4 to 7 are straightforward, in that in each case there is only one significant factor explaining a unique set of variables. In the case of factors 1 and 2, some of the job score variables are relevant to both the mental abilities and skill factors, so we need to extract two factors from the joint set of job scores. There are two significant factors, as expected, and these have been obliquely rotated to confine, as far as possible, the direct relationship of mathematical and verbal ability to one factor, and of manual dexterity and concentration to the other.[3] It will be seen from the factor pattern that the data group clearly in this way. These pairs of variables were then dropped from the calculation of the factor to which they were not related, as not relevant. The correlation between the initial factors is 0.34 while that between the measures so calculated becomes 0.65. Some increase in the correlation was expected from dropping the two pairs of variables but not to this extent. This reflects the difficulty in attaining a high level of validity in measuring one factor without also introducing invalidity in the form of correlation with other factors.[4] Factor 3 is somewhat less satisfactory as a "theoretical" factor in that it does combine some fairly disparate aspects of autonomy, and this shows up in the fact that there are two significant factors. However, we believe it does make good theoretical sense to work with a single autonomy variable and measured it accordingly, although it must be recognised that this is a rather less satisfactory measure than the others we have created.

Finally, we may note that in the two variable factors the use of principal factor or principal component analysis makes no differences to the constructed score. In either case the variables are given equal weight. The loadings for principal factors, as shown, are lower, but the correlations between the constructed measure and the variables are the same as the loadings on the first component. In general, the correlations between the constructed measures and relevant variables are the loadings divided by the validity. The constructed measures from principal component analysis, being precisely defined mathematically with perfect validity, reproduce the loadings exactly when correlated with the relevant variables. For principal factors, however, validity is less than one, so the correlations are greater than the corresponding loadings and each measure explains more variance than the factor it represents. The limiting case, which we have seen occurs in the two variable factors, is when the maximum possible variance is explained, which means that the measure is a principal component. Otherwise, there is a tendency for the measure to be closer to the component than is the unmeasured factor. We see, then, that in practice the two approaches lead to less difference in the construction of measures than might be imagined. Perhaps we should regard it as reassuring that lack of validity produces errors in this direction.

Appendix IV
Background Factors
Related to Orientations

In table A IV.1 we set out the various background factors – both work and non-work – which we found to be related to each orientation. The measures of orientations used are indicated in the table. These are the ones we found most useful in Chapter 7. In all cases we have used the weak form of the orientation but have taken account of the distribution over the measure. Thus we have considered the effects of groupings where numbers are small, and of using the strong form where this might be appropriate. (In the case of intrinsic quality and security we also considered a different basis for the strong form.) The effects of these extra tests were slight, other than to confirm the trend in the initial observation, but they did raise the significance level once or twice, mainly with unusual orientations like fringe benefits.

We do not present coefficients of association, as in this case we believe they would be too misleading. Because of the widely differing distributions of the measures used there are very considerable differences in the magnitudes of coefficients, which may have little to do with the degrees of association between the corresponding theoretical variables. Accordingly, we have placed greater emphasis on the level of significance, which is comparable in all cases, in the sense that it gives the probability, on random principles, of the occurrence of a degree of association as great as, or greater than, that observed, and it is based on a virtually constant number of cases. Unfortunately, significance is not independent of distributions either, and where they are highly skewed the value may be misleadingly low, with the danger that we may overlook or underestimate a relationship. However, it is safer to rely on significance levels. Higher levels not only lead to greater confidence in the existence of a relationship but indicate greater reliability for the degree of association. Of course, the coefficients of association do tend to vary with the significance level (here the constant number of cases is very relevant), with tau being closest and gamma least related. Tau is a measure of association which essentially reflects the degree of deviation from random expectation within the range up to total deviation (perfect association), and with a sample of over 900 a quite small amount of deviation goes with a high level of significance. But a coefficient such as gamma, which sets the deviation within the maximum possible range for the observed (marginal) distributions of the variables (which itself may be quite small for variables with skewed distributions, like strong orientations), may be large for quite low levels of significance. Accordingly, we have also taken some account of the values of gamma.

We have included all relationships significant at the 5 per cent level ($p \leq 0.05$), which should cover the important ones for all orientations but may in some cases allow one or two unimportant ones to creep in. The values of gamma are in the range 0.05 to 0.62, with the majority between 0.1 and 0.3. The relations are subdivided into high, medium and low, with respective levels of significance at $p < 0.001$ (for the majority $p < 0.0001$), $0.001 \leq p < 0.01$ and $0.01 \leq p \leq 0.05$. We also examined all cases of a gamma > 0.4 to see if there was a case for classing at a higher level. However, taking account of values of D and the trend over the whole orientation score (these high values only occur for dichotomised, strong forms) this seemed undesirable. Most were at least at the medium level, anyway.

Significance is measured using a one-tail test. This is appropriate in some cases where there is a clearly expected direction of association, but not in others. It is obviously desirable to be consistent and the one-tail was more convenient to use. Where a two-tail test would be more appropriate it simply means that the significance levels are $p < 0.002$, $p < 0.02$ and $p \leq 0.1$. We have looked at the doubtful cases, i.e. where $0.05 < p \leq 0.1$, and where the level of association is also low we have indicated this in the table with a (†). Clearly we should not give too much weight to these relationships, although in many cases they fit into a definite pattern. In fact, our main reason for including any relationships at this low level of significance is that they do tend to fit and amplify the patterns of association. It is perhaps worth mentioning that on the whole the relationships not included in the table are very clearly not significant, with $p > 0.4$ (two-tail) in most cases. Few fall just outside the range we have taken as significant.

The analysis is, of course, confined to our "unqualified" sample, so all relationships are relative to the sample as a whole. Thus, for example, most non-skilled workers have not previously been self-employed and certainly not more than once or twice, but when an orientation is related to having had few self-employed jobs, we mean few even in this content. Similarly, mobility is always relative to the other workers; for example, when we say that those with a given orientation tend to have "moved up from their highest previous job", a more complete statement would be that they have tended to move up further or moved down less than the other workers. There are a few relationships, such as those involving the number of dependent children, which would probably hold in relation to the entire working population. On the whole, however, it is essential to bear in mind that when we identify a relevant background factor we mean that it is more likely to characterise the unqualified workers who have the orientation compared with other unqualified workers. No doubt we would find some stronger relationships in a more diverse sample, but this would not be relevant to our purpose, since we are concerned with differentiation among those with essentially the same occupational choices available to them.

Table A IV.1   Background Factors Related to Each Orientation

Orientation	Relation	Background factors
Outdoors (Preference—taking account of persistent preference)	High	Born locally – especially not an immigrant from overseas; Religion Protestant; Good housing arrangements (particularly council tenancy); Rarely goes out alone; Low union involvement; Rarely late for work; Low proportion of downward job changes.
	Medium	Age – older workers and not those around 35 to 40; Has relatives working in the same firm; Rarely feels reluctant to go to work; Best-liked job was relatively low status; Moved up from highest previous job; Low proportion of upward job changes; Few jobs in manufacturing industry; Few non-manual jobs.
	Low	Not married; Few dependents; Visits and goes out with relatives; Little church or club membership; Satisfied with life in general; Rarely thinks of work problems outside work; Moved up from best-liked job; Few self-employed jobs; Worked for few firms; Little long-term unemployment.

Orientation	Relation	Background factors
Indoors (Preference)	Medium	Visits relatives; Moved up from father's job; High proportion of downward job changes.
	Low	Immigrant from Pakistan; Father's job was low status; Right-wing ideology; Often late for work; Relatives' jobs are low status, and below his own; High proportion of jobs in manufacturing industry.
Autonomy (Preference)	High	Born locally – especially not an immigrant from overseas; Often late for work; Few previous jobs in agriculture.
	Medium	Born in (large) town; Few dependent children; Often visits the pub; Rarely goes out alone; Often absent from work; Present job is relatively high status.
	Low	Religion not Moslem, and Protestant sect or none rather than Roman Catholic; Lives in an urban area; Goes out with friends; High club or church membership; Poor health; Worked for few firms; Friends' jobs are relatively high status.
Intrinsic Job Quality (Composite Ch —taking account of importance maximum as a strong measure)	High	Not an immigrant from overseas; Born in a (large) town; Religion Protestant (especially C. of E.) or none; Rarely goes out alone; Present job, friends' job, relatives' jobs and best-liked job all relatively high status; Few jobs in agriculture.
	Medium	Father's job was high status; Not buying his home; Satisfied with life in general; Friends are rarely men he works with; Has relatives working in the same firm; Has some occupational qualification; Rarely absent from work; Moved down from best-liked job.
	Low	Stayed at school beyond minimum age; Few dependent children; Goes out with friends; Trade union family background; Rarely late for work; Moved up from first job; High proportion of upward job changes; Several non-manual jobs; Worked for few firms.
Type of Work or Industry (Preference)	High	Not an immigrant from overseas, especially not from Italy or Pakistan; Religion Protestant; Present job and friends' jobs are relatively high status.

Orientation	Relation	Background factors
	Medium	Lives in a rural area; Few dependents; Often thinks of work problems outside work; Best-liked job was relatively high status; Moved up from first job; Worked for few firms.
	Low	Not married; Visits relatives and friends; Goes out with relatives; High club or church membership; Rarely absent from work; Relatives' jobs are lower status than his own; High proportion of upward job changes; Few self-employed jobs.
Worthwhileness (Importance)	High	Not an immigrant from overseas, especially not from Eastern Europe or Pakistan; Religion Protestant; Rarely goes out alone; Satisfied with life in general; Present job, friends' jobs and best-liked job all relatively high status; Moved up from first job.
	Medium	Older; Born in a (large) town; Goes out with family; Relatives' jobs are lower status than his own; High proportion of upward job changes; Little time unemployed since the war.
	Low	Married; Few dependent children; Visits relatives; Has relatives working in the same firm; Has some occupational qualification; Often thinks of work problems outside work; Rarely absent from work†; Moved up from father's job; Low proportion of involuntary job changes.
Work people (Composite Cb)	High	Not an immigrant from overseas, especially not from Italy; Religion Protestant; Satisfied with life in general; Present job is relatively high status.
	Medium	Age – older workers and not those in 40s or late 30s; Good housing arrangements (particularly council tenancy); Few dependent children; Rarely goes out alone; Friends' jobs are relatively high status; Best-liked job was relatively high status; Moved up from first job; High proportion of upward job changes.
	Low	Rarely visits friends; High club or church membership.
Working Conditions (Importance* and Preference*)	High	Not an immigrant from overseas, especially not from Italy (I); Religion Protestant (I); Good housing arrangements (particularly council tenancy) (I); Present job is relatively high status;

Orientation	Relation	Background factors
		(I); Relatives' jobs are relatively low status; (P); High proportion of jobs in agriculture and few in manufacturing industry (P).
	Medium	Born in (large) town (I); Born in village or small town (P); Father's job was low status (P); Visists relatives (I); Rarely goes out alone (I); High union involvement; Radical ideology (I); Good health (I); Poor health (P); Often feels reluctant to go to work (I); Relatives' jobs are lower status than his own (P); Best-liked job was relatively high status (I); Moved up from first job; High proportion of upward job changes (I).
	Low	Stayed at school beyond minimum age (I); Left school at earliest opportunity (P); Visits friends (P); Goes out with family (I)†; Goes out with relatives and friends (P)†; High club or church membership (I); Trade-union family background (P); Satisfied with life in general (I)†; Often absent from work; Often late for work (I); Moved up from father's job (P); Few non-manual jobs (P).
Effort disliked (Preference)	High	Poor health; No occupational qualifications.
	Medium	Lives in an urban area.
	Low	Has dependents; Visits pub; Trade-union family background; Rarely late for work; Spent some time unemployed.
Wages (Economism) (Composite *Cb* – taking account of strong form *CC*)	High	Age – generally younger but especially around 35 to 40; Married; Has dependents, especially children; Radical ideology; Often feels reluctant to go to work:
	Medium	Worked for many firms.
	Low	Immigrant from Italy or eastern Europe; Religion Roman Catholic; Often visits the pub; Goes out with family; High club or church membership†; High union involvement; Rarely thinks of work problems outside work; Often absent from work†; Present job, friends' jobs and best-liked job all relatively low status; High proportion of downward job changes; Few self-employed or non-manual jobs; High proportion of previous jobs in manufacturing industry.

Orientation	Relation	Background factors
Security (Composite *Cb* — taking account of persistent preference)	High	Born locally — especially not an immigrant from overseas; Religion Protestant; Good housing arrangements (particularly council tenancy); Married; Rarely goes out alone; High club or church membership and frequent attendance; Trade-union family background; Present job, friends' jobs and best-liked job all relatively high status; Few previous jobs in agriculture.
	Medium	Visits relatives; Goes out with family, relatives and friends; Satisfied with life in general; Has relatives working in the same firm; Relatives' jobs are lower status than his own; Moved up from father's job.
	Low	Age around 35 to 40; Born in (large) town; Left school at earliest opportunity; Often visits the pub†; High union involvement; Good health; Rarely feels reluctant to go to work (goes with either strong or no orientation); Often thinks of work problems outside work; Moved down from best-liked job; Moved up from first† and from highest previous job; Rarely been unemployed.
Hours (Importance* and Preference*)	High	Born locally — especially not an immigrant from overseas (P); High union involvement (P).
	Medium	Lives in an urban area; Good housing arrangements (particularly council tenancy) (P); Married (I); Visits and goes out with relatives (I); Radical ideology (P); Satisfied with life in general (I); Friends are men he works with (P); Friends' jobs are lower status than his own (I).
	Low	Age around 35 to 40 (I); Religion Protestant (P); Has dependent children (I); Visits pub (P); Goes out with family (I); High club or church membership (P); Frequent club or church attendance (I); Trade union family background (I); Often feels reluctant to go to work (P); Present job is relatively high status (I)†; Friends' jobs are relatively low status (I)†; Relatives' jobs are lower status than his own (I); Moved up from father's job†, first job and highest previous job (I); High proportion of downward job changes (P); Few non-manual jobs (I).

Orientation	Relation	Background factors
Promotion (Importance – taking account of max. as a strong form)	High	Younger; Visits and goes out with friends; Present job and best-liked job are relatively high status.
	Medium	Born in (large) town; Religion Protestant; Visits relatives; Rarely goes out alone; High club or church membership; High union involvement; Friends' jobs are relatively high status; Worked for few firms; Not unemployed often or for a long time.
	Low	Not an immigrant from eastern Europe or Italy; Father's job was high status†; Stayed at school beyond minimum age; buying home or renting from the council; Goes out with family and relatives; Frequent club or church attendance; Radical ideology; Satisfied with life in general; Good health; Rarely absent; Often late; Relatives' jobs are relatively high status; Friends' jobs are lower status than his own†; Moved up from father's job and first job; Moved down from best-liked job; Few jobs in agriculture; Some non-manual jobs.
Status (Preference)	High	Not an immigrant from overseas; Present job, friends' jobs and best-liked job all relatively high status; Few jobs in agriculture.
	Medium	Age – generally younger, but especially around early 40s; Has dependent children; High club or church membership; High interview rating; Some non-manual jobs.
	Low	Visits friends; Visits the pub; Trade union family background; Has relatives working in the same firm; Good health; Relatives' jobs are relatively high status; Worked for few firms; Low proportion of involuntary job changes.
Management Quality (inc. relations with management) (Composite Cb)	High	Right wing ideology
	Medium	Not an immigrant from overseas; Older; Married; Satisfied with life in general; High proportion of upward job changes.

Orientation	Relation	Background factors
	Low	Visits relatives; Goes out with family; Has some qualification; Often thinks about work problems outside work; Present job, friends' jobs, relatives' jobs and best-liked job all relatively high status.
Fringe benefits (Preference)	Medium	Born in (large) town; Goes out with friends; Few jobs in agriculture.
	Low	Not an immigrant from overseas; Lives in village or small town; High union involvement; Radical ideology; Has relatives working in the same firm; Often feels reluctant to go to work; Often absent from work; Present job is relatively high status; Few involuntary changes of jobs.
Trade-union strength. (Importance)	High	Immigrant from Italy; Religion Roman Catholic; Lives in urban area; High trade-union involvement; Radical ideology; Often absent from work; Worked for few firms.
	Medium	Father's job was low status; Trade-union family background; No qualifications; Low interview rating; Moved up from highest previous job; Few non-manual jobs.
	Low	Age – not young (under 25 or even 30) or over 60; Left school at earliest opportunity; Often goes out alone; Satisfied with life in general†; Has relatives working in the same firm; Rarely late for work; Best-liked job was relatively low status, and below present one; Moved up from father's job; Low proportion of downward job changes; Few self-employed jobs.
Personal Suitability (Preference— taking account of persistent preference)	High	Immigrant to the region – especially from overseas (Pakistan, eastern Europe, Italy, in order); Older.
	Medium	Born in village or small town; Rarely feels reluctant to go to work; Friends' jobs are relatively low status; Relatives' jobs are higher status than his own; Moved down from highest previous job; Worked for many firms.
	Low	Poor housing arrangements (mainly buying or renting privately); Married; Rarely visits friends or the pub; High club or church membership; Low union involvement; Friends are men he

Orientation	Relation	Background factors
		works with; Present job is relatively low status; Relatives' jobs are relatively high status; High proportion of downward job changes; Some self-employed and non-manual jobs.

* For working conditions and hours the importance and preference scores were not sufficiently well related to combine and there was no basis to choose between them. Accordingly, we have used both, and where they do not give the same significant result we have indicated after the entry:

(P) = Preference score only.
(I) = Importance score only.

† Marginal relationship, i.e. weak association of relatively low significance ($0.05 < p < 0.1$, 2-tail).

Notes

1. For the moment we are using the term "preference" to indicate a set of relative priorities with respect to the various aspects of a job, which includes the case where a single aspect is dominant. Later on we shall introduce the concept of orientations, in a weak or strong sense, to cover this (see Chapter 6) and use "preference" a little differently (see Chapter 5).
2. The jobs occupy different positions on an indifference curve, or more precisely multi-dimensional surface.
3. For a more detailed, and rather narrowly-based, critique of the orientations approach see Whelan (1976).
4. For convenience we will refer to this as a strong orientation of the type defined by the job aspect, e.g. a strong intrinsic job-quality orientation, and similarly we shall refer to weak orientations, although – particularly with respect to the weak sense – it would really be more precise to regard a worker as having a single orientation with components relating to the different aspects.
5. Though some food processing now involves highly automated production and capital-intensity – and therefore internal labour markets. For an example of this, see Mann (1973b). For a full industrial classification according to type of internal labour market, se Alexander (1974: 67–74).
6. These data are given somewhat obliquely and it is not possible to give comparable figures for internal promotion from semi-skilled to skilled, except for manufacturing industry, where it occurred in just under half the cases. The apparently large difference between manufacturing and other industries may support a dual theory, of course.
7. We assume that Piore also found this in his study of Puerto Ricans. Though he does not give details, he says that their jobs were broadly in the secondary sector, but the diversity of jobs was large (apart from the low promotion chances). He concludes, in rather puzzled fashion, that this is "troubling analytically" (Piore, 1973: 11).

CHAPTER 2

1. To be precise, we did find two or three women holding on to "male jobs" they had filled since the Second World War. They were regarded by all concerned as exceptions who would be replaced by men once they left.
2. Data kindly provided by Professor Peter Townsend, University of Essex,

343

from his research on poverty to be published under the title *Poverty in the United Kingdom* (forthcoming).

3. Precise measurement of changes in pay differentials is not generally possible but the long-term pattern is unmistakeable, see e.g. OECD, 1965:34.

4. Jenkins *et al.* (1975) have undertaken an experimental analysis to examine this sort of approach where job characteristics are measured by systematic observation. This was too late for us to take account of in our research design, but their conclusions do support the usefulness of our procedure.

5. Probably the worst case was the engine test shop at Perkins. In order to "talk" here a man would place his arm round the shoulders of his listener and shout just behind his ear.

6. We are grateful to Ms. Paola Begey, Dr Mario Nuti, and Professor Luciano Gallino for their help in our Italian venture.

7. We were told that this is due to deposits of dinosaur oil, since many dinosaurs gathered and died there, in what was one of the last river valleys when the earth was drying up. The story is supported by innumerable fossil remains, so why should mere sociologists doubt it?

8. One yard we were studying closed unexpectedly in 1970. As the local management had no idea about this when they helped us to select the yard a little earlier, how much more of a bombshell must it have been to the workers!

9. Traditionally, bricks were set and drawn by hand in the chambers. This was extremely arduous, hot work. At the time of our fieldwork the method was still in use in some yards, but was not covered in our sample.

10. See Department of Employment (1976:40) for an analysis of the ethnic composition of the London Brick labour force at Stewartby from 1947 to 1976. It seems probable that the composition in the Peterborough area was very little different, except that the proportion of immigrants from Asia was lower, at least in 1970.

11. However, this tradition seems to be passing; we encountered no dogs.

12. This was the most technically advanced section of plant we studied, falling squarely within the Phase C stage of technological development in the scheme of Alain Touraine. Yet it existed surrounded by Phase B (routine mass production) technology which dominated the firm and its conditions of employment. Its effects upon the workers were therefore minimal (for an exposition and criticism of the "technological determinism" of Touraine and others, see Mann, 1973 b: Chapters 4 and 10).

13. The point may be easily illustrated by the simple example of tossing a coin. If the person tossing continually predicts how the coin will land – heads or tails – we become suspicious, perhaps hypothesising some cheating. We can calculate the probability of 7 consecutive successes is quite low. We cannot conclude definitely that the tosser is cheating (though this would seem most likely if he were making money from it) but we would certainly look for an explanation other than 'chance' i.e. other than pure guesses. We would not make any inference about some larger population of coin-tosses.

CHAPTER 3

1. The correlation coefficients used here are the familiar Pearson coefficients. Since most of the variables have only five values a non-parametric coefficient might be thought more suitable, although the latter are not without disadvantages (see the discussion in Chapter 7). In fact, the results would be very similar: Kendal's tau would give an almost identical result except for slightly lower values of the coefficients, or alternatively Goodman & Krushkal's gamma would give slightly higher values. We have taken care to establish the appropriateness of the Pearson coefficient since it is useful in subsequent analysis (see Table 3.3 and the factor analysis). However, it cannot strictly be interpreted in terms of the proportion of variance explained.

2. The 368 jobs can be used for the Objective Job Scores, but only the 275 jobs have hours and wages data, so for consistency we present the latter. However, to improve reliability both sets have been used to determine hierarchical and compensatory relations, the criteria being a significance level of at least 5 per cent on one set and 10 per cent on the other. These correspond roughly to 0.12 and 0.10 in Table 3.1. For wages and hours we took the best comparable criterion as > 0.10.

3. The position is rather more complicated for oblique factors, since in that case the factors themselves are inter-correlated. A brief account is given in Appendix III, where oblique factors are derived. However, we do not present details of oblique solutions here.

4. The programme used for the factoring described here is the University of Chicago S.P.S.S., Version 5.01. The number of factors extracted is based on the standard conventions of eigenvalues > 1. We used varimax, quartimax and oblique (delta $= 0$) rotations for the 368 data; varimax for the 275 data, with and without wages and hours, and with the addition of wages alone; and oblique for the 275 data with wages and hours. At an earlier stage, before the S.P.S.S. programme was available to us, we used two other programmes and explored the effect of varying the number of factors.

5. That is, the time spent on work, for we recognise that even in the worst jobs an hour has only 60 minutes.

6. Typical high scoring jobs are those of dilutee craftsmen. At the other extreme are driving jobs, since a driving licence is good with any employer. However, most jobs fall in the middle, being neutral on this attribute.

7. The respective loadings become 0.51, 0.43 and 0.38.

8. The oblique factors used to measure these two characteristics are correlated, $r = 0.34$. See Appendix III.

9. Relationships are recorded as significant (hierarchical or compensatory) for unweighted data if significant at least at the 5 per cent level in one and the 10 per cent level in the other of the 275 and 368 job analyses, except for wages and hours where the criterion is $r > 0.10$ (see note relating to Table 3.1). For weighted data the criterion used is again $r > 0.10$. The larger number of cases gives this a higher level of significance, though a precise estimate is impossible because in some cases it is doubtful if the observations can be regarded as strictly independent.

10. Since the multiple cases of a job are always within a particular firm, the

weighting tends to increase the importance of variance between firms.
11. It will be recalled that with unweighted data the exclusion of wages and hours made very little difference at all (apart from dropping the relevant factor). With the weighted data the differences are inevitably larger, but still quite small.
12. In any case the eigenvalue is 0.99 which is only marginally below the conventional criterion of significance.
13. The loadings on skill variables are rather greater in the versions omitting wages and hours. See Appendix III for the construction of the specific skill factor; Memory and Learning contribute least to this.

CHAPTER 4

1. In this one firm we did not have accurate information, since the men finished as soon as their day's work was completed, so there was no reason for the firm to record hours. Consequently, this figure is an estimate. It may be slightly low, as a man could extend his day considerably by going slowly and taking long breaks. However, we saw no evidence of this happening and so made no allowance in our estimate.
2. Excluding "promotion opportunities" which, as we have already noted, are somewhat artefactual, in a way which makes the variable unsuitable for this purpose.
3. A criterion roughly comparable to that of a difference of 0.5 between a firm and the mean of all firms in the relevant direction for job scores was estimated as a difference of 0.43 standard deviations, which was used as a guide.
4. Drivers of electric-powered milk floats scored below this level and are not included in this analysis.
5. To have used the specific 'skill' factor (2) would have made road drivers appear relatively more skilful, but might be regarded as a biased result. In any case the difference is not large.
6. The questionnaire did formally require literacy at one point, where respondants were asked to choose between statements written on cards (Question 34). Several workers asked the interviewer to read these out, always because "I've forgotten my glasses".
7. Except for those jobs which exist recognisably across firms and industries: driver, building worker, etc.
8. See also Table 9.5 below.

CHAPTER 5

1. Having confirmed in our pilot survey an impression that Bettles was not well-known locally, we gave respondents the opportunity to reply to the Bettles question in terms of their knowledge of any other local building firm. The responses did not differ significantly, and have been conflated here.
2. It is also possible that, despite our carefully-worded question, several responded in terms of net earnings instead of gross.

3. We can still think of no adequate reason why Bettles wages appeared so low and this may be an error. One possibility is that extra bonuses were distributed in an *ad hoc* way at building sites, which were not recorded in the company's main wages registers at head office. The explanation is not sample bias, for we attempted to interview all non-skilled workers at Bettle's and the wages of the non-respondents did not differ significantly from those of the respondents. Since the sample size here was only 16, if the figures are inaccurate this will have little effect on analyses of the total sample.

4. The list of studies is actually enormous; Daniel, 1974: 70–3; Freedman, 1969: 29–31; Hill *et al.*, 1973: 104–7; Kahn, 1964: 94; Mackay *et al.*, 1971: 357; Martin and Fryer, 1973: 141–7; Miernyk, 1955: 22; Parker *et al.*, 1971: 183, 196; Rees and Schultz, 1970: 199–206; Sheppard and Belitsky, 1966: 89–96; Reynolds, 1951: 84, 106; Wedderburn, 1965: 147; Wilcock and Franke, 1962: 128–30.

5. This relationship remains mysterious to us, though controlling for two variables, interviewer rating (see Chapter 9 for an explanation of this variable) and status in firm, did somewhat reduce the relationship in a way that we could interpret. As we will argue in later chapters successful workers, in terms of status level achieved, are also more self-confident, articulate and co-operative, and – we would suspect here – more knowledgeable. Note that age was not responsible for the relationship: it is not the case that mere length of experience in employment increases knowledge of the market.

6. We have excluded the fourth possible type, agreement that the firm does not seem extreme, as this could derive partly from silence on the worker's part! To include it would, of course, greatly increase the extent of exact agreement.

7. Remember, however, that we conflated the responses relating to Bettle's and other building firms.

8. We explore the reality of their situation in Chapter 9 below.

9. The total possible mentions of one item is twenty (two reasons of the same type for all ten firms), but in practice when workers gave two reasons for a firm they tended to be of different types. Thus the normal maximum is ten mentions.

10. The factor programmes derived from the University of Chicago S.P.S.S., Version 5.01, using varimax, quartimax and oblique (with three different delta values) rotation.

CHAPTER 6

1. See especially Goldthorpe, 1966; Goldthorpe *et al.*, 1968, and also Goldthorpe *et al.*, 1969. Other relevant works include Touraine, 1964; Ingham, 1970; Beynon and Blackburn, 1972; and in a somewhat different vein, Gouldner, 1959.

2. We are grateful to John Goldthorpe for bringing this point to our attention.

3. The usage in Beynon and Blackburn (1972) was essentially the same as here, although this point was not made explicit.

4. In measuring instrumentalism they also use lack of involvement in social

relationships and organisations, but the element of economism is measured by reasons for staying at the present firm (Goldthorpe *et al.*, 1968: 160–2).

5. Security is by far the most common of the three, and we shall see later it is a moderately important orientation, but there is no basis to see it as part of a "bureaucratic" orientation.

6. The only person who seems to have appreciated its relevance at all is Ashton (1973).

7. This methodology is explained more fully in a previous article (Blackburn and Mann, 1975), where these complaints are labelled "Generalised Demands".

8. We did not include conscripted service as a job, and in some cases workers returned to the same job. (Firms were legally required to make the job available after National Service.) However, in many cases the disruption of being "called up" was the cause of a job change.

9. For further discussion see Blackburn and Mann, 1975.

10. An alternative way to overcome the problems of raw scores is, for each individual, to control for his mean for 12 aspects. This is done most simply by dividing by or subtracting the mean; additionally, in the latter case, we may divide by the standard deviation for the 12 aspects. However, such adjustments create distortion because the raw scale is bounded, with the upper bound frequently used. This may be met to some extent by holding the upper limit constant (at 24) and proportionately adjusting lower scores to make all the individual means equal (at 12, "average importance"). This is perhaps the best standardisation, but all have essentially the same sort of drawbacks as ranking, though less acutely, and in practice seem to have little or no advantage over the raw scores. So, as raw scores are easier to interpret we have preferred to present results using them.

11. This is taking the total frequencies on the two measures as given, although it might well be argued that on random principles the expected frequency of "most important" would be substantially higher (depending on other assumptions). This would increase the expected number of congruent cases, possibly to 35 or even more.

12. A very similar pattern of results emerged from extending the definition of high importance to include score 23.

13. It is worth pointing out that relationships no greater than these have often been used, in previous literature, as the basis for strong arguments about trends when the data have been presented in tabular form.

14. Because of the difficulties associated with individual variation in the zero point it is not possible to determine the sign of correlations between the importance of various aspects (for raw importance scores all inter-correlations are significantly positive), but for these two aspects the relationship is particularly low. In fact, the pattern of correlations between importance scores seem to be entirely in keeping with our account of their relations with preference scores.

15. In line with this pattern, some forms of standardisation of the importance measure give positive relations between the indoor preference and importance of conditions and between outdoor preference and importance of interest.

16. See, for example, Stewart and Blackburn (1975).

17. This may be seen clearly in the attitudes of many married women working part-time; see Beynon and Blackburn (1972).
18. See Beynon and Blackburn, 1972, where short convenient hours were particularly important among women with family commitments.
19. See Hauser and Goldberger (1971) for a full discussion of the method.
20. See Blackburn and Mann (1975) for further information on these measures.
21. See Blackburn and Mann (1978) for a full discussion of this question. Other writers, e.g. Ewen (1967), Blood (1971), have come to similar conclusions about "importance" weighting, although they have not taken account of many of the methodological problems.
22. Using an entirely different sort of approach to evaluation of job characteristics, one of us has shown previously that salience is very relevant to overall attitudes; see Beynon and Blackburn (1972).

CHAPTER 7

1. Our use of the term "socialisation" may appear a little unconventional, but in fact it refers to the transformation "into a person suitable to perform the activities of society" (Brim and Wheeler, 1966: 4), in this case through the acquisition of dispositions appropriate to acceptance of his work role, which may be regarded as an aspect of adult socialisation.
2. This includes a hierarchy of needs, as in Maslow (1954).
3. While the notion of weak orientations involves the range of possible rewards for each individual, it will be convenient to take aspects singly to relate them to the actual rewards.
4. If we use dummy variables for strong orientations, with 1 indicating presence and 0 absence, we may express the new measures formally as follows:

$CA = 1$ if (importance rank = 1 and importance score = 23 or 24)
     or preference frequency> 4
$CA = 0$ in all other cases
$Cb = \frac{1}{2}$ (importance score) + preference frequency
$CC = 1$ if $Cb \geqslant 14$
$CC = 1$ if $Cb < 14$

5. It is usual to use tau C only where variables have a limited number of values, appropriate for presentation in tabular form. Tau B is also used for such data, but in addition is used where variables have many values.

6. Tau $C = \dfrac{2m(P - Q)}{N^2(m - 1)}$ where m is the number of values on the variable with less

values, P is the number of pairs ordered the same way on both variables and Q the number of reverse orderings.

$$\text{Tau } C \text{ max} = \frac{2m \sum\limits_{1}^{m-1} \sum\limits_{2}^{m} a_i a_j}{N^2(m - 1)}, i < j, \text{ where the '}a\text{' are the marginal totals on}$$

the variable with less values. Thus the standardised tau

$$C = P - Q \bigg/ \sum_1^{m-1} \sum_2^m a_i a_j, \ i < j$$

7. The formula for D_{xy} (i.e. x dependent) is usually in the form

$D_{xy} - \dfrac{P - Q}{P + Q + Tx}$, where P and Q are again the number of concordant and

discordant pairs respectively, and Tx is the number of ties on x. Thus it may be seen as taking account of ties on the "dependent" variable and the two values follow from which ties are allowed for. This formula can easily be shown to be the same as the one we derived above for the standardised tau C.

8. The totals do not even need to be in the same order on each variable.

9. Gamma $= P - Q/P + Q$ where P and Q are the numbers of concordand and discordant pairs, as before. This is the same as D and tau B, apart from containing no figure for ties. It has the advantage of a proportional-reduction-in-error interpretation (See Costner 1965; for a more general discussion see Mueller *et al.*, 1970: 297–92).

10. In addition to the measures referred to, use was made of Cramer's V and eta for guidance on non-linear relationships, and tests of significance were applied. Relations are taken as significant where $P > 0.05$, applying a one-tail test in accordance with a hypothesis of congruence.

11. We frequently only report one coefficient for simplicity, but all arguments are based on a consideration of at least three.

12. There were too few cases to use a persistent preference.

13. In this case ordinary product-moment correlations with the job factors can be regarded as roughly correct. They give coefficients slightly lower than the gammas.

14. One advantage of using the Cb form is that we can use the more readily interpretable Pearson product-moment correlation coefficient with considerable confidence. Its values are shown in Table 7.4.

15. The authors are aware of this, although they do think that their measure of instrumentalism differentiates *within* their sample (p. 160).

16. It should be recognised that the notion of "instrumental orientation" entails more than just "economism". However, the pecuniary aspect is central to the argument and a crucial part of the measure of instrumentalism. The Vauxhall assembly workers were the most economistic group, and it is largely on the basis of this that they are classed as the most instrumental group.

17. Some caution is needed in this interpretation since the workers were asked to estimate their overtime "at present", and this was seasonally low for assemblers (Vol. 3, 1969; 61n). The estimates of earnings were "average" and may have reflected the low overtime – giving below-average figures – or they may have been based on longer hours – thus exaggerating the hourly rate. However, the pattern is clear and it would require considerable errors to alter the general argument. What is more likely is that the situation is closer to that we found in Peterborough than the figures imply. In any case, there is no such problem with process workers, or with the difference

between machinists and setters, which follows the same pattern.

18. There is no single unambiguous way in which we can measure the relative sizes of our firms, but whatever criterion is used the result is much the same.
19. This addition was explained in Chapter 5.
20. Strictly speaking, we were able to identify two classes, using all four indicators, but they were poorly related to the indicators and made no theoretical sense. Certainly neither class could be seen as comprising workers with an hours-of-work orientation.
21. Though the numbers are too small to give much weight to the figures.
22. Similarly, *The Affluent Worker* the authors of, in response to our query on this point, wrote in their last volume that a decrease in instrumentalism occurs in their sample with length of service. As all were earning relatively high wages this may be seen as a decline in congruence (Goldthorpe *et al.*, 1969; 68).

CHAPTER 8

1. It is interesting to relate this to the findings of Prandy (1979b) using data from the 1971 Census (i.e. collected at about the same time). On the data from five English cities the Pakistanis emerge at the opposite extreme from the English on a scale of ethnic distance, while the Poles (the only eastern European group) are rather closer to the English than the Italians. When social distance between ethnic groups (based on residential segregation) is presented in two dimensions for each city, while the Pakistanis are always at the extreme on the first dimension (defined by closeness of relation to ethnic distance) the Italians consistently occupy the extreme position on the second. The Poles are not particularly extreme on either.
2. Their allocation was on the basis of types of surname.
3. See Chapter 9 for a general discussion of these characteristics.
4. For a discussion of some of the issues see Stewart *et al.* (forthcoming).
5. It might be objected that they are the sort of people who reply to sociologists' questions! Indeed we would expect this to be so, to some extent. But this does not negate our findings, as may be seen from the negative relation of "personal suitability", and more directly from the lack of relationship of orientations with the interview rating based on answering the questions.

CHAPTER 9

1. We ought perhaps to add that we have no cases of white and obviously "British" workers born abroad, or of black or brown British-born workers. Either might have confused this dichotomy.
2. The notion that long hours and shiftwork might be inter-changeable aspects of the immigrant's employment situation receives support from Cohen and Jenner's (1968–69) study of textile employment in a Yorkshire town in which the decision to employ immigrants was related to their supposed willingness to work shifts or long hours.

3. Remember, however, that our sample excluded trained apprentices still working in the same trade.

4. A slight reservation is perhaps necessary. Younger workers tend to have slightly better qualifications but to have worse jobs (see below). It is thus possible that controlling for age would reveal a slight positive relationship between qualifications and work rewards. However, the number of qualified workers in our sample is too small for us to perform this analysis adequately.

5. The distribution of "number of firms", while not quite normal, is only slightly skewed.

6. Full details of this variable ("Ideology F") can be found in our article on worker's ideologies (Blackburn and Mann, 1975: especially pp. 135–7). Although we there provided a detailed breakdown of job characteristics as they relate to radicalism, our factor measures (which we consider to be our best measures of work rewards) were not then available. We also collected data on two other matters of concern to the employer, absence and lateness records, although we have not used them here for the reason that they are characteristics of *present* job situation. The only significant differences were that those with worse absence records used fewer mental abilities, while the latecomers were very much less autonomous in their work.

7. The decline at four to six years service should not be given much weight, as it is largely an effect of the grouping and of fairly small numbers. The important feature is the overall trend.

8. The former was based on the proportion of our original sampling populations that we rejected because of inadequate English (with a correction for the Italians we actually interviewed); the latter is explained below. The other two "worker quality" measures were the proportion of unhealthy workers in each firm's sample and the average interviewer rating.

9. Note that we are not discussing here "hierarchy within the firm", for which our Job Factor No. 6 is the appropriate measure, but a general occupational hierarchy across firms. We have already briefly discussed this in Chapter 8.

10. It may be that raising drivers from 5 to 3 or 4 would alone raise the correlation to near-perfection.

11. The rather different distributions of fathers' and sons' occupations may be partly an artefact. The "recall' method, of which asking sons about their fathers' jobs is an example, tends to inflate the numbers of unskilled. However, a more genuine cause also operates; the large number of fathers who were agricultural labourers.

12. The numbers responding to the items differs somewhat, due to the lack of precise recall the respondents could manage for fathers' jobs and the number of first jobs that had to be excluded from analysis because they were distinctively "juvenile" in nature.

CHAPTER 10

1. As our sample of immigrants is an unusual one, the reader should bear in mind the reservations we make about these conclusions in Chapter 9 itself.

2. We remember a journey through Peterborough in the company of David

Lockwood after we had been emphasising "random" labour market processes at a conference. "Ah," said Lockwood, "this is the black hole of Peterborough where all known physical and social laws are in abeyance!"

3. Actually, however, no really penetrating or detailed research on this process has yet been undertaken. An ambitiously designed project on ageing and worker behaviour would seem to us to be an invaluable contribution to knowledge.

APPENDIX III

1. See the discussion of factor patterns in Chapter 3.
2. See Harman (1967), p 14–16, 135–43 for a discussion of the general principles involved here. The programmes used were SPSS types PA2 and PA1, the former being principal factor with interations.
3. Rotation was direct oblimin with delta set to −0.6.
4. See Heermann (1963), and Heise and Bohrnstedt (1970), on invalidity.

Bibliography

Abel-Smith, B. and Townsend, P., *The Poor and the Poorest* (London: G. Bell and Sons, 1965).

Aiken, M., Ferman, L. A. and Sheppard, H. A., *Economic Failure, Alienation and Extremism* (Ann Arbor: University of Michigan Press, 1968).

Alexander, A., "Income, Experience and the Structure of Internal Labour Markets", *Quarterly Journal of Economics*, Vol. 88, 1974.

Andreano, R. L. (ed.), *Superconcentration/Supercorporation* (Andover, Mass.: Warner Modular Publications, 1973).

Argyris, C., *Personality and Organization* (New York: Harper, 1957).

Arrow, K., "Models of Job Discrimination" in A. H. Pascal, *Racial Discrimination in Economic Life* (Lexington: D. C. Heath, 1972).

Ashton, N., "The Transitions from School to Work: Notes on the Development of Different Frames of Reference among Young Workers", *The Sociological Review*, 21.1, February 1973.

Baldamus, W., *Efficiency and Effort* (London: Tavistock, 1961).

Barron, R. and Norris, G., "Sexual Divisions in the Dual Labour Market", in D. L. Barker and S. Allen (eds.), *Dependence and Exploitation in Work and Marriage* (London: Longman, 1976).

Berger, S., "The Uses of the Traditional Sector: Why the Declining Classes Survive", unpublished paper, M.I.T., November 1972.

Beynon, H. and Blackburn, R. M., *Perceptions of Work* (London: Cambridge University Press, 1972).

Birnbaum, I. "Greater Indeterminism in Causal Analysis", *Quality & Quantity*, Vol. II, 1977.

Blackburn, R. M. and Mann, M., "The Ideologies of Non-Skilled Workers" in M. Bulmer (ed.), *Working Class Images of Society* (London: Routledge, 1975).

Blackburn, R. M. and Mann, M., "The Relevance of Workers' Priorities in the Theory and Measurement of Job Satisfaction", forthcoming.

Blau, P. M. and Duncan, O. D., *The American Occupational Structure* (New York: Wiley, 1967).

Blood, M. R., "The Validity of Importance", *Journal of Applied Psychology*, Vol 55, No. 5, 1971.

Bolle De Bal, M., "The Psycho-Sociology of Wage Incentives", *British Journal of Industrial Relations*, Vol. 7, November 1969.

Bosanquer, N. and Doeringer, P. B., "Is There a Dual Labour Market in Great Britain?", *Economic Journal*, Vol. 83, 1973.

Brim, O. G. and Wheeler, S., *Socialisation After Childhood* (New York: Wiley, 1966).

Carchedi, G., "On the Economic Identification of the New Middle Class", *Economy and Society*, Vol. 4, 1975.

Castles, S. and Kosack, G., *Immigrant Workers and the Class Structure in Western Europe* (London: Oxford University Press, 1973).

Census, 1971: (a) *County Reports: Huntingdon and Peterborough* (London: H.M.S.O., 1972) (b) *Great Britain, Economic Activity Tables, Part V(10/sample)* (London: H.M.S.O., 1975) (c) *England and Wales, New Towns: Economic Activity, Workplace and Transport to Work Tables (10% sample)* (London: H.M.S.O., 1976).

Cohen, B. G. and Jenner, P. J., "The Employment of Immigrants: a Case Study in the Wool Industry," *Race*, Vol. 10, 1968–9.

Cole, D. and Utting, J. E. G., "Estimating Expenditure, Saving and Income from Household Budgets", *Journal of the Royal Statistical Society*, Series A, Vol. 119, 1956.

Collins, R., "Functional and Conflict Theories of Educational Stratification", *American Sociological Review*, Vol. 36, 1971.

Costner, H. L., "Criteria for Measures of Association", *American Sociological Review*, Vol. 30, No. 3, June 1965.

Dalton, M., *Men Who Manage* (New York: Wiley, 1959).

Daniel, W. W., *A National Survey of the Unemployed* (London: P. E. P., 1974).

Department of Employment, "On the quality of Working Life", *Manpower Paper No. 7*, (London: H.M.S.O., 1973).

Department of Employment and Productivity, *Labour Costs in Great Britain* (London: H.M.S.O., 1968).

Department of Employment, Project Report by the Unit for Manpower Studies, *The Role of Immigrants in the Labour Market* (London: author, 1977).

Department of Education and Science, *A Language for Life* (Report of the Committee of Inquiry under the Chairmanship of Sir Alan Bullock) (London: H.M.S.O., 1975).

Department of Trade, *Report of the Committee of Inquiry on Industrial Democracy* (the Bullock Report) (London: H.M.S.O., 1977).

Doeringer, P. B., "Low Pay, Labor Market Dualism, and Industrial Relations Systems", *Harvard Institute of Economic Research*, Discussion Paper No. 271, April 1973.

Doeringer, P. B. and Piore, M. J., *Internal Labor Markets and Manpower Analysis* (Lexington: D. C. Heath, 1971).

Duncan, O. D., 'A Socio-economic Index for All Occupations", in A. J. Reiss, *Occupations & Social Status* (New York: Free Press, 1961).

Edwards, R. C., Reich, M. and Gordon, D. M. (èds.), *Labor Market Segmentation* (Lexington: D. C. Heath, 1975).

Emmanuel A. *Unequal Exchange* (New York: Monthly Review Press, 1972).

Ewen R. B., "Weighting Components of Job Satisfaction", *Journal of Applied Psychology*, Vol. 51, No. 1, 1967.

Form, W. H. and Geschwender, J. A., "Social Reference Basis of Job Satisfaction", *American Sociological Review*, Vol. 27, April 1962.

Freedman, M., *The Process of Work Establishment* (New York: Columbia University Press, 1969).

Freeman, R. B., "Decline of Labor Market Discrimination and Economic Analysis", *American Economic Review*, Vol. 63, Papers and Proceedings of the 85th meeting, 1973.

Garson, G. D., *Handbook of Political Science Methods* (Boston: Holbrook Press, 1971).

Gayer, P. and Goldfarb, R. S., "Job Search, the Duration of Unemployment and the Phillips Curve: Comment", *American Economic Review*, Vol. 62, 1972.

Gintis, H., "Education, Technology and the Characteristics of Worker Productivity", *American Economic Review*, Vol. 61, Papers and Proceedings of the 83rd Meeting, 1971.

Goldthorpe, J. H., "Attitudes and Behaviour of Car Assembly Workers: a Deviant Case and a Theoretical Critique", *British Journal of Sociology*, September 1966.

Goldthorpe, J. H. and Hope, K. "Occupational Grading and Occupational Prestige", in Hope, K. (ed), *The Analysis of Social Mobility* (Oxford: Clarendon Press, 1972).

Goldthorpe, J. H., Lockwood, D., Bechhofer, F. and Platt, J., *The Affluent Worker: Industrial Attitudes and Behaviour* (London: Cambridge University Press, 1968).

Gordon, D. M., *Theories of Poverty and Underemployment* (Lexington: D. C. Heath, 1972).

Gordon, M. S. and Thal-Larsen, M., *Employer Policies in a Changing Labor Market* (Berkeley: Institute of Industrial Relations, 1969).

Gouldner, A. W., *Patterns of Industrial Bureaucracy* (Glencoe: Free Press, 1954).

Gouldner, A. W., "Organisational Analysis", in R. K. Merton, L. Broom and L. S. Cottrell Jr. (eds.), *Sociology Today: Problems & Prospects*, Vol. II (New York: Harper & Row, 1959).

Gray, R. Q., "The Labour Aristocracy in the Victorian Class Structure", in F. Parkin (ed.), *The Social Analysis of Class Structure* (London: Tavistock, 1974).

Hancock, Hawkes and Associates, *Greater Peterborough: Draft Basic Plan* (London: authors, 1967).

Harman, H. H., *Modern Factor Analysis* (Chicago University Press, 1967).

Harrison, B., *Education, Training and the Urban Ghetto* (Baltimore: Johns Hopkins Press, 1972).

Harrison, B., "Ghetto Economic Development: A Survey", *Journal of Economic Literature*, Vol. 12, 1974.

Hauser, R. M. and Goldberger, A. S., "The Treatment of Unobservable Variables in Path Analysis", in H. L. Costner (ed.), *Sociological Methodology 1971* (San Francisco: Jossey-Bass, 1971).

Heermann, E. F., "Univocal or Orthogonal Estimates of Orthogonal Factors", *Psychometrika*, Vol. 28, 1963.

Heise, D. R. and Bohrnstedt, G. W., "Validity, Invalidity and Reliability", in E. F. Borgatta and G. W. Bohrnstedt (eds.), *Sociological Methodology, 1970* (San Francisco: Jossey-Bass, 1970).

Herron, F., *Labour Market in Crisis: Redundancy at Upper Clyde Shipbuilders* (London: Macmillan, 1975).

Herzberg, F., *Work and the Nature of Man* (London: Staples Press, 1968).

Hill, M. J., *Men Out of Work: A Study of Unemployment in Three English Towns* (London: Cambridge University Press, 1973).

Hollowell, D., *The Lorry Driver* (London: Routledge, 1968).

Hunter, L. C. and Reid, G. L., *Urban Worker Mobility* (Paris: O.E.C.D., 1968).

Ingham, G. K., *Size of Industrial Organization and Worker Behaviour* (London: Cambridge University Press, 1970).

Jenkins, G. D., Nadler, D. A., Lawler III, E. E. and Cammann, C., "Standardized Observations: An Approach to Measuring the Nature of Jobs", *Journal of Applied Psychology*, Vol. 60, No. 2, 1975.

Jones, K. and Smith, A. D., *The Economic Impact of Commonwealth Immigration* (Cambridge: National Institute of Economic and Social Research and Cambridge University Press, 1970).

Kahn, H., *Repercussions of Redundancy* (London: Allen & Unwin, 1964).

Kerr, C., "The Balkanization of Labor Markets", in E. W. Bakke *et al.*, *Labor Mobility and Economic Opportunity* (Cambridge, Mass.: M.I.T. Press, 1954).

Kornhauser, A., *The Mental Health of the Industrial Worker* (New York: Wiley, 1965).

Kunin, T., "The Construction of a New Type of Attitude Measure", *Personnel Psychology*, 8, 1955.

Lampman, R., "Comment on Choice in Labor Markets", in W. Galenson and S. M. Lipset, *Labor and Trade Unionism* (New York: Wiley, 1960).

Lazarsfeld, P. F. and Henry, N. W., *Latent Structure Analysis* (Boston: Houghton Mifflin, 1968).

Lenski, G., *The Religious Factor* (Garden City, N. Y.: Doubleday, Anchor Books edn, 1963).

Lester, R., "A range theory of wage differentials", *Industrial and Labor Relations Review*, Vol. 5, 1952.

Lester, R., *Hiring Practices and Labor Competition*, (Princeton University Press, 1954).

Mackay, D. I., "Wages and Labour Turnover" in Robinson, 1970.

Mackay, D. I., "Internal Wage Structures" in Robinson, 1970.

Mackay, D. I., *et al.*, *Labor Markets Under Different Employment Conditions* (London: Allen & Unwin, 1971).

MacPherson, C. B., *The Real World of Democracy* (Oxford: Clarendon Press, 1966).

Mann, M., *Consciousness and Action in the Western Working Class* (London: Macmillan, 1973a).

Mann, M., *Workers on the Move* (London: Cambridge University Press, 1973b).

Marsden, D, and Duff, E., *Workless* (Harmondsworth: Penguin Books, 1975).

Martin, R. and Fryer, R. H., *Redundancy and Paternalist Capitalism* (London: Allen & Unwin, 1973).

Maslow, A. H., *Motivation and Personality* (New York: Harper, 1954).

Miernyk, W. H., *Inter-Industry Labor Mobility* (Boston: Northeastern University Press, 1955).

Morgan, J. N., *5,000 American Families – Patterns of Economic Progress* (University of Michigan, Survey Research Centre, Institute for Social Research, 1974).

Morrison, D. E. and Henkel, R. E., *The Significance Test Controversy*

(London: Butterworth, 1970).

Mueller J. Schuessler K. and Costner, H., *Statistical Reasoning in Sociology*, 2nd ed. (Boston: Houghton Mifflin, 1970).

Myers, C. A. and MacLaurin, W. R., *The Movement of Factory Workers* (New York: Wiley, 1943).

Myers, C. A. and Shultz, G. P., *The Dynamics of a Labor Market* (New York: Prentice-Hall, 1951).

Office of Population Censuses and Surveys, Social Survey Division, *The General Household Survey, Introductory Report* (London: H.M.S.O., 1973).

Organisation for Economic Co-operation and Development, *Wages and Labour Mobility* (Paris: O.E.C.D., 1965).

Organization for Economic Co-operation and Development, *The 1973– 4 Recession and the Employment of Women* (Paris: O.E.C.D., 1976).

Palmer, G., *Labor Mobility in Six Cities* (New York: Social Science Research Council, 1954).

Palmer, G., (ed.), *The Reluctant Job-Changer* (Philadelphia: University of Pennsylvania Press, 1962).

Parker, S. R., Thomas, C. G., Ellis, N. D. and McCarthy, W. E. J., *Effects of the Redundancy Payments Act* (London: H.M.S.O., 1971).

Parnes, H. S., *Research on Labor Mobility* (New York: Social Science Research Council, 1954).

Parnes, H. S., (ed.), *The Pre-Retirement Years: a longitudinal study of the labor market experience of men*, U.S. Department of Labor, Manpower Administration Research Monograph No. 15 (Washington: U. S. Government Printing Office, 3 vols., 1970).

Parsons, T. and Shils, E. A., (eds.), *Towards a General Theory of Action* (New York: Harper & Row, 1962).

Piore, M. J., "The Role of Immigration in Industrial Growth: a Case Study of the Origins and Character of Puerto Rican Migration to Boston", *M.I.T. Working Paper*, No. 112a, May 1973.

Piore, M. J., "On the Technological Foundations of Economic Dualism", *M.I.T. Working Paper*, No. 110, May 1973.

Political and Economic Planning, "The Facts of Racial Disadvantage", *P.E.P. Broadsheet No. 560* (by D. J. Smith), February 1976.

Poulantzas, N., *Classes in Contemporary Capitalism* (London: New Left Books, 1975).

Prager, J., "White Racial Privilege and Social Change: an Examination of Theories of Racism", *Berkeley Journal of Sociology*, Vol. 17, 1972–3.

Prandy, K., "Ethnic Discrimination in Employment & Housing:

Evidence from the 1966 British Census", *Ethnic and Racial Studies,* Vol. 2, No. 1, January 1979a.

Prandy, K., "Residential Segregation & Ethnicity in British Cities", (forthcoming 1979b).

Rees, A. J., "Information Networks in Labor Markets", *American Economic Review,* Vol. 51, Papers and Proceedings of the 78th Meeting, 1966.

Rees, A. J. and Shultz, G. P., *Workers and Wages in an Urban Labor Market* (Chicago: Chicago University Press, 1970).

Reich, M., Gordon, D. M. and Edwards, R. C., "Dual Labor Markets: a Theory of Labor Market Segmentation", *American Economic Review,* Vol. 63, Papers and Proceedings of the 85th Meeting, 1973.

Reynolds, L., *The Structure of Labor Markets* (New York: Harper, 1951).

Reynolds, L. G. and Shister, J., *Job Horizons: A study of job satisfaction and labor mobility* (New York: Harper, 1949).

Rex, J. and Moore, R., *Race, Community & Conflict* (London: Oxford University Press, 1967).

Robinson, D., (ed.), *Local Labour Markets and Wage Structures* (London: Gower Press, 1970).

Robinson, D. and Conboy, W. M., 'Wage Structures and Internal Labour Markets', in Robinson, 1970.

Rottenberg, S., "On Choice in Labor Markets", in W. Galenson and S. M. Lipset, *Labor and Trade Unionism* (New York: Wiley, 1960).

Sheppard, D., "Characteristics of Drivers obtained from Large-scale Enquiries", *Road Research Laboratory Report, LR 389,* 1971.

Sheppard, H. L. and Belitsky, A. H., *The Job Hunt: Job-seeking behaviour of unemployed workers in a local economy* (Baltimore: Johns Hopkins Press, 1966).

Shimmin, S., "Extra-mural Factors Influencing Behaviour at Work", *Occupational Psychology,* Vol. 36, July 1962.

Skelly, G. B., Skinner, K., Sheppard, D. and Mackie, A., "A Study of Drivers Taking the Driving Test and the Ways they Learnt to Drive", *Transport and Road Research Laboratory, Technical Note TN 710,* May 1972.

Somers, R. H., "A New Asymmetric Measure of Association for Ordinal Variables", *American Sociological Review,* Vol. XXVII, Dec. 1962.

Special Task Force Report to the Secretary of Health, Education and Welfare, *Work in America* (Cambridge, Mass.: M.I.T. Press, 1973).

Stewart, A. and Blackburn, R. M., "The Stability of Structural

Inequality", *Sociological Review* Vol. 23, No. 3, August 1975.

Stewart, A. Prandy K. and Blackburn R. M., "Measuring the Class Structure", *Nature*, 26 October 1973.

Stewart, A., Prandy, K. and Blackburn, R. M., *Social Stratification and Occupational Structure* (London: Macmillan, forthcoming).

Stone, K., "The Origins of Job Structures in the Steel Industry", in Edwards, R. C., Reich, M. and Gordon, D. M., (eds.), *Labor Market Segmentation* (Lexington, Mass.: D. C. Heath, 1975).

Szymanski, A., "Trends in Economic Discrimination against Blacks in the U.S. Working Class", *The Review of Radical Political Economics*, Vol. 7, 1975.

Thomas, G., *Labour Mobility in Great Britain, 1945–1949*, Government Social Survey Report No. 134, n.d.

Touraine, A., *Sociologie d'Action* (Paris: Le Seuil, 1965).

Touraine, A. and Ragazzi, O., *Ouvriers d'Origine Agricole* (Paris: Le Seuil, 1961).

Turner, A. and Lawrence, P. R., *Industrial Jobs and the Worker* (Harvard University Press, 1965).

Wallerstein, I., *The Modern World-System* (New York: Academic Press, 1974).

Wedderburn, D., *Rudundancy and the Railwaymen* (London: Cambridge University Press, 1965).

Whelan, C. T., "Orientations to Work: Some Theoretical and Methodological Problems", *British Journal of Industrial Relations*, Vol. 14, 1976.

Wilcock, R. C. and Franke, W. H., *Unwanted Workers* (New York: Glencoe Free Press, 1963).

Wilensky, H. L., "Orderly Careers and Social Participation: the Impact of Work History on Social Integration in the Middle Mass", *American Sociological Review*, Vol. 26, 1961.

Wilkinson, F. N., "Collective Bargaining in the Steel Industry in the 1920s", in J. Saville (ed.), *Essays in Honour of Asa Briggs*, Vol. 3 (London: Croom Helm, 1977).

Wohlstetter, A. and Coleman, S., "Race Differences in Income", in A. H. Pascal, *Racial Discrimination in Economic Life* (Lexington: D. C. Heath, 1972).

Wright, E. O., "Class Boundaries in Advanced Capitalist Societies", *New Left Review*, No. 98, 1976.

Wright, P. L., *The Coloured Worker in British Industry* (London: Institute of Race Relations and Oxford University Press, 1968).

Author Index

Subject Index

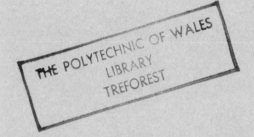